All Religion Is Inter-Religion

Also available from Bloomsbury

Interreligious Comparisons in Religious Studies and Theology,
edited by Perry Schmidt-Leukel and Andreas Nehring
New Patterns for Comparative Religion, William E. Paden
The Problem with Interreligious Dialogue, Muthuraj Swamy

All Religion Is Inter-Religion

*Engaging the Work of
Steven M. Wasserstrom*

Edited by
Kambiz GhaneaBassiri and Paul Robertson

BLOOMSBURY ACADEMIC
LONDON · NEW YORK · OXFORD · NEW DELHI · SYDNEY

BLOOMSBURY ACADEMIC
Bloomsbury Publishing Plc
50 Bedford Square, London, WC1B 3DP, UK
1385 Broadway, New York, NY 10018, USA
29 Earlsfort Terrace, Dublin 2, Ireland

BLOOMSBURY, BLOOMSBURY ACADEMIC and the Diana logo
are trademarks of Bloomsbury Publishing Plc

First published in Great Britain 2019
Paperback edition first published 2021

Copyright © Kambiz GhaneaBassiri, Paul Robertson and Contributors, 2019

Kambiz GhaneaBassiri and Paul Robertson have asserted their right under the Copyright, Designs and Patents Act, 1988, to be identified as Editors of this work.

For legal purposes the Acknowledgements on p. x constitute
an extension of this copyright page.

All rights reserved. No part of this publication may be reproduced or transmitted in any form or by any means, electronic or mechanical, including photocopying, recording, or any information storage or retrieval system, without prior permission in writing from the publishers.

Bloomsbury Publishing Plc does not have any control over, or responsibility for, any third-party websites referred to or in this book. All internet addresses given in this book were correct at the time of going to press. The author and publisher regret any inconvenience caused if addresses have changed or sites have ceased to exist, but can accept no responsibility for any such changes.

A catalogue record for this book is available from the British Library.

Library of Congress Cataloging-in-Publication Data
Names: GhaneaBassiri, Kambiz, editor. | Robertson, Paul (Paul Mark), editor. | Wasserstrom, Steven M., honoree.
Title: All religion is inter-religion: engaging the work of Steven M. Wasserstrom / edited by Kambiz GhaneaBassiri and Paul Robertson.
Description: London; New York: Bloomsbury Academic, 2019. | Includes bibliographical references and index.
Identifiers: LCCN 2019003572 | ISBN 9781350062214 (hardback) | ISBN 9781350062238 (ebk.) | ISBN 9781350062221 (ePDF)
Subjects: LCSH: Religions–Relations.
Classification: LCC BL410 .A425 2019 | DDC 201/.5–dc23
LC record available at https://lccn.loc.gov/2019003572

ISBN: HB: 978-1-3500-6221-4
PB: 978-1-3502-3685-1
ePDF: 978-1-3500-6222-1
eBook: 978-1-3500-6223-8

Typeset by Integra Software Services Pvt. Ltd.

To find out more about our authors and books visit
www.bloomsbury.com and sign up for our newsletters.

Contents

Notes on Contributors   vii
Acknowledgments   x

1   Introducing Wasserstrom's Work on Religion   *Kambiz GhaneaBassiri*   1
2   Nine Theses on the Study of Religion   *Steven M. Wasserstrom*   9

Part One   Conversing

3   Anxiety, Lament, and the Language of Silence: Poetic Redemption and Gnostic Alienation   *Elliot R. Wolfson*   17
4   The Study of Religion in a Postmetaphysical Age: Philosophical and Political Reflections   *Peter E. Gordon*   39
5   Taxonomy Is Epistemology: Theorizing Religion and Hermeticism Polythetically with Wasserstrom's *Theses*   *Paul Robertson*   45
6   *Metrosophy*: Rereading Walter Benjamin in Light of *Religion after Religion*   *Jeremy F. Walton*   57
7   "La Perversión de la Cábala Judía": Gershom Scholem and Anti-Kabbalistic Polemic in the Argentine Catholic Nationalism of Julio Meinvielle   *Jeremy P. Brown*   65

Part Two   Mediating

8   Before Religion? The Zoroastrian Concept of *Daēnā* and Two Myths about It   *Bruce Lincoln*   77
9   Nag Hammadi at Eranos: Rediscovering Gnosticism among the Historians of Religions   *J. Gregory Given*   87
10   Where the Center of the Rupture Is Called Judaism: Maurice Blanchot and *Religion after Religion*   *Kirsten Collins*   99
11   Abrahamic Encounters in the Weimar *Wüste*   *Ruchama Johnston-Bloom*   109
12   Far Too Close: Religion and Reality in the Work of Erich Auerbach and Muhammad Asad   *Sam Kigar*   117

Part Three Rethinking

13 Is Sethian Gnosticism an Abrahamic Religion? Abraham, Sodom, and
    the Parabiblical in Ancient Gnostic Literature *Dylan M. Burns*   127
14 The Repentant Magician: "Esoteric Intimacies" and the Enchantment of
    Religious Difference *Noah Salomon*   137
15 On the Possibility of Jewish Politics in Our Time: Scholem, Exile, and
    Early Modern Transformations *Anne Oravetz Albert*   147
16 Medieval Spanish Jews and the Dangers of Wealth *Andrew D. Berns*   159
17 *Luksus* and the Hasidic Critique of Postwar American Capitalism
    Michael Casper   171

Epilogue: Nine Riddles *Steven M. Wasserstrom*   181

Notes   194
Publications of Steven M. Wasserstrom   268
Bibliography   272
Index   300

Contributors

Anne Oravetz Albert is the Klatt Family Director for Public Programs at the Herbert D. Katz Center for Advanced Judaic Studies, University of Pennsylvania. She is a historian of early modern Jewry, focusing on political thought and Jewish-Christian relations. She is currently completing a book on communal politics and political ideas among Spanish and Portuguese Jews in Amsterdam in the time of Spinoza and Shabbetai Tsvi.

Andrew D. Berns is Assistant Professor of History at the University of South Carolina. His research investigates the intellectual and cultural history of Jews in the medieval and early modern Mediterranean, especially Italy and Spain. He is the author of *The Bible and Natural Philosophy in Renaissance Italy: Jewish and Christian Physicians in Search of Truth* (2015).

Jeremy P. Brown is Simon and Ethel Flegg Postdoctoral Fellow in Jewish Studies at McGill University. He earned his PhD in Hebrew and Judaic Studies from New York University. His research and teaching interests include kabbalah, religion in medieval Iberia, and the historical intersections of Judaism, Christianity, and Islam. Brown has also taught at the University of San Francisco.

Dylan M. Burns is Research Associate at the Freie Universität Berlin, in the Egyptological Seminar. His research focuses on Nag Hammadi and Gnosticism, later Greek Philosophy, and religion in late antiquity. He is co-editor of Nag Hammadi and Manichaean Studies, and author of *Apocalypse of the Alien God: Platonism and the Exile of Sethian Gnosticism* (2014).

Michael Casper is Doctoral Candidate in History at the University of California, Los Angeles. His research focuses on modern Eastern European Jewish politics and culture, especially through Yiddish sources. He is currently working on a book on the history of Hasidic Williamsburg with Nathaniel Deutsch.

Kirsten Collins is Doctoral Student in the Divinity School at the University of Chicago. Her research concerns French and Hebrew literature and theory after the Second World War, focusing on how the concepts of Judaism that developed in these cultural spheres challenge the boundaries between the religious and the secular.

Kambiz GhaneaBassiri is Professor of Religion and Humanities at Reed College. A specialist in Islamic social and intellectual history, Islam in America, material dimensions of religion, and religious diversity in US history, GhaneaBassiri is the author of numerous publications including *A History of Islam in America: From the New World to the New World Order* (2010).

J. Gregory Given is Doctoral Candidate in the Study of Religion at Harvard University, specializing in New Testament and Early Christianity. His research primarily focuses on Christian literary culture in late antiquity, Coptic language and literature, and historiography, and he is currently completing a dissertation on the letters of Ignatius of Antioch. He has recently published articles in the *Journal of Early Christian Studies*, *Journal of Coptic Studies*, and *Archiv für Religionsgeschichte*.

Peter E. Gordon is the Amabel B. James Professor of History and Faculty Affiliate in the Department of Philosophy at Harvard University. His books include *Rosenzweig and Heidegger: Between Judaism and German Philosophy* (2003); *The Cambridge Companion to Modern Jewish Philosophy*, co-edited with Michael Morgan (2017); *Continental Divide: Heidegger, Cassirer, Davos* (2010); *Adorno and Existence* (2016); and *The Routledge Companion to the Frankfurt School* (2018).

Ruchama Johnston-Bloom is Associate Director of Academic Affairs at CAPA: The Global Education Network's London center. Her research focuses on Jewish responses to, and engagements with, European imperialism, colonialism, and Orientalism. She has published on Gustav Weil's *Koranforschung*, Kurban Said's *Ali und Nino*, and the relocation of German-Jewish Orientalist scholarship to Israel and the United States.

Sam Kigar is Assistant Professor of Religion at the University of Puget Sound. He specializes in modern Islamic thought and politics in the Maghreb.

Bruce Lincoln is Caroline E. Haskell Distinguished Service Professor Emeritus of the History Religions in the University of Chicago Divinity School. At various times, he has taught Humanities at the University of Minnesota, Cultural Anthropology at the Università degli Studi di Siena, World History at Novosibirsk State Pedagogical Institute, History of Religions at Uppsala University and the University of Copenhagen, Ancient Iranian Philology at the Collège de France, and Anthropology, Classics, and Middle Eastern Studies at the University of Chicago, as well as offerings in his home department. The author of numerous books and articles, his most recent book is *Apples & Oranges: Experiments in, on, and with Comparison* (2018).

Paul Robertson is Lecturer in Classics and Humanities at the University of New Hampshire. His research includes ancient Mediterranean thought and theorizing religion. He is the author of *Paul's Letters and Contemporary Greco-Roman Literature: Theorizing a New Taxonomy* (2016).

Noah Salomon is Associate Professor of Religion and Director of Middle East Studies at Carleton College and the author of *For Love of the Prophet: An Ethnography of Sudan's Islamic State* (2016). A recent recipient of a Mellon New Directions Fellowship,

Salomon is currently exploring mechanisms for negotiating Islamic difference across several sites in Europe, Africa, and the Middle East.

Jeremy F. Walton is the Leader of the Max Planck Research Group, "Empires of Memory: The Cultural Politics of Historicity in Former Habsburg and Ottoman Cities," at the Max Planck Institute for the Study of Religious and Ethnic Diversity (MPI-MMG) in Göttingen, Germany. He received his PhD in Anthropology from the University of Chicago in 2009. His first book, *Muslim Civil Society and the Politics of Religious Freedom in Turkey* (2017), is an ethnographic exploration of the relationship among Muslim civil society organizations, state institutions, and secularism in contemporary Turkey.

Steven M. Wasserstrom is the Moe and Izetta Tonkon Professor of Judaic Studies and Humanities at Reed College. A specialist in Jewish Studies, Islamic Studies, and the history of the study of religion, Wasserstrom is the author of *Between Muslim and Jew: The Problem of Symbiosis under Early Islam* (1995) and *Religion after Religion: Gershom Scholem, Mircea Eliade, and Henry Corbin at Eranos* (1999).

Elliot R. Wolfson, a Fellow of the American Academy of Jewish Research and the American Academy of Arts and Sciences, is the Marsha and Jay Glazer Endowed Chair in Jewish Studies and Distinguished Professor of Religion at University of California, Santa Barbara. His is the author of many publications, the most recent of which include: *Giving beyond the Gift: Apophasis and Overcoming Theomania* (2014); *The Duplicity of Philosophy's Shadow: Heidegger, Nazism and the Jewish Other* (2018) and *Heidegger and Kabbalah: Hidden Gnosis and the Path of Poiesis* (2019).

Acknowledgments

A heartfelt thanks to Judy, Pesha, and Shuly for sharing Steve!

Thanks to John Kenney for his wisdom to hire Steve in the Religion Department at Reed College,
   ... to Steven Koblik for his foresight in creating the conditions to keep him at Reed,
   ... to Michael Foat, Ken Brashier, and Kristin Scheible (as well as visiting faculty in Religion) for sharing in the journey,
   ... to the Greenberg Distinguished Scholar Program and Brittney Corrigan-McElroy for their support of the conference from which this book emerged,
   ... to Tehniyat Naveed, Alma Flores, Delainey Myers, and Pat Hanley for their assistance in finalizing the manuscript.

Lastly, a special thanks to Reedies of the past three decades whose insatiable curiosity and dedication to intellectual work made this book possible. This book is dedicated to Steve by all the Reedies whose intellectual lives he has impacted.

1

Introducing Wasserstrom's Work on Religion

Kambiz GhaneaBassiri

Steven M. Wasserstrom argues that religion is "a vocation worth the work."[1] So, it is only fitting that an introduction to his influence on the study of religion begins with placing him at work. Wasserstrom is a world-class historian of religions who teaches at a liberal arts college. Liberal arts college professors pride themselves in being teacher-scholars—in that order. The precedence teaching takes in their careers means that they rarely have the opportunity to pursue specialized research interests with their students who, unlike doctoral students of their counterparts at research universities, possess neither the necessary background knowledge nor the requisite research languages. They also do not have ready access to research libraries, and while, in recent years, more and more archives and specialized journals are becoming available online, they still have not replaced the need for visits to research libraries. Wasserstrom, in fact, has made these research trips a regular part of his scholarly regime. Once, when I was a graduate student and had invited him to give a talk at Harvard, he tacked on a few extra days to his trip on his own dime so that he could spend time reading at Widener library.

For all these reasons, fewer liberal arts college professors write field-changing works like Wasserstrom's *Between Muslim and Jew* and *Religion after Religion*. If they do produce such scholarship, their careers usually take a sharp turn toward research universities, where they are called on to help train a new generation of specialists. Of the very few who write field-changing books and opt to remain at liberal arts colleges, fewer still have the influence Wasserstrom has had on their field through training undergraduate students. This is not to suggest that Wasserstrom regards undergraduate teaching a burden. On the contrary, he dedicated *Religion after Religion* to "Reedies everywhere."[2] Inquisitive and thoughtful undergraduates provided him an audience with whom he has worked for more than three decades to close the gap between "the manifest power of religion in the 'real world'" and Religious Studies' ability to communicate its findings to a wider audience.[3] This is all by way of saying, you hold a rare volume in your hands that is a product of an exceptional career in Religious Studies. In it, thirteen of Wasserstrom's students at Reed College who went on to pursue careers in the academy and two colleagues of his generation whose professional life and scholarship have fruitfully intersected with Wasserstrom's come together not just to celebrate Wasserstrom's contributions to the study of religion but also to think with him about the vocation of Religious Studies.

The idea of this book originated at the annual conferences of the American Academy of Religion in the 2010s when I (and Kristin Scheible, after she joined the department in 2014) gathered informally with graduates of Reed's Religion Department to talk about research, to track careers, and to reminisce. In these gatherings, Steve's (for we are all on a first-name basis at Reed) pedagogy and scholarship loomed large. It did not take long before these graduates began to float the idea that they should mark his impact on their own intellectual lives and the study of religion more generally. As Steve's thirty-year anniversary at Reed approached, I offered to help organize a conference in his honor, and Paul Robertson volunteered to help with editing the *Festschrift*. We received financial support from Reed's Religion Department and Reed's Greenberg Distinguished Scholar Program to gather about two dozen of Steve's students and colleagues at Reed College in October 2017 for a three-day academic conference centered around Steve's pithy provocation that "all religion is inter-religion." This provocation encapsulates the collective thesis of the essays gathered here. The principal argument of the present book is that religion is always relational and plural. There is no religion in the singular, nor is there any religion outside of human society, economy, politics, psychology, or ethics. The study of religion is thus tasked with making philosophical sense of the complex relations and differences that humans have managed in history without compartmentalizing them or essentializing them and thus erasing the relations and differences that constitute religion as a subject of study.

Steve had penned the notion that all religion is inter-religion in an essay titled "Nine Theses on the Study of Religion," which is published in this volume for the first time. He had submitted the essay for an edited volume that never reached the printing presses. The large number of these unpublished manuscripts on Steve's shelves and hard drive is mind-boggling. Were it not for Steve sharing this piece with me when we co-taught "Theories and Methods in the Study of Religion," it is very likely that it would not have seen the light of day. Wasserstrom has a long and illustrious curriculum vitae (CV), but Steve does not write to add a publication line to his CV. He researches because he hungers for answers to big humanistic questions, and he writes to think through his research findings. Not many can keep up with the speed with which he thinks and devours books, and while he willingly works to bring inquisitive students along with him in the classroom, he does not slow down for the publishing industry.

We were fortunate that Bruce Lincoln and Elliot Wolfson—two scholars who travel in the fast lane with Steve—readily agreed to give the two keynote lectures for the conference, which have been reproduced with some minor edits in this volume. Lincoln's lecture, "Before Religion? The Zoroastrian Concept of *Daēnā* and Two Myths about It," inaugurated the conference. In it, Lincoln paid homage to the argument of *Religion after Religion* that the concept of religion used by such founding figures of Religious Studies as Mircea Eliade, Henry Corbin, and Gershom Scholem does not reflect the historical realities of the subjects they studied. Lincoln asked whether or not the concept of religion as it is used in the academy today has a pre-history that is reflected in the Avestan word *daēnā*, which scholars often render as "religion." He demonstrated that *daēnā* has multiple meanings in ancient Zoroastrian texts, some of which affirm contemporary presuppositions about religion as primordial and interior and others that problematize such an understanding by historicizing *daēnā*. Lincoln's essay shows that defining *daēnā* as "religion," in the singular, obfuscates the multifarious uses of the term in our historical sources and thus, like the founding figures Wasserstrom studied, imposes contemporary ideologies of religion on the term.

Wolfson's keynote lecture closed out the public portion of the conference and paid homage to Wasserstrom, less through agreement and more by showing how Wasserstrom's conclusions have challenged Wolfson to think and articulate his own ideas about Jewish mysticism. As such, Wolfson's chapter is more programmatic and longer than the other chapters in the book. Wolfson examines Martin Heidegger's "philosophical ruminations" on language as a way of moderating the strong link that Wasserstrom sees between fascism and the mythic/symbolic language through which fascist ideas were buttressed and popularized in the twentieth century. By comparing Heidegger, a well-known supporter of Hitler, with kabbalists, Wolfson seeks to demonstrate that, in careful philosophical work, truths reveal themselves despite the moral shortcomings of the philosopher. Wolfson does not rehabilitate Heidegger for Jewish Studies, but he tries to make sense of similarities he finds between Heidegger's philosophy and the kabbalah in light of Wasserstrom's admonishment that Heideggerian discourses on phenomenology of religion have been "contaminated" by fascism.[4] "What is dark," Wolfson writes, "is not dissolved brightness; it remains concealed and comes to appearance in the light … By illuminating the dark light and uncovering the shadow as shadow, one is emancipated."[5]

The longstanding conversations between Wolfson and Wasserstrom reverberate in Jeremy Brown's essay. Brown studied with Wasserstrom before completing his PhD in Jewish Studies with Wolfson at New York University. He examines the polemical work of the Argentinian nationalist cleric Julio Meinvielle, bringing a concrete example to bear on his two teachers' different approaches to mysticism. More specifically, he examines Meinvielle's use of Scholem to advance a polemic against kabbalah informed by the anti-gnostic framework of ancient Christian heresiology. On the one hand, he demonstrates that Scholem's "mystocentric"[6] scholarship, regardless of the scholar's own Jewishness and anti-fascist intentions, has had a direct effect on the development of fascist and anti-Jewish ideology in Argentina; on the other hand, he interrogates discursive similarities between Meinvielle's heresy hunting and the anti-gnostic pitch of Wasserstrom's critique of mystagoguery in the academic study of religion.

Lincoln's historicizing approach to the study of religion could not be more different than Wolfson's philosophical approach. The fact that they both admire and think with Wasserstrom, just as Wasserstrom admires and thinks with them,[7] not only speaks to how widely Steve reads but also bears witness to how his work seeks to "negotiate … the transdisciplinary space between history and philosophy."[8] Indeed, during one of the evening events of the conference, a trialogue on the "Past, Present, and Future of the Study of Religion,"[9] Wasserstrom sat between Lincoln and Wolfson, physically performing "the dialectic of the Historian of Religion … be[ing] at once historical and philosophical."[10]

We had hoped that Peter Gordon would also offer a keynote lecture that would reflect on his experiences with Wasserstrom as someone who was Steve's first thesis student and now could look back on his oeuvre as a full professor and a prominent intellectual historian of modern Europe. Gordon, however, was unable to make the conference, but graciously contributed a chapter to the volume that "take[s] comfort" in Wasserstrom's assertion that "all religion is inter-religion," because it suggests that the secular, liberal-democratic "promise of interreligious coexistence today has its historical origin in the phenomenon of interreligion itself."[11]

For Steve's students, friends, and colleagues, the conference culminated in a private lecture that Steve delivered titled "Nine Riddles." A word about this lecture for it reveals much about Wasserstrom's pedagogical and scholarly temperament! When I asked Steve if he would be willing to give a lecture at the end of the conference just to his former and current students as well as his colleagues and close friends, he magnanimously agreed. He titled his lecture "The Vocation of Religion." However, three weeks before the conference, he decided to completely scrap this talk, which had already been written. He worked fastidiously during these three weeks to write a completely new lecture titled "Nine Riddles." Following his lecture, which received a standing ovation, someone asked him why he changed his lecture. He explained that when he read the drafts of his former students' papers that were circulated a few weeks before the conference, he was struck by how sophisticated and erudite they were. He wondered what he could possibly say about the study of religion that they have not yet figured out for themselves. So, he decided to write a completely different talk at the last minute, one that was more personal and expressed his gratitude to his students for all that he had learned from them.

The present volume is thus bookended with nine theses about how religion ought to be studied, and nine riddles that question whether anyone could ever know how religion ought to be studied. As Anne Albert explains in her essay, the number nine in kabbalistic schemes of divine emanation anticipates the tenth emanation that interconnects the whole through the "messianic restoration" of the world.[12] Form and content have always been inseparable in Wasserstrom's pedagogy and scholarship. This is likely why he has trepidations about the freedom Wolfson suggests could be uncovered in the "dark light" of a Nazi-sympathizer's writings. Wasserstrom finds freedom in the labor over the mundane. He asserts, "Reoccupation is significance itself" in "Nine Riddles." In the lecture version at the conference, he gestured from behind the lectern, as though he were picking up a book from a shelf and quoted from Theodore Reik's *Pagan Rites in Judaism*: "I get up from the chair and am aware of making the same slow motions" that Reik made when he picked up a book of Sigmund Freud's that talked about Freud picking up a book of Goethe's that talked about Goethe picking up *King Lear* to read.[13] By describing his work on religion as the "reoccupation" of earlier scholars' writings on religion, Wasserstrom differentiates his own approach to the study of religion from those scholars who believe they could overcome their mortality through grandiose, all-encompassing theories of religion. Wasserstrom's work on religion has been a form of resistance to such apotheoses in Religious Studies. To claim to have prevailed over death is to deny the shared humanity that death represents. Wasserstrom's "Nine Theses" orients one in studying religion as a vocation preoccupied with human relations, human responsibility, and human memories that are datable, nameable, and the result of a variety of types of contact.

If the theses communicate how Wasserstrom grapples with the ways religion is defined and evoked in human history, the riddles reveal the personal relations and stakes of his work. The political, ethical, and epistemological implications of definitions of religion are personal for this "little Jewish professor"[14] coming of age during the "cultural wars" and civil rights struggles of the 1970s and thinking about Judaism, Islam, and Religious Studies in the aftermath of the Holocaust and the formation of the state of Israel. In the introduction to his contribution to this volume, Wolfson quotes from a 1994 letter Steve wrote him: "Our forays into gender-sensitive revisions of scholarship demand that we be alert to the ideologies built into scholarship." I read this sentence as evidence of the influence feminist critiques have had on Steve's thought. "The personal is political." Although in the "Nine Riddles" Steve does not speak about his relation to Israel in the same detail as he does about his familial connections to the Holocaust, his scholarship on Judaism and Jewish–Muslim relations is telling insofar as it uses the study of Jews and Judaism under Muslim rule as a way of asking questions that are of universal import for the humanities as well as counter trends toward insularity and self-referentiality in Jewish Studies in America. One of the conference attendees mentioned that when he studied Judaism with Steve, his studies always opened outward, but when he went on to study Judaism in graduate school, he found the field too inwardly oriented to stick with it.

****

Were I ever able to make any claims to fame, one of them would have to be that my office shares a wall with Steve Wasserstrom's. When I came to Reed in 2002, any religionist who heard about my job immediately retorted: "That's where Wasserstrom teaches, isn't it?" I myself was excited about teaching at Reed because "Wasserstrom teaches there." One of the unexpected perks of sharing an office wall with Steve is that I get to see the cool postings on his door. For a period of time a few years ago, he had posted a small cartoon of an old man with spectacles hunched over a desk poring over a big book with a magnifying glass. Its caption read something like, "For a second, it all made sense!" Reading Steve's "Nine Riddles" alongside his "Nine Theses," one sees the futility and perils of a scholar one day thinking "it" all makes sense. The general provocations put forth at the beginning of this book are particularized and historicized in the riddles that end it. "The final veil to lift," Wolfson writes, "is the veil that there is a final veil to lift."[15] Whatever truths Steve managed to unveil about the study of religion through his theses, he veiled them at the end with his riddles. The book begins with the axioms around which Steve has learned to orient his scholarship and pedagogy in Religious Studies, and it ends with prioritizing learning and labor over making truth-claims. It is precisely because of the complexity and vastness of religion and the fact that Religious Studies asks big questions about meaning, eternality, and ultimacy that its study must be grounded in verifiable data and in careful study of texts and practices with methodologies that are teachable and reproducible. When Wasserstrom's former students gathered to honor him, they did so by critically engaging his ideas rather than idolizing him or remarking on his charisma.

It is because the study of religion demands the scholar understand and explain people whose core beliefs and ways differ from one's own that we need to mind our critical distance from our subject of study and be vigilant of the ethics and politics of our vocation. Steve, throughout his career and in his writings, has astutely and empathetically tended to these differences. As Gordon notes, his methodology and pedagogy center on "dialectical understanding."[16] To understand religion dialectically is to see it not only as work on negotiations between different folks or between folks and their old ways but also as work on negotiations between disciplines, between history and philosophy/theology, between science and politics. If Gordon is right, and I think he is, when he suggests that "strong" disciplines no longer occupy a space in the academy, the longstanding transdisciplinarity of Religious Studies rooted in "dialectical understanding" may have something to teach other faculties at the university. We do not just have "something to say … that needs to be said,"[17] but rather what we have to say needs to be heard.

All religion is inter-religion! The brevity of this thesis belies the enormity of the task it assigns to scholars of religion. The intricacies of this task quickly become evident if one does not just read the text of one of Wasserstrom's publications but also tends to his footnotes. It is here that we see the number of languages one needs to master, the archives one needs to sift, the hidden ideologies and presumptions about religion that one needs to uncover and explain, all in order to piece together the "real human relationships"[18] through which religious arguments and experiences are expressed and contested. But the task of the scholar of religion does not end with piecing together relations; we must also, Wasserstrom argues, reflect critically and philosophically on those relations so as to arrive at "species-wide generalizations."[19]

Each of the contributors to this volume has sought to rise up to the challenge Wasserstrom's theses pose by taking up his provocation that "all religion is inter-religion" through the lens of their specific field of study. They have different areas of specialization and are at different career stages. Despite their differences, however, they are all trained philologically and historically and share a commitment to the pursuit of intellectual insight into religion as a self-sufficient endeavor—indeed, a vocation. The scholarly revisions and insights they offer serve as proof of the intellectual value of studying religion as always relational.

Keeping in mind that footnotes are not just the ancillary apparatus of scholarship but also the place where scholars differentiate their work from ideology by providing evidence for their arguments and revealing the depth and extent of their labors,[20] each of the chapters of this volume could be read as a footnote to Wasserstrom's opus. Insofar as Wasserstrom's work has been generative of numerous *conversations* about how religion ought to be studied, it is fitting that a number of the contributors to the volume focus on bringing their own theoretical concerns into conversation with his work. Others build on Wasserstrom's assertions regarding the *mediatory* role religion plays in history to show how social, political, economic, and intellectual relations are constructed or impeded through scholarly work on religion(s). Another group urges us to *rethink* aspects of their respective areas of specialization in relation to Wasserstrom's opus and theses on religion. Rather than summarizing each of the chapters, I conclude by highlighting the principal themes I see running through them. Collectively they give the reader a good sense of the impact Wasserstrom's scholarly interventions have had not just on his students but on Religious Studies more broadly.

First, a number of these chapters build on the work Wasserstrom did in *Between Muslim and Jew*. They demonstrate that insofar as any attempt at self-differentiation results from historical encounters with difference, identity formation necessarily involves the incorporation of others' perspectives of one's self into one's own self-understanding.

Second, these essays are particularly conscious of analytical framings embedded in the terms used to study religion. In *Between Muslim and Jew*, Wasserstrom also subjected the analytical concept "symbiosis" to detailed historical and philological study to show its limitations in explaining the complexity of the relations between Jews and Muslims under early Islam. In *Religion after Religion*, he furthered this work by subjecting the founding figures of History of Religions and the analytical frames and concepts they bestowed upon the field to the same scrutiny. This work has served as an admonishment to the authors of the chapters of this book. They have responded to it prophylactically by subjecting Religious Studies concepts—ranging from gnosis and the Abrahamic to messianism and magic—to detailed empirical and philological analysis. By testing analytical concepts against the mettle of empirical evidence, human memories, and history, they have sought to overcome the myopia of analytical framings that often blind researchers to the actual roles the gods, revelations, invocations, and healing practices—just to name a few of religionists' subjects—play in shaping human societies. Consequently, they instantiate the notion that Gnosticism, Hermeticism, Sufism, the kabbalah, and other phenomena associated with esotericism need not remain mysterious and beyond the realm of critical inquiry and empirical verification. Rather, they are products of political decisions that have ethical implications, or conversely, of ethical decisions that have political consequences. They also function as spaces of intimacy between contradictory views of religion, which scholars could trace in real time and space.

Third and significantly, unlike some critiques of religion as ideology, these essays do not linger on critique to the point of debilitation. Rather, their authors work to further the field. They offer revisions and constructive insights into the study of religion by examining the encounters, continuities, and historical changes that shape religion. They thus focus not just on what religious people do or what they say about religion but also on how scholars and practitioners explain what they do through the idioms of religion. Following Wasserstrom, they approach the study of religion with the assumption that both the way religion is conceptualized and expressed and the context and ways in which it is experienced communicate significance, and therefore must be studied in relation to one another. Using multiple languages and archives, the authors doggedly follow how scholars *and* their sources express identity, behavior, and community as well as aspirations and memories in the idioms and rites of religion. They follow Wasserstrom and offer historically grounded and relational understandings and explications of religions. By doing so, they demonstrate—albeit at times with minor caveats—that discourses that define "religion" as the experience of "the sacred" divorce religions from their economic, social, political, and ethical contexts and reduce them to an ahistorical essence of the scholar's own imagining: constructing a perennial religion in the aftermath historical religions.

In conclusion, the essays in this volume collectively demonstrate the power of a relational approach to the study of religion that regards the methodologies, conceptual framings, and sources used in the study of religion as routes through which scholars of religion relate not only to their subjects but also to other disciplines within the academy and the world at large. Rather than trying to assert the autonomy of Religious Studies by demarcating its domain through such unverifiable categories as hierophany, mystical experience, and perennial truths, the study of religion as inter-religion emphasizes the unique responsibilities and the distinctive work involved in understanding the complex relations humans create and manage through religion.

2

Nine Theses on the Study of Religion

Steven M. Wasserstrom

> I think the peculiar office of scholars in a careful and gloomy generation is to be (as the poets were called in the Middle Ages) Professors of the Joyous Science, defectors and delineators of occult symmetries and unpublished beauties; heralds of civility, mobility, learning and wisdom; affirmers of the one law, yet as those who should affirm if in music and dancing; expressors themselves of that firm and cheerful temper, infinitely removed from sadness, which reigns through the kingdoms of chemistry, vegetation and animal life.
> —Ralph Waldo Emerson[1]

1

Religious Studies, in so far as it is philosophically defensible, seeks a general perspective.[2] The study of religion strives for philosophical understanding of the human as such and seeks species-wide generalizations. The contributions of Religious Studies to the growth of knowledge as such, alone, shall determine its ultimate place in faculties of the university. To earn its rightful place as an intellectually necessary pursuit—not rightful till earned—it must be at least an honest broker in deriving its general case from the fullness of evidence.

The purpose of our science, like that of any science, is first to apprehend reality accurately.[3] "Ultimacy" *per se* is nowhere near the object of our studies, not even at its end. Nor can the "authenticity" of religious experience detain our attention. And not replication either. Rather, as Hans J. Blumenberg analogously observed in another context, "it is a question not of duplicating experience that, with some effort, would also be possible 'in the original' for anyone at any time, but rather of augmenting *what can be seen at all.*"[4]

The critical study of religion is a science of the human plural. There is no privilege, no singularity inherent in a secure Religious Studies. To practice *Religion* is no less absurd than it is to speak *Language*. Max Müller announced our professional motto in his *Introduction to the Science of Religion* (1873): "He who knows one, knows none."

When the students of Comparative Philology boldly adapted Goethe's paradox, "He who knows one language, knows none." People were startled at first; but they soon began to feel the truth which was hidden beneath the paradox. Could Goethe have meant that Homer did not know Greek, or that Shakespeare did not know English, because neither of them knew more than his mother tongue? No! what was meant was that neither Homer nor Shakespeare knew what the language really was which he handled with so much power and cunning.[5]

Not that this ever will be easy. Müller himself recognized the obstacles. "There is a strong feeling, I know, in the minds of all people against any attempt to treat their own religion as a member of a class, and, in one sense, that feeling is perfectly justified … [, however,] in the history of the world, our religion, like our own language, is but one of many."[6] It is epistemologically incoherent to "understand" a religious singularity. As an old scientific principle had it, *once is never* (*einmal ist keinmal*).[7] To grasp the "reality" of *a religion itself*, to seize one religion in some putatively pure singularity is an incoherent proposition, therefore, *a priori*.

A correlate: *All religion susceptible of our study is in a situation of contact.* There is no religion in the singular and the study of religion must suspect every assertion for the unique, the autonomous, the untouched, the monad, the alone. Inter-relational complexity constitutes our subject.

Religious Studies must do more than sponsor congeries of area studies and more, also, than acquiesce to being bastard of grander enterprises—philosophy of religion, psychology of religion, and the like. Religious Studies seeks to understand religion, nothing less. There is no study of a singular religion that does not employ a hermeneutic derived from sources distant from its object of inquiry. Without being seen from outside, there is no communication. If it is to stay situated at an appropriately Archimedean hermeneutical distance, the study of religion cannot identify with any one religion but rather with religion as inter-religion.

2

Against those who believe that "religion" resides in "eternal verities": There is no reducibly essential religion any more than there is such a person. Religion is a function of folks meeting other folks—*contact*—and folks maintaining their old ways—*continuity*.[8] There is no essence to be sought.[9]

Religion is always inter-religion. These, then, are the complexities of mediation: in space, *contact*, and in time, *continuity*. Religious-life-in-history, *continuity*, is mediated by collective memory; religious-life-as-interaction, *contact*, by inter-religious negotiability.

Whether the stress in its governing trope, *contact*, falls on conversation, war, economic transaction, negotiation, rape, or conquest, a critical study of religion applies itself to continuous cross-fertilizations of identity. Religion remakes itself in challenges to identity that provide identity, in being seen and making contact, offering *cortesia*, in short, becoming "human."[10]

3

Identity politics, so-called, led not to solipsism necessarily, although it did sometimes result in tautology: oneself as yardstick, one's group as measure of oneself. A pedagogical imperative of the study of religion therefore must be to inculcate not only a sense of appreciation but also equally a capacity for distanciation. Distance is needed for perspective not just on others but especially on one's own identity, in order *to think religion in the plural*.

Identification and distance, the existential analogues of theory and practice, anchor our bipedal position as observers of religious phenomena. Both theory and practice locate us as observers, but theory is impractically locative while practice is untheoretically locative. Too close and you burn, too far and you freeze.

4

To put the point even more broadly and bluntly, the dual constraints for the critical study of religions are those of science and politics. As modes of human action, science and politics are extensions of theory and practice. The governing assumption here is that naturalistic explanation, from within, and political hegemonies, from without, stretch Religious Studies between two asymmetrical imperatives.

What unites them—and here the shock of Religious Studies millennially inserts itself—is entertainment.

> The easiest way to imagine the future of writing, if the present trend toward a culture of techno-images goes on, is to imagine culture as a gigantic transcoder from text to image. It will be a sort of black box that has texts for input and images for output … which is to say that history will flow into the box, and that it will come out of it under the form of myth and magic. From the point of view of the texts that will flow into the box, this will be a utopian situation: *the box is the 'fullness of time,'* because it devours linear time and freezes it into images.[11]

The entertainment state re-narrativizes our texts and our history. It makes myth live. The vocation of Religious Studies in such a social situation is to mediate two powers centrally necessary for the functioning of the state: science and politics.

Religious Studies inherits the solar breadth of myth but follows it not as guiding light. If we are to do something more than to perpetuate ancient tales of legitimation, Religious Studies must integrate internal complexities on a scale comparable to, or at least intelligibly commensurate with, the science and the politics with which it lives. We start here.

5

Religious Studies is a weak discipline. We must negotiate other university faculties—philosophy, history, social sciences, natural sciences—to understand our primary materials.

The miniature status of Religious Studies in our university stands in inverse proportion to the manifest power of religion in the "real world." Our marginal enterprise has yet to produce works read widely, not to speak of necessarily, outside its classrooms. Faced now with the *glocalization* of cultural illiteracy, this limit-condition is likely to harden outside the academy.

We persist because we have something to say, something that needs to be said. Only connect: inter-religious cognitive bargaining is our classroom norm. Only what we communicate and understand is what we study.

To remember what we have to say we study our own genealogy, the thought of our predecessors, rethinking with them the steps that arrived at us. These steps in a dialectic—one skeptical and then the next understanding—keep us upright and carry us along. If presently we are lost in the labyrinth, then it is not regressive to retrace our own path, and in fact tracking backward may locate the only egress. To enter understanding, the Religious Studies redoubles its paces. To arrive, finally, at understanding religion, we might first recall the oracle. "When Zeno asked the Delphic oracle what was the best way to live, the answer he was given was: 'To mate with the dead.' Which he understood as the equivalent of to *read* the *ancients*."[12]

6

For the critical study of religion, the theologico-political predicament becomes a question of discerning whether only threatless irrationalities are tolerable. Construed trivially as merely the reality of religious difference, it might not mean much. Students of religions, however, have no choice but to recognize the intractability of inter-religion as the baseline assumption of any self-aware study of "religion." This assumption, perhaps, might be called *Deep Pluralism*. *Deep Pluralism* engages inter-religious processes, negotiations, as they reveal themselves routinely in human relations.

The *Deep Pluralism* of Religious Studies is predicated, among other things, on negotiations between "enemy-brothers"—for example, Judaism and Islam.[13] Religious Studies works these negotiations in the *transdisciplinary space between history and philosophy*. The dialectic of the Historian of Religions must be at once historical and philosophical—its original stuff was the historical dialectic of revelational divergence and negotiation. Religious Studies, quite simply, is that historical activity both descended from and reflecting on inter-religion.[14] Theologians study god-talk, anthropologists read tribal life in kinship terms, and Religious Studies not only compares religions but also reflects on that comparison.[15] It must compare historically and then reflect philosophically on the results of that comparison.

If it does so, Religious Studies might play a role in clarifying inter-religion as a cultural discourse—although it can do so only if it takes revelations seriously enough to affirm enemy-brothers all their polemic and apologetic ferocity. To elide these self-defenses is impetuously to minimize the civilizational self-sufficiency revealed respectively to these opposing traditions.

Surrendering to this necessity, then, the new Religious Studies must "abjure such prescribed choices" between opposing revelations.[16] That is, it studies enemies but without a reification of enmity.[17] It is concerned, rather, with the multiplicity of religions and with the meaning of that multiplicity. Religious Studies, by its very definition, seeks to understand religious reality in its plurality: *To know one is to know none.*[18]

7

By its very miscegenated character, it has no defining method of its own.[19] But Religious Studies rejects both existentialism and positivism, both the emotive and the logical criteria as exclusive guides to meaning.[20] That is, we reject the persuasions of mere vision equally with all incomprehending scientisms.

The trans-disciplinary commission of *Religious Studies is to sponsor encounters between philosophical claims to truth and historical claims to power.* Here may be a re-orientation capable, perhaps, of catalyzing a new Religious Studies. On the one hand, naturalistic explanations of religious phenomena suffice only for the naturalistic explanation wing of Religious Studies, while theological self-explanations are sufficient for the opposite end of the intellectual spectrum.[21] Stuck, thus, without the unequivocal support either of reason or of revelation, it would seem that there is no middle arena in which Religious Studies intellectually suffices.

But in fact *interreligious contact itself* provides all the stuff we need: when it comes to *historical exempla of philosophical incommensurates*, here only Religious Studies suffices. Religious Studies seeks, or should seek, the deep meaning of such superficial pluralisms. There is virtually no religious situation that is not a situation of contact, and no Religious Studies that does not make sense of contact.

Quite distinct from the myth of myth, the fatally flawed misapprehension of a putatively sacral isolation, the real, in fact, locates its fate only through orienteering the dense social atmosphere of complicated relations. So Religious Studies cannot decide if witches fly, but can explicate friendships between spell-casters and hex-makers—it can locate witches as neighbors.[22]

To achieve this deepening, we would need, in the arena of the Religious Studies, a *Deep Naturalism*. Addressing this need implies a turn toward the processes, psychological, biological, and social, that gave and keep giving revelations.

8

What does it mean to "deepen?" Here, again, our age of the marvel must be kept in mind. Inversion of scale—quantum mechanics and nanotechnology and genomics—and the attendant shock of recognition as microscopic worlds swim newly blinking into our ken, now large enough to loom unavoidably; "micro" and "thick," the infinitesimally textured surface of ordinary life is not a base substructure to which we would "reduce" religion. Rather, it is the dream combed throughout daily routine, hyper-reality, that demands this new deepening.

What would be the alternative? What choice do we have? "We" have changed. The normal enormity joins crisis as everyday condition. A new numbed but exciting conditioning to ordinary impossibilities is our daily fare. Accordingly, what we need is not a tepidly liberal ecumenicism, but rather the moral equivalent of crisis-consciousness in our anathestized/hyper-stimulated times. William James (who called for the moral equivalent of war) championed a "radical empiricism," and this call was advanced, in other venues, by none other than Franz Rosenzweig.[23] The more the brain sciences, artificial life, artificial intelligence, neural networkings, collective intelligence, cloning, nanotechnology, advanced robotics, the more these continue to accelerate the rate of their own advances—then any serious religious empiricism of this "actual civilizational situation" must acknowledge that human self-definition is itself unfolding into an almost miraculous remaking of itself.

9

Religious Studies might finally become a deeply human science. It will only do so, as social scientists have always insisted, by taking seriously the deeps of naturalism; by taking seriously the deeps of naturalism can we plumb the fullness of the human. Deep Naturalism means that ancient, hidden recesses and present, mind-blowing surfaces should be scrutinized. But it does not assume that we can reach bottom. Deep Naturalism is, in fact, a naturalism without bottom. The trap door on the stage of history may or may not imply that some director in the wings is still at work. But Deep Naturalistic explanations suspend the belief in the end of depths. We plumb depths but bracket the bottom. Like deep pluralism that brackets ultimacy on the social level, deep naturalism on the biological level brackets the "deeps" of revelational claims.

As an empiricism, it starts from the facts, in this case the facts of the new human—new to the exponential increases in information overload, to the cyber-spatialization of time and to the trans-temporalization of space.[24] Given these stimuli, we cannot be content unless Religious Studies continues to widen the area of consciousness, to explore all available dimensions of the human, to submit to the *kairos* of our moment with neither faddishness nor foolish utopianism.

Religion after religion starts from the end of history and its science, Religious Studies, similarly begins from inter-religion as a given. Beginning here, only a trans-disciplinary deepening will now make sense of this, our given, our fantastic hyper-reality. The new Religious Studies is raised on and thus conditioned to inter-religion, especially sensitive, in the reign of the marvelous, hyper-real inversion of surfaces, to the deep surfaces of the past. The deep present is found on the surfaces of ritual, practice, the usual and the routine. This rediscovery of the ordinary will surprise us insofar as we can feel newly in it the depth of the real, deeply textured surprises like those hiding now around us on the surfaces of the hyper-real.

Part One

Conversing

3

Anxiety, Lament, and the Language of Silence: Poetic Redemption and Gnostic Alienation

Elliot R. Wolfson

Tout cela, mon ami,
Vivre, qui noue
Hier, notre illusion,
À demain, nos ombres.
—Yves Bonnefoy

Before beginning my analysis, I would like to add a personal note. The decision to choose the topic of this chapter was informed by an ongoing conversation that began a long time ago with the honoree of this *Festschrift*, a conversation that exposed a fundamental methodological difference that strengthened the enduring intellectual bond of our friendship. From early on, Steven Wasserstrom was concerned about my attraction to Martin Heidegger's thought, given his well-known and documented support of Hitler and the National Socialist agenda. I will refrain from entering into the intricacies of that topic because it would take us too far afield. Needless to say, I understood Steve's trepidations, which extended to the fascist affiliations of other thinkers as well, including Mircea Eliade and Julius Evola. To offer one example that I pulled out from my personal archives, in a letter from April 2, 1994, Steve wrote, in response to my study on the kabbalistic motif of the tree of divine potencies specularized as the male androgyne,[1]

> Where does this complex of imagery come from? The answer is *Sol Invictus*. I can only sketch some of the sources on this important comparative perspective (on your brilliant work from the kabbalistic side). As it turns out, the sexualized Man of Light was a trope of fascist rhetoric. The usage was remarkably interwoven throughout the fascist theory of religion … So too did National Socialism—the swastika is a solar symbol—if you recall the video of Hitler's speech in 1939 when he threatens the annihilation of the Jews, behind him is a massive swastika with rays emanating as from the sun. And this imagery was then taken up by theorists of religion.

After providing an abundant amount of textual support for his contention, Steve gets to the main point related to my own essay upon which he was commenting,

> The discourse on androgyny has been contaminated by some of this stuff, which is what prompted these lubrications of mine. Our forays into gender-sensitive revisions of scholarship demand that we be alert to the ideologies built into scholarship. Thus, while these materials might not be strictly pertinent to your motif of an androgynous phallus, they may nonetheless provide contexts for reflection on that motif.

Many more of our conversations in the next two decades went this way, Steve constantly pushing me to consider the ideological biases that may have buttressed the symbolic and mythical ideas I was explicating in my interpretation of kabbalistic esotericism. I always listened carefully and struggled sincerely with the position promulgated by my comrade and colleague, but in the end, I harbored a different view, not because I ever wished to defend the obvious moral failings of Heidegger, but because I did not, and still do not, think that one's philosophical ruminations are determined monolithically by political affiliations. To be sure, the political and the philosophical cannot be completely separated; this does not mean, however, that the latter is only an epiphenomenon of the former. The space we must inhabit, as uncomfortable as it might be, is to acknowledge that Heidegger was both a Nazi given to anti-Semitic stereotypes and an incisive philosopher whose thinking not only was responding to the urgencies of his epoch but also contains the potential to unravel the thorny knot of politics and philosophy. Heidegger, in short, is neither defensible nor disposable; his thinking—and this includes, above all, his scapegoating of Jews under the rubric of *das Judentum*—demands reflective analysis and critical questioning.[2] As Heidegger himself surmised, extrapolating from the specific example of Nietzsche's doctrine of the eternal recurrence of the same attributed to Zarathustra, a thinker's essential thought can be envisioned (*Gesichtetes*) but remains an enigma (*Rätsel*) worthy of questioning (*fragwürdig*).[3] Before one presumes an indissoluble link between Heidegger's flirtation with Nazism and his thought, one is obligated to submit oneself—in the sacrificial spirit of the piety of thinking—to the subtleties and complexities of his writings and, most of all, to be faithful to the centrality of the Socratic method of questioning by questioning the questions so that new questions emerge to elucidate what is left unquestioned. To paraphrase Habermas, one must think with Heidegger against Heidegger.[4] This chapter is in many respects the continuation of the *Sprachdenken* with Steve that began in the dawning of our academic careers. The specific focus on the intertwining of the themes of language, silence, redemption, and alienation captures the cadence of our dialogue and the focal point of the divergent congruence of our shared vision.

Turning first to Heidegger, let me commence with the well-known fact that in his thought after the so-called turn in the 1930s, he ascribed to Dasein the special role of guarding the clearing (*Lichtung*), the primal space of the between, wherein language and being are juxtaposed in the sameness of their difference. The showing-saying of language reveals the name of the namelessness that remains hidden as a result of being exposed as the beyng that cannot be exposed within the plethora of beings that constitute the world. The poet is privileged as the purveyor of the mystery of language that bears witness to the breakaway (*Aufbruch*) through which beyng originarily becomes word and the nameless dons the attire of the name.⁵ For Heidegger, as for the kabbalists, the origin of language is the ability to keep silent. Consider this striking meditation in the *Beiträge zur Philosophie (Vom Ereignis)* on restraint (*Verhaltenheit*), silence (*Schweigen*), and language (*Sprache*):

> Words fail us; they do so originally and not merely occasionally, whereby some discourse or assertion could indeed be carried out but is left unuttered, i.e., where the saying of something sayable or the re-saying of something already said is simply not carried through. Words do not yet come to speech at all, but it is precisely in failing us that they arrive at the first leap. This failing is the event as intimation and incursion of beyng. This failing us is the inceptual condition for the self-unfolding possibility of an original (poetic) naming of beyng.⁶

Heidegger's notion of ineffability does not entail the saying of the unsayable if the latter is understood as something potentially sayable that is presently not spoken. What he proposed rather is the unsaying of the sayable, which is to say, the belief that every utterance falls short of articulating the words that have yet to assume the character of speech, but this failure is what makes possible the poetic naming of being.⁷ Insofar as the naming cannot be severed from the nameless that defies naming, the mystery to which language can only allude, the apophatic and the kataphatic are inextricably conjoined in what Heidegger refers to as the possibility of language to express itself as the "telling silence,"⁸ or literally, the "saying not-saying" (*sagenden Nichtsagens*).⁹ By saying the unsaid in unsaying the said, the poem mimics the simultaneous appearing and disappearing that is characteristic of the spatiotemporal construction of being,¹⁰ and in that respect, the poet ideally fulfills the task allocated to the human being—the messenger who bears the unconcealment of the twofold (*der Botengänger der Botschaft der Entbergung der Zwiefalt*)—to seek the mystery of the boundary (*das Geheimnis der Grenze*) on the path of thinking by testing the limit of the boundary of the boundless (*der Grenzgänger des Grenzenlosen*).¹¹ Poetic language dramatizes into a narratological form the giving of the nongiven, the withholding bestowal of the nihilating ground of the nonground, the unconcealment of being as it conceals itself in the unpresentability of truth that constitutes the condition of the possibility of its presentation as nonpresentable.¹² More than the philosopher and the scientist, the poet knows that language manifests the wholly invisible (*ganz Unsichtbare*) that, above all, determines everything to which the human must correspond out of the ground of his existence (*jedoch allem zuvor alles Bestimmende, dem der Mensch aus dem Grunde seines Daseins entsprechen muß*),¹³ the nothing that is more originary than the "not" of negation (*das Nichts ist ursprünglicher als das Nicht und die Verneinung*),¹⁴ the advent of the retreat of the appropriating event, the nullity that precedes the fissure into being and nonbeing.¹⁵ The revealing of nothing perforce must be a concealing, for only by being concealed can nothing be revealed.¹⁶

Heidegger's identifying the primary task of language as poiēsis, understood as the unconcealment of the concealed, suggests a striking similarity to the kabbalists, who likewise view language—and in particular the matrix language Hebrew—principally as the unconcealing of the concealment that is the namelessness unveiled through the veil of the name.[17] The nameless name posited by the kabbalists corresponds to Heidegger's understanding of the nothing that is the beyng given in but recoiling from the superfluity of beings that make up the multiverse, what he referred to in *Was ist Metaphysik?* (1929) as the repelling gesture (*abweisende Verweisung*) of the nothing in relation to beings as a whole.[18] The fundamental occurrence of Dasein is identified as the unveiling of this beyng through the beings that "conceal from us the nothing we are seeking." Hence, the nothing is not placed before us as a consequence of the "complete negation of the totality of beings," but rather it is the disclosure of the latter that "makes manifest the nothing."[19] For the nothing to be manifest as nothing, it must remain unmanifest in the manifestation of the plethora of beings in which it is manifest.

The beyng of which Heidegger speaks, as the *Ein Sof* of the kabbalists, is not akin to the differential void that may be envisioned either as the something of nothingness or as the nothingness of something.[20] We become attuned to this nothing by way of anxiety, which is not the fear of any determinate something, but the sense of uncanniness that arises when indeterminateness comes to the fore, that is, when we cannot say anything definitive about that before which we feel uncanny. This feeling of the *unheimlich* is a continuation of what Heidegger analyzed in *Sein und Zeit* in conjunction with the basic attunement (*Grundbefindlichkeit*) to the mood of anxiety that leaves one disoriented as the tranquility and self-assurance of "being-at-home" (*Zuhause-sein*) in the everyday world slip away and one enters the existential state of "uncanniness" (*Unheimlichkeit*), the sense of "not-being-at-home" (*Nicht-zuhause-sein*),[21] an ontological condition in which the familiar becomes strange.[22] In addition, the *Unheimlichkeit* in confronting the nothing bears a phenomenological resemblance to the gnostically infected *Bekümmerung*, the sense of distress or disquietude, the term that Heidegger used in an early phase—as a precursor to Augustine's *cura* rendered as *Sorge*—to name the "original motivation to philosophize in the face of the very facticity of life."[23] In this state of suspicion, we have no hold on the certainty of the self or of entities in the world—in the *Phänomenologische Interpretationen zu Aristoteles: Einführung in die Phänomenologische Forschung*, the lecture course from the winter semester 1921–1922, Heidegger describes this as the "genuine loss" of "letting oneself be diverted from facticity" (*Sichabringenlassen der Faktizität*), which constitutes the existence (*Existenz*) of the "radical existentiell worry" (*radikale existenzielle Bekümmerung*)[24]—and hence the philosophical disposition arises as the clear demarcation of being fades from our purview; in this sense, the unrest of anxiety reveals the nothing that nothing is not in virtue of not being the nothing that nothing is.[25]

In an extraordinary passage from the *Schwarze Hefte*, Heidegger avails himself of language that is even more strikingly gnostic: the delusion we must break through is that it is impossible to step outside the relation of humankind to being; on the contrary, it is the vocation of the thinker "to question disclosively [*erfragen*] the whole of this relation." To do so requires that "one would step into nothingness [*das Nichts*]. Yet as long as this is allowed merely as something misthought, contrived, it is only the semblance of that semblance [*der Schein jenes Scheins*]." If, however, the outermost [*Äußerste*] is only the innermost [*Innerste*] of the human being, then the outside [*Außerhalb*] becomes the inside of the innermost and deepest [*Innerhalb des Innersten und Tiefsten*], becomes that place where the human being has forsaken himself the longest [*sich längst verlassen*] and in the highest mission of his essence has found himself [*in den höchsten Auftrag seines Wesens gefunden hat*]. Have to come back from there as a complete alien [*ein ganz Fremder*] and bring along—set down—the most alien [*das Befremdlichste*].[26]

When the external is internalized, the internal is externalized, and one is thus centered in the marginality of alienation, the unsettling experience of being situated in the disconcerting place where one finds oneself by discovering the abandonment of self. Heidegger's formulation is evocative of the notion of the redeemed redeemer, the redeemer who is in need of redemption as a consequence of attempting to redeem others trapped in the material world of darkness, an interpretation of ancient Gnosticism undoubtedly known to Heidegger from the German *Religionsgeschichtliche Schule* and particularly Richard Reitzenstein,[27] whose perspective was accepted and elaborated by Rudolf Bultmann in his presentation of the unfolding of Hellenistic Christianity by means of gnostic terminology,[28] and continued by his students, including Hans Jonas in his portrayal of the gnostic image of the alien.[29] The degree to which Heidegger was informed by a similar myth of estrangement in the world is made even more explicit in the subsequent entry in notebooks:

The alien (*the human being*) and the great fortuitiveness (*being*). The throwing into being and the trembling of the thrownness into the essence as *language*. Language: *the hearth of the world* ... Here the uniqueness of the revealing-concealing isolation in the simplicity of the aloneness of Dasein. (The unison.)[30]

The kinship of Heidegger's worldview and what German historians of religion in the early twentieth century considered to be the essence of Gnosticism are brought to light when we consider the following summation of Bultmann:

For the essence of Gnosticism does not lie in its syncretistic mythology but rather in a new understanding ... of man and the world; its mythology is only the expression of this understanding. Whereas to ancient man the world had been home ... the *utter difference of human existence from all worldly existence* was recognized for the first time in Gnosticism and Christianity, and thus the world became foreign soil to the human self ... in fact, in Gnosticism, his prison. Gnostic thought is so radical that to it the impulses of one's own senses, instincts, and desires, by which man is bound to the world, appear alien and hostile—hostile to man's real self, which cannot achieve its own nature in this world at all, and to which this world is a prison in which his real self, related to and derived from the divine world of light, is shackled by the demonic powers of darkness.[31]

In Heidegger's philosophical translation of this myth, the human being (*der Mensch*) is labeled the alien (*der Fremdling*) vis-à-vis the great happenstance (*der große Zufall*) of being (*das Sein*). The existential state of this alienation is further described as the "throwing into being" (*der Wurf in das Sein*) and as "the trembling of the thrownness into the essence as *language*" (*das Erzittern der Geworfenheit in das Wesen als* Sprache).[32] Language is the hearth of the world wherein one finds "the uniqueness [*Einzigkeit*] of the revealing-concealing isolation [*entbergend-verbergenden Vereinzelung*] in the simplicity [*Einfache*] of the aloneness [*Allein-heit*] of Dasein."[33] Paradoxically, language is the home that is not only the place of isolation and aloneness but also the place of unison (*Ein-klang*), the haven of solitude, and the womb of relationality. Moreover, as Heidegger put it in *Was ist Metaphysik?*, the experience of being hurled into the abode of language is disquieting, as it "robs us of speech. Because beings as a whole slip away, so that precisely the nothing crowds around, all utterance of the 'is' falls silent in the face of the nothing. That in the uncanniness of anxiety we often try to shatter the vacant stillness with compulsive talk only proves the presence of the nothing."[34] In the postscript to the 1943 edition of this essay, Heidegger reiterates the central point of his argument: "One of the essential sites of speechlessness [*Sprachlosigkeit*] is anxiety in the sense of the horror to which the abyss of the nothing [*Abgrund des Nichts*] attunes human beings."[35]

In spite of Scholem's explicit disavowal of and occasional ridiculing of Heidegger,[36] there is a remarkable affinity between the Heideggerian discussion of the mood of anxiety with which one is overcome when mutely confronting the nothing of being and what Scholem—perhaps influenced by Benjamin's reflections on the nexus of language and lament[37]—argued in the youthful cogitation "On Lament and Lamentation," composed in 1917:

> All language is infinite. But there is one language whose infinity is deeper and different from all others (besides the language of God). For whereas every language is a positive expression of a being, and its infinity resides in the two bordering lands of the revealed [*Offenbarten*] and the silenced [*Verschwiegenen*], such that it actually stretches out over both realms, this language is different from any other language in that it remains throughout on the border [*Grenze*], exactly on the border between these two realms. This language reveals nothing [*offenbart Nichts*], because the being that reveals itself in it has no content (and for that reason one can also say that it reveals everything) and conceals nothing [*verschweigt nichts*], because its entire existence [*Dasein*] is based on a revolution of silence. It is not symbolic, but only points toward the symbol; it is not concrete [*nicht gegenständlich*], but annihilates the object [*vernichtet den Gegenstand*]. This language is lament.[38]

The description of the infinity of language residing between concealment and disclosure—a theme that Scholem would later connect more specifically to the linguistic theory of the kabbalah[39]—is reminiscent of Heidegger's positioning poiēsis on the boundary between speech and speechlessness; that is, poetry is a form of keeping silent by speaking rather than speaking by keeping silent, or in Heidegger's precise formulation, a projective saying through which the preparation of the sayable facilitates the coming to fruition of the unsayable in the world.[40] Analogously, Scholem identifies lament as "nothing other than a language on the border, language of the border itself. Everything it says is infinite, but just and only infinite with regard to the symbol. In lament, nothing is expressed and everything is implied."[41] What is particular about this language is that it does not refer to anything particular but to the condition of being that enframes all beings in a singularly universal as opposed to a universally singular way: "To be is to be the source of lament [*Sein heißt: Quell von Klage sein*]. Origin and border, as in birth in the sphere of life, converge in the sphere of language within lament."[42]

Moreover, just as for Heidegger anxiety has no specific object and hence the linguistic response it occasions is, at best, a metaphor of what cannot be rendered metaphorically—the metaphor par excellence that serves as a metaphor for everything being a metaphor that nothing is metaphorical—so for Scholem, lament is a language that both reveals nothing because the being that it reveals has no content and conceals nothing because its entire existence is based on a revolution of silence through which there is a restoration (*Zurückführung*) of the symbolic to the revelation that induces mourning's self-overturning (*Sichselbst-überschlagen*) and the consequent reversal (*Umkehrung*) that "allows for the course toward language to emerge as expression."[43] The expression that emerges from this revolution, however, is an expression of the inexpressible, the language of silence, an apophatic proclamation. This act of unsaying or speaking-away, which paradoxically reaches its climactic enunciation in speaking the unspeakable, is predicated on the agonizing assumption—both liberating and inhibiting—that what is said can never be what is spoken insofar as what is spoken can never be what is said.[44] This is what Scholem intends when he writes that lament is

> a completely unsymbolic language, since there is no symbol of a symbol. It is only symbolic in relation to that in mourning, which itself is neither a symbol nor an object, but was a symbol and an object; now, however, in annihilation, it signifies the infinite nothing [*das unendliche Nichts*], the zero to an infinite degree [*die Null vom Grade Unendlich*]: the expressionless [*das Ausdruckslose*], the extinguished [*das Erloschene*].[45]

To identify lament as the language of annihilation (*die Sprache der Vernichtung*) means not only that what is declaimed is erased in its very declamation but that the erasure, too, can be erased—and hence be itself—merely through declamation. As Heidegger somewhat enigmatically remarked about the dictum on the basis of which the attunement of the beginning is to be experienced: "*The concealed deep mourning over the veiled decaying of the essence into being as presence* [Die verborgene tiefe Trauer über das verhüllte Ver-wesen des Wesens zum Sein als Anwesenheit]."[46]

It is worth comparing Scholem's tantalizing characterization of lament as an unsymbolic language to the following depiction of language in Heidegger's "Brief über den 'Humanismus'" (1946):

> In its essence, language is not the utterance [*Äußerung*] of an organism; nor is it the expression [*Ausdruck*] of a living thing. Nor can it ever be thought in an essentially correct way in terms of symbolic character [*Zeichencharakter*], perhaps not even

in terms of the character of signification [*Bedeutungscharakter*]. Language is the clearing-concealing advent of being itself [*lichtend-verbergende Ankunft des Seins selbst*].⁴⁷

I do not intend to collapse all the differences between Heidegger and Scholem, but the points of commonality are not without import. For both, language is not primarily a form of chatter or communication nor is it a matter of symbolization or signification. It is the opening that reveals and conceals the event of being whose nucleus is nothing. Although the more mature Scholem used the idea of the symbol to depict what he considered to be at the heart of the kabbalistic theory of language, it is important to note that his use of symbol corresponds conceptually to his earlier locution "unsymbolic," that is, the signifier that points to that which is beyond signification. This, in turn, is in the neighborhood of Heidegger's way of speaking about language as the clearing in which beings are disclosed in their hiddenness and hidden in their disclosure.

Here it is well to recall Wittgenstein's quip in the preface of the *Tractatus*, the second part of which corresponds verbatim to the conclusion of that treatise, that the whole meaning of the book can be summed up as follows: "What can be said at all can be said clearly; and whereof one cannot speak thereof one must be silent." The philosophical burden, then, is to draw the limit (*Grenze*) to the expression of thought (*Ausdruck der Gedanken*), to establish the dividing line "to be able to think both sides of this limit," which is to say to be able to assess what we are capable of thinking and what cannot be thought. The other side to the border of speech, or the limit to thinking, is nonsense (*Unsinn*).⁴⁸ Conversely, for both Scholem and Heidegger, the limit is the differentiating point that demarcates the borderline between being and nonbeing. From Scholem's standpoint, only lament, the language of the border that marks the liminality of speech, enables one to cross from the silence that has descended into speech to the speech that has ascended unto silence. In contrast to revelation, whereby "each language is absolutely positive and expresses nothing more than the positivity of the linguistic world," lament entails that "each language suffers death in a truly tragic sense, in that this language expresses nothing, absolutely nothing positive, but only the pure border."⁴⁹ Lament is thus the tragic point (*tragischen Punkt*) of all language, repeatedly attempting to become symbolic but failing, since as the language of annihilation, every attempt at articulation is, *ipso facto*, self-annihilation.⁵⁰ Alternatively expressed, lament is the silence that cannot be silenced, but, as such, it is the purest and truest form of speech, rendered theologically as the word of God.⁵¹

> There is no answer to lament, which is to say, there is only one: falling mute [*das Verstummen*]. Here again lament shows itself to be the deep opposition of revelation, which is the linguistic form that absolutely demands an answer and enables one ... The teaching that is not expressed, nor alluded to in lament, but that is kept silent, is silence itself. And therefore lament can usurp any language: it is the not empty, but extinguished expression, in which its death wish and its inability to die join together. The expression of the innermost expressionlessness [*der Ausdruck des innerlichst Ausdruckslosen*], the language of silence [*die Sprache des Schweigens*] is lament. The language is infinite, but it has the infinity of

annihilation [*die Unendlichkeit der Vernichtung*], which is, as it were, the ultimate power [*Potenz*] of what has been extinguished.[52]

Significantly, as I noted above, Heidegger understood poiēsis as a form of *saying not-saying*. Scholem likewise referred to lament as the *language of silence*, the *expression of the innermost expressionlessness*, the speechlessness (*das Sprachlose*) that reveals and thereby conceals the nothing at the innermost center (*Mittelpunktes*) of that which has no core (*Kern*).[53] Moreover, in consonance with Heidegger's view that poetic language is "not supposed to express anything, but to leave the unsayable unsaid, and to do so in and through its saying,"[54] Scholem's grappling with the seemingly implacable snare of the apophatic need to speak about not speaking is exemplified in poetic language: "Every lament can be expressed as poetry, since its particular liminality [*Grenzhaftigkeit*] between the linguistic realms, its tragic paradox makes it so … Perhaps, indeed, the languages of symbolic objects have no other possibility to become languages of poetry except in the state of lament."[55]

With respect to poetizing in particular and, by extension, language more generally, there is a commingling of the apophatic and the kataphatic: precisely through the act of saying the poet leaves the unsayable unsaid, not by being reticent but by saying the unsayable in the unsaying of the sayable. The infinite force that is in each word of lament

> negates itself and sinks back into the infinity of silence, in which the word's emptiness [*Leere*] becomes teaching [*Lehre*] … The silent rhythm, the monotony of lament is the only thing that remains: as the only thing that is symbolic in lament—a symbol, namely, of being extinguished [*Erloschenseins*] in the revolution of morning … But the very inviolability of rhythm in relation to words is what, in the most elementary sense, constitutes all poetry … Lament is thus in poetry what death is in the sphere of life.[56]

Just as death constitutes the only hope in reconciliation in life, lamentation is the restitution of language that occurs through the annihilation of language, that is, the symbolic expression of the inexpressible, which is a form of speaking-not and not falling into silence characteristic of not speaking.[57] The mystical nature of lamentation compels us to discern that the wealth of images utilized by the poet relate only to the apparent and not to the objectively real because what the images reveal is the zero point (*Nullpunkt*), expressed mathematically by Scholem as $X \times 0 = 0$.[58] Translating this calculus of the incalculable into an optical metaphor, language is the mirror that cannot mirror itself and thus mirrors the image of the nothing that everything is not, the real appearance of what appears to be real.[59]

One can discern here the seeds for what Scholem came to identify as the core of the meaning of language in the Jewish mystical tradition. As he wrote in the letter to Rosenzweig dated December 26, 1926: "The power of the language is hidden within the name; its abyss is sealed therein."[60] Scholem's main concern in the letter is to express the challenge of the secularization of the holiness of the Hebrew language posed by Zionism and the return of the Jewish people to the modern nationalist state.

Hence, the language to which Scholem refers in the aforecited remark is Hebrew and the name alludes to the Tetragrammaton. Reworking a rabbinic tradition concerning the sealing of the cosmic abyss by the letters of the divine name, Scholem speaks of the abyss of language sealed by the name. That abyss, we can assume, is itself inchoate and therefore nameless, an idea that he would later express in a letter to Benjamin, written on September 20, 1934, as the "nothingness of revelation" (*Nichts der Offenbarung*), which he elucidates as

> a state in which revelation appears to be without meaning, in which it still asserts itself, in which it has *validity* but no *significance*. A state in which the wealth of meaning is lost and what is in the process of appearing (for revelation is such a process) still does not disappear, even though it is reduced to the zero point of its own content, so to speak.[61]

The connection to Scholem's earlier speculation on lament is obvious: in both instances, he avails himself of the algebraic-geometric concept of the zero point—the inflection point that demarcates the originary nonzero in relation to which all coordinates of the surrounding vector are determined—in order to express the essence of language as the revelation of nothing to be revealed, the appearance of nonappearance, which is to be distinguished from disappearance, for the nonapparent appears, albeit as what does not appear. The nothingness of revelation lays bare language in its most rudimentary form as essentially insignificant—called by some its naked truth but which I prefer to designate its primal investiture, since I do not think we can behold the nakedness of truth except through the veil of truth that unveils the truth of the veil; that is, at its core, divine language has the potential for limitless meaning and, consequently, it cannot be limited to any specific meaning. From the kabbalistic perspective in Scholem's presentation, *Ein Sof* (*das Unendliche*), the concealed Godhead (*verborgene Gottheit*) without form (*gestaltlos*), dwells indecipherably (*unerkennbar*) in the depths of its being, and thus can only be described negatively, indeed through the negation of all negations (*der Negation aller Negationen*).[62] However, insofar as every expression of the infinite contains the inexpressible, there is a play of doubleness (*Doppelspiel*), a coincidence of opposites that is labeled by Scholem the *dialectic of form*. To avoid interpreting this dialectic in Hegelian terms, I would suggest renaming the phenomenon in Heideggerian jargon as the juxtaposition wherein the autonomous identity of the contraries remains intact: every disclosure is concealment without the concealment being sublated into disclosure; every conferral on creation is a withdrawing from creation without the withdrawal being sublated into conferral.

The concurrent concealment of the infinite and its omnipresence thus yields the cosmological paradox that God is present in the world from which God is absent—not that God is absent after being present but present and absent at the same time. This paradox, in turn, undergirds what Scholem calls the "mystical nihilism" (*mystische Nihilismus*) that has informed kabbalistic metaphysics: inasmuch as the "formless substance" (*gestaltlose Substanz*) is manifest in every stage of emanation and creation, "there is no thoroughly shaped image [*durchgestaltete Gestalt*] that can completely detach itself from the depths of the formless … The truer the form the more powerful the life of the formless within it."⁶³ Invoking Benjamin, albeit anonymously as a great thinker (*ein großer Denker*),⁶⁴ Scholem writes that the kabbalists, by comparing the theory of emanation with mystical linguistic theory of the name of God, were able to grasp that imagelessness is the refuge of all images.⁶⁵ Scholem was certainly correct to detect that Benjamin's claim that the yearning that crosses the threshold of the image to the imageless refuge of all images is the power of the name reverberates with the kabbalistic perspective. But perhaps even more pertinent is another observation of Benjamin in a fragment on the imagination written in 1920–1921, every apparition is a "de-formation [*Entstaltung*] of what has been formed. It is a characteristic of all imagination that it plays a game of dissolution with its forms."⁶⁶ These words cast a light on the central paradox of kabbalistic theosophy underscored by Scholem, and one that, in my opinion, echoes Heidegger's contention regarding the refusal of beyng from the beings it bestows: the imagelessness of *Ein Sof* is manifestly concealed in the images of the *sefirot*. Immanuel Ḥai Ricchi succinctly expressed the premise underlying this principle, "the inwardness of the secret [*penimiyyut ha-sod*] is the secret of *Ein Sof*, which sustains the *sefirot*, corresponding to the brain that is within the substance."⁶⁷ This insight applies whether the *sefirot* are interpreted as consubstantial with the essence (*aṣmut*) of the divine light or as instruments (*kelim*) through which that light is channeled. That is, whether one adopts the essentialist or the instrumentalist perspective—the two dominant theoretical models to explain the relationship of the sefirotic gradations to *Ein Sof*—one must profess the paradox that the concealment of the infinite can be revealed only insofar as it is concealed, for what is concealed cannot be revealed unless it persists in being concealed. Every act of bestowal, therefore, is concomitantly a withholding. From the perspective of the visionary, the ascent to the pleroma of form is a descent into the abyss of formlessness, and the mystical language that ensues therefrom is a speaking that is an unspeaking, the communication of the incommunicable, the imaginal fabrication of a myriad of images in the attempt to reveal and thereby conceal the imagelessness that is devoid of positive content. The imagelessness is preserved in the images by which it is unseen.

Scholem would later identify the symbolic nature of language as naming the absolute concreteness of the word of God that can never assume any particular semantic form as the shared characteristic and inner dimension of all mystical traditions. As he put it in "The Name of God and the Linguistic Theory of the Kabbala," based on the lecture given at the Eranos meeting in Ascona, 1970:

> The linguistic theories of mystics frequently diverge when it comes to determining this symbolic nature. But all mystics in quest of the secret of language come to share a common basis, namely the fact that language is used to communicate something which goes beyond the sphere which allows for expression and formation; the fact, also, that a certain inexpressible something, which only manifests itself in symbols, resonates in every manner of expression; that this something is fundamental to every manner of expression, and … flashes through the chinks which exist in the universal structure of expression.⁶⁸

A direct line can be drawn from the earlier reflection on the nature of lament and the later speculation on the nature of mystical language.[69] Specifically as it relates to the kabbalah, the original source of all language is the essential name, the name that names the essence but which is not indicative of any specific activity. The name, therefore, is the infinitely interpretable wellspring of all meaning that itself has no fixed significance.[70] As Scholem expressed it elsewhere,

> The word of God must be infinite, or, to put it in a different way, the absolute word is as such meaningless, but it is *pregnant* with meaning. Under human eyes it enters into significant finite embodiments which mark innumerable layers of meaning ... Authority no longer resides in a single unmistakable "meaning" of the divine communication, but in its infinite capacity to take on new form.[71]

Just as the younger Scholem identified lament as the speechlessness at the innermost center of language, so the older Scholem identified the Tetragrammaton, the central point of revelation, as the meaninglessness that enables meaning to be decipherable through exegesis. The primary meaningfulness of language, both human and divine, is not a matter of communication but appeal.[72] This is the crux of Scholem's well-known view that the mystical symbol "'signifies' nothing and communicates nothing, but makes something transparent which is beyond all expression ... It is a 'momentary totality' which is perceived intuitively in a mystical *now*—the dimension of time proper to the symbol."[73] What is rendered transparent is not a thing at all; it is the nothingness of revelation, which refers not to the inaccessible transcendence of ontotheological speculation, as some have argued,[74] but to the being exposed in the concealment of its being. The transparency of the symbolic exposure is linked temporally to the now, the modality of time beyond the partition of time, the equiprimordiality of past, present, and future.

The crisis of modernity is that with the falling silent of tradition, the name of God is withdrawn from language, and the mystery of ineffability is no longer retrievable. In an oratorical flourish that again calls to mind Heidegger, Scholem insists that poets are the ones who can address this crisis:

> For poets do not share the doubt that most mystics have in regard to language. And poets have one link with the masters of the Kabbala, even when they reject Kabbalistic theological formulation as being still too emphatic. The link is their belief in language as an absolute, which is as if constantly flung open by dialectics. It is their belief in the mystery of language which has become audible.[75]

Much attention has been paid to the affinities and differences between Benjamin's theory of language and what Scholem elicits about language from the kabbalistic material.[76] There is good historical and textual justification for this comparison. However, I want to suggest, by way of addition and not substitution, that more consideration be given to the views proffered respectively by Scholem and Heidegger. For both, the power of the poet is connected to disclosing the noncommunicable essence of language, the mystery of the nameless that is coiled in the unspoken core of every word spoken. Furthermore, not only were both thinkers keenly attuned to the fact that there is no unconcealment that is not a concealment, but they equally understood the current predicament of humanity as one in which the absence—for Heidegger, signifying the obfuscation of being by metaphysics, and for Scholem, the removal of God from history by secularization—is the most profound presence. Consider Scholem's assessment in his memorial address for Rosenzweig delivered in January 1930:

> The divinity, banished from man by psychology and from the world by sociology, no longer wanting to reside in the heavens, has handed over the throne of justice to dialectical materialism and the seat of mercy to psychoanalysis and has withdrawn to some hidden place and does not disclose Himself. Is He truly undisclosed? Perhaps this last withdrawal is His revelation. Perhaps God's removal to the point of nothingness was a higher need, and He will reveal His kingship only to a world that has been emptied.[77]

Here it is worthwhile recalling Scholem's quip years later in the interview with Ehud Ben Ezer that the atheistic religion brought forth by the secular world endorses the ironic belief that *God will appear as non-God*.[78] In *Religion after Religion*, Wasserstrom detects in this comment a *coincidentia oppositorum* of the skeptic and the gnostic.[79] In a slightly different terminological register, I would say that Scholem was articulating the sentiment that the atheistic surmounting of theolatry is the highest level of faith. This truism may be culled from Adorno's comment in his *Negative Dialektik* that the supreme metaphysical idea of truth leads us to the proposition that the "one who believes in God cannot believe in God,"[80] and hence "the possibility represented by the divine name is maintained, rather, by him who does not believe. Once upon a time the image ban extended to pronouncing the name; now the ban itself has in that form come to evoke suspicions of superstition."[81] The philosophical implications of the Jewish notion of *Bilderverbot*, the denunciation of any imagistic representation of God as idolatrous, is corroborated by the conclusion of Adorno's essay "Vernunft und Offenbarung" that the "paradoxical purity" of revealed religion is such that "it would dissolve into something completely indeterminate, a nothingness that could hardly be distinguished from religion's liquidation ... Therefore, I see no other possibility than an extreme ascesis toward any type of revealed faith, an extreme loyalty to the prohibition of images, far beyond what this once originally meant."[82] The paradox of the atheistic culmination of the theistic iconoclasm, buttressed by the apophatic reformation of the scriptural faith, has been expressed in recent times by Henri Atlan, "the ultimate idol is the personal God of theology ... the only discourse about God that is not idolatrous is necessarily an atheistic discourse. Alternatively, whatever the discourse, *the only God who is not an idol is a God who is not a God*."[83] Even agnostic claims that all we can know is that we cannot know and apophatic utterances that all we can speak is that we cannot speak are, in the last analysis, self-refuting human fabrications—they are true only if untrue and untrue only if true.

Heidegger was less inclined to use such explicit theological terminology, and of course he showed no overt interest in patterns of Jewish thought, let alone the complex kabbalistic symbolism lurking behind Scholem's impassioned appraisal of the current existential situation as one in which the name of God has been removed from human language. There is, however, an intriguing correspondence between Scholem's perspective and Heidegger's mystifying conception of the last god.[84] Briefly, this notion is his way of coming to terms with Nietzsche's death of god, which signifies "the abandonment of being in the current appearance of beings";[85] that is, the last god is the god after there are no more gods,[86] the god depleted of godhood, the god that signals the overcoming of ontotheology and hence the setting of philosophy on the new course of thinking about the open concealedness (*offene Verborgenheit*) of the essential occurrence of beyng, a mode of contemplation set against calculative reasoning and to which he refers by various names, to wit, "originary meditation" (*ursprünglichen Besinnung*),[87] "thoughtful meditation" (*denkerische Besinnung*),[88] and "thoughtful configuration" (*denkerische Gestaltung*).[89] In the liminal epoch between the presence of what is absent and the absence of what is present, Heidegger saw his task as preparing the "future ones" to stand in the "remotest proximity of the last god" by remaining silent about what is essential,[90] but the last god is the god that is to come, and therefore can be proximate only by being infinitely remote. In a way suggestive of the Jewish belief that the possibility of the messiah's coming is predicated on the impossibility of the messiah's arrival—the hope in the return of what is interminably still to come, the quintessential event of the nonevent—Heidegger maintains that the lastness of the last god consists of the fact that the god is relentlessly coming, which provokes a state of continual waiting.

> He brings nothing, unless himself; yet even then only as the most coming of that which comes [*den Kommendsten des Kommenden*]. Ahead of himself, he bears the to-come of the future [*Zu-kunft*], his time-play-space is beyng, a time-play-space that itself waits for the god, in coming, to fulfill it and in coming to come [*im Kommen komme*]. Thus is the god, of his necessity choosing beyng, the most extreme god, who knows no making [*Machen*] or providence [*Vorsehen*].[91]

The last god is the symbolic enactment of the demise of god. As Heidegger observes in another passage, in language that resounds rhetorically with the aforecited words of Scholem, the "advancing secularism" of the "disempowerment of the beginning," which proceeds from the inceptual entanglement in beyng, requires the "pushing away of beings" and this "will then carry over even to God—as the creator."[92] Simply put, the last god is manifest when what is manifest is no longer the theistically conceived god. Heidegger's intention is expressed unequivocally in the following comment:

> The most intrinsic finitude of beyng reveals itself here: in the intimation of the last god [*Hier enthüllt sich die innerste Endlichkeit des Seyns: im Wink des letzten Gottes*] ... The last god has his own most unique uniqueness [*einzigste Einzigkeit*] and stands outside of the calculative determination [*verrechnenden Bestimmung*] expressed in the labels "mono-theism," "pan-theism," and "a-theism." There has been "monotheism," and every other sort of "theism," only since the emergence of Judeo-Christian "apologetics," whose thinking presupposes "metaphysics."

With the death of this God, all theisms wither away. The multiplicity of gods is not subject to enumeration but, instead, to the inner richness of the grounds and abysses in the site of the moment [*Augenblicksstätte*] for the lighting up and concealment of the intimation of the last god.[93]

Those who would use Heidegger as a foundation to construct a new theological edifice have not grasped the collapse of the polarity of theism and atheism intimated by the intimation of the last god and thus they have not taken to heart the deep-rooted and far-reaching finitude disclosed by this god, an epiphany of nothing to see that imparts knowledge of "the *most concealed* essence of the '*not*' [Nicht], as the 'not yet' [*Noch-nicht*] and the 'not any longer' [*Nicht-mehr*]," the site of the moment that bespeaks the concealing-revealing of the "intimacy and pervasiveness of the negative [*Nichthaften*] in beyng," the "truth of the *not* itself, and consequently also of *nothingness* [*Nichts*]."[94] Heidegger would have agreed with Scholem's anarchistic atheology[95] that, in a world emptied of all but its own emptiness, occlusion might be the highest form of manifestation. Both thinkers, moreover, seemed keenly aware of the fact that the postphilosophical and metapolitical calling of linguistically revealing the concealment of concealment belongs particularly to the poet, who is endowed with the soteriological task to impel others to awaken from being oblivious to the need to be redeemed.

In my view, neither Scholem nor Heidegger ever abandoned the allure of the world-negating orientation of Gnosticism, even though in the case of Scholem it was tempered somewhat by the embrace of Zionism and the affirmation of Palestine, later the state of Israel, as the homeland of the Jewish people and Hebrew as the linguistic correlate that grounds the essence of the national identity.[96] One could say that this is equivalent to Heidegger's embrace of Germany and German as the language most conducive to the disclosure of being, and therefore the most effective language for philosophy and poetry.[97] Just as in the case of Scholem's cultural Zionism, so in the case of Heidegger's attraction to National Socialism, there is a presumed synergy between language and land—the destiny of one is determinative of and determined by the other. Yet, reading between the lines, one could argue that both Scholem and Heidegger continued to be beleaguered by a disjointedness that was askew with their respective ethno-nationalist ideologies, a melancholic dislocation that led each to feel like a *stranger in a strange land*,[98] even when entrenched in the native soil of either Germany or Palestine-Israel. Moreover, the unassailable sense of the tragic and cataclysmic nature of reality and the saturnine distrust[99] in the prospect of rectification of the world's blemish apart from the restitution of all things to the infinite beyond space and time were critical to Scholem's use of the term "gnostic" as a tool of historical and phenomenological inquiry of kabbalistic sources, especially the depiction of the cosmic drama as a crisis within the inner workings of the Godhead according to the Lurianic teaching.[100] Scholem's celebrated remark that the messianic idea in Judaism "compelled a life lived in deferment, in which nothing can be done definitively, nothing can be irrevocably accomplished"[101] is indicative of a pessimistic utopianism that rejects the possibility of an enduring sociopolitical redemption.[102] The constant postponement—referred to by Scholem as the "anti-existentialist idea"—accounts for both the greatness and the constitutional weakness of Jewish messianism: whenever the tension between the expectation and the delay has been alleviated by an actual messianic movement, when the abyss that separates the internal symbolic and the external historical has been crossed, it has been decried or unmasked as pseudo-messianism.[103] The Zionist establishment of the modern state may have been born out of horror and destruction, but it jeopardizes the metahistorical and antipolitical nature of traditional Jewish eschatology, compromising its anarchic and antinomian lifeblood. Scholem thus wondered if Jewish history "will be able to endure this entry into the concrete realm without perishing in the crisis of the Messianic claim."[104] The apocalyptic spirit stems from the infinite negativity of time, the impossible possibility that makes it always possible that the future that is coming threatens not to be the future one has anticipated. The hopelessness of hope proceeds from the fact that the future we are awaiting can never transpire in time and the homeland we are coveting can never materialize in space.

I note, parenthetically, that the gnostic outlook I ascribe to these two thinkers concurs as well with Rosenzweig's characterization of poetry as "at home neither in time nor in space, but where time and space have their inner origin, in imagistic thinking."[105] The poet, constitutionally, is in a state of *Unheimlichkeit*, a condition that is especially germane to the Jews, since they do not feel at home even in the land promised to them as their inheritance.[106] It should come as no surprise that Rosenzweig signals out the Jewish poet as one who disproportionately bears a sense of disaffection in the world to the point that even language is experienced as a source of exile since it is surrounded by the scriptural word.[107] But beyond just the poet, the whole of the Jewish nation, as the metahistorical reference point in history, is fundamentally at odds with the wheeling and dealing of the sociopolitical world. Curiously, the metahistorical status Rosenzweig assigned to the Jews as the eternal people can be compared profitably to the metapolitical role Heidegger ascribed to the poetic dwelling through which one withdraws from the maneuverings of the mundane. Of course, I do not deny that Rosenzweig advocated a return to life as a conquering of death, but this return is rooted in the belief that redemption is not the consequence of historical development, the effect of a causal chain that links the retention of the past and the protention of the future, but rather the corollary of an expectation that is realized as the expectation of what cannot be realized. Salvation comes by way of eternity diremptively breaking into rather than naturally progressing out of history. In the ritualistic lifecycle of the Jew, typified by the Sabbath, time has been proleptically redeemed. This prolepsis entails the suspension of time, which does not imply an abrogation of temporality but its radical deepening, an eradication of time by rooting oneself more squarely in the ground of time. Eternity is not the metaphysical overthrowing of or existential exodus from the fluctuations of time into some stationary heavenly kingdom of heaven; it is rather the compresence of the three dimensions of lived temporality through the eternalization of the present in the continuous becoming of the past that has always been the future that is yet to come.[108]

The notion of time as a linear circularity operative in Rosenzweig's new thinking militates against the belief that history has the potential to redeem itself. There is thus congruity between Rosenzweig's sense of Jewish existence as an inherently exilic state of spatiotemporal ungroundedness, Scholem's insistence on the deferral that is essential to Jewish messianism, and Heidegger's emphasis on the unhomeliness of the human condition in the face of the nothingness of being—an affinity that becomes even more pronounced in Heidegger's later thought, due primarily to the influence of Hölderlin, wherein the poet is idealized as the most suitable guide to the thinker trying to find the language that allows one to be at home in a thinking underway. It is important to recall Heidegger's statement, "A poem: something flimsy, without resistance, evanescent, abstruse, and without substance—such a thing belongs nowhere anymore."[109] *To belong nowhere anymore* is surely referring to the alienation and homelessness that mark the contemporary existential condition. Heidegger's intent, however, exceeds that meaning; the role accorded the uncanny in his understanding of homelessness and homecoming is not constricted by the geopolitical sense of the homeland. Quite to the contrary, the sense of being at home is connected ontologically—or perhaps metaontologically—to that which is foreign.

The entwining of *Heimliche* and *Unheimliche* is elaborated by Heidegger in the section on "becoming homely" in the exposition of Hölderlin's "Der Ister" in the lecture course delivered in the summer semester of 1942 at the University of Freiburg. For Germans, to come into one's own is to belong to the fatherland, but whatever is of the fatherland is at home only in relation to what is alien to it in the mother earth. To be at home depends on an encounter between these two axes:

> This *coming to be* at home in one's own in itself entails that human beings are initially, and for a long time, and sometimes forever, not at home. And this in turn entails that human beings fail to recognize, that they deny, and perhaps even have to deny and flee what belongs to the home. Coming to be at home is thus a passage through the foreign. And if the becoming homely of a particular humankind sustains the historicality of its history, then the law of the encounter [*Auseinandersetzung*] between the foreign and one's own is the fundamental truth of history, a truth from out of which the essence of history must unveil itself.[110]

Coming to be at home is thus a passage through the foreign—the precise obverse of the Nazi conception of the indigenous and the demeaning of the non-Aryan, an idea affirmed by Heidegger himself in his insistence that the homeland is not only "rootedness in the soil" but also the "way of Being of a people ... when it interacts with the outside—when it becomes a state,"[111] a conception that lead him to denigrate the "Semitic nomads" as individuals to whom the nature of the "German space" would likely never be revealed.[112] A few months after making this statement on February 16, 1934, Heidegger educes from Hölderlin's reading of Sophocles in the lecture course on "Germania," delivered in the winter semester of 1934–1935 at the University of Freiburg, that the presence of being at home can be experienced most acutely in the absence of not being at home, occupying the other place that is always the place of the other.

> The uncanny means that which is not "at home," not homely within whatever is homely [*Das Unheimliche meint das, was nicht »daheim«, nicht im Heimischen heimisch ist*]. Accordingly, we must therefore think the extraordinary not as the

immense, nor merely as that which is not the ordinary, but as that which, without the ordinary, resides within that which is not ordinary … Being unhomely is no mere deviance from the homely, but rather the converse: a seeking and searching out the homely, a seeking that at times does not know itself.[113]

Confrontation with the barbarian—the outside that is not merely the expansion of the homeland into the state but a genuine sense of the extrinsic—affords one the opportunity to attain the state of not being at home within the home, to discover the extraordinary as that which is not ordinary within the ordinary. Moreover, only through this engagement with the foreign—the disposition proper to the poeticizing of the poet— can one recover the historical event that is the question of origin (*Ursprungsfrage*),[114] the "original strife" (*ursprüngliche Streit*) that arises from "the intimacy of the 'not' in beyng [*der Innigkeit des* Nicht im Seyn]," that is, the struggle of the oscillation (*Gegenschwung*) between being (*Seyn*) and nonbeing (*Nichtseyn*) in the essence of being.[115] The law of destiny that sends forth the poet into the foundation of the history of the fatherland is the love of not being at home for the sake of becoming at home in what is one's own. The truth of which the essence of history unveils itself—an unveiling that is always also a veiling, indeed, an unveiling of the veiling—is the encounter between the foreign and one's own, the unfamiliar and the familiar, the unordinary and the ordinary. The binaries are pointedly destabilized by Heidegger's creative exegesis of Hölderlin.

As scholars have duly noted, Heidegger's espousal of the Greek-German symbiosis tends toward a racial component as his Germanism, and we can assume his sense of Greekism, is not inclusive of the other precipitously condemned as the barbarian. Heidegger's insistence that Greek and German are the philosophical languages par excellence is further evidence of his ethnocentrism. To cite one illustration from the *Einführung in die Metaphysik* (published in 1953 based on the lecture course given in the summer of 1935): "For along with the German language, Greek (in regard to the possibilities of thinking) is at once the most powerful and the most spiritual of languages."[116] Despite his growing dissatisfaction with the execution of the Nazi agenda, Heidegger never wavered from the conviction that the retrieval of thinking— the second beginning that is the confrontation with the first beginning and the return to the origin concealed therein—must be realized by the German people through their indigenous language and preferably, I surmise, in their native land. Nor did he abandon the belief that German derives its ultimate worth from being the most applicable means to reclaim Greek, the language of "the intimate people" (*das innige Volk*), according to Hölderlin, "armed with the spirit of the gods."[117] In the Le Thor seminar from 1969, Heidegger offered the following romanticized version of Hellenic thought: "The Greeks are those human beings who lived immediately in the openness of phenomena—through the expressly ek-static capacity of letting the phenomena speak to them (modern man, Cartesian man, *se solum alloquendo*, only talks to himself). No one has ever again reached the heights of the Greek experience of being as phenomenon."[118]

The crucial players in the gnostic drama—the ones called upon to sacrifice for the preservation and transformation of the essence of the truth of being—are the Germans; to them exclusively belongs the historical destiny to ameliorate the forgetfulness by heeding the voice of being. Just as kabbalists have categorically assumed that Hebrew, the language of creation and revelation, is the most appropriate means to declaim the ineffable and to conceive the inconceivable, so Heidegger had no compunction about identifying German humanity as the historical humanity: the universal task to unveil the veiling of the veil of unveiling, to disclose the concealment of the unconcealment, can be accomplished only through the language of this particular ethnos. In his sustained analysis of Hölderlin's "Andenken," Heidegger reiterates once again his belief that the universal vocation for the futural humanity can be achieved only through the particular destiny of the German people:

> The dwelling near the origin that prepares a foundation is the original dwelling, in which the poetic is first grounded, upon whose ground the sons of the earth are then to dwell, at least if they are *to dwell poetically upon this earth*. The poesis *of the poets* is now what founds everything that remains. What remains is the originary *remembrance* [*das ursprüngliche* Andenken] ... That which remains prepares the historical place in which German humanity [*das Menschentum der Deutschen*] must first learn to become at home, so that, when it is time, it will be able to linger in the moment when destiny lies in the balance ... *Remembrance* is a poetic abiding in the essence of what is fitting to poetic activity, which, in the secure destiny of Germany's future history, festively shows the ground of its origin.[119]

This passage buttresses the view that Heidegger did come to reject the purely geopolitical understanding of the ideal of the German homeland and the German people, especially in the distorted and vulgar way disseminated by the Nazis, in favor of a theological-political-poetical sensibility, to paraphrase Lacoue-Labarthe.[120] To be at home means, first and foremost, to dwell poetically on earth. The menacing solitude of the wayward path of poiēsis that Heidegger elicits from Hölderlin—at once overwhelmingly individualistic and compellingly collectivistic—forges a breach that destabilizes the nexus between territorialism and exceptionalism, a crack that opens from the weight of the cultural prejudices themselves and seeks to affirm the homelessness of being at home in contrast to the homeliness of being banished from home. Heidegger unearths from Hölderlin the notion of remembrance as a poetic abiding that secures the destiny of the future history of the German people by dwelling in proximity to the origin.[121] And yet, the meditative act of remembrance demands that the foreign element—what was concealed in the origin—is preserved in its foreignness even as it is appropriated as his own by the poet, who in a sense is representative of Germany at large. At the heart of the appropriation is the disappropriated and unassimilable element of the alien. The return to origin comes about by way of the excursion through the foreign. The mandate is thus for the German poet

> to learn the free use of what is his own. That is why the foreign must remain near. That is why, for the future poets, the journey preserves what is unavoidable according to the law whereby they must become-at-home [*Gesetz des Heimischwerdens*]. That is why he who is alone and ponders what is his own at the same time commemorates his companions.[122]

From the intricate relationship of the Greeks and the Germans—a relationship dependent on the essential foreignness of one culture to the other and therefore resistant to either identification or assimilation[123]—Heidegger postulates that instead of integrating or obliterating what is alien, the *modus operandi* is to acknowledge the foreign in its "essential oppositional character" (*wesenhaften Gegensätzlichkeit*), for only by doing so is there

> the possibility of a genuine relationship, that is, of a uniting [*der Einigung*] that is not a confused mixing [*wirre Vermischung*] but a conjoining in distinction [*fügende Unterscheidung*]. By contrast, where it remains only a matter of refuting, or even of annihilating the foreign, what necessarily gets lost is the possibility of a passage through the foreign, and thereby the possibility of a return home into one's own [*der Heimkehr ins Eigene*], and thereby that which is one's own self.[124]

Although Heidegger's analysis proceeds from his consideration of the specific relationship of ancient Greece and modern Germany, it seems valid to extend the discussion: the homecoming that he articulates presumes that the essence of one's own "unfolds its ownmost essential wealth only from out of a supremely thoughtful acknowledgement of the foreign."[125] The relationship with the other should not foster union or a muddled mixture, but rather genuine opposition, a conjoining through distinction. If the confrontation results in the refutation or the annihilation of the foreign, then the possibility of the passage through the foreign is compromised and the journey home curtailed.

The highlighting of the need to confront the foreign as an essential component of the principle of homecoming enunciated by Heidegger stands in blatant contrast to the biological racism propagandized by the Nazis and their denunciation and subjugation of the non-Aryan. This is nowhere more strikingly articulated than in Heidegger's view of translation as a transmogrification of the *Muttersprache* by means of its colliding with the *Fremdsprache*, the transference of the sojourner to the alien shore. "Every translation," therefore, "must necessarily accomplish the transition from the spirit of one language into that of another." The transition is tempered by the fact that it is impossible to substitute the word of one language for a word in another language; however, precisely because equivalency is not feasible, all translating must be an interpreting, and conversely, all interpreting must be a translating. This leads Heidegger to the astounding conclusion, "translating does not only move between two different language, but there is a translating within one and the same language."[126] There is still a privileging of German as the essential language; the "concealed shrine that, in belonging to being, preserves within it the essence of human beings,"[127] but the lingering linguistic ethnocentrism is modified to the extent that the encounter with the foreign language through translation is necessary for the sake of appropriating one's own language.[128] The practice of translation as confrontation with the foreign sheds light on the fact that translation is not only the transposition of one language into another but that every verbal utterance is an act of translation of the language into itself. "To speak and to say is in itself a translation, the essence of which can by no means be divided without remainder into those situations where the translating and translated words belong to different languages. In every dialogue and in every soliloquy an original translating holds sway."[129] In pursuit of the dispossession of the possessed, we can unearth a genuine sense of alterity—the affirmation of the other as the other to the same rather than as the same to the other—that would depend on the inclusion of exclusiveness in the inclusiveness of the exclusion as opposed to the exclusion of inclusiveness in the exclusiveness of the inclusion.

Poetic redemption, on this score, is not the overcoming of alienation, but rather the discernment that the deepest homelessness is felt when the feeling of homesickness has died out because one finds oneself at home everywhere and nowhere, a curious modification of the claim of Novalis that philosophy is homesickness because it expresses the *urge to be at home everywhere*.[130] For Rosenzweig and Heidegger, and I believe Scholem as well, enlightenment in the inherently unredeemable world consists of casting light on the shadow so that the shadow is illumined as light. Departing from the Platonic underpinning of the gnostic mythos, there is no escaping the shadowy world by fleeing to the realm of radiant and everlasting truth.[131] The task of the great thinker, Heidegger reminds us, demands jumping over one's shadow, for only through the leap does one surpass the shadow.[132] The surpassing, however, involves abiding within rather than dispelling the shadow. What is dark, Heidegger conjectures, is not dissolved in brightness; it remains concealed and comes to appearance in the light. True thinking dwells inceptually in the essential space of a dark light.[133] By illumining the dark light and uncovering the shadow as shadow, one is emancipated and thereby reveals that in the showing of the unhidden, beings hide themselves; what is finally disclosed is the concealment that conceals itself in its disclosure. "All revealing," writes Heidegger in a decidedly kabbalistic tone, "belongs within a harboring and a concealing. But that which frees—the mystery—is concealed and concealing itself ... Freedom is that which conceals in a way that opens to light, in whose clearing shimmers the veil that hides the essential occurrence of all truth and lets the veil appear as what veils."[134] *To let the veil appear as what veils*—lifting the veil, ostensibly to see the face beneath the veil, amounts to discerning that there is no way to see the face but through the veil of the face. The final veil to lift is the veil that there is a final veil to lift.

4

The Study of Religion in a Postmetaphysical Age: Philosophical and Political Reflections

Peter E. Gordon

The modern liberal arts college in North America has at least one distinctive advantage over other educational institutions: it lays greatest stress on intimate, seminar-style instruction. Professors are afforded the time and space to convene in small groups with students so that the careful study of texts becomes a cooperative venture in which any anxiety about tests or grades loses its relevance. The sheer passion for learning takes over and sweeps aside nearly all other concerns. When I arrived at Reed College as a sophomore transfer student in the mid-1980s, Steven Wasserstrom was still at the early stages of his career. He arrived at Reed in the same year as I did, with his newly minted PhD from the University of Toronto. No doubt both of us were still finding our bearings. The clean-shaven young man whom I first encountered in his office had an earnest look and a soft-spoken voice with only the faintest trace of his Midwestern origins. To his students he was eager to impart the crucial lesson that scholarship is a vocation that one should pursue not for prestige or personal gain but for the sake of intellectual insight alone.

For the study of religion I was a complete novice. I pursued coursework in both history and philosophy, and I also gravitated to seminars in which this young professor introduced his students to themes in Jewish mysticism and to the problem of cultural symbiosis between Judaism and Islam. I can still recall my first encounter with works by Gershom Scholem. It felt like a revelation, and I was unprepared for the experience. I was raised in a home that esteemed the natural sciences before all other gods, and I was (and have remained) more or less rationalist in temperament. Professor Wasserstrom—it was Reed after all, and we simply called him "Steve"—was an erudite but gentle guide. He brought to all of his teaching a style of admirable lucidity and candor. But the materials he taught in his seminars were explosive. He succeeded in awakening his students to the basic experience of intellectual wonder that accompanies the study of religion even in the disenchanted space of an undergraduate seminar.

Yosef Hayim Yerushalmi once characterized the academic study of Judaism as "the faith of fallen Jews."[1] This applies quite well to my own experience. I spent many years trying to reckon with the history and philosophy of religion without ever permitting myself to lapse into the belief of my ancestors. Both of my parents were born in observant families, but like many children of immigrants in America the process of assimilation had slackened the bonds of faith. What was left behind were only fragments: I was raised with only the most rudimentary grasp of Hebrew and Yiddish, combined with a peculiar reverence for German language and culture that somehow survived in our home despite all that the Nazis had done. The loss of family members in the Holocaust only seemed to solidify my parents' conviction that it was best to abjure all distinctions of identity and religion. In the classroom Steve was never a proselyte: he sustained an admirable neutrality. But over the span of my senior year at Reed I came to realize that a purely academic encounter with Judaism permitted me to reclaim something of the religious inheritance my parents had abandoned. Under Steve's tutelage, I wrote my senior thesis on problems in Jewish historiography. He seemed to understand that in addressing myself to the academic study of Judaism I found myself in a posture of estrangement that could not be overcome. But it turns out that my own sense of outsidership could be an advantage. Today we live in a political culture that too often turns academics into partisans for identity and tribe. But genuine scholarship must resist the temptations of romantic fusion. Mediation, not immediacy, is the watchword for all academic inquiry and not just for the study of religion. This was a basic lesson in dialectical understanding that I learned from Steve.[2] For this lesson I am profoundly grateful.

In his "Nine Theses on the Study of Religion," we are told that no credence should be given to the notion of the utterly "unique" or the incomparable (§1). Because religions exist in the plural the academic study of religion must value comparison over singularity. But this call for comparison is not as innocent as it seems: it already implies a rupture with the principle of uniqueness that underwrites the traditional ideal of revelation. The major religions that emerged from what Karl Jaspers called the "Axial" age typically grounded their authority in proprietary claims to metaphysical insight.[3] True believers were those who accepted this higher truth; those who did not were condemned as unbelievers or heretics. In the Qumran texts we are told of the war between the Sons of Light and the Sons of Darkness.[4] Every claim to a privileged and exclusive revelation tends to reinforce this ancient distinction between friend and enemy, although the lived experience of religious communities has just as often involved the phenomenon of interreligious symbiosis and dialogue. I would like to add as a parenthetical note that this ranks among the major weaknesses of Carl Schmitt's "political theology." As a political and legal opponent of liberal pluralism, Schmitt projected his own modern preference for political authoritarianism back onto the pre-modern image of God as an absolutist monarch. This predisposed him to conceive of religious conflict as the original template for the existential conflict in politics between friend and enemy. To break with the logic of singularity also means breaking from the established patterns of competition and animosity that have predisposed the more zealous partisans of distinct religions to think of themselves as being potentially, if not actually, at war.

But we should also remember that comparison logically requires a shared standard or at least a common language. In the study of religion today a new spirit of nominalism has taken hold that warns us against even the very notion of "world religions." According to this genealogy, the language of pluralism serves only as a mask for a universalism that has its actual origins in a distinctively European and Protestant model that can be imposed upon other cultural systems only at the cost of great distortion or misunderstanding.[5] Against this nominalist argument it is important to ask how comparison could proceed at all if it did not enlist the aid of ideal types. Although no universalism is entirely free from particularism, it does not follow that all languages of comparison should be condemned. In his "Nine Theses," Wasserstrom tells us that "without being seen from outside there is no communication" (§1). Without some language for comparison among distinctive religious cultures the very ideal of mutual intelligibility becomes inoperative. Each culture becomes as self-referential and self-enclosed as a monad.

The new fashion in skeptical nominalism tells us that there is no such thing as an "outside." But perhaps it would be best to say that there is no such thing as an "inside" either. The ideal of pure interiority is a remnant of a romantic historicism that saw each culture as absolutely unique. Once we overcome this myth of cultural uniqueness we have no other choice but to confront the difficult truth that all cultures are fragments of an imperfect humanity. The solution to a false universalism is not a complacent particularism but a universalism that incorporates self-criticism as part of its own unfinished process of education. Wasserstrom writes, "Distance is needed for perspective, not just on others but especially on one's own identity" (§3). I consider this claim absolutely crucial not only for academic scholarship but also for politics, as I will suggest toward the conclusion of my remarks. To begin I would like to amplify the claim by insisting that no privilege should be awarded to the idea of an "insider's knowledge." The principle of an empathic hermeneutics that makes proximity into an epistemic virtue must be counterbalanced by the virtue of distance and critical reflection. The capacity for taking leave of the familiar is the first step on the dialectical path toward mutual understanding. It has taken centuries for the various religions of the world to awaken to the cognitive but also social challenge of multiple faiths, especially in the modern condition of globalized capitalism where the old walls of separation have crumbled and people of different faiths find themselves living in ever greater proximity to one another in heterogeneous societies. No doubt this adjustment is still ongoing and it is marked by violent reversals. But it is a learning process from which no culture can claim exemption.[6]

The modern research university can trace its historical origins back to the medieval theological seminary in which the skills of critical hermeneutics were first developed in application to religious and classical texts. Eventually these skills assumed a corrosive power that began to compromise the revelatory status of scripture and the traditionalist authority of the ancients over the moderns. Today the combined forces of criticism and naturalism have almost completely displaced the old ideal of the university as a preserve for sacred meaning. Divinity schools still exist but are largely consigned to the periphery of the educational mission. The modern discipline of Religious Studies has absorbed the relativistic lessons of historicism that have become normative throughout the social sciences and the humanities. In his fifth thesis Wasserstrom suggests that Religious Studies is a "weak discipline" that must negotiate with the conceptual instruments of other university faculties if it is to understand its own subject matter (§5). One might ask, however, if any discipline today really qualifies as "strong." Philosophy once saw itself as "queen of the sciences," but nowadays many philosophers would admit that philosophy itself has taken the turn to what Jürgen Habermas calls "post-metaphysical thinking."[7] It is a basic insight shared in common by both Heideggerian and post-structuralist modes of criticism that no discipline can claim for itself a meta-discursive perspective that sets it above the other faculties. The human sciences work best when they work in concert; specialization tends to reproduce only the thoughtless dogmas of a single discipline. The study of religion may enjoy a certain advantage precisely because it borrows so freely from the neighboring disciplines in the human sciences.

The relationship between the discipline of philosophy and the study of religion spans the millennia: metaphysical inquiry into the basic structure of the world still bears the memory trace of older religious and mythical narratives of cosmic creation. It should be obvious that this metaphysical point of departure cannot be awarded to any one people or religious system. The narrative of cosmic creation that was recorded in ancient Sumeria (the "Eridu Genesis") shares in common many themes with the creation-narrative found in the Hebrew Bible.[8] This historical fact of pluralistic origins does not easily harmonize with the self-understanding of individual religions that wish to claim their own metaphysical truths as superior to or exclusive of all others. But it is an important reminder that even the modern discipline of philosophy is not the exclusive property of the West: the comparative study of philosophy goes hand-in-hand with the comparative study of religion. The diversity of religious and philosophical discourse is no less evident in fields of discourse beyond metaphysical inquiry such as ethics and political philosophy. The Platonist theory of Forms originally had a religious meaning. In many cultural systems today, a philosophically informed ethics cannot be easily separated from their originally religious frameworks, although occasionally the very definition of religion remains open to contestation. Herbert Fingarette observed, for example, how in Confucianism the secular itself assumes the category of the sacred.[9] Such cases may serve to remind us that the modern academic distinction between philosophy and religion is hardly uncontroversial.

I want to insist on this point so as to reflect on the ongoing significance of religion for contemporary philosophy. The most recent work by Jürgen Habermas confirms the importance of this relationship and it pushes back against the secularist mind-set that refuses to acknowledge the legitimacy of religion. The manifold cases of troubled and even violent encounter between secularist and revivalist-religious movements across the globe should remind us that "taking religion seriously" is more than an academic slogan. It is a crucial task for all peoples who wish to develop flexible frameworks for democratic coexistence that will allow for something deeper and more enduring than a mere *modus vivendi*. Wasserstrom notes the poignant irony that the "miniature status" of Religious Studies within the university "stands in inverse proportion to the manifest power of religion in the 'real world'" (§5). Philosophers and historians and other scholars who adopt a dismissive attitude toward religion in their own disciplines are ill-equipped to understand the resurgence of fundamentalist religious movements in various cultures.

Philosophers and social theorists, I would suggest, may have a special role to play in helping us to see beyond the current secularist-religious impasse. The urgent question today is whether the specific liberal-democratic distinctions that have informed the modern secular state can suffice for resolving the current conflicts. In recent years critics in the social sciences such as the anthropologists Talal Asad and Saba Mahmood have argued that the legal-political premises of the liberal-democratic state are not universal and that they unfairly impose a culturally particularistic conception of "Western" or chiefly Protestant religion on non-Western religious modes of life that cannot be expected to conform to the liberal framework with its trademark distinction between the private (religious) sphere and the public (secular) sphere.[10] Borrowing theoretically from Foucault and working practically with qualitative ethnography, these critics practice a suspicious "genealogy" of secularism: they seek to expose the non-neutral strategies of governmental and cultural power behind the ostensibly neutral discourse of the liberal-secularist state. The real question that emerges from these studies remains unanswered: even if we grant that our inherited liberal-secularist model of the state may impose great demands on religious communities, we still need to ask whether all such demands are *prima facie* illegitimate.

It is here I think that a comparative understanding of religious history in Europe and North America may be relevant. It is altogether obvious that the various religious communities underwent a sometimes difficult trial of readjustment in the early modern era when they were compelled, often against their will, to accept the authority of the emergent modern state. More often than not this state obviously did not live up to its own ideal of religious neutrality. Well into the nineteenth century most of the ostensibly secular states in Central and Western Europe did not wholly surrender their self-conception as outgrowths of a Christian political culture. But even in failing to realize the ideal, these emergent secularist states could not help but confirm this ideal's legitimacy and in doing so they made it possible for religious minorities to redress cases of discrimination through legal cases and legislative reform. This historical dialectic between failure and improvement remains a typical pattern in liberal-democratic states that have adopted secularism as more than a mere mask for authoritarian power. Today secularism still stands as the most plausible framework for adjudicating the contesting claims of multiple religious parties within "post-secular" society.[11]

To be sure, the oppressive and instrumentalist deployment of secularism remains a great danger especially in political cultures in which democratic norms have not stabilized. This may help to explain why secularism is the object of such suspicion for critics such as Mahmood and Asad. But the charge that secularism can be used selectively and with exclusionary effects does not suffice to dismantle the status of secularism as a normative ideal. It is self-evident that the trial of political secularization has not reached the irenic utopia where multiple faiths and non-religious citizens live side-by-side within the neutral framework of a secular state. Even in the United States the secularist ideal is constantly subjected to challenges, most often from Christian–fundamentalist groups who wish to undermine the modern liberal settlement and reinstall the oppressive mechanisms of a theocratic utopia. An unintended synergy joins together the modern academic critics of secularism with these partisans of theocracy: I do not think much can be expected from the theocrats—they have no interest in the secularist framework nor can they accept the modern fact of religious pluralism. But we should expect that academic critics of secularism work constructively to reconceive the practices of the modern democratic state so as to ensure the equal legal and political status of all religious and non-religious citizens. In recent years the ideal of a democratic state that remains neutral with respect to all its citizens regardless of religious identity has grown precarious. Theorists who devote themselves to a suspicious hermeneutic of liberal-democratic norms perform a crucial service but they cannot exempt themselves from the contemporary situation in which those norms are rapidly losing their authority.

The study of religion also has an important role to play in this situation: it can expand our understanding of what religions are and how they have transformed over time. But the study of religion may contribute an even more pertinent insight. Wasserstrom notes that "religion is always inter-religion" (§2). What he calls "deep pluralism" (§6) suggests that no religion finds itself in a sphere of doctrinal or cultural isolation where it could claim its immunity from the challenges of interreligious contact. Perhaps every religion nourishes in itself a fantasy of authenticity or "purity." The Axial revolution in religious consciousness no doubt aggravated the risk of an exclusionary or chauvinistic self-understanding according to which each religion became captive to the fantasy of privileged metaphysical insight. But the history of the world's religions shows us that from the very beginning this fantasy has been compromised by the lived reality of neighboring faiths. When religious communities cannot shield themselves from the cognitive and practical challenge of interreligious exchange, they begin to incorporate the external perspective of the other into their own self-understanding. This was the crucial insight that informed Wasserstrom's first major book on the phenomenon of symbiosis between Judaism and Islam.[12] The lesson we can learn from the idea of "inter-religion" is of relevance not only for the academic study of religion. This relativization of religious self-consciousness is an early and fragile paradigm for the rise of post-foundationalist and post-metaphysical thinking in contemporary philosophy. But it is also a political lesson that may bear on our understanding of religious pluralism today. If it is right to say that no religion is a monad and if we can regard all claims to religious singularity as essentially fictitious, then we might take some comfort in the thought that the political promise of interreligious coexistence today has its historical origins in the phenomenon of inter-religion itself.

5

Taxonomy Is Epistemology:
Theorizing Religion and Hermeticism Polythetically with Wasserstrom's *Theses*

Paul Robertson

In Steve Wasserstrom's "Nine Theses on the Study of Religion" ("Theses"), he suggests that the discipline of Religious Studies "has no defining method of its own" due to its fundamentally plural character.[1] Wasserstrom embraces this plurality at the heart of Religious Studies, understanding all "religion as inter-religion" (§1). Indeed, he esteems this plurality, for it is through Religious Studies' innate pluralism that the discipline is able to mediate what no other discipline can: first, between science and politics (§4); and second, between history and philosophy (§7). Both types of mediation concern the apparent or alleged contrast between philosophical naturalism (i.e., empiricism, of science and history, respectively) and seemingly incommensurable knowledge-production or knowledge-claims (politics' hegemony constructing truths; philosophy/theology's transcendent or revelatory truth claims that remain unverifiable).

How can we as scholars concretely practice this mediation in our own work? In this chapter, I take Hermeticism as my subject of analysis and ask how Wasserstrom's abstract methodological claims (he calls them "provocations") could come into play? Wasserstrom's suggestions here are important starting points, but they can be built upon. He suggests, for example, that Religious Studies analyzes history and theology in the plural, identifies their incommensurability, but then crucially reflects on that incommensurability.[2] In this way, Wasserstrom seems to argue that the study of religion resists categorization and classification of human phenomena, preferring instead to analyze and reflect on encounter, continuity, change, and negotiation.[3] However, I argue here that categorization and classification—of a certain kind, theorized and applied with proper nuance—are in fact extremely useful for the kind of analysis that Wasserstrom proposes. Put another way: we need an approach to categorization

My thanks to all members of the October 2017 conference at Reed College in Wasserstrom's honor, with particular gratitude to those whose specific feedback was invaluable and widely incorporated into the final copy of this essay: Kambiz GhaneaBassiri, Greg Given, and Dylan Burns.

and classification that contains plurality but also includes self-reflexivity about that very plurality, both methodologically in the large (e.g., what does plurality mean for humanity?) and in terms of specific findings (e.g., what does this particular instance of negotiation/contact explain about our data?). While Wasserstrom attempts to navigate plurality and self-reflexivity via "provocations" ("Nine Theses") and poetics (the "Nine Riddles" concluding this volume), I contend that theorizing an empirical mode of relational taxonomy does this type of work differently and effectively.

In this paper, I forward a specific method of classification and comparison—polythetism—that contains both pluralism and the capacity for self-reflexivity in its very structure. Indeed, I argue that this method is especially well suited for the study of religion due to its inherent ability both to incorporate aspects of different disciplines (linguistics, anthropology, history, philosophy, etc.) and to reconcile hermeneutic dualisms as fundamental, organizing criteria in its very structure.[4] I first make a case for polythetism as method, describing its inherent and deep pluralism. In the interest of concretizing my theorizing, I then apply polythetism to a test case, Hermeticism, which contains Wasserstrom's highlighted challenges of inter-disciplinarity, pluralism, and hermeneutic dualisms (e.g., emic/etic, truth/revelation, science/politics, empiricism/theology, history/philosophy)[5] which I contend are addressed in polythetism's very structure. In fact, Hermeticism was one of Wasserstrom's own research interests for these selfsame reasons.[6] I then use my theorizing and analysis around Hermeticism to provide suggestions for how polythetism might also answer Wasserstrom's call for Religious Studies' needed meta-reflection around seemingly incommensurate categories such as history and philosophy.

Indeed, a polythetic inclusion of both the philosophical and historical may be essential to the study of religion. In response to his "Theses," I propose that a desired integration of the Wasserstromian notions of Deep Pluralism, Deep Naturalism, and contact/negotiation demand a framework where plurality is inherently constitutive of a category's ontology. Only thereby, or perhaps therein, can these aspects of Wasserstrom's "Theses" (which in fact seem to be nine facets of a single hermeneutic of understanding and methodology) be effectively united and thus deployed. In this way, I propose a framework, polythetism, whose nature and very constitutive epistemological and organizing principles reflect and embody the "Theses." If Wasserstrom sees the role of Religious Studies to mediate different disciplines, I propose that this mediation can be theorized, distilled, and articulated in a disciplined way. If our method is pluralism, we must articulate the hidden, pluralistic (i.e., polythetic) taxonomy that epistemologically delineates our data, and by extension our vocation as both scholars and teachers. Religious Studies is polythetism; and its aim is to determine what polythetic form that takes in each instance, phenomenon, tradition, and cultural-historical era.

This discussion also speaks to a larger question broached by Wasserstrom's "Theses," namely whether "religion" in the singular should or can be analyzed as a category, such as to understand and compare Islam, Judaism, Buddhism, and so on. Wasserstrom seems to suggest that religion is not in fact a singular category, and that, instead, religion should be analyzed relationally. By contrast, or perhaps by modification, I suggest that religion *is* in fact an over-arching category that can be fruitfully identified qua singular category, *if* our mode of categorization is understood via the inherent relationality of polythetism. In other words, while I am not committed to Wasserstrom's apparent skepticism around the category/ies of religion, I agree with and build upon his arguments around the centrality of relationality to the objects of our analysis.

Polythetism: Theorizing classification and comparison

The question at stake: how can we apply a consistent methodology that attempts to reconcile and incorporate one of Wasserstrom's identified dialectics, that between the historical and the philosophical?[7] For our test case Hermeticism, there are a host of ways to understand the phenomenon, many of which have radically different disciplinary approaches and epistemological underpinnings. We can see this by framing these different approaches in an abbreviated list:

Historical:
        mention of "Hermes"
        initiatory, dialogic
        abstraction
        secrecy

Philosophical:
        revelation
        unitary original truth
        "as above so below"
        hierarchical ontology

Here we see features of Hermeticism that under "Historical" were empirically evident, in terms of both what takes place in the extant literature and what seems likely to be objectively true in terms of the historical phenomena and social practices underpinning that literature. Under "Philosophical," we see a different type of characteristic, namely what lies behind or is indicated by certain claims (the claims are objectively present, but not objectively true, what we might call a second-order naturalism; see more below), which also seems to have an uncertain relationship to historically evident phenomena and social practices.

To re-ask our question more concretely, what method can incorporate all the objects on both lists, in addition to the many elements I haven't listed? How can we define "Hermeticism" as an object of study that is both naturalistic in its study of the historical realities (our more second order, etic categories in the first list set) and philosophical in its reflections on the types of revelatory truth-claims being made in different times (the more content-based, emic aspects of the second list set), some of which might even contradict? And how might we derive a methodology that also allows a meta-reflective end, namely, for us as scholars to seek "the deep meaning of such superficial pluralisms" (§7), that is, Deep Pluralism?

I have elsewhere fully articulated the notion of a polythetic framework and especially justifications for its utility in studies of complex data in history, religion, social practices, and literature.[8] More prominently, Jonathan Z. Smith, early in his career, also advocated for the use of polythetism,[9] and his arguments have been the subject of scholarly critique.[10] Here I will but briefly summarize.

Polythetism is a type of description and classification. It is a mode of taxonomy that determines a particular grouping of objects based on multiple (*poly-*) criteria (*-thetos*), none of which are necessary or sufficient for membership in a given group. Philosophically speaking, polythetism can be roughly equated with Wittgenstein's notion of "family resemblances."[11] Indeed, the philosophical concept of "family resemblances" has been productively applied in scientific fields to handle complex data sets, such as in biology.[12]

Polythetism is counter-posed to monothetism, which deploys fewer criteria (often just one, *mono-*) that are necessary and sufficient for membership in a given group. Monothetism is useful in instances where clear membership in a group is detected or desired, such as in medicine around the presence of a given gene expression.[13] To briefly look ahead, monothetic classifications would understand Hermeticism, Christianity, and Platonism as distinct entities with a few definable attributes; hybrids might be possible, but they would need all of the monothetic characteristics of different categories to belong to the various groupings. By contrast, a polythetic understanding of Hermeticism would see not only the category of "Hermeticism" itself as flexible and fuzzy, but this polythetic categorization would also allow for a more complex and nuanced understanding of its relationship to other similarly polythetically understood categories such as Platonism and Christianity. Polythetism is especially well suited to such notoriously difficult categories as Hermeticism, Neoplatonism, alchemy, and the like.

In approaches polythetic and monothetic both, taxonomy is epistemology. How we describe and classify objects reflects an understanding, or at least proposed understanding, of their fundamental ontology expressed via their attributes. But crucially it also includes their ontological relationships. To define Hermeticism polythetically is to understand it as fundamentally plural and relational: its ontological attributes are inherently multiple and unstable, diverse across the members of this grouping. Furthermore, each member in the group has an ontological relationship with any other datum (inside or outside its group) that shares at least one attribute, even if this relationship is relatively minor.

Polythetism is useful when the data (i.e., the given sphere of reality in question) is decidedly messy: when each datum is extremely complex (e.g., a long text's style and/or content); when boundary lines between categories are fuzzy (e.g., the nature of social practices and group affiliation in a diverse, complex, pluralistic society); and/or when categories shift due to their particular historical circumstances or simply the passage of time (e.g., biological speciation). Polythetism and monothetism can be used in tandem, an approach seen more often in biology than in the social sciences or humanities: one can hierarchically understand certain criteria in clearer, monothetic ways that are seen as more fundamental (mammal vs. reptile vs. bird); concurrently, other polythetic criteria form an inherently more complex and nuanced bound (species types).[14]

In this paper, I add a crucial piece beyond the type of polythetism we find in biological speciation, social practices, or quantifying literary overlap. Whereas those types of polythetism are of a single qualitative type (respectively: physical characteristics of naturalistic speciation, and second-order form-content literary stylistics), I suggest here that polythetism can be used to integrate qualitatively different types of characteristics in a single schema. By incorporating qualitatively different characteristics, polythetism can thus integrate *both* the philosophical and historical aspects of our data.

It is essential that we recognize that in polythetism, we are not identifying "Hermeticism" per se, any more than Wasserstrom suggests we can identify religion or the sacred per se. Rather, we are identifying objects of study that, in the parlance of polythetism, are "more or less Hermetic," or "closer to or further from other Hermetic texts/idea." It is not entirely clear the definition that Wasserstrom ascribes to religion itself, or to Religious Studies as a vocation. But his "Theses" are certainly suggestive of overlaps with polythetism in this "more/less, closer/further" formulation. To investigate contact and continuity is not to investigate contact qua contact, but to explore the ways, extents, and qualities of this contact. What is more, it is to theorize, delineate, and categorize—as a discipline—what exactly constitutes the data of Religious Studies' contact. What kind of contact counts as data for the study of religion?

Wasserstrom states that there is probably no datum that is absent of contact.[15] Certainly this is true, especially when we think of history in wider terms beyond a singular temporal moment. But his statement seems to come by way of defense, anticipating an objection that some data do not reflect contact. Wasserstrom's pre-reply implies that, yes, there are some instances of less contact than others, that minimal contact occurred, even as it *did* ultimately occur in some way. This is wholly compatible, and I would further contend even fully overlapping, with polythetism in its organizing assertion of degrees instead of essentialized object per se. A wide enough set of polythetic criteria would put all objects in the same, hugely broad class, some closer to each other than others; a wide enough scope of history would put all ideas into some type of contact and continuity. It is up to us to demarcate and explicate spheres and lines of relationality within that broad scope.

A new polythetism of Hermeticism: Reconciling the historical and the philosophical

How, then, are we to bring this theorizing on categorizing and analyzing religion into practice? In what remains, I show how this proposed polythetic framework—attempting to reconcile the historical and the theological/philosophical—works in describing and analyzing the phenomena of Hermeticism. Hopefully this application will help explain polythetic theory by illustrating it via concrete example as well as advance understanding of Hermeticism itself.

Hermeticism, or Hermetism, is a loose term referring to texts, ideas, and seemingly also practices that were variously tied to the mythical figure Hermes.[16] In certain circles of the ancient Mediterranean in the first several centuries of the common era, Hermes was understood not in the sense of anthropomorphic Olympian drama, but rather as something of an intermediary between humanity and the divine. This Hermes bore special knowledge about the universe, the visible realm, the nature of humanity, and its ties with divine powers including God, itself understood in various ways. Hermeticism has features recognizable from a host of other ancient social and intellectual movements, such as Gnosticism, alchemy, magic, Neo/Platonism, and asceticism.

As a result, Hermeticism contains a raft of seeming contradictions: it was both ancient and modern (especially Renaissance), Egyptian and Greek and Persian, contemplative and practical, philosophical and religious, hidden and transmitted, syncretic and unique, textual and oral, and so on. Relevant to Wasserstrom's "Theses," these sets of descriptors contain both the historical and the philosophical/theological. And indeed, these diverse influences, categories, and historic permutations defining Hermeticism present a significant category problem. Put simply, what is it? How do we define Hermeticism, if it is so stretched and splintered across time, place, culture, re-imagination, re-invention, and redaction? Can we define it at all?

Scholars are aware of this category problem, and attempts to solve it generally take one of three forms: (1) re-deploying admittedly problematic categories for the sake of convenience (e.g., technical vs. philosophical Hermetica);[17] (2) minimally defining Hermeticism (e.g., texts with formal mention of Hermes);[18] or (3) maximally defining Hermeticism (e.g., an encyclopedic list of features derived from texts in so-called Hermetic collections).[19]

Picking up my discussion from earlier, I suggest polythetism can effectively bridge these divides. It can not only bring together different strands of Hermetism (so-called technical vs. philosophical) but can also speak to Hermeticism's diverse body of content, which seems to contain doctrinal contradictions. What is more, the extant literature is both highly limited and highly redacted, meaning that narrower, formal criteria (i.e., monothetic classification) such as the presence of the name Hermes becomes untenable; such names could easily have been damaged, excised, or added.[20] What is more, we need criteria that are not overly vague, so as to apply to too many texts to the point of uselessness.[21]

We may take as starting point the various ways that Hermeticism has been classified in scholarship, to then build our own polythetic taxonomy from there. A list of characteristics derived from several of the modern studies referred to above:

Copenhaver:
- origins, nature, and moral properties of the divine, human, and material being
- salvation through knowledge or *gnosis*
- integration of practical and contemplative

Fowden:
- three spheres of being that are hierarchical: God, the World, and Man
- humanity's aspiration to know God
- initiation, often with dialogue
- magic, medicine, and the movements of the stars

- individualist (not institutional)
- sympatheia
- magic
- occult properties and alchemy
- astrology
- philosophical *paideia*
- *gnosis*

Linden:
- name of Hermes
- hylozoistic conception of the universe
- relationship between macrocosm and microcosm
- astrological influences
- transmutation
- correspondences between elements of the cosmos

A couple things stand out. First is the highly diverse understanding across these three authors, expressed through their departing taxonomies.[22] This highlights the category problem I noted earlier with respect to Hermeticism: what is it, and how is useful and collaborative study to be done, if there is such a widely departing understanding across scholars? There are always scholarly disputes around the delineation of categories, of course, but for Hermeticism this problem is especially acute. Polythetism, however, overcomes this purported problem of diversity by embracing diversity as its constitutive organizing and epistemological principle. A polythetic understanding of Hermeticism, in other words, will integrate these different lists into one master list, and do so not out of necessity but by design.

Second, the items on these lists are both historical and philosophical. Historically they manifestly occur in the data, for instance the evident presence of initiatory dialogue. Indeed, such an example seems to provide evidence of some historically occurring social practices, here a type of physical initiation and master–disciple relationship therein. Philosophically, meanwhile, there are elements of the data that are manifestly theological, such as the content of truth-claims about the cosmos and humanity's relationship to it and God. Such claims are historically present in the data (phenomenologically true in that sense), but philosophically uncertain (the ontological claims themselves are ultimately unverifiable/unfalsifiable). What we see, in other words, is the very co-existence of the historical and philosophical-theological that Wasserstrom identified as central to Religious Studies. Polythetism is an approach that captures both aspects, and lends them both substantive weight in its approaches, understandings, and conclusions.

What remains is the application of this wider taxonomy to the data, showing how capturing both aspects (historical; philosophical-theological) in theory works in practice. I have reorganized and edited the above scholarly lists, combining certain elements to eliminate redundancies. I've also reorganized the taxonomical criteria for clarity by grouping together related characteristics to show which related clusters of characteristics have wider and more specific manifestations in this particular polythetic grouping:

Cosmological
- origins, nature, and moral properties of the divine, human, and material being
- hierarchical tri-partite being: God, World, Man
- correspondences between elements of the cosmos
- astrology, movements of the stars
- occult properties and alchemy
- sympatheia
- magic

Practices
- integration of practical and contemplative
- philosophical paideia
- initiation, often with dialogue
- transformation
- individualist (not institutional)
- medicinal

Knowledge
- salvation through knowledge or *gnosis*
- humanity's aspiration to know God
- *gnosis*

Appellation
- name of Hermes

We can see here that characteristics of a more monothetic type, such as the name of Hermes or the specific presence of *gnosis*, have fewer appearances on this list. This should not deceive us into thinking they have less import: a single, broader characteristic may capture many more data points under its umbrella than several, narrower characteristics. A single feature might also define a work conceptually, even without appearing in several explicit occurrences.

We should also recall some of the initial, animating methodological issues grounding this essay, namely the nature of Religious Studies as an interdisciplinary enterprise that brings together many disciplines. As this list shows, we have polythetic characteristics of a variety of types, including linguistics, social practices (sociology), philosophy, theology, and astrology. Hermeticism is defined, in other words, not by any one disciplinary category of characteristic, but rather through the pluralistic inclusion and integration of several of these disciplinary categories. As I will return to in my concluding section, such an inclusion of different disciplinary characteristics also invites a meta-reflection on the nature of our data and taxonomic scheme that can aid in attempting to mediate the philosophical and the historical.

When we map texts onto this new polythetic taxonomy, through a process of close reading and hand-coding the data, we can express our classificatory description in a table. I have analyzed only a few Hermetic texts (*Emerald Tablet*; *Poimandres*; *Discourse on the Eighth and Ninth*; Zosimos, *Of Virtue* 1–3) to illustrate by way of a more manageable and focused treatment of data. Each number represents the total appearances for the respective characteristics in each text, with averages to express ranges of data and hence uncertainty.

To better visualize how the texts compare, we can express this table graphically, with an eye toward the text's "shape." It is important to note that the lines below are an expression of counting statistics, not mathematical functions. The key element to note is whether or not the general shape of the lines match: the different text length will result in different counting statistics (the y-axis), but it is each text's internal, relative counting statistics that produce the line shape. A similar line shape between two texts indicates a similarity in terms of the types and ratios of characteristics present in each text internally. In this way, we can thus describe, visualize, and understand a text's polythetic nature according to these characteristics. Indeed, as we see here, despite some outliers (always expected in polythetic classification) there is a generally shared shape across the four texts:

As discussed earlier, polythetism is always a matter of relative distribution: belonging is a matter of more and less. Some characteristics, in turn, are more

Table 5.1 Aggregate appearances of polythetic characteristics in hermetic texts

	Emerald Tablet	Poimandres	The Discourse on the Eighth and Ninth	Zosimos, Of Virtue 1–3
Cosmological				
origins, nature, and moral properties	4	12	12	3
hierarchical being: God, World, Man	3	12	12	3
correspondences between elements	5	2.5	2	4
astrology, etc.	2	0	2	1
occult properties and alchemy	2	0.5	2.5	4
sympatheia	2	2	2	2
Practices				
practical and contemplative	5	9.5	16	6
propaideutic	1	6	8.5	4
initiation, often with dialogue	1	10.5	21.5	7
transformation	2.5	15.5	9	9
individualist	1	7	11	6
magic	1	1.5	0	1
medicinal	0	0	0	0
Knowledge				
salvation through knowledge/*gnosis*	0	8.5	5	2
humanity's desire to know God	0	4	3.5	2
gnosis	4	16	15.5	6
Appellation				
name of Hermes	1	0	5	0

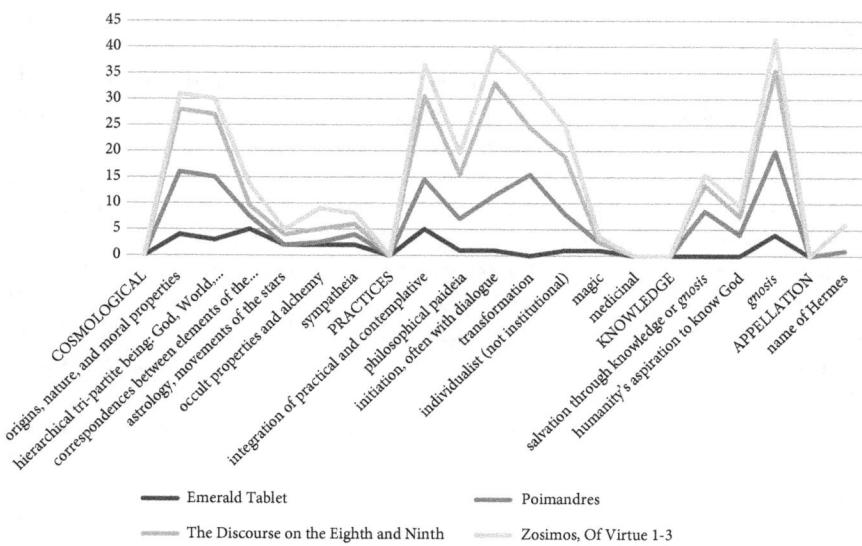

Figure 5.1 Polythetic mapping of Hermetica.

important than others when it comes to membership in a category. We might even combine this polythetic description with a monothetic one, for example, still deciding to retain an explicit mention of Hermes as a *sine qua non*, while deploying something like the above to describe subsequently qualifying texts in a nuanced way.

The above table and graph suggest that several of these textual characteristics are more central to this particularly defined category of Hermeticism, given their relative weight in this polythetic description:

- the origins and nature of hierarchical being
- practical elements in tandem with the philosophical
- propaideutic elements, often related to dialogue with an initiatory telos
- transformation at an individual level
- the centrality of knowledge/*gnosis* itself

Several other characteristics, meanwhile, have comparatively lesser weight:

- astrology, and occult, magical, or medicinal materialism
- the role of desire in aspiring to know God or divinity itself
- the explicit role of Hermes

These latter characteristics are still important—indeed they are present in most of the data—but they simply are not as central. Again we see the type of conclusion gained from using pluralism itself as the organizing principle in a taxonomic-epistemological structure: Hermeticism is not singularly defined, but rather various data points have a complex, nuanced relationship to the category as well as to one another. Derivation of further characteristics and/or inclusion of additional texts would modify the parameters and therefore nature of the category, expressing a different set of relations between texts and the relative centrality of certain characteristics.

Especially relevant to Wasserstrom's "Theses" is the relatively equal weight this polythetic category gives to the historical and the theological-philosophical.[23] The objective presence of certain literary features and seemingly physical practices (e.g., dialogue, initiation) shares space with claims about the nature of the cosmos (e.g., a hierarchically interrelated ontology) that are objectively present but ultimately not empirically verifiable. Hermeticism, in this telling at least, *requires* both the historical and the theological-philosophical to be constituted as such. It is only in this specific clustering of these two types of characteristics (i.e., data) that the object of our study is to be found. What this polythetic approach notably does *not* do is to reflect on the nature of this interrelation between the historical and the theological-philosophical, as Wasserstrom's "Theses" suggest Religious Studies ultimately must.[24] But this approach embraces, concretizes, and clarifies this interrelation in a manner useful as foundation for subsequent reflection. Taxonomy is not reflection, but taxonomy certainly facilitates reflection.

Meta-reflection via taxonomy in the study of religion

My polythetic characteristics draw from varying disciplines, ranging from literary criticism to philosophy to history to sociology. Such an inclusion of different disciplinary characteristics invites a meta-reflection on the nature of our data and taxonomic scheme that can help attempt to mediate the philosophical and the historical. In this concluding section, I will provide some further thoughts and suggestions around how polythetism speaks to other, related aspects of Wasserstrom's "Theses."

I've noted that the type of polythetism I am proposing here differs from the typical biological sort, which is generally composed of a qualitatively singular kind of characteristic. In biology, for example, this qualitative type is generally the empirically physical, such as physical attributes and/or behaviors. What I propose here is that my polythetic taxonomy—what Wasserstrom might call Deep Pluralism; what I might label "self-reflexive polythetism"—not only incorporates characteristics that are naturalistic and present in the object of study per se (Wasserstrom's historical); my proposed type of polythetism also incorporates a reflective and reflexive element (Wasserstrom's philosophical, and also his political) about the nature of description and comparison vis-à-vis the object of study. Which is to say, there will be characteristics in my polythetic category that are historical and philosophical, and the explicit relationship between these two elements is in fact essential to this polythetism's nature and scholarly constitution.

Further, the *relationship* between the historical and philosophical is one of dialectic, and inherently involves reflexivity about categories and the nature of categorization. Labeling a category as philosophical is surely dependent upon the historical in terms of what is objectively present in our data, but it also abstracts and extracts out conceptual frameworks from, imposes a hermeneutic upon, or even does violence to the historical. What is more, the philosophical (a truth-claim of uncertain veracity) is also the political (as knowledge-constitutors, we impose scholarly power over the text to derive our own "truths"). For instance, when my polythetic structure notes the importance of "desire to know God" when these terms are not explicitly in the data, I am making a philosophical abstraction and synthesis around the nature of my data, and such an abstraction is also a hegemonic imposition, that is, a political product.[25] Yet nonetheless, both the political and the philosophical are grounded in the historical: these are categories created not simply for the sake of dialectic mediation, but have an inherent consistency in culture and history. Put differently, this historical-ontological basis of both the political and philosophical suggests that there is, in fact, data for the study of religion. The task of our field is not just to mediate, but to mediate specific and identifiable occurrences of empirical data in inter-relational contact that we can describe polythetically.

The polythetism that I have forwarded in this paper includes both the historical (phenomenologically naturalistic) and the philosophical (what we might call second-order naturalistic, present but not objectively true), the empirical and the radical empirical.[26] It thus attempts to incorporate Wasserstrom's Deep Naturalism (§7), incorporating processes psychological, biological, social, et al., all into a taxonomic description of what (propositionally, at least) best defines Hermeticism. In this way I seek not only (1) to describe (naturalistic phenomenology, basic empirical naturalism) but also (2) to deepen our understanding of an object of study such as Hermeticism by including our own meta-reflections in the very composition of the organizing polythetic structure. My approach here thus accords with Wasserstrom's thesis that we should not reduce religion to mere micro or thick description (the first element above), but should rather seek a sort of radical empiricism in a new age (the second element above).[27]

What is produced by Wasserstrom's attempt to understand Religious Studies as the reconciliation—or perhaps better, integration—of philosophy and history? It is the production of a dialectic between current interests, understandings, and conditions, and past interests, understandings, and conditions. The goal that I forward here is along these same lines: a polythetic taxonomy whose derivation of partly self-reflexive characteristics attempts to express and thereby capture in its very structure the dialectic between current and past, modernity and history, scholarship and scholarly object, and the philosophies of both which are second-order conceptual (radically empirical) just as they always remain grounded in their particular historical, phenomenological contingencies and contexts.

6

Metrosophy: Rereading Walter Benjamin in Light of *Religion after Religion*

Jeremy F. Walton

Not to find one's way in a city may well be uninteresting and banal. It requires ignorance—nothing more. But to lose oneself in a city—as one loses oneself in a forest—that calls for quite a different schooling. Then, signboards and street names, passers-by, roofs, kiosks, or bars must speak to the wanderer like a cracking twig under his feet in the forest, like the startling call of a bittern in the distance, like the sudden stillness of a clearing with a lily standing erect at its center.
—Walter Benjamin, "Berlin Chronicle," 1978[1]

What language does the city speak to those whose ears are attuned to its rhythms, its cadences, its peculiar prosody? Can we read a city allegorically in the manner that we read a text, open to unanticipated exegetical possibilities and hermeneutic outcomes? And what traces of disavowed urban pasts might such a hermeneutics of the city illuminate anew?[2] Walter Benjamin returns to these questions persistently, if obliquely, throughout his oeuvre, from his early essays on cities as various as Berlin, Naples, and Moscow, to his disjointed omnibus, *The Arcades Project*.[3] The passage above, from "Berlin Chronicle," is characteristically evocative: by achieving a mode of absorption in the fluctuating storm and stress of city life—"as one loses oneself in a forest"—the *flâneur* sets out to access meanings that elude the idle urban denizen.

Benjamin's investiture of the *flâneur* as a distinctive hermeneutic subject, drawing on the works of Charles Baudelaire (1821–1867) and Marcel Proust (1871–1922), is well known.[4] More generally, Benjamin remains famous for his staggeringly eclectic philosophical and intellectual synthesis. Marxism—in particular, the concept of the commodity fetish and the method of historical materialism—and German

---

Acknowledgements. The author is exceedingly grateful to Kenneth Brashier, Giulia Carabelli, Karin Doolan, Kambiz GhaneaBassiri, Miloš Jovanović, Annika Kirbis, William Mazzarella, Piro Rexhepi, Paul Robertson, Noah Salomon, and Robert Walton for their incisive, illuminating comments.

Romanticism constitute the central antecedents for his oeuvre; these major currents are complemented and supplemented by a plethora of minor traditions and sources, including the nineteenth-century *feuilleton*, Brechtian radical theatre, and the kabbalah.[5] As Susan Buck-Morss has argued in her indispensable companion to *The Arcades Project*,[6] Benjamin's opus integrates the many strands of his thought, offering a startling interpretation of the built environment and legacies of nineteenth-century Paris as an archive of early capitalist modernity and its constitutive social forms.[7]

Among the various influences on Benjamin's oeuvre, mysticism, occultism, and the kabbalah are often treated gingerly in appraisals of his work. When Benjamin's relationship to the genealogy of mysticism and the kabbalah is pursued, debate and inquiry typically focus on the degree to which he can be considered a "Jewish" thinker, working in the idioms of Jewish discursive traditions.[8] Above all, Benjamin's long friendship with Gershom Scholem, the renowned scholar of Jewish mysticism, and the impact of this comradeship on Benjamin's intellectual trajectory are key concerns in relation to the "mystical" thread of Benjamin's thought. My panoramic task in this essay is to cultivate a new appreciation for Benjamin's inheritance from the minor-key, crepuscular traditions of Western mysticism and esotericism that extend beyond Scholem's direct influence. Although Scholem was undoubtedly a crucial mediator of these traditions for Benjamin,[9] I propose that Benjamin's approach to cities echoes a host of concerns that propelled a broader cadre of scholars of religion of his generation. To put my argument in a blunt nutshell, Benjamin's concept of the urban corresponds to and incorporates many of the motifs of the contemporaneous concept of religion that Scholem and his cohorts espoused. I thus aim to draw out the "elective affinities" between Benjamin's work and that of the early- and mid-century discipline known, somewhat nebulously, as the History of Religions.

What was this concept of religion, then? Steven M. Wasserstrom, whose own remarkable oeuvre this volume celebrates, has identified the circle of intellectuals who composed the Eranos Group—in particular, Henri Corbin, Mircea Eliade, and Scholem—as the proponents of a distinctive form of scholastic spirituality that he dubs "religion after religion."[10] Wasserstrom argues that the scholars of Eranos synthesized Western occultism, as expressed by such thinkers as Nicholas of Cusa and Jacob Böhme, German Romanticism, and the "mystical" traditions specific to the religions they studied: kabbalah in Scholem's case, Shi'ism and Sufism in Corbin's, and a plethora of premodern and non-European traditions in Eliade's. In doing so, they forged a novel concept of religion that was simultaneously esoteric and universalistic, distinguished above all by the privileged gnosis of the scholar-adept. This academic hermeticism forwarded a sharp critique of what Max Weber famously dubbed the "iron cage" of secular modernity.

Benjamin was not a scholar of religion in the manner of Corbin, Eliade, and Scholem;[11] nor was he affiliated directly with Eranos. Nonetheless, he shared a certain world-weary, skeptical sensibility—a postwar generational *zeitgeist*—with the Eranos intellectuals, one that cast a jaundiced eye on the ostensibly self-evident verities of modernist progress and order in the wake of the cataclysm of the Great War.[12] Svetlana Boym poetically describes this sensibility: "There is in fact a tradition of critical reflection on the modern condition ... which I will call *off-modern*. The adverb *off* confuses our sense of direction; it makes us explore sideshadows and back alleys rather than the straight road of progress; it allows us to take a detour from the deterministic narrative of twentieth-century history."[13] For Eranos scholars such as Corbin, Eliade, and Scholem, this off-modern sensibility entailed the reconstitution of religion after its Nietzschean death throes by way of occultism, mysticism, and gnosis; for Benjamin, cities themselves, with their literal "sideshadows and back alleys," were powerful testaments to his off-modern, anti-historicist concept of time and his scathing critique of "the storm ... [that] we call progress."[14]

In what follows, I mine Benjamin's essays on cities—in particular, Naples, Berlin, and Paris—in order to illustrate his "off-modern" concept of the urban in greater detail and clarity. Simultaneously, I place Benjamin's urban writings in conversation with the leitmotifs of Eranos esotericism and "religion after religion" as delineated by Wasserstrom. As we will see, a variety of key concepts that animated Corbin, Eliade, and Scholem's "phenomenology" of religion—*concidentia oppositorum*, a Romantic theory of symbolism—equally illuminate Benjamin's perspective on cities. We might well think of Benjamin as a practitioner of an esotericism of the urban, a "*metrosophy*" rather than a theosophy, even as the emergent, mass forms of city life that he interrogated necessarily demand more open-ended modes of encounter and interpretation than the Ivory Tower excogitations of Eranos.

Coincidentia oppositorum and the porous city

Among the occult concepts that inspired the mid-century Historians of Religions, *coincidentia oppositorum*, the "coincidence of opposites"—a mode of paradox that accentuates the proximity of contrasting elements—was a structuring principle of Eranos esotericism.[15] Although their invocations and deployments of *coincidenta oppositorum* differed—Eliade cited it frequently and liberally, while Corbin and Scholem were more circumspect—Wasserstrom argues that the idea formed the basis of a more pervasive, "new, theosophically derived logic,"[16] which resounded with and responded to the historical predicament of the Generation of 1914. The crucial, double effect of *coincidentia oppositorum* was to destabilize the regency of reason in the study of religion—part of a broader movement away from Neo-Kantian positivism at the time[17]—and to ground the political philosophy of the "conservative revolution," an intellectual movement of the interwar period, associated with the emergence of Heideggerian phenomenology,[18] that romanticized *both* antinomianism *and* authoritarianism.[19]

Benjamin was certainly no friend of "conservative revolution," but he did count thinkers within its ambit as his friends and colleagues. It is perhaps unsurprising, then, that one of his most evocative city essays, on Naples, pivots on a *coincidentia oppositorum*. For Benjamin and his co-author Asja Lacis, the Latvian theorist of revolutionary children's theater who was his muse and occasional *objet d'amour*,[20] the paradoxical coincidence of opposites that distinguishes Naples's cityscape is best captured by the concept of porosity.

To their delight, Benjamin and Lacis discovered that Naples defies, blurs, and reverses the myriad binaries and distinctions that typically structure modern urban space and life: public and private; home and street; work and leisure; sacred and profane; spheres of production and consumption. Naples is an architectural pandemonium where opposites collide and coexist:

> As porous as this stone is the architecture. Building and action interpenetrate in the courtyards, arcades, and stairways. In everything they preserve the scope to become a theater of new, unforeseen constellations. The stamp of the definitive is avoided. No situation appears intended forever, no figure asserts its "thus and not otherwise." This is how architecture, the most binding part of the communal rhythm, comes into being here: civilized, private, and ordered only in the great hotel and warehouse buildings on the quays; anarchical, embroiled, villagelike in the center, into which large networks of streets were hacked only forty years ago.[21]

The kaleidoscopic architectural porosity of Naples suggests an antidote to the sterility of modernist urban planning, with its "large networks of streets"—it was surely no coincidence that "Naples" was published in 1925, a year after one of the definitive documents of modernist urbanism, Le Corbusier's *Toward an Architecture*.[22] Indeed, in Naples, the very temporalities of construction and destruction, design and decay, are indistinguishable. Frequently, "one can scarcely discern where building is still in progress and where dilapidation has already set in."[23] The coincidence of architectural opposites in Naples puts the lie to the Archimedean certitude of modernism and replaces the aspiration to "plan" with a markedly off-modern urban sensibility that celebrates spontaneity, juxtaposition, and decay.

Naples's architectural porosity opens onto other forms of *coincidentia oppositorum*. Neapolitan time is especially porous: "Irresistibly the festival penetrates each and every working day. Porosity is the inexhaustible law of the life of this city, reappearing everywhere. A grain of Sunday is hidden in each weekday, and how much weekday in this Sunday!"[24] Work and play, trade and trick, are enfolded and intermingled. Labor is often a spectacle, and "adheres closely to the holiday."[25] Nor are spaces of production, circulation, and consumption clearly distinguished: "Blissful confusion in the storehouses! For here they are still one with the vendors' stalls: they are bazaars."[26] Finally, and preeminently, Neapolitan social life entails a porous proximity of the "opposites" maintained by bourgeois northern European life. Privacy and publicity are unstable, evanescent, ultimately meaningless: "To exist for the Northern European, the most private of affairs, is here, as in the kraal, a collective matter … Just as the living room reappears on the street, with chairs, hearth, and altar, so only much more loudly, the street migrates into the living room."[27] Even kinship in Naples is porous: "A neighbor takes a child to her table for shorter or longer period, and thus families interpenetrate in relationships that can resemble adoption."[28]

To be sure, the role of *coincidentia oppositorum* in Benjamin's urban theory partakes in a different conceptual grammar than the *coincidentia oppositorum* of the Historians of Religion.[29] Despite his animated friendship and correspondence with Scholem, Benjamin was uninspired by the esoteric quest for gnostic experience, the ontologically "true" *Erlebnis* that oriented and exhilarated the scholar-mystics of Eranos.[30] As I have already proposed, Benjamin practiced a metrosophy rather than a theosophy; concomitantly, his was a mysticism of the everyday rather than the other-worldly. And yet, Benjaminian metrosophy shares a key characteristic with Eranos theosophy: both mount scathing critiques of modernism. Just as "religion after religion" interrogates the capacity of modernist reason to encompass religion, Benjamin's urban theory disdains and destabilizes modernist visions of the city. In order to mount this critique of modernist urbanism—in particular, the naturalization of capitalist modes of production and consumption in the city—Benjamin treated cityscapes as collocations of symbols that, when properly interpreted, express peripheral, subterranean urban histories and genealogies. As I illustrate in the next section, this concept of the urban symbol evinces clear affinities with the concept of the religious symbol that imbued "religion after religion."

Urban symbols and the mystical quotidian

A dynamic theory of religious symbolism, drawn principally from German Romanticism, permeates the work of the Eranos Historians of Religions.[31] Symbols— also referred to as "theophanies" (Eliade's preferred term) and "archetypes" (the Jungian inheritance)—were the ground upon which "religion after religion" staked its claim. Wasserstrom argues that for Corbin, Eliade, and Scholem alike, "*the autonomy of religion rested on the autonomy of the symbol.*"[32] As such, symbols were the hinges between this-worldly and other-worldly realms: "The symbol was not quite empty, but rather in itself was solely an access point into the transcendent realm, a higher reality inaccessible, so it was claimed, by any other means."[33]

Although Benjamin was not metaphysically inclined in the manner of the Historians of Religions, an analogous concept of the symbol, equally redolent of Romanticism, animates his writings on cities. Rather than securing passage between ontic realms, Benjamin's urban symbols form a joint between space and time, between the cityscape and the pasts, personal, and collective, that the city both embodies and conceals. While the Eranos circle and Benjamin proposed quite different objects of symbolism—gnostic religious-existential truth vs. urban historicity—a subjective, "phanic" relationship to symbols unites them. Consider, for instance, the following passage from "Berlin Chronicle" (referring, ironically, to Paris):

> I think of an afternoon in Paris to which I owe *insights into my life that came in a flash, with the force of an illumination.* It was on this very afternoon that my biographical relationships to people, my friendships and comradeships, my passions and love affairs, were revealed to me in their most vivid and hidden intertwinings. I tell myself that it had to be in Paris, where the walls and quays, the places to pause, the collections and the rubbish, the railings and the squares, the arcades and kiosks, teach a language so singular that our relations to people attain, in the solitude encompassing us in our immersion in that world of things, the depths of a sleep in which the dream image waits to show the people their true faces.[34]

Here, a welter of urban sights and sensations induces epiphanic recollections. This is an everyday mode of illumination, through which "the world of things" symbolically triggers memory in a Proustian manner.[35] The passage that I cited at the outset of the essay, also from "Berlin Chronicle," nicely captures what I think of as Benjamin's "mystical quotidian": the manner in which prosaic features of the cityscape "speak" to the *flâneur* like the objects one might encounter on a meditative sylvan stroll.[36]

In "Berlin Chronicle," the symbolic forest of the city opens vistas on Benjamin's own past—fittingly, as this essay is among his most autobiographical works. Elsewhere in his oeuvre, however, Benjamin proposes a hermeneutics of the city that excavates and illuminates collective pasts. *The Arcades Project* inaugurates this hermeneutic project by boldly asserting that mundane objects are symbolic arcana bearing traces and patinas[37] of bygone eras. Susan Buck-Morss eloquently captures Benjamin's insight and intervention:

> Corsets, feather dusters, red and green-colored combs, old photographs, souvenir replicas of the Venus di Milo, collar buttons to shirts long since discarded—these battered historical survivors from the dawn of industrial culture that appeared together in the dying arcades as "a world of secret affinities" *were* the philosophical ideas, as a constellation of concrete, historical referents.[38]

Benjamin's essay, "Paris, Capital of the Nineteenth Century"—the most direct, condensed presentation of the harlequin concerns of *The Arcades Project*—expands on this hermeneutics of everyday objects, this metrosophy rooted in "a world of secret affinities" (a Goethean phrase that Benjamin himself employed in his notes, according to Buck-Morss[39]). One of the key epigraphs for the essay is a quotation from the historian Jules Michelet, "*Chaque époque rêve la suivante*" (Every era dreams its successor).[40] With this observation as his beacon, Benjamin writes as a sort of psychoanalyst interpreting the oneiric visions of nineteenth-century Paris: "In the dream in which, before the eyes of each epoch, that which is to follow appears in images, the latter appears wedded to elements from prehistory ... [they] produce the utopia that has left its traces in thousands of configurations of life, from permanent buildings to fleeting fashions."[41] He returns to this same theme at the close of the essay: "From this epoch stem the arcades and interiors, the exhibitions and panoramas. They are the residues of a dream world. The realization of dream elements in waking is the textbook example of dialectical thinking."[42]

For Benjamin, the iron cathedrals of the arcades are symbols and embodiments of the modern interpolation of industry and architecture, which will only reach an apotheosis in the subsequent century. The nineteenth century "dreamed" these elements; dialectical thinking in the twentieth century treats them "wakefully." Benjamin thus interprets the arcades as features of a "dreamscape" that foreshadows a future that has since come to pass. In doing so, he recasts his own present as a "past future."[43] Reclaimed as an oxymoronic "past future," the present bristles with dialectical tensions.[44] Benjamin's task throughout *The Arcades Project* is to read the cityscape of Paris as a repository of traces of this oneiric "past future" that critically illuminates the present.

It is no far stretch to imagine Corbin, Eliade, and Scholem assenting eagerly to the dialectical historicity that Benjamin exemplifies through *The Arcades Project*. In comparison, however, the "mystic historicity" of the Eranos scholars—particularly Corbin and Eliade—which sought religious reality in the suspension and transcendence of time,[45] is far more static than the dialectical historicity that Benjamin advocates. As Wasserstrom shows, the occult orientation of Eranos skewed into a "mythic ... form of world rejection"[46] that was not so much off-modern as anti-modern. Here, the Historians of Religions and Benjamin necessarily diverge from each other. Benjamin's off-modern sensibility proposes that the past and present always mediate each other—there is no position outside of this temporal dialectic. Relationality and contact, as the contributions to this volume variously illustrate, are ineluctable. There is no place outside of time. Yet such a place is precisely what the anti-modern theosophy of Eranos envisioned and pursued.

Conclusion: Metrosophy and the study of religion (after religion)

Affinity is not identity. When subjects or objects resonate with one another, this resonance equally presupposes and illuminates constitutive differences. With this point in mind, the affinities between the Eranos Historians of Religions and Walter Benjamin that I have traced in this essay demand contextualization within a broader field of contact, debate, and disagreement. These differences emerge most starkly on the political plane. The "antinomian authoritarianism" of the Eranos scholars, as well as their general aestheticization of politics, echoes many fascist motifs, and Eliade in particular flirted with the brutal right-wing Romanian movement of Corneliu Zelea Codreanu, the Iron Guard.[47] By contrast, Benjamin was a consummate thinker of the Left, who memorably championed the politicization of aesthetics as a foil to fascism's aestheticization of the political.[48] Unsurprisingly, the Eranos scholars and Benjamin also diverged on the question of nationalism. While Corbin, Eliade, and Scholem were "importantly engaged in the nationalistic struggles of Iran, Romania, and Israel,"[49] respectively, Benjamin was ill at ease in the Westphalian world of nation-states; cities, rather than nations, provided terrains of identification and inspiration for him.[50]

Theosophical "religion after religion" and Benjaminian metrosophy align most closely in their subjective-epistemological techniques. *Coincidentia oppositorum* and (post-)Romantic symbolism, the motifs that I have focused on here, are two prominent affinities between Eranos theosophy and metrosophy; there are surely others.[51] These sibling concepts share a fundamental function and effect. In William Mazzarella's pithy formulation, they aim "to activate the esoteric potentials of exoteric life."[52] On the basis of this "activation," they stir subjects to awareness of the strictures of positivism and reason (in relation to religion; in relation to urban life) and interrogate the triumphant teleology and rationalist settlement of modernism. It is in this respect that I have described the theosophy of "religion after religion" and Benjamin's metrosophy as "off-modern."

Beyond this common skepticism in relation to modernity and modernism, however, the scholars of Eranos and Benjamin part ways. This divergence is not only a consequence of their disparate objects of scholarly attention. At a more fundamental level, the anti-modernism of "religion after religion" and the off-modernism of metrosophy envision contrary modes of temporality and historicity. For the Eranos scholars, secular modernity necessitated an antithetical re-mystification of life and world that sought to transcend history. The other-worldly, other-timely gnosis they glorified passed beyond the off-modern to become anti-modern. Benjamin, a non-metaphysical thinker despite his flirtations with the occult, could not follow the Historians of Religions to this empyrean aerie beyond the time-space of modernity. For him, there is no point outside of history to which one can return or ascend. To be off-modern for Benjamin is necessarily to be modern, as well. The metrosophic thinker and actor only resides within the maelstrom of history, forever oscillating between the debris of the past and the horizon of the future to grapple dialectically with the present. The modes of knowledge that inspire this endeavor cannot be gnostic. Such knowledge only emerges through the mystical quotidian that one encounters peeking around the crooked corners of Neapolitan alleyways, peering forth from battered Berlin billboards, and suspended in the lacelike wrought iron webs of Parisian arcades.

In its rejection of Gnosticism, Benjaminian metrosophy also salutes contemporary debates and currents in the study of religion. As Wasserstrom has asserted in his provocative, programmatic vision for the discipline of Religious Studies, transcendence, gnosis, or "universal experience" cannot be the coin of our realm: Religious Studies "must compare historically and then reflect philosophically on the results of that comparison."[53] The same might be said for the study of cities. Although Wasserstrom has proposed linguistics as an analogue for Religious Studies, my own preferred counterpart is Urban Studies, especially in a metrosophical, Benjaminian vein. Just as any study of religion is necessarily a study of "inter-religion," as Wasserstrom insists,[54] so too is the study of the urban an inexorably comparative endeavor. To adapt Goethe, we might say that to know one city is to know none.[55] More panoramically, both Religious Studies and Urban Studies necessarily construct their objects of study from the warp and woof of the histories that confront and confound them. Metrosophy, unlike theosophy, acknowledges and reckons with this ineluctable historicity; if we agree with Wasserstrom, so, too, must Religious Studies. It is here, in the maelstrom of past futures, that the rough ores of the urban and the religious provoke, and resist, our efforts of extraction and refinement.

"La Perversión de la Cábala Judía": Gershom Scholem and Anti-Kabbalistic Polemic in the Argentine Catholic Nationalism of Julio Meinvielle

Jeremy P. Brown

> Religious Studies might play a role in clarifying inter-religion as a cultural discourse—though it can do so only if it takes revelations seriously enough to affirm enemy-brothers all their polemic and apologetic ferocity.
> —Steven Wasserstrom, "Nine Theses on the Study of Religion"

The problem of Scholem and fascism

How can scholars working in the modern academic field of Religious Studies effectively subvert the theologico-political complex in which our field is enmeshed? Much of the scholarly reaction to Wasserstrom's *Religion after Religion* has focused on the vector of the work dealing precisely with this question. The 1999 book demonstrated how Henry Corbin, Mircea Eliade, and Gershom Scholem's participation in Olga Fröbe Kapteyn's annual Eranos conferences in Ascona, Switzerland, helped to potentiate an elitist and "mystocentric"[1] image of a "religion after religion," a distorted construction of religion which has nonetheless become somewhat normative in academic accounts.[2] More to the point, the book showed how the mystocentric approach to the study of religion practiced by the three—a cohort of individuals who either flirted with, or overtly endorsed, fascist ideologies—was

---

I dedicate this paper to Wasserstrom, with whom I first read Scholem. His mentorship and scholarship have opened me to worlds within worlds. I wish to thank Benjamin Pollock for inviting me to present an early version of this paper, entitled "Thomism, Gnosticism, and Kabbalah in Argentine Catholic Nationalism (or Did Gershom Scholem Inspire Clerico-Fascism in Latin America?)," at the Hebrew University of Jerusalem, Jewish Thought Faculty Seminar, and to Jonathan Garb for his helpful feedback. I am also grateful to the editors of this volume, to David Biale, and especially to Leonardo Senkman for reading earlier drafts and offering valuable comments.

closely related to these scholars' respective political activities. In a rejoinder to a panel of critical responses to his 1999 book, Wasserstrom epitomized the critical implications of his project in these terms:

> *Religion after Religion* is a critique of these scholars insofar as they conflated historical scholarship with mystocentric theosophy. To assume that mysticism is the center of religion, and then to position the teacher as one who masterfully grasps that center, is not only to mystify the past but also to distort its specific character, its particulars, its historicity. The historians of religions I have studied imply that religion is ruled, as it were, by a mystical elite. The further implication throughout their work is that the contemporary historian of religions can act as a kind of latter-day continuator, a spokesperson, so to speak, for that ancient elite. Here I do object; here, I suppose, I do become … a "moralist." The religious past is peopled with all sorts, and privileging so-called gnostics amounts to a barely concealed privileging of the gnostic teacher now.[3]

In exposing such would-be "gnostics" at the helm of the academy, and laying bare their connections to "the theologico-political dimensions of fascism,"[4] the book is situated at the crossroads where criticism of method and ideology critique converge. *Religion after Religion* urges subsequent scholars and teachers of religion to take leave of the "nurturing authority" of this enchanting, if enchanted, group, even on pain of intellectual orphanage.[5]

On the matter of fascism, however, some readers averred that the book spared Scholem the same standard of criticism that it applied to Corbin and Eliade. One even suggested that Wasserstrom had let Scholem off the hook, or, rather, "redeemed him from the darkness of *Afterreligion*,"[6] insofar as *Religion after Religion* dwells on the manifest fascist activities of the two gentile scholars, while limiting criticism of Scholem, the Jew, to neo-romantic leanings which he preferred to camouflage, as it were, in Zionist clothing.[7] Wasserstrom has responded to this criticism by saying, in effect, that his intention was just the contrary, to focus critical attention on Scholem's otherwise feted career.[8] In this paper, I explore the premise that the problem of Scholem and fascism appears in a different light if we shift our attention from the political life of the scholar to the double political life of his scholarship.[9] I will profile one aspect of Scholem's reception history in 1970s Argentina, where we find a patently fascist reading.

In particular, I will discuss the Argentine Catholic nationalist interpretation of Scholem's history of the kabbalah found in an influential polemical work of Julio Meinvielle (August 31, 1905–August 2, 1973), *De la Cábala al Progresismo* (*DCAP*).[10] This book appeared in 1970, at a time when many prominent *nacionalista* (nationalist) leaders aggressively disseminated a Thomist paradigm of Catholic theocracy as a basis for a totalitarian solution to Argentina's political, social, and economic instabilities. Whereas Wasserstrom stopped short of fingering Scholem as a fascist, his delineation of the Jewish historian's fascistoid neo-romantic affinities prepares us well to make sense of the representation of Scholem's work in Meinvielle's *nacionalista* opus.

Julio Meinvielle: Catholic nationalist ideologue, intellectual combatant

Far from an eccentric outsider, Meinvielle remained close to the most venerated institutions of the Argentine church; and throughout the second and third quarters of twentieth century, he played a key role in the development of both the country's Catholic educational infrastructure and its *nacionalista* intellectual culture. Born in 1905 in Buenos Aires, he trained as a priest and began his lifelong study of the writings of Thomas Aquinas at the Pontifical Seminary in Villa Devoto (Seminario Metropolitano Inmaculada Concepción), the seminary where Jorge Bergoglio later trained. While serving throughout his life as a parish priest in the Versailles neighborhood of Buenos Aires, Meinvielle helped found the Catholic Scouts movement, the *Sociedad Tomista Argentina*, as well as a host of influential Catholic periodicals.[11] In the 1930s, he began teaching at the *Cursos de Cultura Católica*, an institute dedicated to perpetuating the academic study of Christian doctrine after the closure of the Universidad Católica de Buenos Aires in 1922.[12] Meinvielle's first book, *Concepción Católica de la Política* (1932), comprised discourses presented at the *Cursos* in 1931. By 1940, Meinvielle published eight books, which became foundational works of Catholic nationalist ideology. *Concepción Católica de la Economía* (1936) features an appendix "*sobre la cuestión judía*," which anticipated the appearance of *El judío* in 1937.[13] The latter is an incendiary work of modern Catholic anti-Jewish polemic, which by 1999 had undergone six printings in Buenos Aires and two overseas editions in French and German translation.

Scholars have discussed the theme of anti-Judaism in Meinvielle's thought, particularly during the early phase of his career.[14] Generally speaking, scholarly attention has focused on Meinvielle's role as an architect of the Catholic anti-Jewish aspect of the nationalist ideology which was vigorously promoted by the military government of the 1970s and 1980s. None have focused on the status of kabbalah in Meinvielle's thought, which does not become the primary target of his polemic until the end of his career. There are several elements of Meinvielle's early anti-Judaism, which inform his late anti-kabbalistic work. First, his attacks combine scriptural, patristic, and medieval anti-Jewish tropes with elements of modern antisemitism.[15] Of the former, Meinvielle commits himself to the charge of deicide; the Pauline teaching that Israel will play an instrumental role in the final salvation of Christians; the Augustinian typology of the Jews as Cain; as well as medieval anti-Talmudism, blood libel, and the demonization of Jewish usury. The most pervasive element of modern antisemitism is Meinvielle's strong endorsement of the conspiratorial view, associated with the *Protocols of the Elders of Zion* (1903), that the Jews hold the strings of world domination, and have disrupted the natural order of Christian civilization by inoculating the modern world with the ills of liberalism, capitalism, and Bolshevism.[16] The rhetoric of Catholic anti-masonic polemic also colors Meinvielle's conspiratorial characterizations of the Jews.[17] His anxiety over the clandestine influence of the masons meshed with his fears about Jewish esotericism.

Meinvielle's particular brand of anti-Judaism should also be viewed in the context of his rejection of fascism in its National Socialist form. He favored authoritarian political structures which subordinated the state to the church, opposing any absolute statist forms of totalitarianism which threatened the church's primacy, and weakened the divine prerogative over the administration of state and military power. To that extent, he was more receptive to Italian and especially Spanish forms of fascism, which accommodated paradigms of Christian social order—even if only for strategic purposes. Moreover, as a fierce partisan of Catholic tradition, Meinvielle reacted with hostility toward the "new theologians" associated with reform and Vatican II, and, in his writings and orations, took direct aim at Jacques Maritain and Teilhard de Chardin as proponents of a "judaizing" progressivism within the Catholic Church.[18]

By the 1960s, Meinvielle allied himself politically with the Grupo Tacuara de la Juventud Nacional. The Tacuara, initially dedicated to the renewal of Christian public education, and the establishment of Catholic universities, drew membership from the exclusively male members of elite Catholic student organizations in which Meinvielle's authority loomed large. Weekly, Meinvielle convened his Saturday "Grupos de Summa" sessions for the close study of Aquinas's *Summa Theologia*. These sessions attracted some of Argentina's most ambitious, politically conservative students. Increasingly, the Tacuara emerged as a quasi-military organization, which advocated the use of physical violence against leftists and Jews to redeem the nation from both decline and the violation to national sovereignty typified by the Israeli kidnapping of Eichmann.[19] A 1963 police raid of a Tacuara training camp revealed that the works of Aquinas were mainstays of the curriculum, alongside the writings of Argentine nationalist Manuel Galvez, Spanish Falangist José Antonio Primo de Rivera, and Catholic Vichyist Charles Maurras.[20] When the movement began to fracture into various ideological divisions, Meinvielle joined the radical off-shoot Guardia Restauradora Nacionalista (GRN), even serving in an official "advisory role."[21] For a time, members allegedly took part in a ritual of submission to GRN doctrine, which involved visiting the priest's home, kneeling before him, and kissing his hand.[22]

Meinvielle, who represented the violent struggle for influence between the *nacionalistas* and Marxist groups in terms of an impending confrontation between Christian and anti-Christian forces, was arrested in 1971 for involvement in inciting a popular uprising against the newly inaugurated President Alejandro Agustín Lanusse.[23] Meinvielle died in 1973, struck by a car when leaving mass. After his death, Meinvielle's authoritarian vision of a Thomist social order in Argentina was carried forward by Carlos Antonio Sacheri, a professor of philosophy holding influential university posts in Argentina and visiting positions abroad. In the eulogy for his beloved teacher, Sacheri extolled the priest's intellectual vocation as a Christian philosopher, polemicist, and militant, dubbing him an "intellectual combatant" and a defender of Christian civilization. He admonished those present at the burial to the duty of discipleship:

> Today, Father Julio stands before the God whom he consecrated his entire life. Let the youngest ones know to keep the "sacred fire" that he has left for us as an inheritance. Our church and our nation require that the work of the Father continue through the disciples which he formed; the task is arduous in these times in which so many defections of every kind abound. Let them know how to find, in the imitation of his virtues, the impetus to disseminate and deepen his work, so that his youngest proponents may, in their time, discover their Christian and national vocation.[24]

When Marxist guerillas assassinated Sacheri in 1974 (an act attributed to El Ejercito Revolucionario del Pueblo-Agosto 22), he was remembered as a martyr by the *nacionalista* supporters of the neo-fascist military junta of 1976, headed by General Jorge Rafael Videla.[25] In 1979, six years after his death, the military government's Ministerio de Educación y Cultura decreed that Meinvielle's writings be officially authorized for public classroom instruction.[26] Long after the military regime's demise, Meinvielle's legacy continues to flourish, through the efforts of his apologist Carlos Miguel Buela and his Verbo Encarnado clerical institute and publishing house.[27] The Instituto de la Filosofía Practica in Buenos Aires and Centro de Humanidades Josef Pieper in Mar del Plata host regular events on Meinvielle, many of which they disseminate online. His work has invigorated an emergent network of internet-savvy Catholic nationalists, especially those who view the papacy of Francis as the latest episode in a post-conciliar plot corroding the Catholic Church from within.

From kabbalah to progressivism: A Voegelinian heresiology of Jewish Gnosticism

> El viejo me dijo: "A Cristo lo mataron
> Por decir que el lugar más lejano
> Es el que estamos pisando."
> —León Gieco (1976)

In the context of his intensifying political activities throughout the 1960s, Meinvielle seized upon the idea that kabbalah was, in fact, the root of all ills assailing Christian civilization. The many fronts of his intellectual war, he now perceived, encompassed a single territory. What led Meinvielle to adopt this conspiratorial view? And how did Meinvielle find his way to the leading academic kabbalah scholarship of his day? Meinvielle's anti-kabbalistic polemic resulted from the convergence of at least two factors: (1) his assimilation of Eric Voegelin's construction of Gnosticism, and (2) his Voegelinian interpretation of an erudite essay by Gustavo Piemonte on the concept of *Creatio ex nihilo* in John Scotus Eriugena, which appeared in 1968 in *Sapientia: Organo de la Faculdad de Filosofía* , an academic philosophy journal published by Meinvielle's colleagues at the resurrected Universidad Católica Argentina.

From Voegelin, Meinvielle adopted the view that there is a single trajectory of ideational development which runs from the old gnostic "heresies"—those of the second and third centuries as well as those of the Middle Ages—to a host of immanentist modern ideologies. In his widely read book, *The New Science of Politics* (1952), Voegelin framed the matter in this way:

> A line of gradual transformation connects medieval with contemporary gnosticism. And the transformation is so gradual, indeed, that it would be difficult to decide whether contemporary phenomena should be classified as Christian because they are intelligibly an outgrowth of Christian heresies of the Middle Ages or whether medieval phenomena should be classified as anti-Christian because

they are intelligibly the original mode of anti-Christianism. The best course will be to drop such questions and to recognize the essence of modernity as the growth of gnosticism.[28]

Of course, this way of representing Gnosticism as the hidden essence of modernity has been aptly problematized by many, including Voegelin's teacher Hans Kelsen.[29] Nonetheless, in a section of *DCAP* called "El principio de la inmanencia en la política moderna," Meinvielle endorsed Voegelin's theory to the fullest extent.[30] According to this theory, "all gnostic movements are involved in the project of abolishing the constitution of being, with its origin in divine transcendent being, and replacing it with a world-immanent order of being, the perfection of which lies in the realm of human action."[31] This purported gnostic assault on the transcendence of divinity aggravated Meinvielle's Thomist sensibilities, wherefore he alleged that the kabbalists, as authorized custodians of the ancient Jewish gnosis, were in truth its chief perpetrators.[32] Both Voegelin and Meinvielle after him would align this anti-Christian immanentism with secularization, divinization of the individual, the Nietzschean superman, and utopianism.[33]

Furthermore, Meinvielle, to whom his disciples applied Tomás de Torquemada's inquisitorial epithet "the Hammer of the Heretics" (*el martillo de los herejes*),[34] relished the heresiological implications of Voegelin's indictment of gnostic modernity. The gnostic face of modernity is evident, according to Voegelin, in "such movements as progressivism, positivism, Marxism, psychoanalysis, communism, fascism, and national socialism."[35] With the possible exception of fascism, which Meinvielle only opposed in its non-Christian manifestations, these are some of the same ideologies which had vexed the polemicist throughout his career. This is especially true of progressivism, which *DCAP* characterizes as the modern essence of kabbalah, the pernicious Jewish gnosis.[36] Much of the ranging expanse of Meinvielle's argumentation in *DCAP* is aimed at aligning the kabbalah with precisely this Voegelinian construction of Gnosticism.

For Meinvielle, the discovery—at least in its representation by Voegelin—that kabbalah could be conflated with Gnosticism came emphatically through Scholem's studies, which linked certain phases in the development of Jewish mysticism with the very heresies disparaged by the church fathers. Scholem's influence on Meinvielle, however, was mediated through an important Spanish article by the Eriugena scholar Gustavo Piemonte, printed in a journal published by members of the priest's intellectual community. The two-part article was the first by any scholar of Eriugena to place Scholem's theories about the Eriugenist structures of early kabbalistic thought on the agenda for research on medieval Latin scholasticism.[37]

The extent of Meinvielle dependence on Piemonte cannot be deduced from *DCAP*'s stingy nods to his work.[38] Rather, his decisive influence is evident from the fact that in 1970 when *DCAP* was published, it cited the identical French and Italian bibliography of academic kabbalah scholarship that appears in Piemonte's 1968 study. This debt notwithstanding, *DCAP*'s most direct discussion of Piemonte is an audacious correction. According to Meinvielle, the kabbalah is ancient, continuous with the earliest *merkavah* mysticism which Scholem had enticingly labeled "Jewish gnosticism." In fact, Meinvielle claims an even earlier provenance for Jewish Gnosticism: Pharaonic Egypt![39] Thus, he "corrected" both Piemonte and Scholem on their view that the kabbalah emerged in the Middle Ages, in the wake of Eriugena, and argued instead that the direction of influence was not from the Celtic thinker to the kabbalists, but rather the reverse. Thus, he took Piemonte's argument a step further, insinuating that Eriugena took up the *ma'aseh bereshit* (Act of Creation) and therefore merited the ban placed on his writings in the thirteenth century.[40] With reference to ostensibly equivocal language in Scholem and Georges Vajda, and the self-legitimating claims of the kabbalists themselves, Meinvielle built his case for the antiquity of kabbalah. He was uncompromising on his basic conviction that kabbalah is a powerful contagion which has infected Christian civilization from its very inception with an anti-Christian, modernity-engendering immanentism.

Meinvielle's Scholem: Sage Jew, heresiographer

While Meinvielle took issue with certain aspects of Scholem's historical presentation, principally his placement of the kabbalah in the Middle Ages, *DCAP* relied entirely on the scholar's legacy. This is evident in several respects. Meinvielle capitalized on Scholem's scholarly reputation. He seized upon many instances in Scholem's writings which link Jewish mysticism to heterodox streams of Christianity, as well as the latter's references to the kabbalists' flirtations with pantheism. Most important, Meinvielle was wholly receptive to Scholem's delineation of the kabbalah as a sweeping historical phenomenon which potentiated all future ramifications of rabbinic Judaism.

Meinvielle situated Scholem in his typology of modes of discoursing about kabbalah. According to this typology, there are four basic approaches:[41] (1) the Christian kabbalah, that is, the interpretation of kabbalistic lore as a means of demonstrating the truths of Christian doctrine, exemplified by the writings of the apostate French rabbi David Paul Drach;[42] (2) the naturalist or academic interpretation, typified by Scholem, "the sage Jew";[43] (3) the occultist school, associated with Papus (Gérard Encausse) and Eliphas Levi; and (4) the Judaic or "demoniac" interpretation, in other words the traditional rabbinic interpretation.[44] Although he dubbed Scholem "the sage Jew," Meinvielle did not conflate his approach with the traditional rabbinic one. Rather, he followed Piemonte, taking every opportunity to laud Scholem's philological integrity and historical rigor. Founded on a Scholemian framework, the credibility of Meinvielle's anti-kabbalistic polemic depended upon Scholem's "nurturing authority."

Moreover, with respect to Wasserstrom's concerns about the reduction of religions to gnostic essences, Meinvielle's reading of Scholem's narrative illustrates *another* vulnerability to which a mystocentric history of Judaism is prey.[45] When examining aspects of kabbalah which approximated Christian heresies, *DCAP* presented Scholem's narrative as a cautionary tale, with the refrain "Scholem advierte" (Scholem admonishes).[46] In particular, Meinvielle read Scholem as alerting Christian civilization to the ideational and historical threads linking *merkavah* mysticism,[47] the Geronese kabbalah,[48] the Zohar,[49] and the Lurianic kabbalah[50] to dangerous Christian heresies, both ancient as well as medieval (such as those of Simon Magus, Marcion, Saturninus, Basilides, Valentinus, Eriugena, and the Cathars).

Similarly, *DCAP* is acutely attentive to the pantheistic potential of kabbalah,[51] a topic of scholarly debate before and since Scholem.[52] Again, Meinvielle read Scholem's summation of the "spiritual outlook of the Zohar" as a cautionary gesture. "God, the universe and the soul do not lead separate lives, each on its own plane. The original act of creation in fact knows nothing of such clear-cut division which was the cosmic fruit of human sin."[53] Needless to say, for Meinvielle such a "spiritual outlook" was cause for alarm:

> The Zohar does nothing other than explicate—and carry to its furthest limits—the inner and essential conception of the kabbalah, [which is changeless] through the entirety of its existence. This kabbalistic conception encompasses, as its unique patrimony, the idea that God, the world, and humanity move on a single common plane ... This conception translates into monism, emanationism, immanentism, into an intrinsicism of Creator and creature, yes and no, truth and error, nature and grace; good and evil unfold into a unitary world of singular dimension.[54]

One of the many reasons that the pantheistic essence of kabbalah poses such a threat to Christian civilization is that it introduces the specter of *coincidentia oppositorum*, as well as a relativism that weakens the combative resolve of Christian political life.[55] In the conclusion of *DCAP*, Meinvielle delineates no less than twenty-two pathways through which kabbalah has led Christian civilization astray.[56] Insofar as he warns Christians of the true gnostic character of kabbalah, the sage Jew, according to Meinvielle, is a heresiographer.

"Species of misbelief" and scholarly fidelity: Beyond the representation of polemic as shadow discourse

Malicious as Meinvielle's rhetoric may be, my intention is not to simply represent his anti-kabbalistic polemic as a shadow discourse of modern academic kabbalah studies. Nor do I intend to serve a polemicist with a counter-polemic. Insofar as Meinvielle's is a discourse engendered by Scholem, it will be more productive and honest to take stock of the gray area where scholarly criticism and religious polemic intersect.[57] Since, at a general level, both scholarly and polemical approaches tend to inflate the global importance of kabbalah and its impact on the course of human history, it is no wonder that the historical speculations of one discourse fuel the other's conspiracy theories. At a more specific level, though, Meinvielle, without any direct contact with the original textual sources or regard for critical methodology, somehow managed to anticipate several post-Scholemian developments in kabbalah research. It is worthwhile to observe these anticipations.

First, as mentioned above, *DCAP* sought the origin of kabbalah in ancient Egyptian myth, namely in the autoerotic theogony of Atun-Re.[58] While historically impossible, Meinvielle's discernment of the autoerotic dynamics of kabbalistic thought anticipates Elliot Wolfson's work on this mythological facet of kabbalistic theosophy.[59]

Second, in his attempts to trace the ramifications of kabbalah in modern continental thought, Meinvielle presents Schelling, Hegel, and Heidegger as crypto-progenitors of the Jewish gnosis. Meinvielle's demonization of Hegel was especially strong, since he read him as a precursor to Marx, and thus an instigator of anti-*nacionalista* guerilla ideology. The reception of kabbalah by German idealists and romantics, especially via Franz Molitor, has been discussed by scholars since Scholem.[60] And Wolfson, who has long framed his kabbalah research in Heideggerian terms, is preparing a monograph on kabbalah and the German thinker.[61]

Third, Meinvielle's insistence on the essential modernity of kabbalah anticipates the attempts of current researchers to explore the relationship of kabbalah to modernity.[62] Roni Weinstein and Jonathan Garb have argued that the kabbalistic fellowships of early modern Safed, Palestine (sixteenth to seventeenth centuries), introduced sociological and psychological innovations to classical kabbalistic paradigms of theology and religious practice which, they argue, already exemplify Jewish modernity.[63]

Finally, insofar as this study explores the unexpected ways in which academic scholarship has unwittingly sponsored clerico-fascism, I wish to interrogate one additional site of discursive correspondence, pertaining again to the deprecation of Gnosticism. Both Wasserstrom and Meinvielle faced off with an opponent that the writers constructed, *mutatis mutandis*, in terms of "Gnosticism." A careful consideration of the similarities of their respective constructions of Gnosticism begs the question, which I offer with the affection of an immanent critique, of whether *Religion after Religion*'s rhetorical bent verges on a form of "secularized heresiology."[64] Have Wasserstrom's attempts to release Religious Studies from the "privileging [of] so-called gnostics" in effect "ghettoized"[65] Gnosticism in a way structurally analogous to Meinvielle's polemic? Is it possible to heed Wasserstrom's critique of Scholem's mystocentric reduction of religion, without, on the other hand, perpetuating the violence of a clerically constructed polemical category? Or has Wasserstrom effectively articulated his critique in a manner that steers clear of such rhetorical violence? These questions become pressing in consideration of the specific political effects of Meinvielle's polemic during the Argentine *dictadura*. Moreover, these questions are urgent at the most generic level, in light of the long and continuous history of violence directed against groups fingered as "gnostics." As long as we cling to Scholem's characterization of Gnosticism as "metaphysical antisemitism," a characterization which Wasserstrom has avowed,[66] anti-Gnosticism will remain something like a moral imperative. But for Meinvielle, who, like the church fathers, conflated Gnosticism with Judaism (or "judaizing"), the true form of "metaphysical antisemitism"—positively valued—is *anti*-Gnosticism. Where does this leave us as scholars wrestling with the vestiges of heresiology in our own discursive work on religion?

Part Two

Mediating

8

Before Religion? The Zoroastrian Concept of *Daēnā* and Two Myths about It

Bruce Lincoln

I

There are many reasons to admire Steve Wasserstrom's masterful 1999 opus, *Religion after Religion*. Among these are its conceptual boldness, high seriousness (both intellectual and moral), principled argument, tight focus, and vast implications, as well as the clarity and power of its diction. The book succeeds, however, not for any of these reasons, but because of the meticulous research on which all else rests. Over many years of preparatory labor, Steve assembled massive bodies of documentation, then read each text closely and carefully, not only for what it said, but for its omissions and evasions, covert connections, and subtle innuendos. Each item was read, moreover, with keen attention to its historic, social, and political context and import, for Steve rightly understood that the works in question were not just scholarly texts, but attempts—largely successful—to intervene in critical situations by reshaping the consciousness, commitments, and disposition of those who read them or absorbed their content at second hand.

Ultimately, what Wasserstrom demonstrated was that scholars of the Eranos circle, most notably Mircea Eliade, Gershom Scholem, and Henry Corbin, undertook to save modernity from itself by making the world religious again. In an era when religious commitments seemed in terminal decline and the sacred seemed ever more distant, they re-theorized and re-described Judaism, Islam, and religion itself in ways that made them more attractive to alienated moderns. In large measure, this was done by emphasizing those aspects of the religious that have most exoticism and sex appeal—the mythic and mystical—while giving relatively short shrift to ritual, law, and ethics: that is, aspects the disenchanted find tedious, onerous, and problematic, however central they are in and to the life of religious traditions, institutions, and adherents. In doing so, they impoverished, distorted, and tendentiously misrepresented the phenomenon they sought to describe, while trying to function not just as scholars of religion, but as religious leaders—visionaries, reformers, revivalist preachers, and saviors of a sort, who would rekindle the faith and rescue fallen moderns, who so desperately need it.

In the wake of Wasserstrom's interrogation of these scholars' attempt to fabricate a *religion after religion*, others have advanced a similar, but less thorough, thoughtful, and successful critique of what might be called the fabrication of a *religion before religion*. Thus, over the past quarter century, the "linguistic turn" in scholarship, coupled with a belated drive for self-critical reflexivity, has led some colleagues to question our lazy habit of using the term "religion" in pre-modern and non-Western contexts where it carries assumptions that may be unjustified, inappropriate, and misleading; sufficiently so that some have urged the term's abandonment altogether.[1] Well-intentioned though this suggestion might be, it strikes me as misguided, since it exaggerates the problem, proposes a solution that only displaces the difficulty, and fails to comprehend some basic principles of semiotics, mistaking a problem inherent to language for one specific to the word "religion."

Most important, the absence of a signifier does not imply the absence of the signified. Although Sumerian has no word for "oxygen," one may presume the substance was present and it is no mistake—also no act of cultural imperialism—to speak of the Trobriand "economy," even if there be no readily comparable indigenous term. Surely, critics are right when they observe that "religion" is *our* term,[2] but they often confuse two senses the pronoun might have. Thus, if "our" includes all anglophones, an imprecise vernacular term is at issue, in which Protestantism looms large and which is increasingly inappropriate for examples as they deviate from that particular model of "religion."

If, however, the "our" is restricted to academic specialists, we are dealing with a technical (or etic) term, ideally the product of rigorous definitional labor that draws on a great many widely divergent examples. Signifiers of this sort, whether neologisms or common terms that have been reworked and repurposed, operate at a sufficiently high level of abstraction to encompass all members of the category they name, identifying the salient features they share, while allowing for wide variation in their particularities.

Provided that "our" use of the word *religion* is technical and not vernacular, it strikes me as defensible, but admittedly imperfect and precarious to the extent that we (a) base our definition on an inadequate number of examples; (b) confer disproportionate privilege to some examples, while ignoring others; and (c) misconstrue some examples by assimilating them to the ones we know better and to the models we base upon them. For all these reasons, our terms, categories, definitions, and theories always remain provisional at best, desperately needing the challenges and refinements that come from considering new examples and rethinking the old ones.

II

Accordingly, I propose to treat an emic datum found in the Zoroastrian scriptures, which has entered theoretical discussions only infrequently and superficially. This is the Avestan noun *daēnā*, which resembles English "religion" in many ways and has often been translated as such.[3] Intriguingly, however, lexicographers early recognized fluctuations in the usage of this term that make it difficult to arrive at a single, unified definition. Christian Bartholomae, author of the standard reference dictionary, was so troubled by this that he posited two different (homophonic and homographic) nouns. For one—¹*daēnā*, in his notation—he offered the definition "Religion,"⁴ as in passages like the following, where it signifies a body of discourse and practice that adherents accept as authoritative, as well as profoundly important.

> As a Mazdā-worshipper, a Zoroastrian, and one opposed to the demons, I embrace your religion, O Righteous Wise Lord.⁵
> I who am Zarathuštra, may I lead the chiefs of households, clans, tribes, and lands to follow in their thoughts, words, and deeds the religion which is Ahuric and Zoroastrian.⁶

As "religion," Bartholomae's ¹*daēnā* can also be used to signal the community that shares practices and discourse, constructing its identity with reference to these, as in passages that describe the need for one "co-religionist" (*hāmō.daēnā*, literally "one of the same religion") to support another,⁷ or that distinguish the responsibilities of those who "have pledged to and been instructed in the Mazdā-worshipping religion" from those who have not.⁸ A few Avestan passages also make *daēnā* the particular concern of a specialized institution.⁹ Witness an utterance attributed to the Wise Lord (*Ahura Mazdā*) himself.

> I summon priests, who have the greatest wisdom of the Mazdā-worshipping religion to be leaders/models and I summon their teachers also.¹⁰

Daēnā thus includes the four domains I treated as constitutive of "religion" in the technical definition I offered a decade ago: discourse, practice, community, and institution.¹¹ In some passages of the Avesta, however, Bartholomae recognized something that falls outside these domains, which he took to be so different from "religion" that he posited a separate word—²*daēnā*—which he defined as "Inner being, spiritual self, individuality."¹² More recent research supports Bartholomae's identification of an individual *daēnā* in numerous passages, but sees no need to posit a separate lexeme.¹³ Thus, in the most comprehensive monograph devoted to this topic, Firouz-Thomas Lankarany concluded that a single Avestan signifier references two related, but distinguishable, signifieds: "religion" (for Bartholomae's ¹*daēnā*) and "religiosity" (for his ²*daēnā*), as in the following examples.¹⁴

> This I ask you, tell me rightly, Lord:
> How should I perfect the religiosity that is mine?¹⁵
> He who establishes a better and a worse mind, O Wise One,
> Who establishes a better and worse religiosity with his action and speech,
> Whose will follows his preferences and choices—
> He should have a different existence at the end.¹⁶

Apparently, Zoroastrians theorized things more broadly than I did by including a personal "religiosity" alongside the more collective aspects of "religion." It remains to be seen how they understood this.

III

Although the classic phenomenologists of religion generally took religiosity to be a foundational part of the innermost self and an innate attunement to the sacred that provides the basis for the development of collective religions,[17] Avestan accounts suggest something different. Thus, a few texts tell that the Wise Lord initially put religiosity in people,[18] but this is only a potential that will be realized over the course of a life as the individual internalizes the values, dispositions, and *habitus* shared and promoted by the collective. Consider, for example, this prayer Zarathuštra is said to have offered as he sought his first converts.

> Grant me this boon: that I lead the good, well-born lady Hutaosā (wife of King Vištāspa, Zarathuštra's first convert and patron) to follow the religion in thought, to follow the religion in speech, to follow the religion in deed, so she may grasp and place in her heart my Mazdā-worshipping religion.[19]

Or this programmatic statement:

> We teach ... words spoken rightly, Zoroastrian utterances, deeds done well, the preparation of ritual grounds in accordance with truth, the pressing of libations according to truth, sacrificial praise, Mazdā-worshipping religion, and what is thought, said, and done.[20]

As a potential, "religiosity" was considered inherent and god-given. For this to develop into "religion," however, society—which has logical and temporal precedence over the individual—has to instruct, monitor, cultivate, and discipline its individual members, leaving its imprint firmly upon them. *Daēnā* denotes both the incipient potential and its ultimate realization, the latter of which could be judged "good" or "bad,"[21] depending on the extent to which a person's life conformed to the norms of what Zoroastrians call "the Good Religion" (*daēnā vaŋhuuī*).[22]

IV

A myth preserved in several variants helps clarify the ways personal religion was theorized. These texts detail the fate of one's soul (*uruuan*) and one's religion (*daēnā*) following death of the material body. Picking up on the heterosexual complementarity of the two nouns (*uruuan* is masculine, *daēnā* feminine), the story has elements of allegory and romance.[23]

Thus, it is told that for three nights after death, the soul sits a bit anxiously beside the corpse, huddled in prayer and hoping for bliss. On the third morning, it feels a wind, more fragrant than any it has previously encountered.[24]

> Coming forth from this wind, there appears a maiden, who is his own religion (*daēnā*): a maiden whose form is beautiful, radiant, who is white-armed, strong,

shapely, statuesque, tall, high-breasted, able-bodied, noble, of a rich lineage, fifteen years old in growth, with a form as beautiful as the most beautiful creatures.[25]

In response to the question "What kind of maiden are you, you who have the most beautiful form of all the maidens I have ever seen?,"[26] the soul's visitor leaves no doubt regarding her nature: "Verily, I am the religion (*daēnā*) of your very own self, young man, you whose thoughts are good, whose words are good, whose deeds are good, and whose religion is good."[27] Expanding on this statement, she explains that everything this soul has thought, said, and done in life has contributed to her excellence and beauty. Here, the exposition of the Avestan text is less thorough than that of a Pahlavi (Middle Persian) variant, which develops the argument more fully:

> She who was his own religiosity (Pahlavi *dēn* < *daēnā*) gave this answer to him: "I am thus your deeds, O Youth, you whose thoughts are good, whose speech is good, whose deeds are good, and whose religion is good. Because of your desire and your deeds, I am great, good, fragrant, victorious and fearless, as is apparent to you. Because you recited the Gāthās when you were in the material world, because you performed good sacrifices, tended the fire, and praised the truthful men who came from near and far, it had this effect: If I was shapely, I was made more shapely by you. If I was good, I was made better by you. If I was worthy, I was made worthier by you. If I was seated in a place of renown, I was seated in a more renowned place by you. And if I was praiseworthy, I was made more praiseworthy by you, by the good thought, good speech, and good actions you performed, O Righteous Man."[28]

Having revealed her true nature, the maiden carries her partner to the highest heaven, where they are graciously received and will enjoy eternal bliss.[29] In precisely parallel terms, the texts also describe how the soul of an evil person is greeted upon death by a hideous hag who introduces herself as his religion, the product of all his bad thoughts, words, and deeds in life. After which she drags him to hell.[30]

In the image and, more explicitly, in the words of the two maidens, this myth describes the process of a person's religiosity becoming his or her religion. Whatever qualities were initially present as a potential were constantly made better and more beautiful, or uglier and worse, by every aspect of the person's life, depending on how consistently his thought, speech, and conduct reproduced the ideals enjoined on him from childhood by the Zoroastrian priests, scriptures, and community. The moral of the story could not be more pointed. Religion is not a piece of one's life, but the totality. Throughout life one's *daēnā* is constantly under construction and every agentive undertaking, even the smallest, contributes to or detracts from its perfection, which can—and will—be judged by standards that an outsider recognizes as those of the community, but which the community identifies with the will of the deity and the nature of the cosmos.[31]

This is a rather different construction of "religion" than that to which we—scholars of religion, as well as moderns in general—are normally accustomed. Three features strike me as particularly noteworthy. First is the dialectic relation between religion's individual and collective instantiations, each of which is simultaneously dependent on and formative for the other. Second is the all-encompassing, all-pervasive expanse of the category, such that absolutely everything in life is permeated by and constitutive of the religious. Third is the way expectations of eschatological judgment recode a community's evaluation of its members as the inescapable workings of divine justice, a move that provides strong incentive for individuals to embrace everything the collective wishes to inculcate in them.

Given this Zoroastrian evidence (which finds powerful echoes elsewhere), I would now add a fifth domain to my definition, noting that "religion" also includes the subjectivities cultivated in and by members of a religious community, such that individuals' consciousness, values, and sense of identity come to conform with those of the group, a process facilitated by the expectation of rewards and punishments that are often represented as otherworldly, as well as worldly in nature.

V

A second myth provides further insight into Zoroastrian understandings of *daēnā*. This narrative speaks of Yima, a primordial king, during whose reign the world and humanity were closest to the ideal state the Wise Lord intended. As one Avestan text puts it, "In the reign of Yima, there was neither cold, nor heat; there was neither old age, nor death; nor envy, created by demons."[32] Yima's relation to religion, which determined that of humanity itself during his golden age, is reported in a dialogue between Zarathuštra and the deity.

> Zarathuštra asked the Wise Lord: "Wise Lord, most beneficent spirit, creator of truthful incarnate creatures, with whom among mortals did you who are the Wise Lord first converse, other than me, Zarathuštra? To whom did you reveal the religion which is Ahuric and Zoroastrian?"
>
> Then the Wise Lord answered: "O Truthful Zarathuštra, with fair Yima of good pastures—with him among mortals I who am the Wise Lord first conversed, other than you, Zarathuštra. To him I first revealed the religion that is Ahuric and Zoroastrian. Then I said to him, O Zarathuštra, I who am the Wise Lord: 'Get ready, fair Yima, to be the rememberer and bearer of the religion.' Then fair Yima gave me this response, O Zarathuštra: 'I am neither created, nor prepared to be the rememberer and bearer of the religion.'"
>
> Then I said to him, O Zarathuštra, I who am the Wise Lord: "If you are not ready, Yima, to be the rememberer and bearer of the religion, then make my creatures thrive, then make my creatures flourish, then prepare to be protector, preserver, and guardian of the creatures."
>
> Then fair Yima gave me this response, O Zarathuštra: "I will make your creatures thrive, I will make your creatures flourish, I am prepared to be protector, preserver, and guardian of the creatures. Let there be no cold wind in my kingdom, nor a hot one, nor disease, nor death."[33]

Can one without religion still make the world thrive? The myth suggests this may be possible, but only at the dawn of human history and even then, only for a while.[34] Ultimately, King Yima uttered a lie,[35] as a result of which he was usurped by a monstrous foreigner, chased into hiding, then found, killed, and dismembered by his own brother, as the world began its descent into conflict, confusion, and evil.[36] Only after many millennia of increasing woes did the Wise Lord again attempt to bring religion into the world, this time with Zarathuštra as his chosen vehicle.

As the most perfect of priests, Zarathuštra is a more appropriate "rememberer and bearer" (*mərətō bərətaca*) for the religion than was Yima, most perfect of kings, but the world was not transformed immediately when he embraced the Good Religion. Rather, Zoroastrian ideology maintains that the collaboration of priesthood and kingship (righteousness and power) is required for religion to spread, flourish, and accomplish its goals, the support of both institutions being necessary and neither one sufficient in itself. This is expressed quite explicitly in texts like Dēnkart 3.129:

> The battle that is hardest for the Foul Spirit to win is one where the glory of kingship and the good religion come together in the highest degree in one person's body, because this unity would produce his destruction. If in Yima, the glory of sovereignty in the highest degree had come together with the glory of the Good Religion in even higher degree, or if in Zarathuštra, the glory of the Good Religion in the highest degree had come together with the glory of kingship in the highest degree, the Foul Spirit's destruction would be assured, as would the salvation of creatures from his assault, and the desired renovation would come into existence quickly.[37]

A full unpacking of Yima's relation to the religion would go well beyond what can be offered in the present context, since it speaks to the nature of kingship and the proper goals of political action; the extent of kings' competence and their need for priestly guidance; human fallibility and consequent estrangement from the divine; and a great many other themes. What interests me most, however, is the structured contrast the story draws between King Yima—who refused to accept religion, making himself vulnerable to falsehood and setting in motion processes of corruption and decadence—and Zarathuštra—the priest and the founder, who accepted the religion Yima rejected, making truth available, thereby reversing the process of decline and moving the world toward salvation.[38] To put things more schematically, the myth divides cosmic history into four eras, in which the relation of humans to religion varies dramatically (Table 8.1).

Rather than imagining religion as something eternal, inevitable, ubiquitous, and necessary, Zoroastrianism theorizes *daēnā* as contingent: sometimes present, sometimes not, sometimes needed, but often unnecessary. According to this story, religion entered human history relatively late and humanity thrived for a long time, having no interest in or need for religion, until Yima's lie compromised the conditions of existence. With that lie, confusion, corruption, and strife entered our world, putting an end to the golden age, introducing death and all other ills. In these circumstances— which are emphatically theorized as reversible—religion provides moral guidance,

Table 8.1 Eras of cosmic history, as implied in the myth of Yima's rejection of the religion (Vīdēvdāt 2.1–5)

	Temporal period	Need for religion	Presence of religion	Reason
I	from Creation until Yima's lie	–	–	The world is (nearly) perfect
II	from Yima's lie until Zarathuštra	+	–	As king, Yima is unable and unwilling to accept the Wise Lord's offer
III	from Zarathuštra until Ahriman's defeat	+	+	As priest (and prophet), Zarathuštra accepts the Wise Lord's offer and propagates the Good Religion
IV	Eternity following Ahriman's defeat	–	–	The world is perfectly perfect

ritual knowledge, comforting reassurance, and saving grace. Above all, it is human mortality that creates a need for the guidance, solace, and reassurance that religion is uniquely able to provide. Once cosmic perfection has been secured, however, and mortality ended, it is expected that religion can and will disappear.

VI

Consistent with "our" tendency to theorize religion in ways that implicitly take Protestantism as the model, emphasizing doctrinal commitment and ethico-philosophical outlook, most experts on Zoroastrianism have accepted an etymology that derives *daēnā* from the verbal root ^2dāy- (< Indo-Iranian *$dī$-), "to see."[39] Accordingly, a variety of interpretations have been offered that, notwithstanding different nuances, make *daēnā* primarily an internal and intellectual experience, for example, "the religious vision,"[40] "vision(-soul),"[41] "conception,"[42] "conviction,"[43] "conscience,"[44] "that which is seen or recognized (as the truth),"[45] "humanity's contemplation of and attitude toward life's fundamental conditions,"[46] or "seeing with the inner eye of one's mind and, especially, what is produced by such an activity, that is to say 'thought,' 'conviction,' 'belief,' or 'vision.'"[47]

The most sustained attempt to avoid this more or less unconscious projection of Protestant assumptions onto Zoroastrian "religion" has been made by Jean Kellens, the foremost contemporary translator of the Avesta, who has consistently stressed the sacrificial context and ritual concerns of that text. Having noticed that crucial aspects of the sacrifice (for which the most important sections of the Avesta provide the liturgy) are timed to take place at dawn, also that the *daēnā*-maiden appears at dawn and is described with auroral imagery, Kellens has developed a complex interpretation, whereby *daēnā* is "the vision of the beyond obtained in the course of sacrifice,"[48] as well as the "itinerant soul" that is reunited with the "soul" after death and guides the latter to the otherworld, knowledge of which and access to which were gained through the faithful performance of sacrifice.[49]

Although I find Kellens's arguments innovative, ingenious, and attractive in many ways, they fail to persuade me for two reasons. First, all action—indeed, all thoughts, words, and deeds—are encompassed within *daēnā*, not just that related to sacrificial ritual. Second, *daēnā* denotes an entity that can be bad, as well as good. To take but one example, consider Yasna 31.20:

> Whoever attacks a truthful person, his ultimate lot is lamentations,
> A long life of darkness, bad food, the word "Alas"—
> Religion (*daēnā*) leads you to that, liars, by your own deeds.[50]

Where is the sacrificially induced vision in this verse? Are we to imagine that the "liars" in question performed a bad sacrifice, in the course of which they obtained a bad vision, which inspired them to attack truthful others, thereby leading them to the bleak torments of hell? Much simpler to understand this passage as describing an act (attacking the truthful) that is associated with a bad religion (*daēnā*) and has eschatological consequences, but no particular connection to sacrificial rites or visionary experience.[51]

VII

As part of his argument, Kellens took Avestan ²*dāy*- to describe the act of shining, as well as seeing, consistent with ancient theories that make the eyes emitters and not receivers of light.[52] This helped him avoid the danger of importing Protestant models that treat this "religion" as a "concept," "conviction," or "worldview." One can also accomplish that in another fashion, however, by deriving *daēnā* from Avestan ¹*dāy*- (< Indo-European *$dheH_1$-i-*), a verbal root that Bartholomae translated "to nourish and protect, to care for."[53] Supporters of this etymology are in a minority, arguing that its semantic advantage—which permits a view of "religion" as a nourishing and care of the person—offsets the technical factors (particularly a detail of metrics, whose importance is disputed) that favor the other option.[54]

As Bartholomae observed, however, Avestan ¹*dāy*- never denotes nourishment in general; rather, it is used only with reference to cattle.[55] This, plus its relation to such Indo-Iranian cognates as Avestan *daēnu*, Vedic *dhenú* and *dhénā* (all denoting "cow"), Vedic *dhayati*, Ossetic *dæjyn, dæjun*, and Yaghnobi *diy*- (all denoting to suck, suckle, take milk from a mother's breast), Pahlavi *dāyag* and Farsi *dāyah* (both denoting wet-nurse), Kurdish *dā(yk)*, Gurani *dā(ya)*, and Taleshi *dāya* (all denoting mother), has led subsequent philologists to posit a more specific and basic connection to lactation and the consumption of milk.[56] What on earth can that mean?

The answer becomes clear when one considers Zoroastrian myths of alimentation that describe how the first human, Gayōmard, was created perfect by the Wise Lord, such that he needed no nourishment of any form.[57] Only after the Evil Spirit assaulted creation, introducing death, falsehood, appetite, and other evils, did Gayōmard's offspring—Mašya and Mašyānī—experience the need to eat and their first meal consisted of milk, which unlike other foods (save honey) can be procured without injury.[58] As humanity's first food, milk is also analogous to the first food of infants, which makes them grow and thrive, while staving off hunger, unhappiness, and imminent death (all theorized as demonic forces unleashed by the Evil Spirit), while doing no harm to others.[59]

Like infants, Mašya and Mašyānī gradually moved on to other foods, each of which involved them in greater violence and guilt.[60] The story does not end there, however, for the texts observe that toward the end of life, individuals eat less and less, withdrawing from meat first and then milk, subsisting on water until they die. Just so, at the end of cosmic history, righteous humanity will renounce meat first, then milk, and having overcome hunger in this fashion, they will have overcome death. Not only will they live forever, but their acts set in motion the resurrection of the dead, the final conquest of evil, the restoration of a perfect cosmos according to the Wise Lord's plan, the end of history and beginning of eternity.[61]

Milk is thus theorized as the best sustenance available during the time when good and evil struggle. Insofar as the human body is a prime battleground in that struggle, it is constantly in danger of hunger, starvation, and death, while also facing risk from the impurities ("poisons") that all foods contain in varying concentrations, but milk least of all.[62] Although milk thus helps each individual survive, thereby securing the continuity of life, this is true only during the period of conflict and milk will no longer be needed once evil is overcome. In these ways, religion (*daēnā*) and milk can be seen as complementary counterparts of each other, providing the best spiritual and material sustenance, respectively, for people in the era of death, mixture, and other ills, but entities whose importance is expected to disappear with the coming age of peace and perfection.

Which is to say, that although this religion understood and represented itself as the highest good and the best response to the problem of mortality, it also considered itself infantile in ways and theorized its own obsolescence. Such positions are as unusual in the history of religions as they are in the history of theory, but we might do well to recall their implicit modesty when we ourselves turn to theorizing.

9

Nag Hammadi at Eranos: Rediscovering Gnosticism among the Historians of Religions

J. Gregory Given

I

> To remember what we have to say we study our own genealogy, the thought of our predecessors, rethinking with them the steps that arrive at us ... If presently we are lost in the labyrinth, then it is not regressive to retrace our own path, and in fact tracking backwards may locate the only egress.
> —Steven Wasserstrom, "Nine Theses on the Study of Religion"

More so than any other scholar I have read, Steve Wasserstrom has taught me to pay attention to footnotes. In footnotes we find not just the guild-approved research receipts that constitute "evidence" for arguments in the humanities. We also find the textual traces of real human relationships. Sure enough, one of the great truths of humanistic study is the fact that the hermeneutical key, or the spark for a paradigm-shifting realization, could always be lurking in that *next* book in the library or box in the archive. This is why we (re)search; in our footnotes we mark the trails that led us to our discoveries. But it is nevertheless also demonstrably the case that we have a tendency to cite our friends. After all, we tend to know what our friends think, what our friends have said, written, and published. More than we'd ever care to admit, we cite who we know.

This fact of scholarly interaction makes citations exceptionally useful as data when one sets out on a course of inquiry that seeks to scrutinize the intersection of the history of ideas and the history of specific social groups. In the case of the History of Religions, few can wring significance from the complex dynamics of this intersection like Steve

---

I would like to thank all of the participants in the Reed conference for the stimulating conversation throughout the weekend and their thoughtful feedback, especially Dylan Burns and Paul Robertson for their detailed notes on my paper. I thank also Hugo Lundhaug, Maia Kotrosits, and Eliot Stempf for offering comments on an earlier draft of this essay.

Wasserstrom. In his work—and in his footnotes—he has taught us to pay attention not just to the major intellectual statements of scholarly monographs or the archival riches of collected correspondence, but also to who is citing whom, to dedications of books (both printed and inscribed), and to the tables of contents of *Festschriften*.

And so it is appropriate that, in a *tour de force* essay on two overlapping intellectual circles in interwar Jerusalem (incidentally, a contribution to a *Festschrift*), buried in a footnote among publication details and typically fascinating asides, we find the programmatic suggestion: "The social phenomenon of grouped genius is worthy of further study."[1] Here we might sense an echo of the familiar mantra of *Religion after Religion*, framed there as more of a warning than a suggestion: "The greatest scholars require the closest study"[2]—especially, I might add, when they get together.

I do not know what, exactly, Wasserstrom means by "greatness" or by "genius."[3] I doubt that he would adopt a romantic transcendental notion of genius like that of, for example, Harold Bloom.[4] At the probing of Tomoku Masuzawa on the American Academy of Religion review panel for *Religion after Religion*,[5] Wasserstrom clarified that this "greatness is constituted precisely by multiple levels of meaning."[6] Insofar as these multiple levels of meaning are fully realized and elaborated only in the *reception* of the scholarship, it seems clear to me that scholarship attains "greatness"—functionally, anyway—by retrospective consensus. Scholarly genius, like Weberian charisma, is in the eyes of the beholders. It is primarily in the retrospective gaze, then, that the "phenomenon of grouped genius" can be identified and studied, and thus rendered significant. As certain scholars become received as "great," the citations accumulate, appreciation swells—and, with it, critical scrutiny. We start to pay closer attention to their footnotes. And we start to pay closer attention to moments of contact between the "greats," both historical and intellectual.

The greatest scholars require our closest study not because we stand to be enriched by an intense personal encounter with their transformative genius, nor because there is some secret pearl of wisdom to be plucked from a spectacularly obscure moment in the scholarly past. Rather, we study great scholars because it is from them that we inherit our categories, our discourses, our boilerplate common wisdom that is the foundation upon which we build our historical research. This inheritance was accumulated in the all-too-human contexts of mundane daily life—of social interaction, political interestedness, exclusive institutions, and deep-pocketed donors. The idiosyncratic trappings of these human circumstances can have follow-on effects downstream in our work, whether we realize it or not. From the vantage point of the present, then, we recognize moments of "grouped genius," when the "greats" got together, as potential inflection points in the history of our discourses, when one road was collectively chosen instead of another; when categories or concepts that structure our thought were inaugurated; when decisions, whether arbitrary or considered, set constraints and opportunities for scholars in the decades and generations to follow.

What I have learned from Wasserstrom's work is that when you pay attention to these moments of confluence, when you start to correlate the in-person meetings with the publication dates and follow the footnotes, the intellectual contributions fall out into a new arrangement. You see different things and ask different questions. There is rarely a smoking gun to find, because there is rarely a mystery to be solved. There is also rarely an explanatory moment of simple one-to-one transferal; as is the nature of scholars, ideas are shared and picked-up piecemeal, redeployed for uses different than originally intended. What we find instead is a different perspective on the already-known, a different distribution of attention paid. And, occasionally, an opportunity to deconstruct a problematic legacy and build something new.

In this essay, I want to draw attention to two overlapping intellectual circles in the middle of the twentieth century and ponder the implications of their entanglement. One is the Eranos circle in its heyday of the 1950s, a moment of grouped genius familiar to many, not least because of the light shined upon it by *Religion after Religion*. The other group is perhaps less well known to the broader field of the study of religion, although famous in its own historical subfield: the tight circle of scholars who initially assessed, announced, and published the Nag Hammadi Codices, beginning in the late 1940s and early 1950s. In focusing on the intersection between these two groups, I want to pose the question of how, on the one hand, the specific social contingencies of this overlap set the course for the early scholarship on Nag Hammadi (and thus the history of early Christianity), and how, on the other hand, the assimilation of insights from the Nag Hammadi materials may have inflected the broader enterprise of the History of Religions.

II

Now imagine what it is for a scholar to study Valentinus during a whole war and afterwards to acquire a whole manuscript with five authentic and completely new writings of Valentinus and his school. Is that not an act of God?
—Gilles Quispel, "Gnosis and Psychology"

Gilles Quispel's "Original Doctrine"

I begin with the wartime research of a young Dutch scholar, Gilles Quispel. Having studied classical philology at Leiden University, Quispel spent the years during the Second World War teaching Greek and Latin at a Gymnasium in Enschede, eastern Netherlands. During this time, he completed and defended a dissertation at the University of Utrecht on Tertullian's treatise *Against Marcion*, the famous second-century arch-heretic.[7] As Quispel would later reflect on this research, "in the particular constellation of that time and that moment in my life, I found that the heretics were right."[8]

This moment of identification sparked an intense interest in Valentinus, a Christian teacher active in Rome in the middle of the second century, remembered by heresiologists such as Irenaeus and Tertullian as a peddler of "gnosis falsely so-called." Quispel combed through the reports of these heresiologists, compiled the known fragmentary witnesses to Valentinus's thought, and wrote an article on "The Original Doctrine of Valentine." After the war, this article was published in the inaugural issue of a new journal covering early Christian life and literature after the New Testament, *Vigiliae Christianae*, of which Quispel was a founding editor-in-chief.

The article opens with an evocative, if somewhat tragic, account of the state of the evidence for Valentinus's thought, setting up the questions that Quispel aims to tackle:

> The writings of Valentine, the Christian gnostic who lived about 150 [years] after Christ, are lost: only a few fragments remain … This is a deplorable situation, because Valentine seems to have been a person of some importance, who exercised a considerable influence on Christian theology … So Valentinianism offers a tempting problem to the puzzled mind. Are the antiheretic writers to be blamed for dishonesty to their opponents? Is there some evidence in our sources, which leads us to suppose that pupils changed the doctrine of their master? Will the outlines of the original system reappear when these additions have been removed?[9]

Quispel proposes that these questions can only be answered through rigorous application of "the methods of modern criticism, based on philology."[10] Beginning with an enumeration of the already-established points of scholarly consensus of the day, Quispel then sets about a source-critical analysis of the heresiologists, parsing the elements of Valentinian thought that go back to the master himself from those later developed by his disciple Ptolemy and other inheritors of his teaching.

Quispel briefly arrays the different stages of the Valentinian teaching synoptically, then articulates a hypothetical composition history for a document of Valentinian teaching that his followers must have had at their disposal. "Valentine was a visionary mystic," Quispel explains, but "Ptolemaeus took a more reconciliatory attitude towards Christian orthodoxy … This leads us to suppose that Ptolemaeus adopted an existing manuscript by means of corrections, interpolations, and transpositions. The author of this document can hardly have been anyone else than Valentine himself."[11] This document was in turn made available to Theodotus, another follower of Valentinus, and its traces are visible, Quispel suggests, in the *Excerpts* from Theodotus preserved by Clement of Alexandria. Through comparison of the Theodotian sources in Clement with the Ptolemaean sources in Irenaeus, Quispel pieces together a provisional reconstruction of this "Original Doctrine," in Greek with a facing (if avowedly free[12]) English translation.

Quispel is explicit in his goals with this reconstruction. He does not present it as the final word; he expects it to be tested. But his "aim is to show that the Valentinian doctrine was a systematic conception of the universe, poetical, but not disorderly, heretic, but not confused." By virtue of Valentinus's Alexandrian education, philosophical and Hermetic influences could be noted in this teaching, Quispel clarifies, but

> after all these influences were not very important. Hippolytus declares that a vision of Christ was the impulse for the composition of the myth. On the whole this metaphysic poem seems inspired by vivid emotions and personal experiences. Valentine was not a philosopher, not a theologian, but a visionary mystic, who expressed his tragic conception of life in the symbols of creative imagination.[13]

Quispel arrives at Eranos

Proud of his fresh scholarly achievement, Quispel sent offprints of the article to Aldous Huxley, Karl Barth, and Carl Jung.[14] Jung was the only one to reply, but he was enthusiastic enough about Quispel's work to invite him to the Eranos meeting in August 1947.[15] Here Quispel lectured on "The Conception of Man in Valentinian Gnosis."[16] He set the stage for his audience with a broader survey of the current state of the question on the phenomenon of Gnosticism in antiquity. This entailed, of course, an assessment of Hans Jonas's *Gnosis und spätantiker Geist*.[17] Quispel praised Jonas's revolutionary incorporation of phenomenological method to correct and improve Adolf von Harnack's and Richard Reitzenstein's inadequate definitions of "Gnosticism."[18] Jonas, on Quispel's account, had put his finger on what was legitimately distinctive in Gnosticism: the conception of man as "a stranger in a demonic world," *in* this world but not *of* it.[19] What Jonas had neglected in his zeal for phenomenology, however, was the philological data. Echoing his article on the "Original Doctrine," Quispel argued that the tools of philology are the true means by which scholars sort out historical sources and identify influences in the history of religions—without philology, it is impossible to judge what is truly "new."[20] Given the paucity of sources for ancient Gnosticism, Quispel deemed it "prudent not to discuss the conception of man in gnosticism in general, but to limit oneself to the anthropology of a single gnostic," Valentinus.[21] Quispel then launched into a detailed exploration of Valentinian anthropology, rooted in analysis of specific passages in the ancient sources.

The lecture was reportedly well received,[22] and in any event Quispel's newfound connection with Jung immediately paid dividends. Quispel received a Bollingen Fellowship for the year 1948-1949 to study in Rome, where he first met Erik Peterson and Gershom Scholem.[23] He again lectured at Eranos in August 1948.[24] A volume collecting his essays on Valentinianism was soon planned for publication in the Bollingen Series, provisionally titled *Tragic Christianity*, after the final line of his first Eranos lecture.[25] Jung wrote a foreword for the volume, although the book was never actually published.[26]

A discovery in Egypt

In October 1947, just two months after Quispel's first lecture at Ascona, Jean Doresse, a young French coptologist on a research mission at the *Institute Français d'Archéologie Orientale* in Cairo, penned a letter to his doctoral advisor in Paris, the well-known scholar of Gnosticism Henri-Charles Puech.[27] Doresse reported that he had made an exciting discovery: a papyrus codex of some 140 pages, containing among other works the *Apocryphon of John* and *Wisdom of Jesus Christ* in Sahidic Coptic. Although he did not share its location with Puech in this initial letter, the codex was in the possession of Togo Mina, director of the Coptic Museum. Another related codex was also in Cairo, Doresse had learned, in the hands of a dealer intending to try and sell it to Americans for £6,000. "I plan on seeing this volume next week," Doresse writes,

"Perhaps one will be able to prevent it from leaving Egypt and direct it toward an accessible collection."[28]

Unbeknownst to Doresse, he was not the first Frenchman to see the codex in the Coptic Museum. In December of 1946, Mina had shown the codex to François Daumas, a young Egyptologist at the Institute, and Henry Corbin. Daumas recalls (over thirty years later):

> I saw the manuscript in the company of H. Corbin on 5 December 1946, in the office of Togo Mina. The latter was certainly aware that he was holding a very ancient text, doubtless unpublished, having to do with Christianity. That is all. He had clearly been delighted to see the enthusiasm of Henri Corbin, when I read the first leaf of the manuscript that Togo must have placed (or left?) at the front of the book. It was only the title ⲡⲁⲡⲟⲕⲣⲩϕⲟⲛ ⲛ̄ⲓⲱⲁⲛⲛⲏⲥ [*Apocryphon of John*]. I certainly pronounced the word "Gnostic." Corbin was delirious and said to me: If it is Gnosticism, translate that immediately. Alongside [the Gospel of] John, it will be Gnostic mysticism. I do not guarantee the terms, but the meaning.[29]

Whether or not Mina previously considered the codex "Gnostic," he certainly did thereafter.[30] Sworn to secrecy by Mina, Daumas and Corbin kept quiet about what they had seen, lest popular attention to the codex start driving up prices for the other manuscripts still on the market. Daumas returned to Paris in the summer of 1947 with the understanding that he would co-edit the papyrus with Mina.

Evidently unaware of Daumas's involvement, Puech urged Doresse in his reply to collect as much information about both codices as he could and, especially, to seek publication rights.[31] Doresse replaced Daumas as Mina's partner in editing the Museum's codex.[32] As Doresse and Puech's correspondence unfolded through the fall of 1947, Doresse kept his supervisor apprised of the developing story coming into view: ten or so codices had been found together in a jar; the two Doresse had seen were from this find, two had been burned, and rumors were circulating of some six or seven others being privately offered. A fellow resident at the Institute had been shown two codices by a dealer, and had caught a glimpse of the title "Apocalypse of Peter," numerous mentions of the name Seth, and an image of a serpent on the leather cover of one of the ancient books.[33]

This awkward tangle of correspondence, handshake agreements, and private meetings in a Cairo office ultimately delivered the academy its first glimpse at the Nag Hammadi Codices. While the circumstances of their discovery took years to sort out and remain contested, it is clear enough that the codices were first unearthed around the end of 1945 in the vicinity of Jabal al-Tarif, a rocky outcrop across the Nile from the town of Nag Hammadi in Upper Egypt.[34] The first published accounts of the find came in 1948, after Doresse had returned to Paris from his archaeological mission. Puech and Doresse filed a *communiqué* with *l'Académie des Inscriptions et Belles-Lettres* regarding "New Gnostic Writings Discovered in Egypt."[35] The Summer 1948 issue of *Vigiliae Christianae* carried an announcement from Mina on the Coptic Museum's acquisition of a "Papyrus Gnostique," alongside an article by Doresse assessing the "three unedited Gnostic books" contained within it: "the Gospel of the Egyptians, Letter of Eugnostos, and Wisdom of Jesus Christ" (= Nag Hammadi Codex III).³⁶

Thus went the public rollout of the codex in the Coptic Museum. As for the manuscript known to be available for sale, Doresse had been given the opportunity to study and photograph a number of leaves. "But the person who currently possesses it," Puech and Doresse reported, "authorizes him to give only a few details":

> This is a codex of about 150 pages, rather well preserved, and which, as evinced by its binding, was part of the same collection. The format is quite elongated; the pages contain 39 to 41 lines written across the entire width. The writing, extremely clumsy and even uneducated, appears to date to the 4th century. We are this time in the presence of texts written in a subachmimic dialect displaying some new features. At least three works comprise the volume: an *Apocalypse of James*, on a moral subject; a *Gospel of Truth* (is this the *Veritatis Evangelium* of the Valentinians, reported by Saint Irenaeus?) and a *Prayer of the Apostle Peter*,³⁷ both of which treat an abstract genre.³⁸

A year later, far more information about the contours of the discovery was made available, again in the pages of *Vigiliae Christianae*.³⁹ Doresse's travels and inquiries soon led him to identify the approximate location of the find, and learn that there were originally "about a dozen" codices found. Meanwhile dialogue had opened between the owner of the outstanding lot of codices and the Coptic Museum.⁴⁰ Although the owner and the Museum had not yet agreed upon the terms of the purchase, Mina and Doresse received permission to publish a preliminary report—with striking photographs—on the broader "library," now standing at thirteen known volumes: twelve in the hands of the Museum and the codex featuring a *Gospel of Truth* still on the private market.⁴¹ All were understood to date to the late fourth century. In the following year Puech published the first catalog and detailed accounting of the contents of the codices, in the *Festschrift* for the eminent Coptologist Walter Crum.⁴²

Quispel intervenes

Quispel first caught wind of the new codices in Egypt from Puech sometime in the spring of 1948.⁴³ After the initial reports had been published that summer, Quispel contacted Jack D. Barrett, secretary of the Bollingen Foundation, and urged him to consider acquiring the codex that was then on the market; he gave Doresse the address of the Foundation in New York, requesting that it be passed on to the dealer in Egypt, later revealed to be one Joseph Albert Eid.⁴⁴ Meanwhile, Eid was packing the leaves of the codex between sheets of cellophane, stuffing them in a flat envelope, and hiding the envelope among antiquities licensed for export from the Islamic Museum in Cairo. In late 1948 or early 1949, after unsuccessfully trying to sell the codex to the University of Michigan, Eid brought the papyri to the Bollingen Foundation offices in New York City, offering them at the price of $12,000. The Foundation declined. Toward the end of 1949, Eid took the codex back across the Atlantic to Brussels, where he stashed it in a safety deposit box. He returned to Cairo, and died the following year. Quispel and Puech corresponded urgently through the years 1950–1951, trying to arrange a purchase from his estate.[45]

Early in 1951, Quispel was invited to lecture at the Jung Institute in Zurich on the recently announced hoard of new manuscripts.[46] This series of lectures was published as *Gnosis als Weltreligion*.[47] Although the texts were yet to be published and Quispel had not yet seen any of the manuscripts, he did not miss the opportunity to seize the audience's imagination. "A world religion has been rediscovered,"[48] he began, before providing a sweeping overview of the new find and its potential implications. Over the course of five more lectures, Quispel fleshed out different key historical moments in the constitution of this "world religion," culminating in a full lecture devoted to—who else?—Valentinus. "A Gnostic as Pope of Rome," Quispel began, provocatively referencing Tertullian's famous claim that Valentinus had spurned the church after being passed over for the bishopric of Rome.[49] "And even the most important of all Gnostics! Once it really almost came to that."[50]

Although he later characterized *Gnosis alt Weltreligion*, perhaps for its zeal, as "my youthful lapse,"[51] the Jungian conceptualization of the mystical experience of gnosis at its core remained an integral part of Quispel's scholarship for the duration of his career. And he later claimed that it won him at least one prominent fan. At the Oxford Patristics Conference in 1964, so the story goes, a young Roman Catholic priest struck up a conversation with Quispel and asked him how his book had been received. When Quispel replied that it had been shredded by the critics, the priest replied, "'How is it possible? … because I recommended it so strongly in the review of it which I wrote.'" The priest's name, at the time, was Joseph Ratzinger.[52]

Eranos, August 1951

Later in the same year as his Jung Institute lectures, Quispel returned to Eranos. In the three years since his last lecture, several prominent members had joined the group, including Gershom Scholem (1949), Henry Corbin (1949), and Mircea Eliade (1950).[53] The Eranos meeting of August 1951 was a particularly significant occasion.[54] While he would attend a few more times, at this meeting Jung presented his final Eranos lecture, "Über Synchronizität" ("On Synchronicity"). Puech gave what would be remembered as a classic lecture on "La Gnose et le Temps" ("Gnosis and Time"); Quispel offered a contribution on "Zeit und Geschichte im antiken Christentum" ("Time and History in Ancient Christianity").[55] Corbin, Eliade, Louis Massignon, Erich Neumann, Erwin Goodenough, and other prominent European scholars were in attendance.

And some time during the meeting, in the midst of it all, a final agreement was reached that the Bollingen Foundation would fund the purchase of the codex locked away in Brussels, with the guidance and facilitation of Quispel.[56] When the Bollingen Foundation later backed out of the deal for fear of antagonizing the Egyptian authorities, the Jung Institute would ultimately provide for the purchase, with funds from George H. Page, an American expat living in Switzerland.[57]

Presenting the "Jung Codex"

Just six years after he had lamented the dearth of sources for Valentinian thought, Quispel posted a "Note on an Unknown Gnostic Codex" in the October 1953 issue of *Vigiliae Christianae*:

> On May 10th 1952 I acquired after long and patient investigations a coptic codex; which contains the following writings ... It seems rather probable that all these writings were translated from the Greek and in their original form belong to the second century A.D.; the last three certainly were written by adherents to the valentinian schools. There is some reason to suppose that the *Letter to Rheginos* was composed by Valentinus himself. The *Gospel of Truth*, which expounds a rather primitif and uncomplicated stage of valentinian Gnosis, may prove to be of paramount importance both to students of ecclesiastical history and to scholars in the field of the New Testament Canon.[58]

Whereas Puech and Doresse had previously raised the question of whether this *Gospel of Truth* was the same text as mentioned by Irenaeus, Quispel positively affirms the identification.[59] He further characterizes the *Gospel of Truth*, "this esoteric text, which was intended to be a sort of fifth gospel and is in fact the only heretical gospel known up till now, is undoubtedly of valentinian origin and probably goes back to the middle of the second century."[60] The "primitif" nature of the *Gospel*'s Valentinianism suggested its great antiquity, outflanking even the "Original Doctrine" that Quispel had previously reconstructed.

If in this initial announcement the involvement of Jung and his Institute in recovering these Valentinian sources goes unmentioned, the association would soon become crystal clear. On November 15, 1953, Quispel and Puech joined Jung himself at the Jung Institute in Zurich for a formal ceremony presenting the "Jung Codex" [= Nag Hammadi Codex I] to the world. All three men gave brief addresses assessing the significance of the discovery for the understanding of Gnosticism and human psychology.[61] The texts of the Jung Codex were lauded by Puech as likely the oldest writings among the new Nag Hammadi hoard, displaying the "most primitive phase" of Valentinianism.[62] Quispel celebrated their articulation of "the authentic Gnosis of the Valentinian school," in contradistinction to the other Nag Hammadi texts which mostly pertained to the "vulgar Gnosis of the Sethians."[63]

Other scholars had the opportunity to read a lot *about* the codex before they ever had a chance to read the texts themselves. In addition to a 1955 volume collecting essays from the presentation ceremony at the Jung Institute, Puech and Quispel published a fifty-page article in *Vigiliae Christianae* describing the contents of the codex,[64] and another lengthy discourse on the curious fourth text in the collection (now known as the *Tripartite Tractate*).[65]

The first actual text published from the codex was the *Gospel of Truth*, in 1956.[66] In the same year, Puech began giving lectures on another exciting text from the Nag Hammadi find, a collection of sayings of Jesus with the subscript title, "The Gospel According to Thomas."[67] In 1959 the *Gospel of Thomas* was first published, and popular and scholarly attention on the Nag Hammadi find (including that of Puech and Quispel) swiftly re-adjusted around *Thomas* as the gravitational center of the conversation.[68] Editions of the other texts from the Jung Codex trickled out individually over the following decade and a half. Although the Jung Codex was the first manuscript from Nag Hammadi to find its way into scholars' hands in 1952, its texts were not fully accessible to the wider academy until 1975.[69] With the initial editions complete, the codex was repatriated to Egypt by the heirs of Carl Jung on October 12, 1975.[70]

III

> To assume mysticism is the center of religion, and then to position the teacher as one who masterfully grasps that center, is not only to mystify the past but also to distort its specific character, its particulars, its historicity. The historians of religions I have studied imply that religion is ruled, as it were, by a mystical elite … [and] that the contemporary historian of religions can act as a kind of latter-day continuator, a spokesperson, so to speak, for that ancient elite.
>
> —Steven Wasserstrom, "Note to Significance Seekers"

The Nag Hammadi Codices first entered the scholarly consciousness through the filter of this tight circle of scholars, bound together by a common interest in gnostic and mystical expressions of religion, as well as the largesse of the Jung Institute and Bollingen Foundation. Before the texts in these codices were made available to readers, their significance had already been profoundly over-determined. Their specific character—their particulars, their historicity—was distorted by the idiosyncratic fantasies and desires of a small group of men who sought to grasp the mysteries at their center. These men preemptively bypassed the material fact of fourth- or fifth-century papyrus books inscribed in Coptic in favor of hypothetical second-century originals written in Greek by a hypothetical gnostic elite, for which they were the self-styled spokesmen. The "original doctrine" of Valentinus was already divined before the "early Valentinian" texts ever came to light; codices were rendered "Gnostic" at a glance before their contents were even read. Despite Doresse's hope that he might be able "to prevent [the codex containing the *Gospel of Truth*] from leaving Egypt and direct it toward an accessible collection," Puech worked with Quispel to precisely the opposite ends.[71] Jealously territorial, actively anti-pedagogical, they sought legal and intellectual control over the "secret books," and prioritized writing *about* the texts over making the texts themselves accessible to others.[72]

We have only begun to reckon with the effects of these distortions, retracing the steps of our predecessors to rethink the particularities and the historicity of the Nag Hammadi Codices. We have troubled the simple identification of the collection and its contents as "Gnostic" and started to ponder the material and social contexts in which these books were actually produced and used.[73] Much work on these fronts remains to be done. It remains to be explored, as well, how early assessments of these manuscripts, such as those presented at Eranos, inflected the broader theorizations of the Historians of Religions through the pivotal decades of the 1950s and 1960s. Influence, as a scatter of partial appropriations, is a messy thing to chart. But it is worth being attentive to the subtle genealogies that quietly emerge from the webs of citations—and the real human relationships that played out beyond them. In pausing to consider these moments when the "greats" got together, we can see how their idiosyncratic priorities guided their research; we ought to consider, too, the extent to which they still guide our own.

In so doing we are forced to recognize that we, too, continue to reproduce many of the same esotericizing practices, both in our relationship to ancient evidence and in our persistent interest in speaking to our own little specialized circles, our friends.[74] If there is a way to counterbalance this tendency toward solipsistic over-identification, it is through an insistence on practicing scholarship in situations of contact, "folks meeting *other* folks"—purposeful distanciation not only from our objects of study but also from the inward-looking coteries in which we develop our ideas.[75] As Wasserstrom has powerfully demonstrated throughout his career, this effort begins in the classroom. For while there is undoubtedly always a need for technical analysis and specialized discussion in the study of ancient texts, the pedagogical encounter can remind us of the conceptual limits of expertise. But it does so only when we approach teaching with humility, openness, and care, practicing pedagogy in a way that challenges our hypotheses rather than reifying them, decentering our interests rather than imposing them on our students. To the extent that we can follow Wasserstrom's example in adopting such a pedagogical posture toward our students and our colleagues, we—and our histories—will be the better for it.

10

Where the Center of the Rupture Is Called Judaism: Maurice Blanchot and *Religion after Religion*

Kirsten Collins

In 1969, Maurice Blanchot wrote, "The atheist is closer to God than the believer."[1] Embedded in an essay on Simone Weil (1909–1943), this sentence points out that an atheist's confidence in a truth above religion resembles religious belief more closely than the torturous doubts of Weil herself. That doubt, for Blanchot, indicates the awareness of a "rupture" separating God and humanity, truth and language.[2] The concept of rupture emerges from Blanchot's literary criticism of the 1940s, which posits literature as the site at which the distance between language and truth is disclosed as the truth of language. Blanchot constructs awareness of this truth as simultaneously more religious and more atheist than either religion or atheism, through an understanding of the relation between religion and language that becomes clear in the 1960s when he begins to write frequently on Judaism. Drawing on his readings of French-Jewish writers such as André Neher (1914–1988) and Emmanuel Levinas (1906–1995), as well as the philosophical canon of Europe, Blanchot finds the fullest connection between Judaism and language in the poetry of Edmond Jabès (1912–1991), which reconceptualizes Judaism as a literary revelation of the rupture between language and truth. Adopting Jabès's Judaism and pushing it further, Blanchot deploys Judaism as an exemplary form of religion, insofar as it serves as a figure for the distance between divine truth and our historical world—in other words, insofar as it defines boundaries of the secular.

Blanchot's reduction of religion to Judaism, Judaism to literature, and literature to rupture initially appears to define religion out of existence. It is against such projects that Wasserstrom writes: "To grasp the 'reality' of a *religion itself*, to seize one religion in some putatively pure singularity is an incoherent proposition,"[3] because "there is no religion in the singular and the study of religion must suspect every assertion for the unique, the autonomous, the untouched, the monad, the alone."[4] In Wasserstrom's view, "there is no religious situation that is not a situation of contact,"[5] which makes contact the true subject of Religious Studies, one that he has examined in many forms in *Between Muslim and Jew*, and *Religion after Religion*.[6] While Wasserstrom's focus on historical work concerning concrete situations of contact appears irreconcilable with Blanchot's reductionist abstractions, they come together when Blanchot's work is understood as an interrogation of the philosophical presuppositions about language that make contact possible.

Blanchot's definition of rupture refuses conceptualization: to render rupture a singular concept would negate the separation by which it is defined. Because it cannot be properly conceptualized, rupture is split from itself, defined by opposing sides that cannot be unified. The irreducible separation of rupture is, for Blanchot, the precondition of contact between the two opposing sides that does not attempt to unify them. Wasserstrom's notion of contact, understood with reference to Blanchot's concept of rupture, becomes clear as a normative rather than descriptive concept, one that denotes not assimilation, domination, or integration, but something like *conversation*, which recognizes and maintains the differences of its participants. Judaism functions in Blanchot's work as sign demanding the examination of contact as rupture not only because it is the religion of difference par excellence in French philosophical thought,[7] but because it differs from his own definition, and warns against the consequences of erasing such differences.

Blanchot's conceptualization of contact as rupture can be seen as an attempt to confront the political consequences of those theological concepts which Wasserstrom, too, considers dangerous. In *Religion after Religion*, Wasserstrom elucidates the fascist political ideologies hidden within the scholarly field of History of Religions, and in his essay "Nine Theses on the Study of Religion" in this volume, he places this type of work at the center of Religious Studies, whose aim, he writes, is "to sponsor encounters between philosophical claims to truth and historical claims to power."[8] Blanchot's work helps us think about how philosophical claims to truth are always, in one way or another, claims to power, which adds to Wasserstrom's call—to attend to the historical manifestations of those claims—an attempt to undo the philosophical logic presupposed by their entanglement. At the same time, Blanchot's iteration of Judaism is a shadow of a living religion, a concept drawn from an anti-Semitic history of philosophy rather than the history of a religion. His politics, too, had their historical crossing with fascist claims to power,[9] for which his work during the 1960s appears as an impossible attempt to atone by theorizing a language that would prevent the political consequences of a certain ideology with which he associated.

Blanchot's work, in many ways, stands against a central demand in Wassserstrom's work, to "stay within the limits of human knowledge, not to speak of the limits of human dignity ... Without holding on to the first and last traces of the past available to us, the texts of history, we break the chain connecting us to the living past."[10] By placing Judaism at the center of the rupture that is necessitated by contact, Blanchot breaks the chain of Jewish tradition and theorizes the Jewish tradition itself as a break—thus, continuing a tradition of anti-Judaism. And yet it is precisely these dubious intellectual roots that add to Wasserstrom's historical imperative a philosophical imperative to understand religion as a system for the exposure of the doubts that compose the only truth that can remain free of power.

Rupture at the center of language

Blanchot lays out an understanding of language as rupture in his 1948 essay, "La littérature et la droit à la mort" (Literature and the Right to Death), though Judaism does not become a central topic until nearly fifteen years later. By examining that essay in connection with three others published during the early 1960s, it is possible to trace his transformation of the problem of language into that of Judaism through his identification of the figure of the writer with that of the biblical prophet, and later, with "the Jew." While much of Blanchot's information on Judaism is filtered through his readings of Emmanuel Levinas and André Neher, it is the work of Edmond Jabès, a French-Jewish poet born in Egypt, which provides the key to reconstituting Judaism as rupture. Jabès's identification of writing with Judaism provides the grounds for Blanchot to collapse religion with a concept of language as rupture, which in turn questions the essentiality of any concept, including that of religion itself.

In Blanchot's "Literature and the Right to Death," the ostensible question of defining literature leads to the central thesis that literary language seeks to rupture reality, to rewrite it, and, in doing so, to expose the distance separating language from reality. Literary writing has no origin or goal, but is instead defined by the "passage from nothing to everything,"[11] a moment of absolute transformation that leads the writer to seek revolution, "the time during which literature becomes history."[12] Revolution, for Blanchot, is a rupture in history, the recognition of which constitutes the possibility for truth in literature. It is "the moment when 'life endures death and maintains itself in it' in order to gain from death the possibility of speaking and the truth of speech."[13] This statement, which closes the first half of the essay, draws from Alexandre Kojève's interpretation of Hegel's idea that the use of words to name beings—"Adam's first act"[14]—erases the beings themselves in the attempt to grasp their essence through language. The writer seeks to realize in writing the rupture between words and things, an impossible situation, as it requires the writer to capture in words that which is constitutively outside them, but also the basis of literary truth. Judaism provides a concrete figure for the transformation of this failure of language into its highest goal.

Blanchot's first extended meditation on Judaism appears in 1957, under the title "La parole prophétique" (Prophetic Speech).[15] In this piece, the writer is reconceived as the prophet whose speech, Blanchot contends, "announces an impossible future, or makes the future it announces."[16] He goes on to describe the prophet's role as to announce "a momentary interruption of history, to history become an instant of the impossibility of history."[17] The prophet here fulfills the ambition of the writer in entering the moment at which history is suspended and rewriting it. While the writer finds this moment of suspension in the act of writing itself, the prophet encounters it in the attempt to translate the absolute language of God into the limits of human, representative language. The prophet, in Blanchot's conception, speaks from "the Outside itself,"[18] transmitting the language of a God whose "'incessant Word'"[19] has an "absolute of meaning"[20] that no interpretation can claim to exhaust. Locating the source of truth in an untouchable God and reconstituting literature as prophecy, Blanchot recodes the writer as the Jew.

In "Être juif" (Being Jewish), published in 1962, Blanchot places the concept of a Jewish divinity absolutely removed from humanity at the center of his theory of language. In his account, divine distance is the origin of exile and nomadism, the concepts whose presumed centrality to Judaism render that religion an ideal figure for the foundational rupture of language. Indeed, Blanchot's writes, "the Jewish people become a people through the exodus,"[21] suggesting that Judaism, like language, originates from rupture. Exodus and exile, he argues, "indicate a positive relation with exteriority,"[22] which is maintained and made visible in "speech as the place where men hold themselves in relation with what excludes all relation: the infinitely Distant, the absolutely Foreign."[23] Despite the irreducible distance between man and God, Blanchot insists that "God speaks, and man speaks to him."[24] The impossible situation of the writer and the prophet is here presented as that of the Jew, and rendered universal insofar as using language requires holding oneself in relation to what is outside of language, and speaking truth means grasping this chasm at the center of speech. Judaism, reduced to a form of speech, renders the rupture between humanity and truth visible, mapping the distance between them rather than erasing it.

Blanchot completes his identification of writer and Jew through a reversal of the trope of exile, considering it a positive relationship to truth as rupture rather than a negative relationship to God. He draws his identification of Judaism with exile from the first section of Hegel's *The Spirit of Christianity and Its Fate*, entitled "The Spirit of Judaism." In a rare moment of direct citation, Blanchot quotes: "'The God of the Jews is the highest separation, he excludes all union,'" and "'In the Jewish spirit there is an insurmountable abyss.'"[25] In Hegel's essay, these statements portray Judaism as a religion devoid of the aesthetic feeling upon which the connection between the real and the ideal relies.[26] Blanchot reverses the value of Judaism in Hegel in order to show that cognizance of the rupture between ideal and real, rather than synthesis, constitutes the possibility of truth. He argues:

> Hegel ... is merely neglecting the essential, which, for thousands of years, has been given expression in books, in teaching, and in a living tradition: this is the notion that if, in fact, there is infinite separation, it falls to speech to make it a place of understanding; and if there is an unsurmountable abyss, speech crosses this abyss. Distance is not abolished, it is not even diminished; on the contrary, it is maintained, preserved in its purity by the rigor of the speech that upholds the absoluteness of difference ... Speech, in this sense is the promised land where exile fulfills itself in sojourn since it is not a matter of being at home there but of being always Outside, engaged in a movement wherein the Foreign offers itself, yet without disavowing itself.[27]

The God of Judaism, defined as separation itself, is not merely negation, but is the absolute other whose otherness, revealed in speech, makes space for the reconstitution of rupture as contact.[28] Blanchot's neat inversion of Hegel's conception of Judaism as a religion of rupture does not conceal the Christian supersessionism from which the concept developed, but instead preserves it as a warning. Judaism, in his definition, not only contains the exigency to recognize the distance between language and truth, but is itself a figure for that exigency, whose history demands that it be questioned by the speech that is the precondition of contact.

Judaism at the center of the rupture

The Hegelian conception of the Jewish God as irreparably severed from humanity cannot be found in the work of Neher and Levinas, nor would it be possible to draw from their writings an identification of Judaism with literature.[29] While Blanchot develops his equation between those terms in essays that take Neher and Levinas as interlocutors, he leans heavily for his arguments not only on Hegel but also on Edmond Jabès, the Egyptian-born Jewish poet known for focusing on the relation between Judaism and writing. Jabès grew up in an assimilated Cairo family, attending French schools and using French as his everyday language as well as the language of his poetry. Preoccupied with French literary culture, neither Judaism nor Islam— archaic traditions from a modernist perspective—featured prominently in the poetry he published while residing in Cairo.[30] It was only in Paris, to which Jabès and his wife fled after the Suez Crisis, that Jabès formulated his relationship to Judaism as a question, one that would henceforth drive his poetry.

Published when Jabès was fifty-one, *The Book of Questions* adopts formal elements that index Judaism, and reconceptualizes Judaism not only *through* text but also *as* text. Jabès signs his texts with the names of fictional rabbis, which he appends to aphorisms, dialogues, and arguments. To these he adds journal entries and narrative interjections, centering these diverse elements on the tale of two Jewish lovers, Sarah and Yukel, separated by the Holocaust. The constant interruption of one literary voice or genre by another draws attention to the discontinuity between the modes of text, while the motif of rabbinic speech and the story of Sarah and Yukel evoke a Judaism whose essence is sustained through the very experiences that fracture it. The prominence of juxtaposition emphasizes the role of text as the medium that binds the fragments into a paradoxical tradition of continuous interruption. This use of literature to reconstitute tradition through interruption anticipates and provides a basis for Blanchot's use of Judaism to argue for an understanding of rupture as the truth available from within language.

Jabès roots his Judaism in tropes of the Abrahamic, especially that of the desert, a key landscape for religious revival among assimilated Jews, the history and implications of which are treated more extensively by Ruchama Johnston-Bloom in this volume.[31] His desert, however, is not just a physical space, but a figure for textual tradition. In a section of *The Book of Questions* presented as conversation between two rabbis, one says to the other: "The garden means speaking, the desert, writing. In every grain of sand, a sign surprises us."[32] This statement implicitly contrasts an edenic state, in which God is present and speaking, to the desert of language, which can only refer to that which it renders absent. Sand, here, is configured as words. Read with reference to Jean Starobinski, who argues that sand, in Jabès's text, signifies the remains of the "letter of the commandments graven indelibly on stone tablets,"[33] human language appears as the "wearing out" of divine speech.³⁴ To imagine sand as words also modifies the conception of the desert from which, it was imagined, Judaism emerged, and in which it is sustained. Jabès emphasizes language as the Jewish homeland when he writes: "The country of the Jew is on the scale of their world, because it is a book."³⁵ While the Jabès's text reflects on what it is to be Jewish in myriad ways, the collapsing of sand and words into a single figure at the basis of Judaism suggests that what separates Jews from others is simply that "there are people who think to found their future on certitudes, and others who know in advance that they are building on sand."³⁶ Jabès transforms the desert into a metaphor for human language as the worn remains of divine language, and makes Judaism a figure for the navigation of this shifting landscape.

Jabès's book positions itself as the house built on sand, an unstable construction which demands constant rupturing of his identity as a Jew through its building. This is established from the opening dialogue, in which one unnamed voice begs another for entry into the house, which is "in the book."³⁷ This positions the book as home, yet "defeat is the price agreed on"³⁸ for those who would attempt to enter into it. This defeat is the opposition of the self toward itself introduced by the questioning of foundations, a dynamic that Jabès emphasizes later in the text in a dispute between his rabbis and his narrator regarding the definition of Judaism:

> Rejected by your people, robbed of your heritage: who are you?
> For the others you are a Jew but hardly for us.³⁹

The narrator replies:

> I have the wound of the Jew. I was circumcised, as you were, on the eighth day after my birth. I am a Jew, as you are, in each of my wounds.⁴⁰

The wound, here, is not the singular mark of circumcision, but one of many wounds that define Judaism as the pain of a rupture at the center of self. Suspecting that such an understanding of Judaism will not suffice for his interlocutors, the narrator adds, "But is one man not worth the same as any other?"⁴¹ It is as if, in claiming to be Jewish, he wishes to claim at the same time that it should not matter whether he is a Jew—forcing a French conception of egalitarianism on the rabbis, and depriving them of the right to judge his claim to Judaism. Recognizing the trap, the rabbis reply with a question that divides the narrator yet further from Judaism and from himself: "If you make no difference between a Jew and a non-Jew, are you, in fact, still a Jew?"⁴² The narrator, claiming to be a Jew while claiming to find no difference between Jew and non-Jew, finds himself confronting a rupture at the center of his own identity. The Judaism of the writer not only remains in question, but in fact rests entirely in the incessant writing of questions that continually reconstitute the rupture in his identity.

Blanchot picks up on this theme in "L'Interruption," first published in 1964. Divided into two sections, the first introduces the titular concept of interruption while the second illustrates the role of literature in exposing this interruption through a treatment of *The Book of Questions*. Interruption, Blanchot contends, takes two forms: the dialectical pause that facilitates discursive exchange, and the rupture between language and its referent that subtends all discourse and prevents the dialectic from resolving into truth.[43] Blanchot reads *The Book of Questions* as exposing this second interruption, and marking it indelibly as Jewish.[44] Jabès's poetry is the place in which Blanchot finds "the powers of interruption through which that which is called writing (the uninterrupted murmur that never ceases) must be inscribed by interrupting itself."[45] This interruption is not only in the "poetic fragmentation"[46] of Jabès's text, but also in "the history and the writing in the margin of history. In history, where the center of the rupture is called Judaism."[47] This history is the history of Jewish exile that Blanchot, drawing on Hegel, sees as originating from the words of the distant Jewish God; it is the history of the West, in which the Jew is the figure of difference whose presence denies the universality of Christian society; and it is the story that Jabès tells in *The Book of Questions*, in which assimilation has placed a rupture at the center of Jewish identity and the Holocaust has permanently ruptured Jewish community and faith.

In *The Book of Questions*, Blanchot finds an instance of Judaism conceived as a language that "invites man to no longer identify himself with his power,"[48] a rupture in identity that gives him privileged access to "the speech of impossibility,"[49] which exposes the truth of the rupture at the center of language. Blanchot articulates the union between the rupture at the center of language and at the center of Judaism by locating it in the Tablets of Law, which "were broken when still only barely touched by the divine hand … and were written again, but not in their originality, so that it is from an already destroyed word that man learns the demand that must speak to him."[50] Jabès, by rewriting the rabbinic commentary that explicates the "already destroyed word," and recoding his words as the desert that is both the origin and remains of those broken tablets, reconstitutes "that non-original text of origin" as poetry,[51] and indeed identifies Judaism and writing as "the same waiting, the same hope, and the same wearing out."[52] Blanchot, inspired by this collapse of Judaism into writing, argues that Jabès's poetry "introduces a new form, a new interval in which it is now the sacred itself, in its too immediate power, that is held at a distance, and, if we dare to say it, ex-ecrated."[53] In Jabès's positioning of the rupture at the core of Judaism in poetry, Blanchot finds religion reconstituted as the preservation of distance from the sacred, which is to say, secularized.

Rosemarie Waldrop, as she was translating *The Book of Questions*, once challenged Jabès: "'You say you are an atheist. How can you constantly write of God?'" His reply: "'It's a word my culture has given me.'"[54] This answer marks a deep ambivalence regarding the relationship of God to language, and that between religion and culture. "God" may be nothing but a word to Jabès, but it is a word that he cannot do without, for, as he says, "It is a metaphor for nothingness, the infinite, for silence, death, for all that calls us into question. It is the ultimate otherness."[55] If Jabès has inherited "God" as a metaphorical figure for the other, Blanchot has inherited the Jew—and a concept of the radical alterity of the Jewish God—as the metaphor for an inassimilable otherness, other even from itself, whose exposure constitutes the truth of writing. To posit Judaism as nothing but a metaphor for otherness erases, in a rhetorically violent manner, the historical beliefs and practices of Jews, reducing them to a word that marks their difference while effacing their being. Yet Blanchot's conception of language, based on the operation of replacement performed by Adam in naming, implicitly theorizes metaphor as that which exposes the distance of language from truth and crosses it at the same time. Judaism, then, is a metaphor for the metaphorical operation at the base of language, which the Jew, reconceptualized through Jabès as the writer, exposes in an act of writing that pushes religion beyond its boundaries and places it in contact with the secular.

In this case, Judaism is reconceived not only as the metaphor for the rupture that opens the possibility of contact, but as itself the point of contact between the religious and the secular—their point of contact, and at the same time the expression of the rupture between them. *The Book of Questions* makes this contact possible by its endless navigation between France and Egypt, between Christianity and Judaism. In Jabès's text, Judaism is given to us as words referring only to other words, understood through the metaphor of the desert as shifting like sand. It is a religion whose only essence is the navigation of its inessentiality through language. In "Interruption," Blanchot lays out the ethical and epistemological importance of grounding language in rupture and, building on Jabès, locates Judaism as the point at which religion is reconstituted as other than itself, eliminating essence in order to expose rupture as contact.

Rupture at the center of contact

Blanchot's use of Judaism as a figure for rupture can be understood as the remains of religion in the secular, but it is a conception of religion that excludes all *religions*. Religion, in Blanchot's work, is nothing but a metaphor for metaphor—a figure for the operation of replacement whose centrality to language exposes its foundation on rupture. This rupture is both the precondition for contact as conversation, which recognizes the difference between its participants, and a marker of the violence inherent in language, which is the precondition for contact. The use of Judaism to represent this rupture itself does rhetorical violence, but this is the condition of speech for Blanchot. In a startlingly direct parenthetical, he asserts that "all speech is violence, and to pretend to ignore this in claiming to dialogue is to add liberal hypocrisy to the dialectical optimism according to which war is no more than another form of dialogue."[56] If contact is to be able to resist violence, it must recognize its foundation in rupture and the violence inherent to this foundation. Judaism, in Blanchot's iteration, recalls to his readers the history of European anti-Semitism that culminated in the Holocaust, "the history where the center of the rupture is called Judaism."[57] Judaism thus indexes the violence of historical attempts to eliminate difference, and using it as a figure for rupture implicitly demands the rigorous maintenance of difference in situations of contact in order to prevent such a history from being repeated.

While Judaism is at the center of associations linking rupture to violence, it also functions as a term binding the concept of rupture to truth and to God. By recoding literature as Jewish, Blanchot equates the rupture from truth, entailed by language's dependence on metaphor as an operation of replacement, with a rupture from God, blurring the boundaries between religious and secular concepts of the absolute. Blanchot projects his understanding of language as rupture back to the beginning of

Judaism, turning religion into a mode of preserving rupture that finds its highest form in Jabès's poetry: the rupture from religion reconstituted as religion through literature. In Blanchot's corpus, Judaism, since the breaking of the Tablets of Law, *always already has been* a religion after religion.[58] The concept of "religion after religion," then, no longer indicates the smuggling of an esoteric ideology into the definition of religion, but the recoding of religion as a metaphor, in a transparently figural vocabulary that neutralizes mythology by making use of it—which is to say, wearing it out. As such, Blanchot's conception of Judaism not only serves as a marker of his contact with philosophers working on and within religious traditions; it serves as a marker of the contact between the religious and the secular through which their definitions are negotiated.

Wasserstrom's dictum that "religion is always inter-religion" demands that we examine the boundaries of religion itself as we examine the boundaries between different religions and institutions. There is no singular concept of religion that we can identify in its multitude of deceptively different forms; there is only the continuous history of communication and translation from religion to religion, from religion to culture, and from culture to politics that creates the frameworks through which humans understand, and within which the human is understood. Blanchot's use of Judaism to explicate the operation of literary language introduces a framework that refuses to essentialize, insisting instead on an essential rupture that is navigated and maintained by language. In doing so, he opens us to the possibility that Wasserstrom's theorizing of religion as a situation of contact applies not only to historically contingent situations, but also to the philosophical category of religion itself. The concern, inevitably, is political: in "Interruption," Blanchot calls attention to the consequences of uninterrupted speech:

> Let us remember Hitler's terrible monologues. And every head of state participates in the same violence of this *dictare*, the repetition of an imperious monologue, when he enjoys the power of being the only one to speak and, rejoicing in possession of his high solitary word, imposes it without restraint as a superior and a supreme speech upon others.[59]

In accord with Wasserstrom's mistrust of any totalizing conception of religion, Blanchot reconstitutes religion as rupture to provide an antidote to the "imperious monologue" of the "high solitary word." In contrast to an argument made in an earlier chapter by Paul Robertson for examining (inter-)religion as a polythetic—and thus inessential and contingent—category, Blanchot's work suggests that we consider religion inessential in its essence, a category that refuses the reification of categories and which calls the stability of boundaries unceasingly into question.

11

Abrahamic Encounters in the Weimar *Wüste*

Ruchama Johnston-Bloom

In *Religion after Religion*, Wasserstrom explores the interwar shift away from *nomos* and toward myth that was a key component of the development of History of Religions. Characteristic of this shift was the emphasis placed on the *Akedah*: "The collective reception of divine commandments ... was deemphasized in favor of an individual gnostic encounter with a *theophany*."[1] Indeed, as Reuven Firestone suggests, Abraham fits the Eliadian model of *homo religiosus*: a founder of sacred sites, experiencer of hierophany, of "eruptions of the sacred."[2] Not surprisingly, then, Abraham became a key figure for Jewish thinkers of the era, including Martin Buber, Franz Kafka, and Emmanuel Levinas, who all responded to and grappled with Søren Kierkegaard's "knight of faith" and the idea of the "suspension of the ethical."[3]

The move away from *nomos* and the interest in gnosis during the interwar period was, of course, not the final word on how to interpret Abraham, or how to interpret religion. Levinas, for one, ultimately rejected the suspension of the ethical.[4] However, the current preoccupation with the Abrahamic (over and against the Mosaic) in interfaith work and in the academy is partially a legacy of this earlier understanding of Abraham. In order to "remember what we have to say," as Wasserstrom puts it in his "Nine Theses," this chapter examines a strand of how we arrived at the contemporary image of the Abrahamic.[5] Namely, it examines how Jewish thinkers (and converts to Islam) responded to and reworked theories that connected monotheism and the desert, theories in which Abraham is a key figure. While these Jewish thinkers did not necessarily follow Mircea Eliade's "mystocentric"[6] approach, Eliadian impulses—in particular, the critique of modernity—can be identified in their readings of the desert and Abraham.

The desert, the wilderness, the *midbar*, the *Wüste*, the overdetermined site where Abraham and the Abrahamic are located, is a freighted location in the History of Religions. For example, the French geographer de Planhol's entry on "deserts" in the *Encyclopedia of Religion* opens with the statement that "in areas of continuous occupation, the presence of the sacred transcends and resolves the stresses produced by the environment. In the desert, humankind, deprived of the support of social solidarity and helplessly confronted by supernatural forces, is beset by anguish and fear."[7] De Planhol then discusses the desert as a place of danger and exile, as well as of divine revelation and ascetic solitude (particularly for Christian monasticism). He then introduces the argument of Ernest Renan (1823–1892) that monotheism necessarily developed in the desert.[8] While de Planhol complicates Renan's assertions by examining the complex religious milieu of pre-Islamic Arabia, he concludes: "In the historical evolution of humanity in the Old World, the deserts have indeed been the privileged place for the development of the pastoral nomadic cultures that evolved precociously toward monotheism and that constituted an essential component in the genesis of the great monotheistic religions."[9] In this entry, included in the both first (1987) and second (2005) editions of the *Encyclopedia of Religion*, Renan's theory, at the center of which is the idea of an inferior Semitic race, lives on.

The idea of the desert as a privileged site also lives on in the study of religion more widely. For example, the announcement for the 2016 conference of the International Society for Religion, Culture and Literature called for a "renewed exploration of desert spirituality as a way forward in addressing issues of religious and racial conflict, ecological crisis, and economic instability."[10] Issues eminently worthy of address, but what is "desert spirituality" exactly? For the conference organizers it was closely linked to Christian asceticism.[11] One might ask, however, if presenting a Christian concept as universal, and as universally relevant, is really the way forward in addressing conflicts, religious or otherwise. In the UK context, (Christian) Theology has a larger presence in the academy than Religious Studies per se, so the meaning and utility of "desert spirituality" may have seemed self-evident to the organizers.[12] However, their use of the phrase encourages interfaith dialogue while at the same time dictating its terms.

The conference organizers would have done well to historicize "desert spirituality," to think about the history that makes this concept intelligible (or unintelligible) today, and to think about whose "desert spirituality" is deemed acceptable. Nineteenth-century philological and racial discourse ascribed "desert spirituality" of a different kind to both Jews and Muslims. The Semitic "genius" was credited as giving the world monotheism, but Jews and Muslims were seen as lacking mythology, as incapable of science and, in general, as inferior to Christian Europeans. Their (perceived) monomaniacal interest in the divine was deemed the result of their roots in the desert.

This chapter explores the trajectory of this freighted "desert spirituality" and how Jewish thinkers themselves responded to it. The Jewish response to this idea of the Semitic, this Orientalizing of the Jew, relates of course to Wasserstrom's work on Jewish and Muslim "enemy-brothers," to what happens "Between Muslim and Jew."[13] During the *fin de siècle* and interwar periods, some Jewish thinkers embraced the Orient, and turned an admiring eye toward Islam, using engagement with Islam to construct an authentic Judaism.[14] As Wasserstrom has written of S. D. Goitein and his generation: "Young Jewish Orientalists were in some serious sense in love with Islam, a love perhaps not inconsistent with the Orientalist depredations attributed to it by Edward Said and others."[15] For this generation, the Orient—sometimes entirely imagined, sometimes the *Yishuv*, sometimes further east—was enchanted, a place of possibility.[16]

Philology, Semites, and dissimilation

The *fin de siècle* and interwar Jewish thinkers who positioned Jews vis-à-vis the desert and the Orient did so by reworking anti-Semitic tropes that had emerged out of nineteenth-century philological and racial discourse. This discourse categorized Jews and Arabs together as Semites and highlighted the desert as constitutive of the Semitic "genius," which supposedly gave monotheism to humankind. In *Histoire générale des langues sémitiques,* Renan proclaimed: "The desert is monotheistic. Sublime in its immense uniformity, it first revealed to man the idea of infinity, but not the perception of an unceasingly creative life that a more fertile nature inspired in other races."[17] For Renan, Semites were limited because Semitic languages were limited. Indo-European languages were inflected, whereas Semitic languages lacked inflection, and this lack led to "all the limitations that characterized their native speakers as a race."[18] As Tomoko Masuzawa has argued, the creation of the (inferior) category of Semite is key to understanding shifting attitudes toward Arabs and Islam in the nineteenth century. The idea of the linguistically and racially inferior Semites helps us "begin to understand the new logic and renewed momentum behind the particularly harsh condemnation of Islam [in the nineteenth century]. With the emergence of the science of comparative philology, it is as though the age-old European anti-Semitism—or more precisely, negative sentiments against the Jews—took a new turn and found a novel deployment."[19]

Masuzawa argues that this idea of the Semite in some ways solved a problem for Christianity, which had always been troubled by Islam being a younger religion. In conceptualizing and essentializing Islam as Semitic and hence retrograde, Christianity was able to designate Islam as archaic, even though it had developed after the rise of Christianity. These racial ideas also allowed Europe to claim that the only Semitic part of itself was Christianity and that the rest came from Greece (and was therefore Indo-European). Renan would even argue that Jesus was the "ultimate" Aryan and hence that even Christianity was not really Semitic.[20] As Gil Anidjar has argued, the idea of the Semite was integral to the idea of Christian Europe. According to Anidjar, as Semites, Jews and Muslims were conjoined but also differentiated: "in Europe, in 'Christian Europe,' they—the Jew, the Arab on the one hand, religion and politics, on the other, are distinct, but indissociable. Stated in a different idiom: The Jew, the Arab constitute the condition of religion and politics."[21] The idea of the Semite, yoked to claims about the origins of monotheism, is therefore key to a certain, historical self-understanding of the so-called West.

Jewish and Muslim thinkers, including Ignaz Goldziher (1850–1921) and Sayyid Jamal al-Din al-Afghani (1838–1897), responded to this idea of the Semite, refuting accusations of racial inferiority.[22] When Renan claimed in a lecture on Islam and Science (1883) that Arabs were incapable of science and that Islamic science was in fact entirely derivative and borrowed from the Greeks, al-Afghani argued that although contemporary normative Islam was opposed to modern science, Islam had historically achieved great things scientifically and that there was nothing racially inferior about Arabs.[23] In *Mythology among the Hebrews and Its Historical Development* (1877),

Goldziher, for his part, argued against Renan's claim that Semites did not have any mythology.[24] In the beginning of this work, Goldziher shows his cards:

> I start from the conviction that the Myth is something universal, that the faculty of forming it cannot *a priori* be denied to any race as such, and that the coincidence of mythical ideas and modes of expression is the result of the uniformity of the psychological process which is the foundation of the creation of myths in all races; and this very uniformity of mythical ideas may consequently serve to psychologists as an argument for the thesis of the psychological uniformity of all races.[25]

In their responses to Renan, both al-Afghani and Goldziher argue against the view of Semites as radically different and inferior to other peoples. They trace the historical development of Judaism and Islam in order to make a case for viewing these traditions in comparison to other traditions.

In the twentieth century, Jewish thinkers (and Jewish converts to Islam) would use the idea of the Semite to dissimilate. As Volkov has detailed, toward the end of the nineteenth century, Jews in Germany and elsewhere began to have doubts about whether or not complete assimilation was desirable or even possible. As Volkov writes, "the exclusiveness and recurrent hostility of the host society, on the one hand, and the inner dynamics of assimilation itself, on the other," nurtured dissimilation.[26] Hence, assimilated Jews began to reinvent the Jewish tradition. One way they did this was by turning to the Orient for inspiration. This was a more cultural embrace of the Orient than practiced by earlier generations of German-Jewish Islamists who had studied Islam in order to valorize Judaism.[27] Many dissimilated by becoming Zionists, while others simply became involved in a renaissance of Jewish culture.[28]

Martin Buber is a key figure here. As many scholars have noted, in both his celebration of Hasidism and his cultural Zionism, Buber positioned the Jew as Oriental, as capable of providing an antidote to the ills of Western modernity. For Buber, the Jews are a mediating people, capable of traversing the divide between East and West. His strongest statement regarding the Oriental nature of the Jew is the address, entitled *Der Geist des Orients und das Judentum* [*The Spirit of the Orient and Judaism*], which he delivered in 1912 to the Prague Bar Kochba Student association.[29] In this talk, Buber argues that although the Jew has spent time in the West, "the Jew has remained an Oriental. He was driven out of his land and dispersed throughout the lands of the Occident ... the ways of the nations among which he has lived have affected him, and he has spoken their languages; yet, despite all this, he has remained an Oriental."[30] In valorizing the Jew as Oriental, Buber both drew on the "neoromantic, neomystic, and indeed orientalist discourses of the fin de siècle"[31] and pushed back against anti-Semitic tropes connected to the desert. Buber's neo-romanticism is on full display when he begins the address with a reflection on how German Romantics viewed the Orient:

> At the end of the 18th and the beginning of the 19th century, Herder and Goethe, Novalis and Goerres, were aware of the fact that the Orient is a single unit. Though they knew the diversity of its peoples ... these men looked through the shell of

diversity and saw its unified spiritual core. To them, the Orient was no poetic trope but an undivided, efficacious reality whose touch they experienced and of whose greatness they had a first, awe-inspiring inkling.[32]

Buber goes on to affirm this reading of the Orient as unified, and draws heavily on the German romantic tradition in his depiction of the Jew as Oriental. However, he also rejects the idea, circulating at the time, of the Jews as *Nomadenvolk*, roaming the desert. Following on from Renan's characterizations of Semites, Werner Sombart's *The Jews and Modern Capitalism* (1911) blamed Jews for capitalism, and traced this back to their roots as nomads.[33] Buber rejected this depiction of the Jews, envisioning Old Testament figures as warriors and farmers deeply rooted to the Holy Land instead.[34] The Jew may be Oriental, but for Buber he was not the fanatic Semite of Renan and Sombart's fever dreams.

Zionists, Arab drag

If Buber and others rejected the label and connotation of *Nomadenvolk*, some interwar *olim* (pl. someone who makes Aliyah) to Palestine modeled themselves on the nomadic Bedouin they encountered there. For these *olim* (the *Yishuv*—the Jewish community of pre-state Palestine) was an enchanted place where they could remake themselves.[35] Having internalized anti-Semitic tropes about Jews being Oriental, they sought to liberate themselves by reclaiming the label. Bound up in this was an attempt to cast off another anti-Semitic stereotype—that Jews were effeminate.[36] Settlers who tried to remake themselves by adopting Arab dress and culture were drawn to what they considered to be the virility of Bedouin culture and romanticized the Bedouin as "noble savages." The major arena in which this "arabizing" took place was among the young men of *Ha-Shomer* (the Jewish defense organization that guarded the Jewish settlements) and later the Palmach. Gil Eyal describes the *Ha-Shomer* and Palmach culture of "arabizing" as an "exclusive and masculine subculture of virtuosi."[37] These young men adopted Arabic dress and Arabic nicknames, and used Arabic. However, the enchantment of the *Yishuv* and this appropriation was complex. As Oz Almog notes, many of the Arabic words these young men adopted (and which have since become part of Israeli vocabulary) were Arabic curse words and this adoption of language was in some ways mocking.[38] The use of Arabic slang was an inside joke among the Zionist elite, meant to demonstrate that these young men were "native," the new Jews.

Converts to Islam, the desert, Abraham

Two Jewish converts to Islam went further than the young men of *Ha-Shomer*. Rather than simply adopt elements of Arab dress and culture, both Muhammad Asad (born Leopold Weiss) (1900–1992) and Essad Bey (born Lev Nussimbaum) (1905–1942) embraced Islam. They also both wrote about the desert as a key site for the development of monotheism and spiritual awakening. Both men led complex, eventful lives, which I cannot cover in detail here. Nussimbaum was born in Kiev, grew up in Baku, and fled with his family to Berlin in 1920 when the Red Army invaded Azerbaijan. In Berlin he converted to Islam and became a popular author. Today he is best known for his novel *Ali and Nino* (1937), published under the pseudonym Kurban Said.[39]

Weiss was born in Lemberg (now Lviv), relocated to Vienna with his family, and attended university there for a time before dropping out and going to Berlin in 1920. In 1922 he visited Mandatory Palestine (where his uncle, the psychoanalyst Dorian Feigenbaum, had relocated) and began a career as a journalist for German papers. After a second trip to the Middle East in 1924–1926, he converted to Islam in Berlin and returned to the Middle East.[40] He then spent six years in Arabia, before leaving for the Indian subcontinent, where he eventually became the Director of the Department of Islamic Reconstruction in Pakistan. In 1952 he went to New York as Pakistan's ambassador to the UN, but soon after he left his diplomatic position and spent the rest of his life living in America, Europe, and Morocco. He is now known for his biography *The Road to Mecca* (1954), his translation of the Qur'an (1980), and his contributions to twentieth-century Islamic thought.[41]

As Essad Bey and Kurban Said, Nussimbaum wrote popular books on a variety of topics, including Central Asia, the Soviet Union, and Islam. In these books he mobilizes and complicates Orientalist tropes. For example, in *Ali and Nino*, an old Georgian man digresses on the difference between *Waldmenschen* (wood men) and *Wüstenmenschen* (desert men):

> Maybe that is the one real division between men: wood men and desert men. The Orient's dry intoxication comes from the desert, where hot wind and hot sand make men drunk, where the world is simple and without problems. The woods are full of questions. Only the desert does not ask, does not give, and does not promise anything. But the fire of the soul comes from the wood. The desert man—I can see him—has but one face, and knows but one truth, and that truth fulfills him. The woodman has many faces. The fanatic comes from the desert, the creator from the woods. Maybe that is the main difference between East and West.[42]

Here again the desert, the *Wüste*, determines the nature of Muslims, who are painted as fanatical and non-creative.[43] In his biography of Muhammad, Essad Bey also makes the connection between the desert and monotheism, writing of sixth-century Arabs: "No doubt the grandiose desert gives him an inkling of the puissance of some godhead which rules over all things."[44]

In his autobiography, Muhammad Asad also connects the desert to monotheism and authentic religious experience.[45] For Asad, monotheism is the product of the desert: "There are many more beautiful landscapes in the world, but none, I think, that can shape man's spirit in so sovereign a way … Ever since man began to think, the desert has been the cradle of all his beliefs in One God."[46] Here is the same connection between desert and monotheism posited by Renan, but this time with an entirely positive valuation. In keeping with the desert's centrality in *The Road to Mecca*, Abraham is also a key figure for Asad. In his autobiography, Asad writes that upon arriving in Jerusalem in the early 1920s he is struck by the Bedouins he encounters there. One day, near the Old City, Asad imagines that a Bedouin he sees is one of King David's warriors:

> And then I remembered with a start: this man was an Arab, while those others, those figures of the Bible—were Hebrews! But my astonishment was only of a moment's duration; for all at once I knew, with that clarity which sometimes bursts within us like lightning and lights up the world of the length of a heartbeat, that David and David's time, like Abraham and Abraham's time, were closer to their Arabian roots—and also the Bedouin of to-day—than to the Jew of today.[47]

Asad's conversion is an embrace of his authentic roots, and hinges on the figure of Abraham:

> My coming to this land [Arabia]: was it not, in truth, a home-coming? Home-coming of the heart that had espied its old home backward over the curve of thousands of years and now recognizes this sky, my sky, with painful rejoicing? For this Arabian sky ... vaulted over the long trek of my ancestors ... that small Bedouin band of Hebrews, forefathers of that man who was to be born in Ur of the Chaldees. [Abraham] would have well understood why I am here—for he also had to wander through many lands before he could build his life into something that you might grasp with your hands, and had to be a guest at many strange hearths before he was allowed to strike root.[48]

Asad can be and has been read in a variety of ways: as firmly entangled in the Jewish trajectories he endeavored to leave behind, or, simply, as a Muslim thinker.[49] He tried to help "reconstruct" Islam in Pakistan, imagining what a modern Islamic state might look like, but his son Talal Asad has also suggested that, ultimately, Asad's thought can be read as pointing beyond the modern idea of the state.[50] Throughout his oeuvre, Asad posits Islam as the antidote to the ills of modernity, much as Buber suggests cultural Zionism and the Jewish mediation between East and West can provide an escape from the morass of modernity. Although Asad often waxes poetic about the desert and spirituality in his autobiography, he also tended to dismiss mysticism (he was quite critical of Sufism). And ethics are a key concern in his other writings on Islam.[51] The alienation and spiritual searching that drove the History of Religions group *toward* myth led Asad *back* to revelation and law. He spent the last twenty years of his life working on a translation of the Qur'an.[52]

Conclusion

This chapter has mapped Jewish responses to the idea that monotheism necessarily emerged in the desert. This idea hinges on the desert as a sight of theophany, as where God reveals himself to humankind. As discussed above, this idea has a long and ignoble history—replete with racial assumptions about desert fanaticism. Jewish thinkers responded to this history in various ways—some rejecting the very idea of a Semitic "genius," others revaluing the idea, and in the process rethinking the connections *Between Muslim and Jew*. For some Jewish contemporaries of Mircea Eliade, the desert, the site of theophany, offered an escape from modernity. Muhammad Asad "found himself" in the desert, identifying an unbroken (or re-forged) chain from Abraham, to his Bedouin contemporaries, to himself. Martin Buber also looked toward the Holy Land, and mysticism, as a way out of *fin-de-siècle* Europe. For these thinkers, Abraham was a solution, an answer to the question(s) of modernity. We can find traces of this earlier valorization of Abraham in today's embrace of the Abrahamic.

Post-9/11, connections and contestations between the so-called Abrahamic religions have become a key focus of interreligious dialogue and scholarship on religion. The qualifier "Abrahamic" has come to replace "Judeo-Christian," at least in some discourses, as a means to gesture toward shared origins and values. Judeo-Christian, popular during the Cold War, has been set aside as scholars have identified the term's built-in Christian supersessionism and argued that use of the term rhetorically exonerates Europe from perpetration of the Shoah (Holocaust).[53] Abrahamic has been adopted as an alternative, largely for the obvious reason that it makes space for Islam.[54] Abrahamic is not without its critics, however. Aaron Hughes has suggested that while the term may have some utility for interfaith work, it hinders rather than helps the scholar of religion, as "it adds yet another order of monovocality, further homogenizing or leveling our view of what is going on."[55] Jon Levenson has also made a case against the idea of Abrahamic religions, arguing that by extracting Abraham/Ibrahim from each religion's specific texts and traditions, the figure comes to mean nothing.[56] For Levenson, this is a Protestant Abraham, a disembedded Abraham, taken out of the interpretative frameworks and the textual traditions that give meaning.

At this moment in time—this moment of Muslim travel bans and re-invigorated, emboldened anti-Semitism—criticizing interfaith work might seem churlish. However, as scholars of religion, we must understand, as Wasserstrom's work consistently reminds us, the history of our endeavor and the concepts we employ. The conference announcement and the *Encyclopedia of Religion* entry discussed above are evidence that old habits die hard. Whenever the figure of Abraham is embraced as a common ancestor, we need to ask: Which Abraham? The Abraham of the Paul? The Abraham of Kierkegaard? The Abraham of the Qur'an, Genesis, the Talmud? The Abraham of Auerbach or Asad, as Kigar asks in this volume? Following Wasserstrom's dictum that "religion is always inter-religion,"[57] we should also ask how each Abraham serves as a figure of inter-religion. As Wasserstrom writes, "Inter-relational complexity constitutes our subject [the study of religion]."[58] Each of the many different Abrahams referenced above is a product of that inter-relation complexity. Therefore, while we should eschew simplified notions of the Abrahamic, we should nevertheless examine what each specific, complicated Abraham can tell us about "the situation of contact" in which religions are constituted.[59] This emphasis on contact can serve as a corrective to the above idea of the Abrahamic, which obscures differences and historical specificity, and which smuggles in essentializing models of religion—Eliadian or otherwise.

12

Far Too Close:
Religion and Reality in the Work of
Erich Auerbach and Muhammad Asad

Sam Kigar

As a young man, Leopold Weiss left the central European home of his father, a banker, and his grandfather, a rabbi, and went to the Middle East to work as a journalist.[1] Before too many years had elapsed, he converted to Islam, changing his name to Muhammad Asad (1900–1992). His illustrious and varied career as a translator of the Qur'an, Muslim political theorist, and diplomat makes him important to the history of modern Islam.[2] Asad's *The Road to Mecca* is a swashbuckling account of the author's days in Arabia, which is interlaced with sharp religious, sociological, and philosophical reflection. It was composed in the 1950s but recalls a period from the early years of the twentieth century through the Second World War. By contrast, Erich Auerbach's (1892–1957) work, *Mimesis: The Representation of Reality in Western Literature*, is a classic not only in the field of comparative literature, but also in the Euro-American humanities writ large. Auerbach described himself as belonging to "the Jewish faith," while maintaining a commitment to secularism.[3] Auerbach's *Mimesis* was written during his exile in Turkey during early years of the 1940s. It is a scholarly work of enormous breadth and acumen. Despite these differences, Asad and Auerbach had overlapping interests in religion and the relationships between religions.

In *Religion after Religion*, Steven Wasserstrom's analysis of the "Historians of Religions"—Mircea Eliade, Gershom Scholem, and Henry Corbin—is one of comparison but also "orienteering,"[4] a term that will come up again in his "Nine Theses on the Study of Religion," in this volume (§6). In the conclusion to *Religion after Religion*, Wasserstrom writes, "The clarity sought in the foregoing essays may be nothing more than orienteering, trying to locate [the Historians of Religions] in the larger world of thought."[5] For Wasserstrom, their shared location in the world of thought depended on their intermittent shared geography. He plots the coordinates of their annual convergence in Switzerland, at Eranos, showing how those meetings shaped the coincidence of their thought. His focus on the relationships between these men is proleptic affirmation of his later claim that religion only occurs in multiples: "*All religion susceptible of our study is in a situation of contact. There is no religion in* the singular and the study of religion must suspect every assertion for the unique, the autonomous, the untouched, the monad, the alone."[6] Of course, Wasserstrom goes beyond the apparent similarity of these thinkers. By marking their distances from one another he gives the lie to their affirmation of a shared mystical core to religions.

The thinkers under consideration here, Asad and Auerbach, chart a different cartography. These thinkers lived during roughly the same period as the Historians of Religions considered by Wasserstrom and, in some cases, shared friends with them.[7] But they did not meet regularly or, to my knowledge, at all. Unlike the Historians of Religions, their differences are patent, their similarities concealed. More specifically, their shared backgrounds and divergent careers and interests allow for inquiry stemming from Wasserstrom's insight that "all religion is inter-religion." How did these thinkers understand religion and religious difference? Did they share a religious or inter-religious perspective from which they analyzed individual religious formations? This chapter compares their understandings of the figure of Abraham to answer these questions.

On the surface, Asad viewed religion in a supersessionist mode, in which each Abrahamic tradition replaced the preceding historical tradition.[8] This view would square with his theological emphasis on choice, reason, and will. Just as Asad had chosen to accept Islam, so too could society use reason to redeem itself by embracing the final Abrahamic religion. Conversely, Auerbach's forced exile contributed to the formation of an outlook that was resolutely worldly and that continuously deferred solutions.[9] Auerbach accepted the problematical nature of reality, the capriciousness of life, and the idea that the Abrahamic traditions would continue to exist alongside one other, sometimes irreconcilably. In the story of Abraham's binding of his son, Auerbach saw precisely the expression of this reality. Auerbach did not become a Muslim while living in a Muslim-majority country. To do so would have been to think that it was possible to, as Asad says, "exchange one world for another"[10]—a proposition that was unsupportable according to Auerbach's understanding of reality and the ethical. However, this thesis, which takes Asad as a supersessionist and portrays Auerbach as focusing on religious incommensurability, emphasizes only the divergent ways they attended to religion. It ignores what these thinkers shared: a sense of the ethical necessity of thinking inter-religiously.

Reality and inter-religion

Asad's and Auerbach's lives and works testify to Wasserstrom's claim that religion is a function of "contact" and "continuity."[11] Asad's autobiography traces such an encounter. The meaning of its title, *The Road to Mecca*, is twofold. On the one hand, the book stories Asad's life leading up to and immediately following his conversion to Islam. In this case, Mecca is synecdoche for Islam. On the other, it tells the tale of the trek Asad took with his friend and servant, Zayd, through Arabia, many years after Asad had left Europe. Mecca here refers to the city itself, which Asad was suddenly compelled to revisit after he got lost in a life-threatening sandstorm in Egypt. The latter story frames and concludes the former. Asad uses the events of his camel trek to lead to recollections about his initial voyages from Europe to Muslim-majority lands. The two tales weave together, ultimately converging on the same location, Mecca.

Reflecting on his childhood, Asad describes a significant amount of Jewish learning. He studied biblical exegesis, "just as if [he] had been destined for a rabbinical career."[12] But he reports that, well before he became Muslim, he felt discontentment with Judaism. He claims an understanding of Judaism that relies on a reading of the text of the Torah and not his experience in his childhood home, and rehashes many old, anti-Jewish stereotypes including clannishness and slavish following of the external form of the law.[13] He repeatedly underscores Judaism's lack of universality. The arc of *The Road to Mecca* leads steadily away from Jewish particularity and into Islamic universalism. Islam, Asad argues, represents "a more human" landscape.[14]

As Muslim voices steadily grow louder in the book, it becomes clear that they are providing a solution to the problems of disaffection that Asad experienced as a child and a university student.[15] The moment that Asad describes as pivotal in his conversion, even though it predates when he verbalized the declaration of faith, is when an Afghani friend says to him, "You are Muslim, only you do not know it yourself."[16] The expression is meant to signify that an inward change had already occurred as Asad (then Weiss) traveled among Muslim communities. But it also shows how Islam is a solution to problems long ago felt and shared by many Europeans. Islam has a double meaning here. It is taken to be the West's other, both geographically and spiritually. At the same time, Islam is a universal ethical solution to the fundamental problems faced by all human society. Islam as a universal religio-ethical system sometimes contradicts Islam as socially constituted phenomenon that Asad first encountered in the Middle East.[17] This contradiction is manifest in the narration of his own life:

> Sometimes it seems to me that I can almost see the lives of two men when I look back at my life. But, come to think of it, are those two parts of my life really so different from one another—or was there perhaps, beneath all the outward differences of form and direction, always a unity of feeling and a purpose common to both?[18]

Asad asks if his autobiography is the story of one man or two. He means to question the degree to which his conversion to Islam brought about a total change in his person. His tentative answer is that there is unity between the European and Muslim (or Arabian) parts of his biography. In this frame, a belief in one God and a commitment to reason were constants in his life. Islam merely gave name to this "feeling." To recall Wasserstrom's terminology, it was not only contact but also continuity that led Asad to Islam. But this telling must ignore the "outward differences of form" that mark the two phases of his life as distinct. As such, it strips Islam of its ritual particularities and the materiality of its lived expressions. Yet, as we will see below, Asad's lack of certainty about how to answer his own question leaves the door open for continued reflection on religions and the relationships between them.

Auerbach's itinerary through Muslim-majority countries was less culturally immersive than Asad's. He was welcomed to Turkey as part of that country's attempt to Europeanize. In contrast to its regime of isolating and ostracizing Turkish Jews, the

Turkish state did not emphasize the religion of its German Jewish academic guests. Rather, Auerbach and others were viewed simply as Europeans. Auerbach's comment, made in a letter to a friend, is revealing of his situation in Turkey: "The conservatives distrust us as foreigners, the fascists as emigrants [*sic*], the antifascists as Germans, and anti-Semitism exists, too."[19] This statement shows that he was in a precarious place. He must have had to walk a fine line in his public writings and lectures. His role as a representative of Europe in Turkey is evident in *Mimesis*. The scholar of comparative literature Kader Konuk argues that *Mimesis* does not stray from Europe and European subjects for precisely this reason. In his pre-exilic writings, for example, Auerbach had considered the role of Muslim letters on Dante.[20] In *Mimesis*, such consideration drops completely out of sight, a fact that Konuk attributes, in part, to the Turkish state's search for a Europe to mimic.[21] Whatever the reason, Europe is—to borrow Auerbach's language—brilliantly illuminated in *Mimesis*, while the rest of the world remains in the shadows.[22]

The one place where contemporary non-European places and peoples occur in *Mimesis* is in the last few pages, where Auerbach speaks of world historical events. In these pages, Auerbach expresses his hope for a "common life of mankind on earth."[23] He maintains that this goal is still "a long way off," but it "begins to be visible."[24] He writes, "It is most concretely visible now in the unprejudiced, precise, interior and exterior representation of the random moment in the lives of different people."[25] Auerbach stakes his hope for a common life on attunement to the intricate trivialities and necessities of life, which he sees so well demonstrated in the writings of Virginia Woolf.[26] Representations and acknowledgment of these shared experiences, Auerbach wagers, will allow peoples to bridge their differences. Importantly, *Mimesis* posits a connection between Judaism and attention to these quotidian aspects of life.

The question of Auerbach's Judaism is by no means settled. Edward Said sees him primarily as a secular figure.[27] The classicist James Porter, on the other hand, argues vociferously for the centrality of Judaism to Auerbach's work.[28] Surprisingly, there is common ground between these views. Both camps agree that the "concrete" reality of this world was of central importance to Auerbach. Concrete worldliness is an attribute that Auerbach ascribes to both Judaism and secularism. The idea of God, according to Auerbach, is symptomatic of the Jewish tendency to see depth and problems in lived experience. By keeping one eye focused on the deep and contradictory nature of reality—what he understood as the "Jewish way of representing things"—he gained critical perspective on those texts that elided worldly problematics. In other words, Said and Porter can be reconciled if we see that Auerbach's Judaism was his secularism.[29]

Asad and Auerbach seemed, then, to agree on one salient point: the importance of the worldly, the everyday, and the human. They came to this conclusion by different roads and to different ends. For Auerbach, God was a symptom of the deep, subjective, and world-oriented psychology that he found in Jewish texts. To the degree that Auerbach's method mimicked what he understood as the "Jewish way of ... representing things," the real was marked by capriciousness and uncertainty. Asad, by contrast, saw God as a legislator who commanded rational and upright dealings in the world. While sociality was fraught with problems, Asad believed that such problems could be overcome by obeying the rational principles of Islam.

Wasserstrom writes, "Quite distinct from the myth of myth, the fatally-flawed misapprehension of a putatively sacral isolation, the real, in fact, locates its fate only through orienteering the dense social atmosphere of complicated relations."[30] Wasserstrom draws a line between the isolationist tendencies of myth (or those myths that place a certain concept of myth at the center of religion) and the complex social relationality that defines the real. The concept of the real was central to how both Auerbach and Asad thought about religions and their interrelations. Asad saw in Islam a reflection of the "human." In a less direct way, Auerbach saw the human psychic and social reality in Jewish texts. This concern for the real led both men to place ethics at the heart of religion.[31] By contrast, Wasserstrom shows how Eliade, Scholem, and Corbin replaced ethics with ontology. He discusses this as a lack of human *"need"* in their work. "Or rather," he says, "the one primary need they posited by contrast to Durkheim's social needs or Freud's psychological need was an *ontological need.*"[32] By contrast, need is rife in the works of Auerbach and Asad. They agreed that the fundamental need was to address reality. The figure of Abraham provided an example for both men.

Abraham and the ethical

From the first lines of *Mimesis*, we are plunged into Auerbach's masterful analysis. He asks us to recall a scene from the *Odyssey* in which Odysseus has returned home but remains unknown to Penelope. The housekeeper, Euryclea, remarks to her master how much he resembles Odysseus who is "even now wandering somewhere, a stranger."[33] On touching the scar[34] on his ankle as she washes his feet, Euryclea realizes that Odysseus is sitting before her. Auerbach's concern is with how and why the narrative shifts to an explanation of the origin of the scar. Despite the narrative's move to an event that occurred many years prior, everything remains "uniformly illuminated," and in the "foreground."[35] It is a "basic impulse of the Homeric style" to refuse lacunae. Auerbach contrasts the Homeric text with the biblical story of Abraham's binding of Isaac. Far from Homer's "uniform illumination," the biblical text sheds light on only "decisive points of the narrative." Whereas all thoughts are "externalized" in Homer, the examples of direct discourse in the Bible "serve to indicate thoughts which remain unexpressed." The Abrahamic story "remains mysterious and fraught with background."[36]

Auerbach's comparison of these two texts is not impartial. While, on the surface, Auerbach's essay deals with antique literature, Porter demonstrates how National Socialism in Germany weighed heavily on his mind as he composed it in 1942. According to Porter, Auerbach likened the Homeric style to the Nazi process of legend making.[37] Regardless of whether or not Auerbach drew such a strong connection, it is clear that, as *Mimesis* moves into a comparison of Homer and the Binding, the author betrays his sympathetic stance toward the former. He much prefers the "dark" and "obscure" text of the Torah to the "uniformly illuminated" *Odyssey*.[38] The most obvious and convincing example of Auerbach's preference for the biblical text over the Homeric is the degree to which he describes the former as "problematic" and "historical." Auerbach writes:

Abraham, Jacob, or even Moses produces a more concrete, direct, and historical impression than the figures of the Homeric world ... because the confused, contradictory multiplicity of events, the psychological and factual cross-purposes, which true history reveals, have not disappeared in the representation.[39]

In the remaining chapters of *Mimesis*, Auerbach frequently champions the motifs he first identifies in the Bible. By giving preference to the Jewish text over the Greek, he develops a conception of realistic representation against which he can measure other pieces of literature. The fact that the Binding is a horrific and troubling scene is not incidental to Auerbach's belief that it was an accurate representation of the everyday and the real.

Wasserstrom points out that his Historians of Religions were interested in the Binding for precisely its "exceptional" status.[40] "The 'exception' thus variously served the Historians of Religions as an Archimedean point for a cartographer off the map; or a sovereign; or a phenomenologist."[41] Søren Kierkegaard's reading of the Binding linked up with Carl Schmitt's concept of sovereignty: they were the other of ethics and of law, respectively.[42] But Auerbach and Asad were not interested in the "primal scene"[43] of the Binding for its exceptional status—its teleological suspension of the ethical. For them, the near-sacrifice of Abraham's son was indicative of reality and the *need* to address sacrifice ethically. Of a phrase in the story of the Binding of Isaac, Auerbach writes, "So 'early in the morning,' is given, not as an indication of time, but for the sake of its *ethical* significance; it is intended to express the resolution, the promptness, the punctual obedience of the sorely tried Abraham."[44] Abraham's decision, for Auerbach, was not a departure from ethics. Instead, it was the very instantiation of an ethical response to the demands of truth. In his reading of the Binding, Truth trafficked under the name of God; elsewhere, Auerbach called this truth "history."

What of the Christian Abraham? Auerbach claims that the Christian reading of the Binding disrupted the foreground–background dyad by making the older event (the background) always point to the newer event (the foreground). Christianity, for Auerbach, was an attempt to make sense of the messiness of history by reading older events as foreshadowing what was to come. This is what he famously refers to as the *figura*. The *figura* describes an extra-historical connection between events. The most notorious example is the would-be sacrifice of Isaac, which came to stand for the sacrifice of Jesus. Auerbach claims that the figural interpretation of history came to dominate the world. But he cautions that it could not colonize all of reality. The fate of human beings was still caught in the exigencies and contingencies of material and social existence.[45] Auerbach's objection to the *figura* may be likened to Wasserstrom's critique of myth: "Myth, in short, belittles difference; it builds on the drive, in fact, to close the gap of contradictions, to tell one story and not two."[46] The fact that Auerbach undercuts the explanatory power of the *figura*, even as he introduces the concept, shows that he means to destabilize the supersessionist view of religious history. While the Christian figural understanding of history won out, other possibilities remain open.

As Konuk points out, for all of Auerbach's focus on Abraham, it is notable that he did not so much as mention the patriarch's relevance for his Muslim audience in Turkey, neither in *Mimesis* nor in his extant Istanbul lectures.[47] Asad, by contrast, did focus on the significance of Abraham to Muslims. His lengthiest engagement with Abraham and his progeny comes toward the end of *The Road to Mecca*, after Asad and his companion have entered the holy city.[48] He writes:

> All references to the patriarch in the Koran itself are so worded as to leave no doubt that he had been living in the foreground of the Arabian mind ages before Muhammad's time: his name and the outline of his life are always mentioned without any preliminaries or explanation—as something, that is, with which even the earliest listeners to the Koran must have been thoroughly familiar.[49]

Asad's use of the word "foreground" is significant to our reading as it touches Auerbach's use of the foreground–background binary to explain the distinction between the Torah and the *Odyssey*. Asad places Abraham in the foreground of Arab consciousness, indicating that the reality of Abraham lies in his continuous presence in Arabia which the ceremonies of the Hajj commemorate. For Auerbach, the Binding is significant because so much in the story remains unsaid and in the background. He finds an expression of the real in the text's shadowy and elliptical nature. Abraham is real because his motivation is obscured, even to himself. For Asad, the elliptical nature of the qur'anic text of the Sacrifice is indicative only of the Abrahamic text, with which the Qur'an's audience was already intimately familiar.

References to Abraham in Asad's translation and interpretation of the Qur'an (e.g., Q 37:105–15) and in *The Road to Mecca* lack meditation on the more disturbing aspects of the patriarch's story. Rather, he is primarily signified as the genealogical forbearer of most of the Arabs, including Muhammad.[50] This focus on genealogy inverts Auerbach's *figura*. Rather than Abraham's sacrifice of his son prefiguring the Christian event, the pilgrimage to Mecca points back to the story of Abraham. In this way, Islam becomes simultaneously the newest and the oldest of the three Abrahamic faiths. The point for Asad is that Abraham's mark on the land, in the form of the Ka'ba, is unmoving and unaltered.[51] Islam, for Asad, collapses the figural meaning of Abraham with his historical meaning. Abraham prefigures himself. His continued presence in Muslim Arabia is an enduring sign of that region and religion's unique commitment to ethical monotheism.

The irresolution of inter-religion

Asad and Auerbach did not reproduce the myth that religion had an unchanging mystical core, so expertly dispatched by Wasserstrom in *Religion after Religion*. But, in their insistence on the human, the real, and the lived, these scholars constructed other sorts of myths. Auerbach implied that Judaism had a tragic worldliness at its center. Asad portrayed Islam to be essentially rational and therefore able to navigate away from an impending sense of disaster felt after the Great War. Both often missed Wasserstrom's benchmark of paying attention to the "complicated relations" that form not only between people but also between the texts of these commentarial traditions. Instead, they replaced attention to social and commentarial complexity with myths of "the human," "background," and "reason," all of them masquerading as the real. Yet, Auerbach and Asad re-joined Wasserstrom in his insight that the real has a fate yet to be located.[52] Auerbach writes:

> We are constantly endeavoring to give meaning and order to our lives in the past, the present, and the future, to our soundings, the world in which we live; with the result that our lives appear in our own conception as total entities—which to be sure are always changing, more or less radically, more or less rapidly, depending on the extent to which we are obliged, inclined, and able to assimilate the onrush of new experience.[53]

And Asad

> Our destination—our destiny—is not so easily espied: for destiny is the sum of all that has moved in us and moved us, past and present, and all that will move us and within us in the future—and so it can unfold itself only at the end of the way, and must always remain misunderstood or only half understood as long as we are treading the way.[54]

These quotations express the authors' uncertainty about their lives and the worlds in which they lived. In making myths about Judaism, Islam, and Christianity, they essentialized religions and belied their mutually constitutive histories. But they both allowed that history would continue to unfold; and they also exemplified a shared commitment to try to understand it. In their efforts to discern the future by attempting to make sense of the past, they shared the sense that not just religion but also the contact between religious people held some answers. They searched for ways that religion could account for the relationship between past and future. They anticipated an implicit insight of Wasserstrom's comment on ethics regarding the Historians of Religions: if the religionist's method may be shorthanded as "orienteering," then their compass must be an ethical one.

Part Three

Rethinking

13

Is Sethian Gnosticism an Abrahamic Religion? Abraham, Sodom, and the Parabiblical in Ancient Gnostic Literature

Dylan M. Burns

The complex of literary traditions identified by scholars as "Sethian (Gnostic)" has frustrated attempts at scholarly categorization across the spectrum of religions in the late ancient Mediterranean world.[1] While biblical themes and figures—particularly Seth, Jesus of Nazareth, baptism, and the apocalyptic genre—are central to Sethian literature, scholars have struggled to diagnose the "Jewish" and/or "Christian" character of Sethianism.[2] We then presently face a wide range of competing hypotheses concerning the origins and valence of Sethian mythology, understood variously to have been a pre-Christian, Jewish movement subsequently Christianized and Paganized, a "Sethian Christianity," or, as I have argued elsewhere, a literary tradition recalling what we find among "Jewish-Christian" baptismal movements, like the Elchasaites, rich in Jewish apocalyptic motifs and in many respects recalling Manichaeism.[3]

Indeed, scholars have poor terminological options for designating such movements on the borderlines of Judaism and Christianity in the first half of the first millennium CE: Sethianism then joins the ranks of (anti-)baptismal, dualist movements of (late) antiquity, such as Elchasaism, Manichaeism, and Mandaeism, whose relationship with the relatively familiar religions of Judaism, Christianity, and Islam remains tricky to explain. Yet explain it we must! To drive these sources into the corral of "secret tradition," "esotericism"—or, as remains surprisingly fashionable in Europe, a religion called *Gnosis*, distinct from Judaism and Christianity—is to *ghettoize* them, as the honorand of this volume, Steven M. Wasserstrom, once exclaimed to me in his office.[4] Rather, we ought to seek a "species-wide generalization" for treating the phenomenon of Sethian literature, one that makes it intelligible to our students and colleagues while embracing the "deep pluralism" of late ancient religion, and making sense of the "historical exempla of philosophical incommensurates" it

---

The present author thanks the other participants of the conference for stimulating discussion and critique that was helpful in revising this study; particularly invaluable were the suggestions of Gregory Given and Paul Robertson.

poses.⁵ Thereby, we can recover ancient Gnosticism from the twentieth-century History of Religions, where Gershom Scholem understood it as "the greatest case of metaphysical antisemitism."⁶

Now, as Guy Stroumsa has stressed in recent publications, Jewish Christianity, Manichaeism, and, yes, Gnosticism contributed a great deal to the late antique formation of Islam and even the greater body of traditions we might call "Abrahamic religion."⁷ Professor Wasserstrom certainly recognized as much decades ago, in his pioneering work on the emergence of the *ghulat*—Shi'ite "extremists" known as "Gnostics"—in the second Islamic century.⁸ It might then be asked: Was Sethianism an Abrahamic religion? The short answer is: certainly not, Sethian works say nothing about Abraham at all. Instead, they trace divine lineage back past The Flood to Seth himself.

And yet, Sodom. The thread back through Sodom in literature—where Abraham has been erased and his God (re)named Saklas—should lead historians to explore other options for describing the late ancient crucible of Judaism, Christianity, and Islam, as well as the difficult, dualist movements inhabiting their borderlines and borderlands. More specifically, the Sethian texts that discuss Sodom address the figure of Abraham even when they do not explicitly mention him, and this is in keeping with a greater engagement with the figure of Abraham across the exegetic spectra of ancient Gnosticism. Nonetheless, many of these sources, like the Sethian exegeses of the legend of Sodom and Gomorrah, reject an early Christian ethnic reasoning grounded on the figure of Abraham, a fact which I suggest should lead us to focus on classifying this literature not with reference to Abraham, but the Bible. The case of Sethian Gnosticism should lead us to set aside the category of "Abrahamic religion" in favor of "encounters" with biblical traditions.⁹

Sodom and Gomorrah without Abraham, I: *The Apocalypse of Adam*

A story about Abraham—the destruction of Sodom and Gomorrah—figures prominently in two Sethian texts, both of which are difficult to classify as simply "Christian," "Jewish," or "other," and which hold differing but ambivalent views of baptism. It has been argued that these works have no "interest" in Abraham, since the patriarch does not appear in them.¹⁰ I disagree.

The first is an elliptical reference in *The Apocalypse of Adam* (NHC V, 5), a testament where the dying Adam delivers a discourse about primordial times and an *ex eventu* prophecy to his son, Seth. The genre and setting closely recall the apocryphal *Life of Adam and Eve*.¹¹ In *Apoc. Adam*, the satanic world-ruler—simply referred to as "God Almighty (ⲡⲛⲟⲩⲧⲉ ⲡⲁⲛⲧⲟⲕⲣⲁⲧⲱⲣ)" or "Sakla"—has created humanity to be his slaves, but Adam and Eve have managed to engender a race of elect humans outside of his control, apparently beginning with Seth himself.¹² God sends the flood to destroy this elect "seed," and makes a pact with Noah, who will therefore be permitted to survive the flood and rule the earth, in exchange for his obedience: "Therefore, I shall give the [earth to you], you and your sons. [In] royal fashion shall you rule over it, you and your sons. And no seed shall come from you belonging to the people who do shall not stand in my presence, through another glory."[13]

"Then," our narrator, Adam, continues,

> Noah shall divide the whole earth amongst his sons—Ham and Japheth and Shem. He shall say to them: "My sons, listen to my words. Look, I have divided the earth amongst you—but serve him (i.e., God) in fear and slavery, all the days of your life!"[14]

The seed of Ham and Japheth will number "twelve kingdoms" plus "another tribe," yet 400,000 people born from this seed will become elect themselves, "sojourners" (ⲥⲟⲉⲓⲗⲉ), foiling Sakla's plan.[15] Sakla will try again to destroy them: "Then, fire and sulfur and asphalt shall be cast upon those men, and fire and mist shall come upon those generations, and the eyes of the powers of the luminaries shall become dark, and the generations shall not see them in those days."[16] This must be a reference to Sodom.[17] The 400,000 people will be rescued by angels who appear in other Sethian texts (Abrasax, Sablo, and Gamaliel), and "for the third time," an "Illuminator of Knowledge" (ⲫⲱⲥⲧⲏⲣ ⲛ̄ⲧⲉ ϯⲅⲛⲱⲥⲓⲥ) will descend to earth, to create elect among the sons of Ham and Japheth, "redeeming them from the day of death."[18]

The apocalypse ends with a kind of hymn, which describes the ostensibly miraculous births of twelve (apparently) false prophets and their followers ("kingdoms"), concluding each "verse" with the refrain "and thus he came to the water." The thirteenth kingdom appears to be that of the Christians,[19] contrasted with another group—the "kingless race":

> And the thirteenth kingdom says of him that every birth of their ruler [is] a Word (ϭⲓⲛⲙⲓⲥⲉ ⲛⲓⲙ ⲛ̄ⲧⲉ ⲡⲉⲩⲁⲣⲭⲱⲛ ⲟⲩⲗⲟⲅⲟ[ⲥ ⲡⲉ·]). And this Word received a mandate there. He received glory and power. And thus he came to the water, so that the desire of these powers should be satisfied. But the kingless race (ϯⲅⲉⲛⲉⲁ ⲇⲉ ⲛ̄ⲛⲁⲧⲣ̄ ⲣ̄ⲣⲟ ⲉϩⲣⲁⲓ̈ ⲉϫⲱⲥ) says that God chose him from among all the generations.[20]

"God"—the "real" one—"chose" the "great Illuminator," who, notably, does *not* come to the water. Rather, teachings will inspire his followers to battle the "power" and which will awe even the unbelievers; they will not be written down, but shall eventually be brought by angels "on a high mountain, on a rock of truth. Therefore, they shall be named *The Oracles of Immortality [and] Truth*."[21]

The problematic character of *Apoc. Adam*'s cultic filiation is well expressed by one of its leading interpreters, Birger Pearson, who has argued it to have been a "pre-Christian" work with a "lack of obvious Christian influence … a Jewish Gnostic document in the sense that its genre and its building-blocks are derived from Judaism. But in its intentionality it is anti-Jewish in the extreme, a product of the Gnostic revolt against the Jewish religion and the Jewish God."[22] Yet, while its salvation-historical narrative appears to distinguish the elect from the Jews (the first twelve kingdoms) and the Christians (the thirteenth kingdom), it would be misleading to describe the work as *neither* Jewish *nor*

Christian. As Pearson himself notes, it is unintelligible without reference to Judaism and Christianity, not least in its allusion to the destruction of Sodom.

Sodom and Gomorroah without Abraham, II: The Egyptian Gospel

A malevolent creator-god named Saklas also rains fire on the elect—explicitly connected with Sodom and Gomorrah—in *The Egyptian Gospel* (NHC III, 2; IV, 2). Here, as in other Sethian texts such as *The Apocryphon of John*, *The Three Steles of Seth*, or *Zostrianos*, Seth and his "Seed" are two of many pre-existent, celestial beings engaging in a celestial liturgy before the Godhead.[23] Seth follows the generation of the world by the rebel angel Saklas and his demon partner, Nebrouel:

> Then, the Great Seth came, bringing his Seed, and it was sown in the aeons which were begotten, their number being that of Sodom. Some say that "Sodom" means "the pasture"[24] of the Great Seth, which is "Gomorrah." But some (say) that the Great Seth took his plant (ⲧⲱϭⲉ) from Gomorrah, and planted it in the second place, which he named, "Sodom." This is the race which came forth through Edokla, for she gave birth to the Word of Truth and Justice (ϣⲁϫⲉ ⲛ̄ⲧⲁⲗⲏⲑⲉⲓⲁ <ⲙ̄ⲛ̄> ⲟⲉ{ⲛ̄}ⲙⲓⲥⲥⲁ), the source of the seed of eternal life which is with those who shall endure because of the knowledge of their emanation. This is the great, immortal race.[25]

Literary motifs of the Jewish pseudepigrapha appear here, too: like *Apoc. Adam*, the conclusion of *Eg. Gos.* states that this primeval text was left for posterity on a large mountain, so as to better survive the coming cataclysms of the Flood and Fire.[26] Yet here, Jesus of Nazareth appears as the savior, and so *Eg. Gos.* may be called "Christian" in a sense, despite Schenke's belief that the text has only a "Christian veneer."[27] The Seed of Seth, we are told, will undergo terrible trials, but will be guarded by angels,[28] and, above all, The Great Seth himself, incarnated as Jesus Christ:

> He passed into three incarnations (ⲁϥⲟⲩⲱⲧⲃ̄ ⲛ̄ⲧϣⲟⲙⲧⲉ ⲙ̄ⲡⲁⲣⲟⲩⲥⲓⲁ)—which I mentioned before, along with the Flood and the Fire and the Judgment of the Archons and the Powers and the Authorities—in order to save it (i.e., the Immortal Race) that went astray, by means of the reconciliation of the world and baptism, (and) by means of a word-begotten body that the Great Seth prepared for himself in secret, through the virgin … (and) through the immortal, Word-begotten one, and Jesus the Living, and the Great Seth, who put him on. And through him (i.e., Jesus) did he (i.e., the Great Seth) crucify the powers.[29]

Among the gifts of the Great Seth, Jesus Christ is "the reconciliation of the world and baptism." The text even finishes with what appears to be a hymn meant to accompany a ritual, perhaps baptism, although metaphorical as well as physical water could have been intended.[30]

Sodom and Gomorrah without Abraham, III: A response to Genesis 18:16-33

The shared motif in *Apoc. Adam* and *Eg. Gos.* of Saklas's attempted obliteration of the elect at Sodom and Gomorrah—a scenario where the Sodomites are *good*—has long puzzled scholars.[31] It is impossible to locate such a reading in the world of ancient Jewish and Christian exegesis of the legend of Sodom and Gomorrah, which usually focused on the "great sin" of Sodom, vaguely alluded to in Gen. 13:13 and 18:20.[32] This sin was generally understood in two senses: first, as primarily sexual, with some authors focusing on homosexuality and others on a more general sexual profligacy;[33] second, as the absence of kindness and hospitality to those in need, particularly strangers.[34] Although there is one extant Gnostic text whose valorization of the Sodomites as the elect may be tied to sexuality,[35] *Apoc. Adam* and *Eg. Gos.* seem distant from sexual context. I think we are put on the right track by Jenott's observation that the *Eg. Gos.* "marks the beginning of Seth's race ('the seed of eternal life') in world history by the birth of two ethical concepts, 'truth and justice,'" and thus the elect's opposition to "the wicked world-ruler."[36] In one of its few allusions to what characterizes the elect, *Apoc. Adam* says that they did not succumb to "desire (ⲉⲡⲓⲑⲩⲙⲓⲁ)," unlike the "angels"—likely a reference to the fall of the Watchers (Gen. 6:2).[37] Their scriptures will be called *The Oracles of Immortality [and] Truth*.

The identification of the elect of these texts—the Sodomites attacked by Saklas—as humans of great ethical stature brings Abraham, who appeared to have been erased from the legend, back into the picture. The theological upshot of the Sodom myth is not simply that God will wreak vengeance upon sinners. It is that Abraham was chosen to father Israel because he was a good person, as is evident in Abraham's dialogue with God in Gen. 18:16-33.[38] God has decided to smite Sodom, and does not hide his intention from Abraham, "for He knew that he would direct his sons and his entire house after him to keep the ways of the Lord and to do what is right and just (δικαιοσύνην καὶ κρίσιν), so that the Lord would bring about everything He had promised him" (18:19 LXX). Abraham here appeals to God to be a good judge, and not to execute all the inhabitants of the city at once, for some of the citizens might be just after all. God agrees not to destroy the cities, even if there are just ten righteous people in them. The Lord's agents enter Sodom, only to find that Abraham's brother Lot and his daughters are the sole righteous inhabitants. They are removed from the cities, which are then annihilated by fire (18:20-19:29).

The identification of the "Seed of Seth" as the truly righteous race—as opposed to Abraham's "entire house after him"—is fitting within contemporary Christians' self-understanding as a universal *tertium genus*.[39] In the second and third centuries, Christian apologists employed a sort of "ethnic reasoning" to articulate an identity distinct from those of the Jews and Heathens. This ethnic reasoning often concerned the figure of Abraham. The apostle Paul famously offers a novel interpretation of God's pledge of the Covenant to Abraham's son from Sarah (Gen. 17), wherein those who believe in Christ are grafted on to the inheritance of Abraham's blessing (Rom. 9-11; Gal. 4:21-5:1).[40] Justin Martyr (d. circa 165 CE) insisted that while the true lineage of Abraham is spiritual and Christian, Jesus belonged to the biological lineage of Abraham anyways.[41] Of particular significance is the denotation of this Christian ethnicity as a race of "foreigners" or "aliens," strangers to the present cosmos—an exaltation of foreignness rare in religious literature of the Roman world but widespread in early Christianity, and especially in the Sethian corpus where the elect of *Apoc. Adam* are "sojourners."[42] The Great Seth himself—"another seed (σπέρμα ἕτερον)" (Gen. 4:25 LXX) of Adam and Eve, also known as ἀλλογενής, "foreigner"—connoted alienation as well.[43] Such language is not common in Second-Temple Jewish literature, but it is significant that Abraham himself, as a righteous follower of the ways of the Lord prior to the establishment of Israel, is called "stranger" (Heb. גר, Grk. πάροικος).[44] Indeed, Abraham's "foreignness" constituted part of the appeal of the "resident alien motif" among early Christians (e.g. Heb. 11:13).[45]

The "Seed of Seth" may in this light be read as one of many post-Christian instances of ethnic reasoning. Its employment of the "resident alien motif" may have recalled Abraham to readers with the patriarch on the mind. Abraham may also lurk behind the revised legend of Sodom and Gomorrah in *Apoc. Adam* and *Eg. Gos.*, where the Seed of Seth is an ethnicity that promotes righteousness: the Seed of Seth possesses what Gen. 18:19 assigned instead to Abraham and his descendants. It differs, of course, from Abraham's "house" in an obvious way: while the "seed of Abraham" in Gen 17–18 is post-diluvian and biological, the Seed of Seth is ante-diluvian, and, like other Christian "new races," it is universalizing.[46] Moreover, the decision to use a different metaphor—the Seed of Seth—and then *oppose* it to Abraham and his house through reconfiguration of the legend of Sodom was not a random one. It was inspired by exegesis critical of the God of the Jews.

Abraham among Marcionites, Manichaeans, and Gnostics

The crucial figure here is Marcion, who allegedly excised passages from Luke identifying the God of Abraham with the true God and penned a work, the *Antithesis*, which appears to have used Scripture to prove that the Creator of the world could not be the good God whose Son was Jesus of Nazareth.[47] Marcion's teaching likely influenced Mani and his followers, renowned for their excoriation of stories from the Hebrew Bible.[48] As Judith Lieu has recently argued, Marcion's criticism of the vengeful God of the Septuagint was extreme, but not out of place in second-century exegetical debate concerning the problem of God's justice.[49] Other writers interpreted the God of Abraham allegorically: Valentinus was said to have taken the figure of Abraham in the Septuagint to be the demiurge himself, who, upon learning that there is a higher God than him, says, "I am the God of Abraham, my name I did not declare" (cf. Ex. 6:3 LXX), meaning that the demiurge has concealed his true identity.[50] The Valentinian Ptolemy also demarcated the "single good God" and a "just" and vengeful God who nonetheless loves good, and the Marcosians held the ten tribes of Abraham to be code for the decad of aeons (a group of ten primordial realities).[51] The anonymous *Refutatio* says that "Sethians" adduced the threesome of Abraham, Isaac, and Jacob to support their breakdown of all reality into triads.[52] For these Jewish and Christian writers, Abraham remains a central and positive figure in Scriptural exegesis and Jewish or

Christian identity, even as the punitive God of Genesis 18–19 is distinguished from a higher God and the symbol "Abraham" is transmuted, taking on ever more hifalutin referents.

Other writers were more critical. Irenaeus says that the "other (Gnostics)" (often dubbed "Ophites" in scholarship today) teach that the monstrous demiurge, Yaldabaoth, chose Abraham and made a covenant with him. Through Moses, the demiurge brought Abraham's descendants out of Egypt, gave them the Law, and so made them the Jews.[53] Interestingly, the Genesis legend of Abraham and his God is here understood as a historical event,[54] as it was by Marcion. Similarly, the Mandaean *Right Ginza* describes Abraham as well as Moses as prophets of Rūhā, a malevolent female spirit; the Jews, Abraham's children, spread lies through the "works of Abraham."[55] Here too, Abraham is taken as a historical but hostile personage. The same is true of the account given in a stunning polemical homily from Nag Hammadi, the *Second Treatise of the Great Seth (Treat. Seth)*,[56] where the ascended Christ speaks:

> For Adam was a joke, having been created from the image of a pattern of a human being by the hebdomad, as though he had become stronger than me and my brethren. We, we are innocent as regards him, since we did not sin. Now, Abraham was a joke, with Isaac and Jacob, since they were named by the hebdoad 'the fathers deriving from the image,' as if he had become stronger than me and my brethren. We are innocent as regards him, because we have not sinned. David was a joke, because his son was named 'the Son of Man' ... Solomon was a joke, thinking that he was a messiah ... The twelve prophets were jokes ... Moses was a joke.[57]

In fact, all teachers from Adam up through John the Baptist are false, "for a teaching originating from some angels is what they had, to keep dietary rules and bitter slavery."[58]

It is difficult to imagine *Treat. Seth* as any less transgressive in an ancient Mediterranean context than it is today. Rather, despite taking up the notion of Christianity as a *tertium genus* apart from the Jews, most Christians rejected Marcion and *Treat. Seth*. They held on to the metaphors of Israel and the heritage of Israelite cult, seeing themselves as *verus Israel*.[59] In exegetical matters, the majority seemingly agreed with thinkers like Origen, who charged that God's punishment of Sodom was in no way incommensurate with God's goodness.[60] Indeed, Abraham was also an important symbol for several of the heresiographers in describing their own faith: the author of the *Refutatio* attempts to show that the "god-fearers"—the race of Abraham—is older than the earliest philosophers and their sects, and therefore more authoritative.[61] Epiphanius described the "true religion" of Abraham as monotheism, rejecting idolatry.[62] Asked by a Manichaean critic what it means to do "the will of Jesus," Didymus the Blind retorted that it is "to do the works of Abraham and believe in Moses."[63] Abraham's seed, Israel—not a primordial race—was and remains the dominant metaphor for expressing Christian universalism.

Nor should we consider Abraham to be either absent or rebuked across the board in our Coptic Gnostic sources. *The Gospel of Philip* from Nag Hammadi Codex II interprets Abraham's willingness to embrace circumcision as a foreshadowing of Christian asceticism.[64] *Pistis Sophia* states that Jesus has forgiven the sins of Abraham,

Isaac, and Jacob, given them the "mystery of light," and brought them to the aeon of Abraoth, the benevolent brother of the celestial Adam.[65] This evidence reminds us how distinctive it was to reject the God of Abraham in the ancient Mediterranean context.

Unconcluding Coda: Are we Jews?

Distinctive enough that we should refrain from dubbing texts like *Treat. Seth*—as well as *Eg. Gos.* or *Apoc. Adam*—as "Abrahamic"? Yes! Yet as we have seen, these works—by virtue of their grappling with the legends of Abraham and the ethical problems they pose—are unintelligible without reference to Abraham, either. This problem lends us a fundamental insight regarding the complex of religious traditions that critically and even vehemently engage the figure of Abraham and his God: Marcionite Christianity, Manichaeism, Mandaeism, and, yes, Sethian Gnosticism. To wit, the historical interface between these currents and the properly "Abrahamic" religions of Judaism, Christianity, and Islam cannot be the *figure of Abraham* himself, but the *textual traditions in which Abraham figures*, namely the traditions of the *Bible* and *biblical literature*.[66] The fact that the Gnostic texts discussed in this study transgress biblical traditions shows that they regard some biblical texts, especially those pertaining to the God of Abraham, as authoritative in some sense.[67] Here, I wonder if the term "parabiblical"—employed, for instance, by Annette Yoshiko Reed when referring to the "books outside" of early Jewish and Christian canons—may be usefully appropriated to describe religious discourse distinct but utterly inextricable from the thought-world in which biblical texts are authoritative.[68] Diverse Sethian texts employ diverse biblical intertexts; some of them are Christian; many of them deal with baptism; apocalyptic literature is predominant. Sethian literature is not Abrahamic, but it is biblical in some sense—parabiblical, perhaps.[69]

Does it make sense to talk about Sethianism as a *parabiblical religion?* We do not even know for sure if there was a group of "Sethians" who regarded themselves as distinct from "Christians." While previous generations of scholars sought to trace the development of a Sethian Gnostic "movement" by tracking the presence and absence of Jesus Christ and allusions to the New Testament in Sethian texts, any such "Sethian community" is a hypothetical.[70] It may be more prudent to speak of the development of "Sethian literary tradition" as part of the flowering of parabiblical literature among communities who found biblical traditions authoritative and identified with them in some sense. Indeed, the Nag Hammadi manuscripts must be not only contextualized in the world of ancient Gnosticism, but also fourth- to sixth-century Egyptian biblical apocrypha.[71] These apocryphal works appear to have been produced and transmitted—at least at the level of the Coptic manuscripts themselves—among what we might call Christian subcultures.[72]

I have argued elsewhere that the ubiquity of pseudepigrapha (apocalypses, specifically) in the Sethian corpus may also indicate its production by individuals inhabiting the borderlines between Judaism and Christianity and with a relatively low sense of group definition; at least some of these individuals who circulated Sethian literature identified as "Christians."[73] Conversely, the overlap of many "Sethian" mythologoumena with beings invoked in ancient and medieval magical texts reminds us that Sethian characters and themes moved about a greater, late ancient religious *koinē*, dwarfing Christian heretics and their literary manuscripts.[74] This free exchange of parabiblical symbols, incantations, and mythologoumena in the context of magical practice ensured the survival and transformation of Gnostic themes and motifs in medieval Jewish and Islamic contexts alike.[75]

The *Unbeständigkeit* of the parabiblical aside, I conclude with a slice of evidence which, to me, demands of us *some* better terminology for these biblically informed, not-exactly-Abrahamic-or-Mosaic dualisms. A Mandaean goldsmith who fled Saddam Hussein's Iraq in 1980 shows the stakes of this necessity. In an interview with Jorunn Jacobsen Buckley, noted for her fieldwork in contemporary Mandaean communities, Majid 'Arabi al-Khamisi relates that, like so many who come to the United States from abroad, he arrived in New York City. There, he worked for five years as an apprentice to Jewish Hasidic specialists in gold and diamonds. "He loved being with the Hasidim," Buckley writes:

> "We are so similar! The same clothes, the same habits, the same humor—everything! I was amazed!" Majid beams. I ask him whether the Hasidim knew he was a Mandaean, whether they knew what that meant. No, they didn't, and they didn't care, but they knew he was not a Muslim. To the Hasidim, Majid was some kind of Christian. Then Majid asks me the question he seems to have pondered for years, "Are they Mandaeans? Are we Jews?"[76]

The *Right Ginza* notwithstanding, Abraham is not the question in this volume as the figures discussed by Ruchama Johnston-Bloom and Samual Kigar would have it. It is the encounter with Abraham, with Moses, with the Bible—interreligion—that is at issue.[77] We need to coin a word for that.

14

The Repentant Magician:
"Esoteric Intimacies" and the Enchantment of Religious Difference

Noah Salomon

On the outskirts of the Sudanese capital, Khartoum, on a long and dusty road, in a small and unremarkable home, lives a quite remarkable individual. A healer by trade, Shaykh Hamid Adam Musa has a house that is usually buzzing with clients outside his front door or sitting on a stoop in his driveway waiting to meet with him. On entering the home, one often encounters Shaykh Hamid in an outdoor *diwan* flanked by a large new four-wheel-drive vehicle, displaying the material success of his endeavors. Known publicly (due to his several video-discs and appearances on television and in the printed press, and now his many videos on YouTube[1]) by the colorful nickname "The Repentant Magician" (*al-sahir al-ta'ib*), Hamid Adam Musa sees himself as a warner against the dangers of the traditional Sudanse Sufi path and the necessity of following Islam "as the pious forbearers understood it" (*'ala fahm al-salif al-salih*). Shaykh Hamid has come to this conclusion about the error of Sufism and the righteousness of what he calls Salafism (*al-salafiyya*) through an intimate knowledge of the former, as he speaks of having spent many years of his life as a Tijani Sufi shaykh running a center for learning and worship in the eastern desert of neighboring Chad. What one might describe as his "conversion" from the Sufi path to Salafism is evident from his very nickname itself. *Al-sahir*, the magician, is his derisive description of what he was in his earlier years, a leader of a branch of a Sufi order. And *al-ta'ib*, the repentant one, is how he describes his current state: a recognition of his errors and an attempt to make amends for them, an act of *tawba*, of repentance from sin and misguidedness. Indeed, the arrangement of his new life as a public critic and *da'i*, one who attempts to fix the errors of others in their Islam, is a result of this continual repentance, as if putting other Muslims on a correct path might expiate some of his own earlier transgressions.[2]

However, while the Repentant Magician is contrite, it is interesting to note that his conversion does not necessitate an overturning of the "magical" system in which

---

I thank the editors of this volume, Kambiz GhaneaBassiri and Paul Robertson, for their extremely helpful comments on this chapter. It has been greatly improved thanks to their suggestions. I remain responsible for any remaining shortcomings.

he once participated as a fiction, as a myth, as anti-religion, or otherwise. Rather, what has shifted is his relationship to the "magic" and the created beings (the *jinn*) who are said to instrumentalize it, but nevertheless remain very much real for him both before and after his life changes. That the *jinn* would continue to exist for Shaykh Hamid following his experience of religious reform needs no justification. The *jinn* are an integral part of the Muslim tradition from the Qur'an onwards and thus are inescapable even for the modernists (who often see them as internalized psychological states).[3] Nonetheless, the precise universe of the *jinn*, their behaviors, their relationships to humans, and their particular forms are, in many instances, extra-canonical,[4] and would be expected to be highly unstable, particularly in the context of a movement of Islamic reform such as Salafism that demands a return to the Qur'an and the Sunna. What, then, are we to make of the fact that, for Shaykh Hamid, they are not unstable, that his ontology remains the same, even while his sociology has drastically shifted? How might such an observation weigh on our understanding of the nature of the religious difference between Sufi and Salafi that Shaykh Hamid is said to have traversed? In *Between Muslim and Jew*, Wasserstrom's pathbreaking first book, a compelling model is proposed for understanding the nature of the borders and passageways that exist between those who understood themselves as Jews and Muslims in Islam's formative period; in this chapter, I will extend his observations to explore how they might help us think differently about this paradigmatic case of intra-Muslim religious difference, between Sufis and Salafis. Along the way, I will explore the implications of Wasserstrom's thought for our understanding of religious difference in the field of Religious Studies more broadly.

Traditional structures and the structure of traditions

"I am [even after all of this change] still a doctor," Shaykh Hamid told me one afternoon back in 2007 when I first came to know him. He continued:

> I know cures by means of demon spirits (*jinn*) [from my time as a Sufi shaykh] … But I can't engage in that anymore. Even if the ill person will thereby not be cured by me, I say to him: "my brother, God is able to do what he wills, and he didn't create a cure for you on my hands, so you are welcome to look for another." But I cannot return and cure him in a way that is not legitimate (*shar'i*). To do this would be curing [your] body, but making you sick in the firmness of your creed (*'aqida*), which is your soul. And your soul, if I corrupted it, your fate will be the Fire. It is better for you to sit with [the] illness [from which you came to me to be cured] and suffer the test in this world and go to God with a clean creed. Because I, as a Muslim, believe that any torture that does not include the eternal fire is [in fact] good fortune (*'afiya*). And any good thing without the attainment of paradise, is superfluous (*za'id*).[5]

In this small statement, the linearity of Shaykh Hamid's "conversion" is destabilized on two levels. First, his "profession" has remained the same, a healer through the will of God. Second, while Salafi critiques of Sufism (including Shaykh Hamid's own) have focused on the charlatanism and trickery (*dajjal wa shawadha*) of Sufism, Shaykh Hamid does not see Sufism as a means of trickery in the sense of slight-of-hand—indeed he believes that Sufi shaykhs *can* heal and *can* interact with the *jinn*—but that such healing is harmful to one's '*aqida*. Thus the repudiation of Sufism is not in terms of the efficacy of Sufi modes of healing to produce their desired effects, nor is it around the fantasy of the Sufi vision of the world of *jinn*, but rather what is being repudiated here is the moral value of one's relationship to *jinn* and its ultimate weighting within the economy of Judgment Day.

In Shaykh Hamid's story, we can clearly see how conversion to an Islamic reformist personhood, often decried by its detractors as a paradigm shift of a global Islamic trend blotting out local tradition, can be an event that reveals as much continuity as change, here owing as much to popular conceptions of the spirit world as to the modern reform logic of global Salafism. As we will see in a moment, it is this spirit world, intact before and after his change, that in fact *implements* Shaykh Hamid's conversion, remaining very much present both prior and subsequent to it. In the story of his awakening, the features of procedural rationalism and *solo scripura* of his new Salafi identity are set not in opposition to the ephemera of the spirit world, nor do they merely justify it, but rather they are made possible by it, for, as we will see, it is only through a certain encounter with the *jinn* that he comes to embrace the Salafi path. So, while Wasserstrom is correct in his brilliant "Nine Theses" that Religious Studies cannot "decide if witches fly"[6] (or here, if *jinn* sorcerers cure), I would argue that our discipline has at hand the ability to do even more than "locate witches as neighbors," that is, unpack the social relations that structure the supernatural. In the case of Shaykh Hamid, it seems that a fairly constant supernatural, with a long and venerable history within popular Islamic writings and lore (and even before), has come *to structure the social*, to remain a constant variable that endures even in the face of radical sociological change, such as conversion from Sufism to reformist varieties of Islam that have swept across Muslim societies in the modern era. It is the depth and nuance of our discipline's understanding of tradition that may offer it, while not unique purchase on this analytic perspective, the ingredients to substantiate its thickness.

Importantly, Wasserstrom's own writings on the category of what he calls "esoteric intimacies" in *Between Muslim and Jew* in fact offer a model to understand the perseverance of such forms in new ways, as ones that bind not just temporal eras and sociological groupings, but even what we might otherwise understand as discrete religious traditions.[7] In doing so, Wasserstrom offers a model for examining religious difference that extends our capabilities beyond that of social history alone. It is in allowing us to ponder the ability of tradition to structure, *and not just be structured by*, social relations that makes his intervention a particularly powerful one. The remainder of this chapter will look at the case of Shaykh Hamid's religious transition from Sufi shakyh to Salafi preacher (while all along remaining a healer), observing the role of the *jinn* in it. I will conclude by placing Shaykh Hamid's narrative within the framework of Wasserstrom's illuminating analysis of the morphology of religious difference in the cases he discusses in *Between Muslim and Jew*.

An intimate encounter with the *jinn*

Shaykh Hamid's entire life, up until his Salafi awakening, had been a calculated bargain with the *jinn*. As he described it, the Sufi confidence in the superiority of inner-knowledge (*'ilm al-batin*) had blinded him from seeing the obvious waywardness of his path. Indeed, in his community, this concept was taken to an extreme of antinomianism, where seemingly anything exterior was seen to be illusory: in his account, the shaykhs said they could drink alcohol because in the *batin* it was, in fact, Pepsi; the shaykhs said they could sleep with young girls since through taking their virginity they could give them some of their *baraka* (blessing); the shaykhs read the Qur'an "like a sandwich," he said, each word a stack of meaning indicated by letters each of which index other words. Among other things, he related that when he was in seclusion (*khalwa*)[8] he used to pray naked, since he believed that God saw his private parts (*'awra*) anyhow. While his account of the corruption of shaykhs mirrors that of a great deal of modernist anti-Sufis,[9] except in its autobiographical character, and thus should be taken less as a verifiable report and more as part of a genre of polemic, his discussion of the *jinn* is quite different. Here, rather than presenting shaykhs as cunning tricksters, he argued that they were in fact intimately related to a world of spirits that is very much real. While the Sufi shaykhs' relationship to this world was one of subservience or ignorance, rather than animosity, the *jinn* nevertheless were presented as undeniably real participants in the created world and the Sufi shaykh as a powerful figure who could influence the world through his relationship to them. The effect on his *'aqida* might be detrimental, but the idea that he achieved power through the *jinn* seemed undeniable.

In Shaykh Hamid's story of his conversion from Sufism to Salafism it is indeed the *jinn* who are the only stable figures in the narrative.[10] The story is worth retelling: one day in Eastern Chad, a visitor came to the Sufi center where Shaykh Hamid was living. The visitor was a trader from Sudan traveling to Nigeria to buy and sell some goods and arrived unannounced, wanting to see his fellow countryman. When this trader had gone to the market in the nearby village, people told him that there was a Sudanese shaykh in the Sufi center there who not only had the ability to perform *karamat*, miracles, but also had many connections in Nigeria and that a letter from him to any trader in Nigeria would bring great results. The trader went to Shaykh Hamid's house and Shaykh Hamid immediately befriended his countryman and took him in for several nights. One night while the two men were sitting and chatting, the trader asked Shaykh Hamid the following question:

> "Do you do [all these miracles people say you do]?" I said, "Yes, do you want me to do anything for you." He answered, "No." He asked me about my *karama* in which I make ablution jugs (*ibriqs*) walk [and fetch water] by themselves. And I asked him, "Do you want me to send an *ibriq* for you?" And he said, "No." He said to me ... "Oh shaykh, are these miracles ones that we can count as being among the miracles of the righteous friends of God, *al-awliya' al-salihin*?" And I said, "Yes, these are miracles and miracles of God ... " He asked me, "Those who are working with you [in helping you to implement these miracles], are

they spirits (*ruhaniyin*)?" I said to him, "They are spirits." He asked, "What are spirits?" I answered, "Spirits are a kind of angel, our Lord brings them out to *al-awliya' al-salihin* like us." ... [But the guest expressed doubt.] He said, "If I read the Qur'an and you try and interact with [this spirit], he will not interact with you ... In order to prove to you that this is not an angel, I will read a verse from the Qur'an and if he is with you here, he will get up and go far away ... Call him and let him come [so that I can prove this to you]." So I did a particular something [that I would do to call him] and he came ... I said to [my guest] that the spirit was present and he said, "I don't see him." I said, "You wouldn't see him because you haven't reached this level of spiritual perfection (*ma wasil*)." He said, "Okay, I will begin by reading *ayat al-kursi* (Qur'an 2:255) ... I will read it slowly so that the spirit gets up slowly ... " He said [beginning the recitation], "A'uhdu bilahi min al-shaytan al-rajim ..., " and of course his voice was beautiful, he was reading with *tajwid*. And as soon as he began [the spirit] got up [from what he was doing and stopped] ... [My guest] said, "If I read it in a louder voice the spirit will leave." And when he read in this louder voice, indeed the spirit started moving away. He said, "If I raised my voice even more, he will run away as well." He raised his voice, and [the spirit] really ran. I saw it with my bare eyes. He then said to me, "Try calling him now while I am reciting." So he began to read and I did my *du'a* to call [the spirit] and I saw the spirit from far away doing like this [waving his figure to denote a negative]. He was signing to me that "if that [man] is present, I am not coming ... " And from this it was over, like I had been asleep and only now opened my eyes in that moment. After that I began to question myself, to review my entire life. Was it true that I had been working with the *jinn*?

Suddenly, on recognition that he was working with the *jinn* and not angels, as he had imagined, Shaykh Hamid's miracles began to unravel. He used to walk over wells using a small stick as a bridge. The visitor said that this was because the hand of Satan was holding it up. He said, "Try doing it while you are reading *ayat al-kursi* and see what happens." He did and the stick broke and he fell in. And then there was the miracle of the walking *ibriq*. The visitor read the beginning of the second chapter of the Qur'an, *surat al-baqara*, and Shaykh Hamid was no longer able to make the *ibriq* walk by itself. So Shaykh Hamid had come to realize that though his miracles were indeed real, and that he had reached a knowledge of the hidden world that allowed him to interact with it, these miracles were the work of the *jinn*, not of the angels, and by the power of the Qur'an this truth was revealed to him.

Here, the turn to the Qur'an and the Sunna, which the Salafis often request in their demand for evidence (*adilla*),[11] took on a rather different meaning than the kind of hermeneutic with which they are often associated. In Shaykh Hamid's story it was the physical Qur'an itself and its effect on the spirit world that he was indexing, giving a new meaning to the label of scripturalism with which Salafis are often tagged.[12] It is important to point out—only because it is so often a reaction among scholars and average observers alike of Islam in sub-Saharan Africa[13]—that such a vivid description of the spirit world is not some sort of localism. What Shaykh Hamid refers to as *al-ruqya al-shar'iyya*, legitimate or shari'a-based incantation that helps heal from the afflictions of the *jinn*, is in fact a genre of healing with a long history and a broad geographic spread, its primary present-day proselytizers being Saudi Salafi shaykhs. In any Salafi bookstore, one will find manuals devoted to healing with the Qur'an, such as the ubiquitous pocket guide, *Al-duʿa' min al-kitab wa-l-sunna wa yalihu al-ʿilaj bi-l-ruqya min al-kitab wa-l-sunna* by Saʿid bin ʿAli bin Wahaf al-Qahatani, and cassette tapes that provide an oral how-to. I do not raise this point as some sort of justification that what Shaykh Hamid was involved in was a resuscitation or continuation of a pure Islam of the Arabian Peninsula,[14] but to say that the dynamics in Shaykh Hamid's story are not unique, but rather linger in the margins of the history of modern Islamic reform in ways that have far too infrequently been recognized.[15] Indeed, the element of the fantastic on display in Shaykh Hamid's conversation story begs a revaluation of the nature of Islamic reform and its drivers in general.

Shaykh Hamid's biography is also a key site through which we can observe the space between the quotidian construction of religious subjectivity and the propositional arguments for *why one should* construct his or her religious subjectivity in a particular manner that is the stuff of public debates through which Islamic reformism is often approached, and on which analyses of religious difference often rest. Instead of couching his "conversion" in terms of the doctrinal debates between Sufis and Salafis, for example over the reality of hidden knowledge (*al-ʿilm al-laduni*), Shaykh Hamid's change takes place without rejecting its reality. An encounter with the *jinn* themselves leads him into conversion.[16] The presence of a gap between these two approaches to change to which I draw attention seems not insignificant to how we conceptualize the intervention of contemporary Islamic reform movements such as the Salafis. If indeed there is considerable distance between the arguments they make for Islamic reform and the construction of the self (and the means of getting there) for the "reformed Muslim," what might this tell us? That is to say, if individual reform does not always track with the kinds of changes that are seen as characteristic of "modern Islam" in the various studies that have tried to carve out such a category (e.g., democratization of knowledge and authority, objectification of religion, rationalization, politicization), might we need to focus on other factors revealed in such narratives that are not captured by public discourse if we are to draw an accurate picture of such change? What sorts of enchantments do sociological categories of religious difference provide, and might other ways of looking at varieties of religious distinction, such as those suprahuman ones presented in narratives like those of shaykh Hamid, allow us another path forward?

The persistence and consistency of the world of *jinn* both prior and subsequent to Shaykh Hamid's conversion suggests as well a realm of accumulated tradition not shaped by the immediate sociological features of religious change in Sudan, but which in fact shapes them, making them subservient to its demands. In her analysis of *jinn*-inspired poets, Amira El-Zein discusses the concept of "sharing the 'poetical terrain' [wherein] the poet is constantly shifting from absence when it is the 'other' (the *jinni*) who recites poetry, to awareness, when it is the poet himself who declaims the verse."[17] In the story of Shaykh Hamid, we seem to be in a similar terrain: he is present, author and agent, at moments, while his self "recedes" at others, "leaving a blank space to be swiftly filled by another power."[18] Understanding Shaykh Hamid's before and after as not merely sharing in a common idiom, but in fact, as he tells it, directly shaped by an agency not his own, helps us to understand why we must take propositional arguments for religious reform with a grain of salt. Such arguments share space with myriad other forces, worldly and otherworldly, that insist upon continuity as much as change.

Methodological intimacies

In his now-classic volume *Between Muslim and Jew: The Problem of Symbiosis under Early Islam*, Wasserstrom styles the kinds of borrowing and shared resources of the Jewish and Muslim communities he studies under the heading of "intimacies," a certain sort of close relation that led to cross-pollination but nevertheless did not occasion a breakdown in sectarian identity. He writes:

> Esoteric intimacies allowed (among others) sectarians and story-tellers actively to reorganize all knowledge, as it were. In both cases, to say the least, this open attitude did not come in the form of a public pronouncement: they certainly did not preach some transcendental unity of world religions, for the author of the *milal wa nihal* [sects and creeds] treatise, like the gnostic theosophist, always operated within confessional bounds on the basis of a strict and even severe in-group centeredness.[19]

And yet they shared much. Given that Wasserstrom argues elsewhere in that volume that it is pure hubris for orientalists to think that they discovered such borrowing and that Muslims were very much conscious of their use of the old,[20] what are we to make of the tensions between continuity and change in this model, between borders and passage ways? This seems to be the problem we face not only with Wasserstrom's Jewish and Muslim communities in early Islam—who lived in a discursive frame of distinct and uncrossable boundaries, but a ritual life where the lines were far blurrier—but with figures like Shaykh Hamid too. What are we to make of this discourse of radical difference in a landscape of unescapable continuities?[21]

The concept of "intimacy," with which Wasserstrom orders the last third of *Between Muslim and Jew*, may offer a solution to this dilemma if we follow it as a call for methodological innovation. An earlier version of this chapter was delivered at a workshop in May of 2015 at New York University-Abu Dhabi, entitled "Islamism and Intimacy," which shared not only the conceptual frame ("intimacy") but also many concerns with those that Wasserstrom relates. In the conference materials, its organizer, anthropologist J. Andrew Bush, whose work articulates this category with nuance and sophistication,[22] described the methodological stakes of "intimacy" to the study of movements of Islamic reform such as the Salafiyya, as "a shift [in] analytic perspective away from the spectacles of violence and security toward everyday forms of labor and leisure such as household economics, relations with neighbors or *jinn*, and the bearing and rearing of children by families."[23] In Sudan, for example, the unease with Salafism expressed by those who live in communities where it is gaining strength is often not provoked by discourse (indeed, even liberal Muslims appreciate Salafi calls for a radical split with an Islam that requires human intermediaries, as they see Sufism doing), but through a disruption experienced at the level of the senses in intimate spaces of family, leisure, or pleasure: from the tingling of the hand expecting but not getting pressed in a handshake with a non-intimate, to the overly sweet tea served at Salafi gatherings ("*al-mu'min halawi*," the believer is sweet, as the famous, though weak, hadith reminds us), to the scents of the perfumes sold in Salafi bookshops, to the sight of the Salafi beard. That these somatic markers provoke such intense reactions—indeed they are posed as proof-positive of Salafi extremism by their critics—should provide us with some pause as they begin to suggest, as Bush commented in the same document, that a study of such intimate relations "may generate questions that would otherwise be elided by analyses that privilege state and market priorities for understanding the diffusion of [and, I would add, the pushback against] these movements."[24] Such an observation suggests that the topic of intimate and affective relationships engaged (and, significantly, not engaged) by Salafis may be of equal importance to understanding their place within contemporary Muslim societies, and the image of religious difference that they pose, to the kinds theological and political disputes they initiate on which the bulk of the literature focuses.[25]

Shifting our methodological focus in situations of religious change to the intimate, as Wasserstrom encourages us to do in his study of esoteric exchange in *Between Muslim and Jew*, would transform the landscape of how we understand difference in instances of Muslim reform such as the one of which Shaykh Hamid is exemplary as well. The reason, perhaps, that esoteric sites in particular—from Wasserstrom's Geniza magic to the sorcerer's den of this chapter—are often fertile places to study these kinds of exchange, these crossings of sectarian boundaries that seem otherwise sacrosanct, is that they tap into domains that embrace a displacement of human agency: the *jinn* care little for the petty human disputes on which religious difference is founded, curses do not discriminate on the basis of affiliation. The esoteric, often presented as the paradigmatic site of the non-conventional, is shown here to be a place that offers a logic for traditions *to persevere* even across sectarian boundaries that we might otherwise imagine would split them apart.

There is a fascinating line in *Between Muslim and Jew* that may equally apply to the relationship between contemporary Islamic reform movements and the landscape they aim to reform. Wasserstrom writes, "*Jew*, then, served as an essential and necessary catalyst in the self-definition of Islam; and *Muslim* likewise, operated in synergy with a Jewish effort at self-legitimation. The other—whether as myth or history, image or enemy, precursor or opponent, had its uses. The uses of the other, in the end, produced a kind of symbiotic interdefinition."[26] Shaykh Hamid's Salafism too is impossible to imagine without his Sufism. It is only as an expert in dealing with the *jinn*—recall, in his "conversion" tale, it is only he who can even see them—gained through his years as a "magician," that he is able to recognize the truth of the Salafi path.

A focus on everyday relationships with *jinn* among Salafis, as I have tried to show, complicates two common paradigms through which religious difference in Islam is often studied: that of conversion, on the one hand, and that of reform on the other.

Salafism, and revivalist Islamic movements in general, are often understood to be trends that blot out local relationships (to kin, to religious authorities, to sacred geographies) in favor of a global homogenizing logic that grounds itself in the practices of seventh-century Arabia projected toward the future as universals. When we look to spaces of intimacy among such movements, as Wasserstrom encourages us to do, we can observe a far more complicated landscape, however, one in which, as we have seen, the tradition bridges or even outright ignores the kind of sociological difference said to be traversed by conversion or reform, even across boundaries that seem otherwise impenetrable. In doing so, we may come to reassess the landscape of such difference in the study of religion more broadly, recognizing the multiplicity and complexity of the relations present in even the most bounded locations.

15

On the Possibility of Jewish Politics in Our Time: Scholem, Exile, and Early Modern Transformations

Anne Oravetz Albert

Gershom Scholem remains a giant in Jewish and Religious Studies, a thinker whose ideas, though contested, continue to establish essential problematics in the study of Judaism and Jewish thought. Scholem's work on Jewish mysticism has now inspired generations of students to enter the field, although many if not most of us find that we must soon leave him behind, as his approach and specific conclusions are increasingly out of step with the historiographical standards of the day. My own journey to and through Scholem was mediated from the start by Steve Wasserstrom's insights, as expressed in *Religion after Religion* and impressed upon me in my undergraduate studies with him while he was completing that work.

One of Wasserstrom's central critiques is that Scholem privileged myth over historical actuality—that he saw mysticism as the true core of Judaism as opposed to legal or communal traditions, a move with problematic implications in both scholarly and political terms. In this essay I explore Scholem's depiction of the early modern transformation of Jewish politics, which centers on an attitude toward exile that in turn defines his view of Jewish politics in his own day. I confront Scholem's monolithic claims with the very different thinking of an early modern figure, Daniel Levi de Barrios, a onetime follower of the Sabbatian messianic movement to which Scholem accords so much significance. Treating the Jewish politics of his own day, de Barrios offers an alternative to Scholem's paradigmatic view of modernity.

A familiar characterization of modern Jewish history implies that Jewish politics did not really exist before modernity. Tied to a Zionist paradigm treating the creation of a Jewish state as a "return to history," understood as a return of the Jewish people to geopolitical relevance, this view casts diaspora Jewish life as an existence outside of history in which Jews lived as dependent yet detached subjects of powerful states and rulers, largely indifferent to their political times. Although this depiction may be somewhat caricatured, an attitude much like it permeated scholarly treatments of pre-modern Jewish civilization at least until the final decades of the twentieth century. Throughout the infancy and golden age of modern Jewish historiography, from the *Wissenschaft des Judentums* through the mid-century historians at the Hebrew University of Jerusalem, the subject was analyzed in "social" or "communal," not political, terms in addition to religious, intellectual, and legal ones.[1] More recently, a number of sensitive textual interpreters and historians have recognized the political in Judaism not only before Zionism but even before the Enlightenment and Emancipation made some Jews into citizens of secular nation-states. The field continues to expand.[2]

A certain tension persists, however, not least because the analytical utility of the category of Jewish politics, that is, a form or tradition of politics that is particularly Jewish, is problematic. If one accepts the basic premise—as most students of politics would today—that politics are not limited to the context of a state, then Jewish politics are visible everywhere in the pre-modern world, from family structures to rabbinic authority to the advocacy of court Jews, taking forms as many and diverse as those among non-Jews. The old idea that exile, understood as political subjugation or the total lack of politics, marked the Jews as essentially different therefore disappears. One way of salvaging the notion of a particular Jewish politics is to argue that Jewish politics share a referential relationship to the texts and practices of the Jewish religion. In his introduction to the path-breaking multivolume series *The Jewish Political Tradition*, Michael Walzer explains that his subject is a "tradition of thought, theological and legal rather than autonomously political in its form, but political in substance nonetheless," emphasizing that the tradition's "point of departure is always the Hebrew Bible, understood as the revealed word of God."[3]

Political and mystical exile

In his 1963 essay "On the Possibility of Mysticism in Our Time," Scholem describes Jewish mysticism as dependent on the same belief in revelation that is privileged by Walzer. But unlike Walzer, who sees continuity in Jewish politics from antiquity through modernity, Scholem suggests that Jewish mysticism was broken along the way: "We do not [any longer] believe in Torah from heaven in the specific sense of a fixed body of revelation having infinite significance. And without this basic assumption one cannot move."[4] A casual reader of "On the Possibility" alone might assume its existential despair to be the result of modern crises like secularism and the Holocaust, but Scholem's earlier works locate the change in the seismic shifts of the sixteenth through eighteenth centuries, a period now usually referred to as early modernity. As he presented it, the intense disruption of the Sabbatian messianic movement, itself precipitated by the crisis of the Spanish expulsion and the spread of Lurianic kabbalah, was responsible for shattering the previously coherent mystical-messianic structure and changing the Jewish world by creating a politics stripped of myth as well as a messianism stripped of political action. These events constituted a shift in mysticism—and thus in the very lifeblood of Judaism itself—from a literal, external messianism to an internal, spiritual one, tearing messianism apart from politics, and thereby breaking both of them.

In tying his view of Jewish politics to the fate of Jewish messianism, Scholem makes exile a key concept—beginning with the experience of exile that was compounded by the expulsion from Spain in 1492. At the start of his main essay on Lurianic kabbalah, Scholem declares:

> After the Exodus from Spain, Kabbalism underwent a complete transformation. A catastrophe of this dimension, which uprooted one of the main branches of the Jewish people, could hardly take place without affecting every sphere of Jewish life and feeling. In the great material and spiritual upheaval of that crisis, Kabbalism established its claim to spiritual domination in Judaism. This fact became immediately obvious in its transformation from an esoteric into a popular doctrine.[5]

In particular, Scholem suggests, the previously marginal messianic or apocalyptic tendencies in kabbalah came to the fore, as the exile-minded Luria and his circle "laid the emphasis on the final stage of the cosmological process"; "the 'beginning' and the 'end' were linked together."[6] Later in the same essay, Scholem dramatically described Lurianic emphasis on the negative experience of exile:

> The exiles from Spain must have held an intense belief in the fiendish realities of Exile, a belief that was bound to destroy the illusion that it was possible to live peacefully under the Holy Law in Exile ... Life was conceived as Existence in Exile and in self-contradiction, and the sufferings of Exile were linked up with the central Kabbalistic doctrines about God and man.[7]

As is well known, Scholem interprets the Lurianic notion of *tsimtsum*, or contraction, wherein the divine removes itself from the universe, as a reflection on exile, where the resolution and restitution of proper order can be achieved through *tikkun*, or repair. Scholem comments: "In an age in which the historical exile of the Jewish people was a terrible and fundamental reality of life, the old idea of an exile of the Shekhinah [divine indwelling] gained a far greater importance than before."[8] Scholem suggests that the Spanish expulsion and subsequent hardships broke down a millennium-long equilibrium between myth and messianism, wherein exile was both real and tolerable. That is, exile was understood as part of the divine myth and hence only a prelude to messianic redemption, but on the other hand redemption could comfortably be postponed indefinitely so exile need not be immediately disrupted.

The new mystical outlook became a mass movement in the next century, as the would-be messiah Shabbetai Tsvi rallied most of European Jewry behind his aspiration to end the exile in the literal sense of ingathering and acquisition of earthly kingship—a movement that Scholem details in a thick historical work, the most extended investigation of a single topic in his oeuvre.[9] But in Scholem's reading, this movement quickly turned into an irrational and antinomian movement characterized by mob rule, and Scholem is especially interested in how the mystical messianic expectation, pushed to a moment of political reality, could not stand. That break—separating myth from worldly experience—was definitive of everything that followed.

In Scholem's telling, after the disappointment of the failed messianic bid of Shabbetai Tsvi in the mid-1660s, the mythical and messianic core of Judaism was perpetuated through Hasidism, which sublimated the messianic dream into a spiritual and individualistic, rather than a geo-political, view of redemption. The other path, which Scholem so wholly rejected as to all but ignore, he identified with Spinoza, followed by Moses Mendelssohn and then social historians and assimilationist thinkers from *Wissenschaft* up to his own day.[10] Scholem saw such rationalists as abandoning the particularistic relationship to revelation as a source of Jewish symbols and myth, in favor of participation in the world's politics. His view was that there had been a decisive split by the nineteenth century between that path and the course of Jewish mystical activity, which was by then buried within Hasidism.[11] His view of Hasidism was decidedly mixed: Jewish myth and mysticism continue to live on in it since its adherents still viewed revelation without skepticism, but on the other hand, Hasidism had "neutralized" the "messianic element" of mysticism, meaning that it had popularized kabbalah without the apocalypticism that made earlier forms dynamic and imbued them with the potential for eruption into a redemptive movement.[12]

Operative here is the tension between inner and outer, or between mystical and political, dimensions of Jewish life. Scholem emphasizes that messianic redemption was traditionally conceived in Judaism as an outward, public, collective event,[13] and identifies it with the popularization of mystical innovation in his essay, "On the Possibility." He writes that some mystics—those "whose eyes have been opened" and who understand "something of the root of our being"—try to share their knowledge: "Those who felt such impulses attempted to energize human beings toward new forms of organization and society" and thus essentially drove the entire "history of religions"[14] by creating movements.[15] Somehow, the sparks ignited by the mystics do make their way to what he calls the "public": "Thus, even if we are concerned here with a particular individual and a personal matter, it nevertheless imbues a particular spirit upon entire phenomena, upon entire communities, upon certain circles within society, or upon the public as a whole." Much of the essay "On the Possibility," in fact, concerns the conditions that facilitate mystical movements in the sense of appealing to the masses and stimulating social and institutional changes.

In other words, inner and spiritual (mystical) processes can erupt into the political sphere by achieving the status of mass movements. The trifecta of expulsion, failed messianic movement, and spiritualization of redemption formed the conditions for an inner, spiritual rupture to produce its counterpart in outer, social and cultural experience. As Joseph Dan summarizes Scholem's work in this area, "Scholem saw the Sabbatian movement as a key to the development of Jewish society, culture, and beliefs in modern times."[16] Specifically, Scholem describes the previously bound pair of politics and messianic redemption as having been sundered. After Sabbatianism, politics could only be external and redemption could only be internal. Scholem's view accords with the widely held impression, discussed at the start of this essay, that an inexorable political transformation occurred in Jewish early modernity—but instead of modernity being marked by a new Jewish embrace of politics, he sees in it the excision of the political in the sense that the mass, external, social, and historical dimensions of experience were torn asunder from the mystical and mythical core of Judaism, which he saw as the only true Judaism.

Adherents of Hasidism, according to this scheme of Scholem's, had no interest in worldly politics; politically minded Jews were on a secular path. What about Zionism? After all, Scholem indicates that in his own day, the Holocaust and mass migration of Jews to Palestine constitute a crisis of the sort that gives rise to mystical-messianic movements. He notes that the time is ripe for such a movement to arise because it has been two centuries since the last flowering of mysticism. He acknowledges that there is usually a delay of some few generations between a seismic shock and the composition of a creative response to it, so he still awaits the movement of his own day. In fact, strikingly: "We hope that this shock will be productive, and it is for this reason that we live here, in this country [Israel]."[17] What Scholem is considering when he asks about the possibility for "mysticism" in his day is really the question of whether a messianic politics in the form of a social movement based on mystical insight could occur. It would depend on a renewal of Jewish myth where the narrative was made literally real and present.

Scholem is decidedly pessimistic in his answer. In another essay on the subject, he describes exile in similar terms, explaining that the objective and subjective experiences of exile are no longer aligned—meaning that while exile is still an objective reality for some (i.e., some still live outside of the Holy Land), it has ceased to be a powerful idea to them; whereas for others, those living in the state of Israel, the exile is no longer physically real but remains subjectively so.[18] It is a neat dichotomy that plays to Scholem's use of intertwined symbolic opposites, and reflects the complexity of his own Zionism.[19] He sees the experience of exile after Sabbatianism as no longer capable of being both literal and meaningful at the same time, a fact that goes just as much for the experience of redemption. This suggests that the Jewish politics of his day—even the politics of Zionism and the state of Israel—are still exilic politics, meaning that they are not imbued with a direct experience of myth and mystical renewal.

Messianism and diaspora

The two paths that Scholem presents as the legacy of Sabbatianism are, in broad strokes, the secularization of the political, entailing an embrace of power but a loss of Jewish particularity; and the abandonment of politics, turning toward a Jewish ethos that is mystical but not messianic, separatist but not in a national sense. This duality depends on a limited definition of Jewish myth that does not account for Jewish politics and history apart from the messianic. To illuminate a third path, I offer a close reading of a Jewish thinker who experienced Sabbatian excitement and disappointment himself, who lived the conditions that Scholem and others have called "double exile," and yet who saw an alternative resolution.

Daniel Levi de Barrios (*c.* 1625–1701) was a charismatic and idiosyncratic poet who made himself popular with governing elites, including Christian nobility as well as Sephardi Jewish lay leaders, by praising them in florid Baroque poetic and prose compositions.[20] He was born into a *converso* family in Spain under the

Inquisition, and went to the Low Countries as an adult to take up a Jewish life in the famously tolerant city of Amsterdam. The Jewish community built there by Spanish and Portuguese immigrants fleeing from the Inquisition was also home to Benedict Spinoza (1632–1677), and much has been made of this cultural context in terms of the shaping of Jewish modernity. In addition to Scholem's theory that Sabbatianism was connected to the experience of Spanish Jews, scholars have attributed a kind of innate secularism or skepticism, "double exile," or "disputed soul," to those who lived as hidden Jews in a Catholic land and then as open Jews in a Protestant land.[21]

Whatever one concludes about their psychological state or their relationship to the Enlightenment, it is true that these Jews were highly *au courant* in the Christian ideas and events of their day, and that the late seventeenth century was a moment of rapid change among both Jews and Christians, witnessing the first inklings of modern forms of religious toleration, liberal democracy, mass politics, and citizenship. The concomitant changes in Jewish culture were enormous, including new forms of communal organization and leadership, new senses of self and self-differentiation from non-Jews, and even fundamentally new narratives of Jewish history and destiny.[22]

De Barrios himself was an ardent believer in Sabbatianism in the years between Shabbetai's apostasy in 1666 and his death in 1676; Scholem, in fact, relates a brief but colorful story about de Barrios from this period,[23] but the then-troubled poet seems to have given up on the movement soon after.[24] In his chronicle and panegyric ode, *Triumpho del govierno popular y de la antiguedad Holandesa* (The triumph of popular government and Dutch antiquity, 1683), de Barrios locates his exilic community in a global history of Jewish forms of government, in actual historical terms and in connection with a broad Jewish theo-politics. The arc of his story travels from original monarchy to present-day democracy and eventually to messianically restored monarchy, so that exilic regimes appear as a legitimate form of Jewish self-government during a long interregnum. In doing so, he turns the classical tripartite classification of polities as monarchies, aristocracies, and democracies into a chronological scheme in Jewish history, with a final, transcendent era that circles back to origins.

De Barrios lays out this scheme at the very start of the dedicatory poem at the head of his book. He praises the seven lay leaders of his community, who made up a governing council called the *Mahamad*.

[1] *Democracy* means popular
dominion in Greek; *monarchy*
government of one; and *aristocracy*
designates that of the noble betters.

2 The politics of the last are strict,
those of imperial sovereignty are severe.
Democracy is more gentle,
and better to the high patron.

3   He chooses the Judge whose rule is wise,
    who teaches with example and just proof,
    more than with words.

4   He who governs this way improves and elevates,
    because the voice of the people is a divine voice,
    and fortunate is the judge who knows to take it up.

5   God created the universe in six days,

6   and divided it into three worlds: the first
    monarchy with high hierarchies;
    the second noble with celestial privilege.
    The third shows itself to be of elements in mixed
    and proportional groups.
    A propitious bond now holds all in the *six*,*   *parnassim[25]
    With unity, with nobility, and with judgment.

7   On the seventh day, God rested;
    his people did well to rest with Joseph.*   *Gabbai[26]
    From the six Parnassim, justice comes
    piously to Joseph, who is the seventh:
    these are the seven Judaizing marvels
    that the tree of the law constantly signifies.

The seven numbered stanzas correspond to the seven leaders as well as the seven sections of the ensuing text and the seven days of creation. As a group of seven, the *Mahamad* is compared to a tree of life, comprising all of creation and holding it together in connections that span worlds, eons—and forms of government.[27] At the same time, the *Mahamad*'s identification with the democratic form, "the voice of the people," is specifically associated with the time of creation of earthly things, beneath the divine and celestial realms. The image overall is a kabbalistic vision of sefirotic emanation, where descent into the human realm correlates with increasing popular participation. That realm is still integrated into the whole by means of the organizing and life-giving properties of the *Mahamad*, as he characterizes its members as "sustainers."

De Barrios imbues this scheme with a historical dimension as well. Although the following is framed as a classification, it offers a chronological account of the political history of the Jewish people.

> Political peoples in general can be divided into three main categories. The first is monarchy, or government of one, like that of Moses, Saul, David and Solomon. The second is aristocratic, or noble, like that of Joshua, the holy Judges, and the Maccabeans. The third is democratic, or popular, like that of the Israelites in Egypt, Babylonia, and everywhere they are found in the Mosaic Law, ever since the Assyrians dispersed those of Israel, and the Romans those of Jerusalem.[28]

Here, as in the dedication, de Barrios says that monarchy gave way to aristocracy, which gave way to democracy, the current form. The exilic portion of the divine history has particular prominence and glory in de Barrios' depiction.

> There were three popular, or lower [i.e., plebeian]
> Israelite governments: one among Egyptians,
> Called the pastoral dynasty;
> Another among Babylonians and Phoenicians.
> The third is that of the Sustainers
> Or Parnassim, shining outward
> In various temples among various nations,
> Lights of God within them.[29]

Here again, the "lower" government means the rule of the people. Jews have experienced three popular regimes or "governments" that correspond to three exiles: the Egyptian, the Babylonian, and now one that he refers to as the time of the "sustainers," in which individual communities are compared to so many temples spread out all over the world, each one governed "as a republic unto itself"[30]—shining beacons of democracy before that was a cliché. Their by-the-people, for-the-people government is particularly close to God in a way that suggests cleaving to the *shekhinah*, or divine indwelling: de Barrios writes in another work, *Govierno popular Judayco*, that "those who govern the Israelite republics are like those who, with Moses in Chapter 24 of Exodus, *saw the God of Israel: and there was under his feet as it were a paved work of a sapphire stone, and as it were the body of heaven in his clearness.*"[31]

Like the sapphire floors that are also the heavens, democracies are both the "lowest" form in the sense of nobility and cosmic emanation, and also paradoxically the highest. Likewise, de Barrios treats them as highest in terms of political theory, so that as history has progressed Jewish politics have improved. Citing classical and contemporary sources, he says that monarchy inevitably devolves into tyranny—at least after Moses, who was the last truly God-fearing king, setting a standard for proper kingship that cannot be met except by a prophet. In a parallel to the three democratic regimes of the exile, de Barrios tells of three true (godly) monarchies: that of Hanoch son of Yerek, "who reduced to his religious empire all of the descendants of Adam"; that of "Ioctan son of Heber (brother of Peleg), captain or emperor of all of the successors of Shem, as Philo certified in his *Antiquities*";[32] and the third, "most perfect" monarchy—that of Moses.[33] He describes these ancient geopolitical events at length,[34] showing how the monarchical form became closer to God as it progressed. Then, he goes on to describe the transition from monarchy to the "Jerusalem aristocracy" (also with three stages) and then to democracy.[35] De Barrios has set up a kabbalistic scheme of nine[36] parts that become a complete, interconnected whole when united with a tenth.

That tenth, of course, is the anticipated messianic restoration, which will witness a return to kingship that possesses the prophetic dimension as with Moses. Although de Barrios does not spell it out, the circle is completed when this glorious restoration brings the whole world and all of the people with it. Thematically, this messianism is intimately related to the Sabbatian messianism that Scholem explored so deeply in essays like "Redemption through Sin," as the redemption that de Barrios describes is achieved through a process of delving into "lower" realms in order to redeem them. This is a messianic vision, but it is also a concrete historiographical one. The political circumstances of the diaspora that it describes are not merely the politics of the nations, but rather Jewish politics in all their glory. The point of it all is to show that the present form of Jewish politics, that which he calls "democratic" in distinction from the divinely mandated monarchy, is itself also a manifestation of God's will. De Barrios describes the period of Jewish dispersion in a way that is not defined by its lack of political self-determination or longing for monarchical restoration, but essentially positively, as a period in which the people were to be taken just as seriously as kings. It is a vision in which the exile is not only an apex of Jewish life, and a compelling arena for Jewish politics, but also a shining example of politics for any people.

At least as regards de Barrios, Scholem was right about messianism losing its apocalyptic dimension and being replaced by a vision of a long, slow process of cosmic reparation in the world and through the world. However, de Barrios also reveals Scholem's misapprehension of such a vision as necessarily apolitical or inherently opposed to a particularly Jewish myth based on biblical revelation. De Barrios's Jewish theo-politics glorified the exilic community, embracing the concrete forms of Jewish collectivity and authority as significant both geopolitically and religiously, within traditional Jewish narratives of universal history.

Possibilities

Scholem writes that exile is "that state of the universe in which there is no *tikkun* or harmony, and by which everything is damaged and harmed. Exile and redemption are thus transformed into powerful symbols, acquiring the background of cosmic myth. This may explain the tremendous attraction to these ideas until the period of the Enlightenment."[37] But de Barrios, on the tail end of Sabbatianism and the eve of the Enlightenment, finds the harmony in and *of* exile. The perfect and deeply iterated set of correspondences that describe the universe are, for de Barrios, not damaged by Sabbatian failure or even by exile in general; rather, the unfolding of history nestles into the scheme. (So, for that matter, do Jewish migrations, European languages, and classical myths.) De Barrios certainly accords special significance to exile in his scheme, but it has a different quality than the objects of Scholem's focus. De Barrios treats exile (or diaspora) as a political alternative, rather than a political lack, and even so does not abandon the central mythological narrative that ends with ingathering.

The tension between these two thinkers' visions centers on the question of what exilic Jewish politics are: specifically, on the apparent impossibility of a full embrace of worldly affairs in anything other than a messianic era. Total acceptance of revelation seems to entail the expectation of a political messiah and the rejection of any other politics; total acceptance of non-messianic worldly politics suggests the abandonment of the particular, national, political narrative that ends messianically. But de Barrios is not trapped by that opposition. Instead, he offers a vision that is at once messianic and deeply political. Seemingly having absorbed the hard truth that Shabbetai Tsvi would not return to govern the world as a Jewish messianic king, de Barrios finds an equivalent political fulfillment for Jews in exile. It is a vision that relates messianic kingship to a distant, unspecified future; but what differentiates it from the exile is not the presence or absence, but rather the style, of politics that characterizes Jewish experience. In exile, Jews were to enjoy not monarchy but democracy.

De Barrios was a unique character, but his exploration of diaspora as a legitimate arena for Jewish politics was part of a widespread attitude at a particular moment. His peers included Abraham Pereyra, a merchant who wrote whole sections of his ethical and pietistic works on the proper workings of Jewish "republics," by which he meant exilic communities;[38] Isaac Orobio de Castro, a physician who drew on Christian political theory to argue, among other things, that Jews still possessed the scepter of Judah;[39] and Isaac Aboab da Fonseca, the prominent rabbi who defended the *Mahamad*'s absolute rule over the community, treating diaspora communal politics along the lines of Christian intellectual debates about the social contract and the right of resistance.[40] These figures all wrote in the decades during and just after the Sabbatian movement, engaging with many of the same Christian political ideas as Spinoza. All of them find Jewish politics in exile—not innocently, as Scholem imagines pre-modern Jews to do before the Sabbatian crisis, but rather with a high degree of self-awareness— creating sophisticated responses to the questions they raised. And in so doing they all maintain intimate connections to the core texts and myths of Jewish tradition.

Their political discourse shows that other possibilities existed apart from exile and myth, which are the two paths Scholem saw. Other narratives could compete, ones that did not pit the diaspora against Jewish myth, and that were not determinedly removed from the world of ethical, legal, and social action. On the contrary, the vision of exilic Judaism in de Barrios's *Triumpho* is holistic and integrated with the messianic vision, but it also plays itself out in the minutiae and realia of life in the world—not only in the synagogue but also in the chambers of the lay leaders, in the Spanish literary academies, and in the communal charity coffers. De Barrios offers a powerful rebuttal to Scholem's privileging of myth over history, of text over lived experience.

This critique has a deep affinity to Wasserstrom's views, not only of Scholem but of the study of religion in general. As Wasserstrom writes in *Religion after Religion*:

> It remains impossible, finally, to imagine that we critical students of religion can meet that challenge by surrendering to theophany, theosophy, or even theology. Without holding on to the first and last traces of the past available to us, the texts of history, we break the chain connecting us to the living past. This past was not crowded with mystics, but rather with detailed practices and personalities of all types. Remaining traces of these ancestors are our only evidence, the stuff that provides our purpose, and to it we must yield and then yield again. The history of religions, I conclude, must end up being a historical study or it may be no study at all.[41]

Religion must be understood as existing inherently within the world, among people, practices, and happenings, which, unlike mystical experience, are intelligible and accessible. And in their quality of being embodied, they are also mixed. In his "Nine

Theses," Wasserstrom emphasizes that all religion takes place in contact between people, as a function of contact and continuity.[42] De Barrios does not mourn his *converso* background any more than he mourns the pluralistic Dutch setting or the influence of Roman oratory. Rather than creating religious confusion, skepticism, or tragically doubled identity, these abundant contacts created him and his world and he sees them as worthy of Jewish mythical elaboration.

It seems appropriate that de Barrios fixes on democracy as the form of politics most suited to the exile. His "voice of the people" expresses the sense of politics dwelling in the actions and desires of the masses rather than the elites, in much the way that Wasserstrom insists that the history of religions must pay attention to all people, and not only the mystics. De Barrios's and his peers' discussions of Jewish law, self-government, group belonging, and religious self-differentiation reflected a different kind of crisis than the mythical ones through which Scholem saw Jewish history as developing its core "ideas." To Scholem, their writings would not have seemed relevant to the essential questions of Jewish myth and messianism, dwelling as they did in the realm of the historical, the contingent, the hybrid. But their writings show that those things *are* the exile, and as such they are all the more essentially Jewish—not less so.

In two fascinating final paragraphs of "On the Possibility," Scholem turns to the future. He allows for the possibility that Jewish mysticism may take nontraditional forms, but ultimately he cannot imagine how such activity would be continuous with the past. He writes:

> Who knows where the boundaries of holiness lie? ... Perhaps mysticism will be revealed, not in the traditional garb of holiness, but ... within the innermost sanctums of this secularity?[43]

Immediately thereafter, Scholem—remarkably—cites Walt Whitman as an example of secular spirituality. He seems to see Whitman as a kind of American analogue to spiritual Zionists, but laments that neither can partake of the "traditional concepts" that have formed Judaism. I suggest that de Barrios reveals mysticism and holiness in what Scholem saw as the "innermost sanctums of ... secularity," namely diaspora history and geo-politics. Yet de Barrios still makes them intelligible using the "traditional concepts" of exile and redemption, kabbalah and scriptural hermeneutics. For Scholem, politics—understood as movements of the masses, states, governments, declarations, treaties, and social conditions—may be the outward or literal realm that only intersects at intervals with the workings of a mysterious and eternal, inner or mystical core of reality. For de Barrios, on the other hand, the political is itself the mystery. The unfolding of history and the story of Jewish migration, tribulation, survival, and glory, and even the details of lay communal administration—treasurers and conflict arbiters and such—hold symbolic mystical significance and form a matrix through which God's special relationship with the people Israel can be perceived.

For Scholem, exile was a catch-22. His way of understanding modernity meant that if there was messianism there could be no politics, and vice versa. But de Barrios did not sublimate the geopolitical after Sabbatianism: he reinterpreted it into a democratic and multiplicitous vision the likes of which Scholem could not imagine. Scholem entered the Holy Land, yet he could not see the floors of sapphire that de Barrios saw in the institutions of Jewish justice and charity in the city of Amsterdam. But even Scholem acknowledged his limits, writing optimistically in 1967: "I am numbered among those who think that Judaism is filled with an abundance of vitality, and that with all its rich past, it still has a rich future, stretching unto eternity; that it is a phenomenon in which the not-yet-revealed, the hidden, and the anticipated, flowing like the remnants of the riches of the past, are still present."[44] Perhaps what was hidden to Scholem was visible to de Barrios, and might, in turn, be so to us.

16

Medieval Spanish Jews and the Dangers of Wealth

Andrew D. Berns

In March of 1492, King Ferdinand and Queen Isabella of Spain promulgated their edict of expulsion, forcing the kingdom's Jews to convert to Christianity or depart forever. By the end of that summer, fifteen hundred years of Jewish life in Spain had come to an abrupt end. The crises Spanish Jews lived through—from mass conversion to organized violence to their final banishment—led them to reconsider many of their assumptions about how they lived. Hispanic Jewry wrote eloquently about their work, their lifestyles, and their goals. They expressed concern about rampant wealth acquisition, and mused that their pursuit of riches and power led directly to their misfortunes.

This essay explores how one prominent Spanish Jew—Isaac Abravanel—and several of his peers came to grips with the shock of their expulsion from Spain. By studying the responses of Spanish Jews to the catastrophes they witnessed, I hope to underscore and extend two of Steven Wasserstrom's "Nine Theses," particularly his first and ninth. In his first thesis, Wasserstrom posits that the professional study of religion should seek "a general perspective," and strive for a "philosophical understanding of the human as such."[1] The Hebrew writings of the Spanish-Jewish authors that I study in this paper speak to a universal human preoccupation: what are the proper ends of life.[2] To Wasserstrom's mind, the study of religion seeks "species-wide generalizations."[3] Doubts about the redemptive powers of wealth and status are common across the world's religions and cultures: they are truly "species-wide." In Jewish history one finds them in the Bible, and in recent critiques of materialism. One set of recent denunciations is brilliantly presented in this volume by Michael Casper, whose essay on how twentieth-century Hasidim in Brooklyn demonized money, materialism, and luxury goods presents a compelling analogue to the fifteenth-century texts I discuss in this contribution. Sephardic Jews had a unique view of this subject, one clearly framed by the ethical traditions of the Hebrew Bible, but also informed by their lived experience as exiles from Spain and Portugal.

Wasserstrom also calls for Religious Studies to be a "deeply human science." He argues that such depth may be found in "the usual and the routine," and advocates "the rediscovery of the ordinary."[4] Many of the issues that animated the writers I discuss in this essay were closely connected to their everyday experiences. Wealth was linked to work, and questions regarding how to live were both practical and existential: answering them required close examination of contemporary Jews' lives and careers, as well as biblical history and mythology. Stories from the Bible, seen through the prism of Sephardic Jews' experiences, convinced writers such as Isaac Abravanel and other Hebrew authors that they were not victims of intolerance; they were the authors of their own tragedy.

In the centuries since the edict was issued, historians have argued endlessly about the causes of this trauma. They tend to focus on a few themes: the fervid Catholicism of Ferdinand and Isabella, which understood Judaism as a heresy that needed to be stamped out; populist anger, fueled by economic dislocation and recession, which found a convenient scapegoat in Spain's Jews; or the monarchs' belief that in order to run a world-wide empire they had to demonstrate absolute authority, and that evicting a prominent minority was an easy way to accomplish that.[5] These theories share a common denominator: the Jews were passive subjects, rather than active agents who thought critically about their role in their dislocation by examining their lives in light of Jewish traditions. Abravanel and his peers saw things differently. They thought that the Jews brought the expulsion upon themselves. They thought that one particular sin doomed them: greed.

Isaac Abravanel was born in 1437 and died in 1508, and is best known as a commentator on most of the Hebrew Bible, as well as author of a series of philosophical works.[6] In Spain, he advised Ferdinand and Isabella until he was exiled from Iberia in 1492. The boat he boarded in Valencia dropped anchor in Naples, and Abravanel found himself in a dusty refugee camp in Campania during the dog days of August, suffering alongside his sick fellow Jews.[7] This experience marked a sharp deviation from the former trajectory of Abravanel's life. Born in Portugal to an exiled Castilian family, Abravanel had not only cultivated his precocious literary talents (as a teenager he wrote his first philosophical treatise in elegant Hebrew prose), but had become fabulously wealthy. Working as a tax farmer and advisor to the noble Braganza family prior to his flight from Portugal in 1483 (Abravanel was falsely implicated in an anti-monarchical conspiracy), he became the owner of vast estates, some of which were gifts from his grateful and magnanimous friends. There is more evidence of his wealth during his Portuguese young adulthood: after a costly war against Castile in 1480 that drained the Portuguese treasury, a band of nobles loaned 12,000,000 *reals* to the Portuguese king. Abravanel's contribution was more than a tenth of that sum.[8]

Abravanel was not unique in his wealth and success; many Jews lived lavishly in fifteenth-century Spain. In the words of a sixteenth-century Jewish historian who looked back at life in Spain with nostalgia, there was "no end to the grandeur and greatness of their courtyards and homes."[9] By the middle of the fifteenth century, it was common knowledge that the Jewish upper classes, especially courtiers, enjoyed extravagant parties, sumptuous dances with women, and illicit concubines. Affluent Jews even got a daily allowance of meat from city officials. Such privileges were hereditary, passed from father to son.[10]

Some Jews in fifteenth-century Spain were fabulously wealthy. One was Abraham Senior—Abravanel's friend and fellow financial advisor to the Catholic monarchs who later converted and took the name Fernán Núñez Coronel. Shortly before the expulsion, one of Senior's Catholic friends estimated the Jew's fortune at a million *maravedís*.[11] One modern historian posits that Senior's riches were equal to those of 100 noblemen who enjoyed state incomes of between 100,000 and 500,000 *maravedís*.[12] A 1492 inventory of his possessions, including his house in Segovia, reads like a lusty real estate advertisement. It notes that the home had an elegant chamber in which Senior could converse with visitors or pray. His wine cellar had multiple entrances, and a tall fence enclosed a sun-spackled porch.[13]

Senior's wealth brought him power, but could not save him. When the expulsion decree was issued Senior and his fellow Jews offered an enormous bribe to Ferdinand and Isabella, imploring them to rescind the edict. Abravanel, Senior, and Senior's son-in-law Abraham Melamed offered the monarchs 300,000 gold ducats, or 112 million *maravedís*, which was fifty times the projected cost of Columbus's expedition to the New World.[14] The proposal failed; Ferdinand and Isabella's hearts only hardened. A chronicler who wrote in Hebrew from the safety of Crete a generation after the expulsion imagined Abravanel's conversation with the Queen. In this dramatic recreation of Abravanel's audience with Her Majesty, the disgraced statesman warned Isabella that all those who wish ill upon the Jews "will perish"—a dark prophecy of Spain's eventual imperial decline. In that same Cretan chronicle we read that even the king's own advisors were said to have remarked, "what is it that you've done, sending away a numerous nation like this, to depart from your land with their money and properties! Your forefathers gathered much treasure from them, and now you squander it?"[15]

The "treasure" that Ferdinand and Isabella squandered was amassed in a variety of ways: in fifteenth-century Spain Jews held many jobs. These ranged from working-class trades such as artisans and small shopkeepers in Iberian cities and towns, to farmers and agricultural laborers, to financiers and political advisors. One boon to historians that resulted from the expulsion of the Jews is that we possess detailed lists of Jewish property. In fact, such lists reflect many agricultural pursuits. After the expulsion, agriculture continued to attract and employ many Jews: a sixteenth-century rabbi writing in Ottoman Safed expressed concern that if he interpreted certain laws stringently he would deter the Spanish exiles from cultivating land.[16] The implication, of course, is that they were already farming. Even popular ballads in expulsion-era Spain confirm the involvement of Sephardi Jews in agriculture.[17] In the middle of the fifteenth century it was said of Jews of Huerta, a small town in Castile along the Tormes river, that they were "for the most part laborers and cultivators of fields and vineyards."[18] Such data rebut comments made by contemporary Christians to the effect that Jews would not stoop to the level of manual labor. Consider the tirade of Andrés Bernáldez, a Spanish bishop and historian at the time of the expulsion, against the Jews:

> For the most part, they were a profiteering people, with many arts and deceits, because they all lived from idle jobs and they had no conscience when buying

or selling with Christians. They never wanted to take jobs such as ploughing or digging, or walking through the fields looking after flocks, nor did they teach such things to their children, but rather [they took] jobs in the town, and sitting down making their living with little effort. In these kingdoms, many of them gained great wealth and property in a short time, because they had no conscience about profit and usury.[19]

There is an element of truth to Bernáldez's words: some Jews did "gain great wealth." But many more farmed. This propensity to work the land must have escaped the attention of Catholic polemicists even while it shaped Abravanel's own caustic remarks about the morally degenerate nature of such work.[20]

It was in finance, however, that the Jews made their real mark in Spanish society. As one historian put it, they "involved themselves in all the ramifications of the urban, seigneurial and royal financial administrations."[21] Registers of royal revenues contain the names of families that could be described as veritable dynasties of tax farmers and collectors, including the Abenamías, Abenxuxen, Abudaran, Baquex, Bienveniste, Çabaco, Levi, Leyva, and Nasçi.[22] By some estimates, at this time Jews controlled two thirds of the indirect taxes and customs within the country.[23]

Tax farming—collecting taxes on behalf of someone else, usually a political figure— may have been lucrative, but it carried risks, and could be socially disadvantageous. For one thing, such positions were seen in Spanish society as incompatible with true *hidalguía*, or nobility.[24] A nobleman, so the thinking went, would not stoop to sullying his hands with money. For another, it isolated Jews and incited popular ire. As one historian has put it, "like other merchants and tax collectors," Jews were "hated."[25] At this time foreign observers noted that Spanish Jews were closely associated with wealth. The Italian historian and diplomat Francesco Guicciardini, writing in 1513, wrote that half a century before "the whole kingdom [of Castile] was full of Jews and heretics ... who had in their hands all the main offices and wealth."[26] And it was not only Catholics who felt this way. Solomon ibn Verga, a Jewish historian looking back at the tragedy of Jewish life in Spain from the vantage point of the sixteenth century, "saw the jealousy of Christians for Jews excited by Jewish thirst for riches and power, the pride and luxury displayed in their dress, far richer than that of Christian nobles."[27]

Ibn Verga was not the first Sephardic Jew to say this; Abraham Saba, a contemporary of Isaac Abravanel, made a similar point.[28] Like Abravanel he was an accomplished intellectual—a philosopher and exegete who wrote polished Hebrew prose. He too left Spain in 1492 rather than convert to Christianity, and like Abravanel he endured the indignities of a rough sea voyage from Spain to Italy. After docking at Livorno, Saba made his way to Ferrara, where the ruling Este duke welcomed Jewish refugees. For unknown reasons, Saba later made his way to Adrianople (Edirne in present-day Turkey), which was home to a large and growing population of exiled Sephardic Jews. In his Bible commentary, Saba explained, in his words, "the cause for the expulsion," and inveighed against "the arrogance and domination that existed in Israel, as though they were living on their own land."[29] Such arrogance, Saba thought, meant that the Jews "were building ruins for themselves."[30] Those ruins were deceptive; they were not crumbling edifices. They took the form of "houses panelled with cedar and with beautiful crafts, like kings' palaces, for the sake of which they bowed down and worshipped idolatry."[31]

Saba's insistence that the Jews brought expulsion and exile upon themselves as a result of their vanity and by virtue of their ostentatious dwellings echoed earlier responses to other tragedies that befell Iberian Jewry. A century before their final expulsion in 1492, Jews suffered violent persecutions and forced conversions after a series of riots throughout Castile in 1391. Saba's criticism of luxurious houses is reminiscent of another Jew who wrote three quarters of a century before Solomon Alami. Alami penned a lapidary letter to Spain's Jews in 1414 excoriating them for their greed and imploring them to embrace a life of spiritual, rather than physical, pleasures. "Those who sat in their paneled houses," Alami moaned, "were expelled from pleasant palaces. And we were expelled because we built wide houses with spacious, beautiful rooms in our exile."[32] The connection between gaudy real estate and expulsion was a Spanish-Jewish topos.

Biblical commentary

From the persecutions of 1391 to the final expulsion of 1492, Sephardic Jews analyzed the causes for their sufferings. They did so in ethical letters and historical writings. But the fullest articulation of their claim that greed, along with its subsidiary sins of pride and pomposity, was to blame for their national downfall came in another genre: biblical commentary. Sephardic Jews saw the Bible as a manual for their own times. Biblical heroes were models worthy of emulation; biblical villains were typologies of evil. One theme that Spanish Jews saw constantly repeated in Scripture was that of greed and its consequences.

Abravanel and his peers reflected on many biblical passages that warned of the dangers of excessive wealth. The first I would like to consider is the story of manna in the desert.

Almost 2,000 years before the Jews were expelled from Spain, their Israelite ancestors lived through the dramatic exodus from Egypt. Shortly after the Children of Israel left the land of the Pharaohs, and immediately after they witnessed the parting of the Red Sea, they started to complain. "Would that we had died by the hand of the LORD in the land of Egypt, when we sat by the fleshpots, when we did eat bread to the full; for ye have brought us forth into this wilderness, to kill this whole assembly with hunger."[33] They were camped at Elim, where gurgling brooks provided water, and a grove of date-palms satisfied their hunger. Still, they missed Egyptian cuisine.

God's response was to give the Israelites manna. "The people shall go out and gather a day's portion every day," God was quick to stipulate.[34] The Israelites were specifically instructed not to gather more than they needed, and not to leave any for the next morning. But they didn't listen. The Book of Exodus tells us that "they hearkened not unto Moses; but some of them left of it until the morning." Divine punishment was swift: the manna "bred worms, and rotted." Moses was irate.[35]

Abravanel interpreted this tale as a warning about the evils of acquisitiveness. He had seen those evils first hand, and was even guilty of yielding to their siren song. Writing ten years after the expulsion, from the tranquility of the Venetian lagoon,[36] Abravanel reflected on his people's expulsion from Spain, and the original Exodus that served as its backdrop. "The Holy One, Blessed be He, did not want the Israelites to conduct themselves as was their wont with material things, namely to pile them up and conduct trade with the surplus."[37] For Abravanel it was the nature of Israelites to accumulate possessions, and use them to trade. But that wasn't all: to his mind generating surplus was an unfortunate reality of all societies. God did not want the Israelites to "bequeath it [surplus] to their children until they had a human society. For the nature of surplus and its evil is to trap you: excess in material things is a great impediment and drain in attaining spiritual perfection."[38]

In Abravanel's analysis God foresaw what the Jews' tendency would be: like all human societies, theirs would save and preserve wealth in order to pass it on to future generations. Knowing that excess would only bring out the worst in people, God commanded Jews to gather only what they needed:

> When the Holy One limited the Israelite's food in the desert he allotted their supply such that they would lack nothing. Indeed, he inflicted an organic defect on their share of food, so that nothing would remain that they could store up, trade, and grow wealthy from, as in storehouses of produce, oil, and wine. In this way they could avoid the anxiety and inconvenience that result from unnecessary accumulation. For this reason He commanded that they "gather of it what they need to eat," in other words that they not store it up or trade it.[39]

Abravanel proposed that God saw capitalist exploitation as the natural consequence of people taking more than they need. The Spanish commentator underscored the moral lesson inherent in this story: Moses told the Israelites not to leave manna over until morning so that "no one would fritter away their time in gathering superfluous things: it is proper for man to be content in his provisions with what is necessary."[40] If man is not content with what he needs, a proto-capitalist society would not be the only result; man's downfall would be next. The Bible stated that there were worms in the manna and it stank, "like living meat that had died" according to Abravanel. In an era before refrigeration everybody knew the smell of rotting flesh; it must have pervaded the marketplaces and abattoirs of late-medieval Spain. But the smell was not only an aesthetic offense: its purpose was "to hint at what is the end of any man who chases after superfluous things."[41]

The manna that rotted was more than a tit-for-tat punishment; it was a visceral reminder of the futility of a life devoted to accumulation. Abravanel thought that Jews, like all humans, have a natural tendency to hoard. Although that hoarding might be well intended—as in the example of Jews who wished to pass on their estates to their progeny—it would ultimately amount to nothing. The man who had known great opulence and splendor, and who had helped Europe's first major empire enrich itself, thought at the end of his days that a life of accumulating material possessions was a life in vain.

The Hebrew Bible presents many tales warning readers of the allures and traps of materialism. The most famous is the story of the Golden Calf. In it our Spanish commentators found a rich vein of insights to mine.

The Golden Calf

For a generation of intellectuals who had seen precipitous accumulation of wealth, and then the sudden loss of that wealth, followed by an ignominious exile from their native land, the Bible's story of the Israelites building a Golden Calf resonated powerfully and painfully. In Exodus' tale, Moses tarried on Mount Sinai while God spoke to him and delivered instructions. Growing impatient with his delay, the Israelites grumbled to Aaron and asked him to "make a God" for them, since Moses seemed to have disappeared. Aaron yielded to their wishes, asked them to remove their jewelry and bring it to him, and he forged it into an idol, and then created an altar upon which they could worship that idol.[42]

Centuries of commentators had asked why Aaron was so quick to do his fellow Jews' bidding, especially since what they were asking for was a flagrant violation of all the laws they had recently heard—and a glaring contradiction of the first two of the Ten Commandments. Abravanel did his best to exonerate Aaron's behavior in his commentary on this episode: Aaron stalled for time, putting off the Israelites' demands and avoiding construction of the calf. When he could no longer do that,

> in order to delay them he urged them to "take off the gold rings that are on the ears of your wives and sons and daughters and bring them to me." For he told them that since they were desirous of a talisman that would channel the power of the higher forces it would have to be of gold, and constructed from the most precious and dear possessions.[43]

In the Bible's story the Israelites did not request an idol made of precious metals; they only wanted something tangible to worship. Aaron knew that one way to make them delay was to force them to part with that which was dearest: their gold jewelry. He essentially lied, convincing the Israelites that in order to be efficacious the idol had to be gold. His real goal was merely to buy time.

In Abravanel's reconstruction of these events, so relevant to his own age, Aaron was zealous to do the will of the people and build an idol so that "they would ultimately see that there is no substance to it, and nothing within it."[44] He wanted the people to see that the talisman "knows nothing and informs of nothing."[45] In other words, Aaron wanted his fellow Jews to know that no material object could function as an oracle or prognosticator. Once they grasped this, Abravanel points out, "they would be ashamed of their counsels and embarrassed of their own thoughts, and their base desire would cease."[46] Aaron's intention was to "reveal to them that they were chasing after vanity."[47] Indeed, among the Israelites who had just recently witnessed God's appearance on Mount Sinai "there were brutish men with no knowledge or understanding who, when they saw the image of the calf and the beauty of the gold and the craftsmanship of it, bowed down before it."⁴⁸ Aaron was painfully aware of the Jews' "foolishness, for they were bowing before that trifling piece of gold that had no knowledge, no understanding, and no divine quality."⁴⁹ Placing hope in the salvific power of money was bad, but believing in a talisman—an object that purports to convey divine forces from the heavens to the earth—was even worse. To Abravanel's mind, worship of money was merely one ritual in the cult of materialism.

Abravanel knew that for the Jews idolization of material splendor was mistaken for spiritual elevation. It was a tendency that had not changed in 2,000 years. In his lifetime he even witnessed a scene that recalled the deficit of values which the worship of a golden calf embodied. In the summer of 1495, Abravanel took refuge for a few months on the Mediterranean island of Corfu, then under Venetian control. There were a number of Sephardic exiles there, and the scene was not a heartening one. In his commentary on the *Ethics of the Fathers*, a rabbinic text popular among Sephardic Jews, he painted a grim picture of what the Spanish exiles were up to, lamenting:

> [The refugees] neglect eternal values and are interested in temporal affairs only, like dissolute slaves. They spend all their days either in diligent pursuit of money and the comforts they desire ... or in the ways of the sinful, in the company of the lightheaded. They breathe forth lies, and play games with dice, and they band together with irreverence. And as for the work of the Lord, which is the beginning of His way and the gift of His Torah, they see not even in their dreams.⁵⁰

One response to challenging circumstances would have been for the Jews to devote themselves to their spiritual convalescence. Instead, they chose the path of least resistance, and dedicated themselves to a life of ease, cupidity, and sin.

Epilogue: Avarice

Exile helped Abravanel to recognize the futility of the path he and his fellow Spanish Jews were on. The expulsion was a teachable moment for him; he seems to have mended his ways. In a letter to his friend Saul Ashkenazi, he wrote "who is the man who in his youth did not journey to the ends of the earth for two years or three ... to trade and increase his wealth?"⁵¹ Youth, clearly, is a time for acquisitiveness. Abravanel says of young men that "their desire is for money."⁵² Philosophy, however, was fit for any time of life: "As for this glorified science, trade in it is better than gold, than fine gold."⁵³ Abravanel dedicated the final years of his life to feverish writing: he composed his best-known commentaries in this period, and largely turned away from tax farming and other business activities that brought him wealth and renown in Portugal and Spain.

Clearly not everyone could earn a living from their pens. So what profession did Sephardic commentators of the late fifteenth and early sixteenth century think Jews should practice? Shepherding. The man who articulated this vision most clearly was an inveterate urbanite: Isaac Abravanel. In a commentary on *Pirqe Avot*, he exclaimed, "how beautiful are the words of Solomon, who said 'be diligent to know the state of thy flocks, and look well to thy herds.'" He did this "to praise and crown and glorify the life of a man engaged in the field in the profession of shepherding, who flees from government work and authority amongst urban dwellers." Abravanel knew the temptation of placing the care of one's land and flocks in another's hands, and was quick to point out that King Solomon knew that "this means do not say 'I will entrust my flocks to the shepherds and make myself lord of the city.' Do not do this! You yourself should 'know the state of thy flocks.'"[54] To Abravanel there was a redemptive quality to life lived on the land.

Urban jobs, on the other hand, that led to wealth acquisition were to be avoided. Abravanel cites an apposite biblical verse: "For riches are not forever; and doth the crown endure unto all generations?"[55] He explains it as referring to precisely the kind of city-based work he and his fellow Spanish Jews used to excel in: "This means that work with authorities and in offices of the state is not permanent, and the crown of political power will not last from generation to generation." No one knew this better than Abravanel: shifting political winds forced him from Portugal to Castile, and from Castile away from Iberia forever. "The good and perpetual prosperity" is to be found "in the pasture of the flock." When King Solomon exalted the day "when the hay is mown and the tender grass showeth itself, and the herbs of the mountains are gathered in," Abravanel saw this as propelling a chain of economic events. Writing as an economist might, he notes:

> The hay will come and afterwards grasses of the mountains will be gathered, and the product of wool will be reserved for you from the flock, and this is the point of [Solomon's] saying "the lambs will be for thy clothing," and you won't have any need for affairs of the state, for if you need a garment to wear, do not go to the city merchant to buy it from him; from the wool of sheep you may make a garment to clothe yourself in your own home. If you need gold and silver coins, "the goats the price for a field." This means people will come to you to buy goats, and they will give you money. If you need food there will be goats' milk enough for thy food, for the food of thy household. With all this, there will always be work for your maidens. These are all advantages of labor in the fields.[56]

Abravanel's remarks mingle nostalgia with practical prescriptions for how to live in a world of rapid urbanization and the decline of traditional farming practices.

According to a man with political experience, the best way to live a long and contented life is to work on the land and eschew the temptations of wealth and honor that come from civil service and financial work in cities. In sum, "a man of understanding and knowledge, an intelligent man will lengthen the days of his life with his work and the pasturing of his flock, not with government offices and rulership."[57]

The simple life, as it turns out, held limited appeal to post-expulsion Sephardic Jewry. Soon after 1492, a son of Don Vidal de la Caballeria wrote a Hebrew chronicle about the trauma Jews went through. Speaking of those who converted to preserve their fortunes, he predicted that "they shall increase as they shall increase."[58] In other words, they would be fruitful and multiply in a now *Judenrein* Spain. But all would not be well, for "the paths of their way are turned aside; they go to nothing."[59] Don

Vidal de la Caballería's son didn't finish the verse he cited: the words "go to nothing" come from the Book of Job. Those words are followed by a dark prediction: they "go to nothing *and perish*." But he did not have to cite the full verse: his Hebraically literate audience knew the Bible well. They also likely shared his grim prophecy for the fate of their former co-religionists.

This scion of the de la Caballería family must have known what Saba and Abravanel articulated so clearly: the "alien Gods" of material possessions do not easily relinquish their grasp on men's souls.[60] These Jewish criticisms of *conversos* were more than just that: they were also veiled critiques of the society those *conversos* were eager to assimilate into—Catholic Spain. Jews were not alone in that critique; Muslim scholars contributed to it, too. In 1510 the lawyer Abu al-'Abbas Ahmad al-Wansharisi lamented the corrosive effects of Spanish life on the Muslims of Ávila and elsewhere: "One has to be aware of the pervasive effect of their [Christian] way of life, their language, their dress, their objectionable habits."[61] Al-Wansharisi was particularly concerned about linguistic assimilation, but to his mind the loss of Islam's sacred tongue implied that "when the Arabic language dies out, so does devotion."[62] Wasserstrom reminds us that "there is no religion in the singular," and that "inter-relational complexity constitutes our subject."[63] One wonders to what degree Iberia's fifteenth-century Jews and Muslims shared a distaste for contemporary Spanish mores.

Jews and Muslims alike may have excoriated the pursuit of luxury that characterized life in fifteenth-century Spain. But Catholics, too, could be stern critics of their own culture. For example, Poggio Bracciolini, an Italian humanist two generations older than Abravanel—and, like Abravanel, a resident of an increasingly urbanizing society—wrote a dialogue in the late 1420s entitled *On Avarice*.[64] In it he has Bartolomeo da Montepulciano, one of the dialogue's participants, remark that the vice of greed "is repugnant and contrary to nature, whose laws tell us to put the common welfare before our own, so that we may bring help to as many people as possible."[65] Bracciolini summons a number of earlier authorities on this subject, both Christian and Pagan, to show that the roots of anti-materialism stretch back deep into the past. Bracciolini quotes the ninth-century Christian theologian Andrea of Constantinople, who bemoaned that "greed has made this earthly world unstable, it has confused all things," and Cicero, the first-century BCE Roman orator, who observed that "there is nothing so characteristic of narrowness and smallness of soul as the love of riches."[66] In the intellectual life of this period, condemnations of avarice are hardly unique to exiled Sephardic Jews.

The uniqueness of Spanish-Jewish critiques of wealth may lie in their tendency to project their own life experiences against the backdrop of the biblical narrative. Abravanel had a particular affinity for this: he saw several biblical tales as ciphers for his own life story. In his introduction to *Kings*, for example, Abravanel describes his forced departure from Portugal in 1483 with language that echoed the book of Exodus: "God delivered me from the sword of Pharaoh."[67] From our twenty-first-century perspective, it may seem odd that Renaissance scholars collapsed the distinction between mythology, ancient history, and their lives. In fact that was a norm, rather than an exception, for both Abravanel and his peers. In the premodern world, biblical commentary was an ambitious endeavor remote from today's siloed academic subjects.

A leading scholar of Renaissance biblical commentaries notes that they constitute "a disciplinary matrix where philological, historical, legal, antiquarian, and rhetorical procedures combine and recombine in response to fluctuations within the larger intellectual culture."[68] To extend this point, one might add that biblical commentaries from this period include fundamental observations about the human condition, such as the persistence of greed.

A decade ago Wasserstrom insisted that Religious Studies needed to "earn its rightful place as an intellectually necessary pursuit."[69] By bringing attention to relatively unstudied texts that concern essential issues like how we live and what we value, I hope to have demonstrated one way in which these subjects and sources might be justified as "intellectually necessary." What Isaac Abravanel and his contemporary Abraham Saba had to say about avarice is no less relevant now than at the turn of the sixteenth century.

17

Luksus and the Hasidic Critique of Postwar American Capitalism

Michael Casper

In her memoir of being raised by her grandparents in Williamsburg neighborhood of Brooklyn, New York in the late 1980s, Deborah Feldman wrote, "Bubby has been begging to change the worn blue carpet in the dining room for years now, but Zeidy insists that *luxus*, luxury, is not something to be enjoyed in this lifetime."[1] For much of the second half of the twentieth century, many Hasidim in Williamsburg held to an ethos that demonized money, materialism and luxury goods. The target of this ideology was often distilled into the single Yiddish word *luksus* (frequently spelled *luxus*), which was presented as being incompatible with the Hasidic ideals of modesty, asceticism and unchanging ways. This paper seeks to historicize the term *luksus* and its meaning for Williamsburg Hasidim by looking at its usage in a number of sources including statements by the Satmar Rebbe, Joel Teitelbaum (1887-1979), writings in the Satmar organ, *Der Yid*, and the work of performer Yom Tom Ehrlich (1914-1990). I argue that the discourse on *luksus* was a way to mark Hasidic religious difference in the postwar era of widespread Jewish assimilation, suburbanization, and acculturation to middle-class American mores. At the same time, as some Hasidim became financially successful, the Hasidic attitude towards *luksus* served as a check, internally among Hasidim, against social change in the postwar period. Ultra-Orthodox communal attitudes toward economics, like those on the state, language, neighbor relations, and Israel, cut to the core of Jewish identity. Steve Wasserstrom's "Nine Theses on the Study of Religion" shed light on the emergence of Williamsburg Hasidism in this context. Citing "economic transaction" among several prime examples of modes of interreligious contact, Wasserstrom writes, in his second thesis, "a critical study of religion applies itself to continuous cross-fertilizations of identity. Religion remakes itself in challenges to identity that provide identity."[2]

A large segment of Williamsburg Hasidim arrived in New York in the late 1940s as refugees after surviving the Holocaust, especially in Hungary and Romania. Empty-handed, and in some cases orphaned, many of these Hasidim settled into Williamsburg's "brownstone barracks" and entered blue-collar professions in which the

---

I am grateful to Nathaniel Deutsch, Kambiz GhaneaBassiri, Paul Robertson, and the participants in the October 2017 conference in honor of Steve Wasserstrom for their comments on this paper.

language barrier was not a problem.³ Through extraordinary leadership and vision, the Satmar Rebbe led the transformation of this linguistically, culturally, and religiously heterogeneous group of religious new arrivals into a more unified Yiddish-speaking community with ultra-Orthodox ideals. The ideals espoused by the Satmar Rebbe were often defined against those of other Jews already living in Williamsburg, who were not considered to be "real Jews." As many Jews left Williamsburg for other neighborhoods in Brooklyn, or the suburbs, Hasidim in Williamsburg entrenched themselves in the inner city; as most Jews stopped speaking and reading Yiddish, Hasidim expanded their daily use of the language at home, in schools, and in media; as mainstream Jewry rallied around the cause of the State of Israel, the Satmar Rebbe doubled down on his anti-Zionism, publishing a treatise outlining his views in 1961; and as Jews entered the middle class in large numbers, Williamsburg Hasidim rejected middle-class mores and consumerism that valued personal material gain and non-essential commodities.⁴ Despite a recently renewed interest in historicizing American Jews' relationship to capitalism, the economic behaviors and attitudes of Hasidic Jews—and American Jewish skepticism of capitalism more broadly—remain overlooked within this literature.⁵ Hasidim arrived in the United States at the start of a period of unprecedented economic growth and technological development, along with the rise of a consumer culture that championed innovations in the area of household conveniences.⁶ In this context, *luksus* was widely seen as a serious threat to the very existence of Hasidic Williamsburg. According to sociologist Israel Rubin, the driving force behind the establishment of Kiryas Joel, the major Satmar settlement outside of New York City, was that it would be a place "where the quest for luxury could be more easily tamed."⁷

At the same time that Hasidim cultivated a critique of *luksus*, some Hasidim threw themselves into business and rode the nationwide economic wave of production and spending to success in areas such as electronics, diamonds, and construction, much like other Jewish residents of Williamsburg who had settled there before the war. The Hasidic attitude toward *luksus* thus also served as a check against the growing wealth and changing mores of Williamsburg Hasidim over the course of their first decade in the United States. George Kranzler claimed that, for the Hasidim, the deprivations of the war years "made the newcomers eager to succeed" and even prone to "greediness"; the Satmar Rebbe "complained" about "the money-mindedness" of his flock.⁸ Although the type of self-governing community that the Rebbe favored could not function without wealthy members who subsidized institutions and charities, this "money-mindedness" came along with an attraction to amenities and housing of higher quality, part of a broader trend in "creating a Jewish consumer culture."⁹ For Williamsburg Jews in the 1940s, as Kranzler outlined, "the general trend was to spend more and spend it more casually ... the standard of comfortable living now included things that had been deemed luxuries" previously.¹⁰

The Satmar conception of *luksus* was built on an established tradition of central European Jewish religious animus toward luxury dating back to the early modern period.¹¹ But the word *luksus* also had particular valence in the early twentieth-century central European world in which many Williamsburg Hasidim lived before the Second World War. The term was popularized in the work of German sociologist Werner Sombart (1863–1941), who, though largely discredited today because of his associations with National Socialism, was once widely read and highly regarded. Sombart was a primary interlocutor with Max Weber, in particular over the question of the origins of capitalism. While Weber famously posited the centrality of the "Protestant work ethic" on this question in his now-classic 1905 study, Sombart's theory put Jews in the center of this story.[12] Specifically, Sombart emphasized Jews' role in the international trade of luxury goods. As he put it in a 1911 work, titled *The Jews and Modern Capitalism*, "The Jews for a long time practically monopolized the trade in articles of luxury, and to the fashionable world of the aristocratic seventeenth and eighteenth centuries this trade was of supreme moment. What sort of commodities, then, did the Jews specialize in? Jewelry, precious stones, pearls and silks."[13] Sombart further developed this idea in 1913, in *Luxury and Capitalism* (Luxus und Kapitalismus), which posited that the driving force of capitalism is the luxury taste of bourgeois women. This work had a far reach, and was published in a Yiddish translation in Warsaw as part of a "popular science library," as *Love, Luxus and Capitalism* in 1929. Sombart's works were widely read in Hungary and Romania, but he had close connections to Romania in particular.[14] His wife, Corina Leon, was a native of Iași (she served as Carl Schmitt's translator into Romanian), and Sombart lectured Jewish groups in Romania on his ideas.[15]

In some ways, the Satmar critique of capitalism epitomizes what Rebecca Kobrin has identified as "the fateful encounter of Sombart's exceptionalisms: the Jews and the United States."[16] The Sombartian sense of *luksus* as materialism included fancy household items—such as carpets, furniture, and drapes—which deemed women agents of immorality and cultural change for the worse. This view of materialism was a particularly good fit with the worldview developed by the Satmar Rebbe, who was known for his personal asceticism and fierce antipathy to technology and change both in Romania before the war and also in the United States afterward. Common targets of American Hasidic anti-*luksus* sentiment included furniture, appliances, household fixtures, luxuriant clothing, and extravagant weddings. In this way, the anti-*luksus* position sought specifically to control realms of Hasidic society associated with women, whose bourgeois tastes were blamed for cultural and religious deterioration. Fashion, or style, itself—as a fleeting preference—was antithetical to the benchmark Satmar concept of unchanging ways, and women's materialism was seen as a primary gateway to change.[17]

The Satmar Rebbe dealt with changing attitudes toward money and material goods with characteristic acuity. In a collection of stories of the Rebbe's sayings, the section titled "Against *Luksus*" contains a story in which a man visits the Rebbe to ask if it is permissible to have nice furniture or a "dining room set" in his apartment.[18] The Rebbe answers with a story about how his own grandfather, the Yetev Lev, did not have a table at home but instead used the pasta board as a desk; on Thursdays, when the Yetev Lev's wife would use the pasta board to begin to prepare for the Sabbath, he would hold his book in his hands. "The point is not to tell you that you should live in a home without a table and chairs," the Rebbe concluded, "but that you should hold before your eyes the words of the holy RaMBaN (Nachmanides), who said ... that you should be wary of every material thing lest you fall into *mosres* (excess/luxury)."[19]

The Rebbe was also wary that money could divide his community. Hertz Frankel, in his memoir of working in the Satmar school system, explains why the Satmar Rebbe hesitated to invest in developing a *kollel*, the system that supports a year or more of study for newly married men. The Rebbe's hesitation was against his followers' strong desire for a *kollel* and also a curious anomaly in the context of his indefatigable activities in establishing religious and educational institutions. According to Frankel: "He was afraid that a *kollel* would become a place for wealthy people to send their sons and sons-in-law and the average men would be left out. There simply weren't enough funds to support everyone. He feared it would become a 'rich man's club.'"[20] When the Rebbe did eventually establish a *kollel*, he interviewed applicants himself so as to make sure his fears about *kollel* wouldn't come true. According to one recollection of these interviews, "The first candidate came in, nervously anticipating a grueling *farher* (examination). 'How many people did you invite to your wedding?' began the Rebbe, 'at how much per couple? ... How much did your furniture cost? ... So much? And you want the community to support you? *Kollel* is not for you.'"[21] In other words, the Rebbe sought to limit, or at least control and manage, the emergence of a wealthy and powerful elite.

The problem of the corrupting influence of money was central to the founding mission of the Hisachdus Harabonim, one of the cornerstones of the Rebbe's organizational structure. The Hisachdus Harabonim, also known as the Central Rabbinical Congress of the United States and Canada, was created by the Satmar Rebbe and the Krasner Rebbe, Hillel Lichtenstein, as a more controlling alternative to the umbrella organization of Jewish communities that existed in Hungary. "We have to look back at all the great rabbis who came to this country before us and see what mistakes they made that led to the current situation in *kashrus, mikvaos*, and *chinuch* (kosher standards, ritual baths, and education)," the Satmar Rebbe said in his address at the organization's founding conference, held at the Satmar Beis Medresh in January of 1955.[22] Three months later, at the first convention of the Hisachdus Harabonim, the Rebbe announced that he thought most rabbis were under the influence of money and therefore compromised. "The influence of money is so great," he declared, "that to fear Hashem, love truth and hate money is not enough. An upright but poor judge may still rule incorrectly, due to his reliance on the money of others."[23] By contrast, the Satmar Rebbe himself, according to a member of his inner circle, could "not be bribed."[24]

On May 24, 1961, the Satmar Rebbe organized a large meeting of rabbis at which "the plague of *luksus*" was addressed directly. Called the "Kinus klali," or "General Assembly," the gathering was held in a ballroom at the Hotel St. George in Brooklyn. Hundreds of rabbis and an overflowing crowd of around 4,000 audience members were present to hear leaders of North American Orthodoxy address the major issues of the day.[25] In the opening address that evening, the Tzelemer Rav, Levi Yitzchok Greenwald, warned about the dangers of the free street. He was followed by the Voideslaver Rav, Yissachar Ber Rottenberg, who made a few announcements and read aloud telegrammed greetings from President John F. Kennedy, Vice President Lyndon B. Johnson, Senator Kenneth Keating, and Mayor Robert Wagner. *Der Yid* reported a mood of "optimism."

Although *luksus* was one of many issues addressed that day, including modesty, Zionism, and unisex bathrooms, the dangerous lure of money was of central importance. According to Dovid Meisels, a biographer of the Satmar Rebbe, Teitelbaum opened his address at the meeting with a quote from Exodus 5:1: "Command the children of Israel and let them expel from the camp." Meisels summarized: "The message for this generation, said the Rebbe, is to expel violators of the Torah from our camp, and not to accept their money to fund Torah institutions. When *rabbanim* and *roshei yeshiva* (rabbis and heads of rabbinical academies) accept money from sinners, they no longer feel able to denounce their sins." The Rebbe went on to connect the corruption of money to the problem of *luksus*. As Meisels paraphrased, "Hundreds of thousands of dollars are invested into a new house with all the latest luxuries, yet the *mezuzos* that adorn the doorposts are of the cheapest quality, sometimes not even kosher. He denounced expensive bar mitzvahs and cheap, unkosher *tefillin* (phylacteries)."[26]

The *luksus* issue was highlighted at the Kinus Klali in a speech made by the Voidislaver Rav. The Voidislaver was close to the Satmar Rebbe—the Rebbe had sent him to meet with Vice President Richard Nixon in 1956.[27] *Der Yid* summarized his speech, which, using characteristically militaristic language, was called "Battle against the Plague of *Luksus*":

> The Voidislaver Rav [...] focused on the plague of *luksus* that corrupts and ruins every good achievement and every hard-won position and undermines the existence of the Jewish home. / [He] stressed that there are some more areas where some shared actions will be planned by the Hisachdus HaRabonim together with Agudas HaRabonim (Union of Orthodox Rabbis), [Yeshiva] Keren Torah and [Congregation] Chizuk Hadas. / The Voidislaver Rav also called on the Jewish communities to conduct themselves in the same manner as was done in the old country.[28]

By calling *luksus* a plague, the Voidislaver established it as part of a religious cosmology, in this case as an external force of change threatening the holy community and its customs. In his contrast between the United States and "the old country," he also framed the accumulation of capital and wanton spending as an innovation to be shunned within the Satmar-driven ideology against cultural change in the United States.

This de facto official position against *luksus* set the tone of negative attitudes toward money for the rest of the 1960s. In a study of Williamsburg published the year after the Kinus Klali, sociologist Solomon Poll noted that "the Hasidim are constantly exhorted to resist Americanization" and also identified the desire for monetary gain as the driving force behind assimilation and the potential breakdown of the community's hard-won coherence.[29] "Will the Hasidim be able to hold another generation in the community," Poll asked, "or will the tremendous lures of personal advancement and profit bring the young men out fully into the secular world?"[30] A 1963 study of Hasidic Williamsburg by the Anthropology Workshop of the Brooklyn Children's Museum observed, "At present the Hasidic community still regards the American value, which is based on monetary success, as unacceptable."[31]

One of the primary exponents of the concept of *luksus* in Hasidic Williamsburg was Yom Tov Ehrlich, a wedding entertainer, or *badkhn*—a communal role with a long history in Hasidism.[32] Ehrlich produced a number of popular recordings of his original compositions, including three albums of recorded music in the 1960s, that dealt directly with the topic of *luksus*: "Ameritchke," produced in 5724 (1963–4) and "Luksus" Parts 1 and 2, which came out at the end of 5726 (the summer of 1966). The prologue to "Ameritchke"—or, "America" with a diminutive suffix—states, "This cassette came out in 5724/its clear goal is to ridicule and make fun of, in the manner of

[Talmudic] 'mockery of idolatry,' the *treyf* (non-kosher) American way of life/so that real Jews [erlikhe yidn] won't be drawn, God forbid, into bad customs of materialism [geshmies], desire and licentiousness but live ... just like in the old country in Europe."[33]

Ehrlich was born just before the outbreak of the First World War in Kazan Horodok, a shtetl near the Pripet Marshes in the White Russian region of the Russian Empire, today in southwestern Belarus.[34] After spending the Second World War years in Samarkand, Ehrlich went to Paris, where he was exposed to the culture of materialism he would later critique. As he states in "Luksus" Part 1: "The mother of 'luksus' is 'style,' is fashion/As I'm sure you know/Its center is in Paris."[35] Once he had settled in Williamsburg, Ehrlich began his work as a *badkhn*, performing as a jester at weddings and festivities such as Purim.[36] After "consulting" with rabbinic authorities, Ehrlich began producing recordings of his *badkhones* (wedding rhymes) to satisfy the demand for his tunes. Over his long career, Ehrlich recorded hundreds of 78s, LPs, and tapes, which were compiled into thirty-six albums.[37] Ehrlich's geographic origins and Yiddish dialect differed from most Williamsburg Hasidim, and he remained a Hasid of the Stolin-Karlin sect. However, he was close to the Satmar Rebbe, and his recordings gave Williamsburg Hasidim of all denominations a common vocabulary to describe *luksus*.

While Ehrlich was known for his *badkhones*, he actually only moonlighted as an entertainer, at least at first; by day he worked as a diamond cutter in Manhattan, following the path of many postwar immigrants. This meant that he would have seen firsthand the rapid increase and later plateauing of wealth among diamond merchants in the 1940s. George Kranzler provided the most detailed account of the diamond boom, writing, "More than any other single factor—even the general economic boom due to the war situation—the rise of the diamond trade was responsible for the greatest material as well as spiritual boom Jewish Williamsburg has known."[38] According to Kranzler, men with no previous experience in the diamond trade, including "religious functionaries," joined the business in droves as "salaries increased by leaps and bounds."[39] The diamond boom "affected practically every aspect of the community life of Jewish Williamsburg," in Kranzler's assessment, "and changed the entire economic pattern described [earlier]. Not only did it introduce a new social elite and reform the social valuations, it changed the community's appearance and standards of living."[40] Ehrlich also apparently had *yikhes*—or some inherited social standing, and perhaps money—through his marriage to the daughter of R. Elimelech Moskowitz "of the respected Williamsburg *balebatim* (ruling class)."[41]

In addition to having some knowledge of the Hasidic and non-Hasidic Jewish *nouveau riche* of Williamsburg, Ehrlich had a front-row seat to the changes in Hasidic wedding customs that so angered the Satmar Rebbe. Jerome Mintz and George Kranzler both point to extravagant weddings, and, in Mintz's astute observation, "press photos of opulent weddings," as significant performances of wealth and status within the Hasidic community.[42] One of the *badkhn*'s primary roles was to be "a moralizing entertainer at weddings, whose songs were often rendered in quasi speech-like style" that held up a mirror to the community's contradictions.[43] According to Kranzler, the Williamsburg *badkhn* "'says Gramen,' rhymed humorous stanzas" about the couple and "makes light comments about the guests, public figures, current events, or issues in Jewish communal life."⁴⁴ As Herbert Gans observed in his study of performer Mickey Katz, mid-century Jewish wedding entertainers had an audience of "the restless children of unassuming east-European immigrants who have with amazing speed moved up in the American middle-class society their parents never entered," people for whom economic striving and the "criticism of the mass media culture" were incisive topics.⁴⁵ The *badkhn*'s role in these performances of wealth and power gave him a unique position—sanctioned by the community and sanctified by tradition—to criticize and sometimes ridicule the community in ways that even rabbis and *Der Yid* could not. Ironically, Ehrlich spread his message against innovation through the latest recording technology, and worked as a professional wedding entertainer whose main *shtik*, as it were, was to denounce the attention and money people gave to their weddings. Yet, Ehrlich was approved by no higher authority than the Satmar Rebbe himself, who was known to have Ehrlich entertain at his own Purim table, where *badkhonim* would give "Purim Torah," a humorous mock sermon featuring faux etymologies and Talmudic bon mots that strongly informed Ehrlich's style.⁴⁶ The Satmar Rebbe himself was known for his own sharp wit, which, like Ehrlich, frequently inverted the absurdities of modern life with wordplay.⁴⁷ To give just one example, in a speech the Rebbe gave on Yom Kippur in 1954, he said, "'Television' lives up to its name; it makes a *'tel,'* a mound, out of a *Yiddishe* home."⁴⁸

Much of Ehrlich's work deals with the problem of *luksus* in the Hasidic community. For example, in "Ameritchke," Ehrlich gives a humorous faux etymology of the word "capitalism" as "kaput iz ales" (everything is broken) and says, "although every country upholds it/it will grow big and fat/but this is an old way/to stuff a goose for slaughter."⁴⁹ Ehrlich also declares, "The unluckiest man in America is the millionaire."⁵⁰ In America, according to Ehrlich, people work too much in order to buy material things; *luksus*, then, becomes a distraction from traditional Hasidic values of learning and piety, and also the deeply ingrained frugality and pragmatism of Eastern Europeans, and of Holocaust survivors. "Luksus" Part 1 begins with a long parody of the desires of a newly married bride and groom, including an expensive ring, telephones, and dining rooms, part of what he calls, "the *luksus* epidemic."⁵¹ Ehrlich calls *luksus* "the new paradise" and unpacks its meaning in a subsection in which Satan leads a young Hasidic man astray:

> He sees a fresh, young, maybe newly married man,
> or a new Jewish immigrant from the other side of the ocean,
> He arrives with advice, a plan,
> There are a lot of dollars in this land,
> You can quickly become a millionaire,
> You don't have to sit and learn
> You need to have lines of credit
> You need to run around here and there
> In real estate, horses and stocks,
> Have a jewelry box,
> And not a year will go by
> And you'll become a millionaire.⁵²

Ehrlich provides tongue-in-cheek religious justification for working less. The word "busy," he says, "comes from the word 'bizas Mitzrayim,' and 'bizas ha-yam,'" or the "spoils of Egypt and spoils of the sea," a reference to the objects taken by the Israelites from the Egyptians, in Exodus, and items which washed ashore after the Egyptians drowned."[53] Ehrlich continues, "There is another religious interpretation of 'busy,' for us in this country/Busy comes from the word *bizoyen* [disgrace]/a shame and a pity/ Work through both day and night, and never take a holy book in your hand."[54] In a section called "A Conversation about *Luksus*," Ehrlich gives the term *luksus* this same treatment:

> The name *luksus* is a mix/of the holy language and English/and it only has value together, "luk" is in English "look" and "sus" is in the holy tongue "a horse"/so together it means, "luk-sus"—"look a horse"/and the meaning is very true! Don't work like a horse, on things that have no value because they only have a value if the other doesn't have it, and I tell you the truth, when people get a lot of stuff, it comes from *luksus*, it's a natural thing, ten years ago a Frigidaire was a *luksus* item, today there's no house in which you won't see one. *Luksus* is a thing, that may be pretty, but you can also live without it, you don't buy it for its own sake, but for others, for the world, so everyone understands that the guy has money.[55]

Elsewhere, Ehrlich goes into greater detail about how things were better in the past, before technological advances:

> Once the Jewish housewife knew/how to wash a mountain of clothes with her own hands/Rubbing, soaping, squeezing, here and back, and just when she hung up a healthy load, she was full of happiness, and for so long, a housewife used to buy a stick of ice for a quarter, and cool the food on it, today every house needs a Frigidaire, nothing happens without a washing machine, and a washing machine without a dryer, is like a cantor without a choir, and she can't make anything without a mixer, and a dishwasher is no longer even a *luksus* item.[56]

"Luksus" Part 2 includes a piece entitled "Luksus" that describes how immigrant Jews act in American stores:

> Drapes, with Persian carpets near them,
> All the best of Uncle Sam,
> The finest crystal, silver in the world.
> It is a sin
> To leave them in the store
> Especially when you pay "without cash."
>
> Luksus—a living world!
> Luksus—you go around and brag!
> Grandchildren of Auntie Sorah
> Look just like, *keyn a hora* (no evil eye, i.e. knock on wood)

The husband doesn't know who they are.
And the house is like a mirror,
Like it's just been ironed,
You're afraid to set foot in it.⁵⁷

Ehrlich defines and redefines *luksus* throughout the poem. "Luksus is the fashion today"; "Luksus is a sorrow on the world"; "Luksus—everything is covered in plastic"; "Luksus is today more important than anything else [*haynt iberal*]"; "Luksus is only a *khaye sha'a* (a hedonistic pleasure in the present), today it is here, tomorrow it's gone."⁵⁸

By the late 1960s, large-scale flight of non-Hasidic Jews from Williamsburg and other parts of Brooklyn only deepened the social and economic chasm between Hasidim and other Jews. Phyllis Franck opened her 1969 study of the neighborhood by highlighting how definitional Hasidic opposition to luxuries had become, writing, "25,000 ultra-orthodox Jews live without televisions, movies or miniskirts, in what they feel is a special communion with God."⁵⁹ Contempt for *luksus* remained a common topic of Hasidic editorials. In a 1969 article in *Der Yid* called "The American Exile," R. Elchanan Yosef Hertzman wrote that America is so prosperous that people sometimes forget that they are in exile. Hertzman criticized the individual, stereotypical Jewish immigrant who says he "wants a million dollars for me and my children" while the broader Jewish community disintegrates. "If the shame of something from the past, remembered by familiar neighbors who knew my parents, bothers you a little—well, you just move away, and you keep moving further and further." Unlike the "old fashioned" older generation sitting in their darkened home, today, Hertzman lamented, "people turn two windows into one big window, across from a crystal lamp, and in front of a case full of silver, so everyone can see."⁶⁰

A Yiddish tractate published anonymously in Williamsburg in 1975–1976 (5736) continued the rabbinic criticism of *luksus*. This book, called *We Search for Our Path*, placed *luksus* second in a long list of the major issues of the day. The chapter called "Mosros (Luksus)" contains a multipart breakdown of common *luksus* violations. The list included, in summary:

1-Buying expensive clothing, especially in popular *goyishe* styles; shopping
2-Paying for expensive and extravagant weddings, including wedding halls and feasts; "a day later it is all forgotten"
2a-Buying expensive rings, wedding invitations, flowers, wedding photos, "which is really not a Jewish thing," and theatrical ceremony
2b-Buying expensive, foreign furniture only because it is expensive; also *shtraymls* (fur hats); "people throw thousands in hard-earned money at nothing"
3-"In the same way, the apartment has become royally decked out as if for the Kaiser himself," with chandeliers, flowers, etc.
[...]
5-Working overtime; "working like a dog" to earn money to buy all the things, "and it's all in order to be able to yield to womanly and—*lehavdil* (pardon the comparison)—*goyishe* caprices."⁶¹

These examples demonstrate how men often considered women to be drivers of *luksus* and the bridge to non-Jewish styles.

In the 1990s, animus against *luksus* was still strong. One Hasidic woman in Williamsburg told George Kranzler, "Thank God, we have what we need because we have higher values and goals than luxuries, going out, and attending the movies and eating out at fancy restaurants."[62] This attitude toward *luksus* appears to have survived into the era of Deborah Feldman's late twentieth-century childhood, but not much further. With the spread of gentrification and the internet into Hasidic Williamsburg, modern devices and mores have become more commonplace in Hasidic homes. The 2006 obituary of a well-known 93-year-old Williamsburg Hasidic woman highlighted the shift: "With so many children, Mrs. Schwartz had to make six loaves of challah for every Sabbath, using 12 pounds of dough—in later years, she was aided by Kitchenaid or Hobart appliances. (Mrs. Mayer said her mother had weaknesses for modern conveniences, and for elegant head scarves.)"[63] Deborah Feldman warned, "It is luxury that leads to sin, Zeidy used to say, because it makes us comfortable and lazy, turns our bones soft and our minds numb," but she herself became captivated by the "shimmering glass condominiums" that sprouted in Williamsburg during her lifetime.[64] Upstate Hasidic enclaves did not become bastions of economic modesty; on the contrary, families who live there, according to a stereotype articulated in an interview with a Williamsburg woman, "have to show off with their clothes, cars, and chandeliers."[65] As some Williamsburg Hasidim have recently accumulated large amounts of wealth, much of it derived from the explosion of the neighborhood's real estate market around the turn of the century, luxuries such as expensive *shtrayml*s and sumptuously appointed apartments are widely advertised in the Yiddish press. Indeed, these advertisements, such as one for a home goods store on the front page of *Der Yid* in November 2016, sometimes use the word "luxuries" as a selling point.

Epilogue: Nine Riddles

Steven M. Wasserstrom

> I pursued a maiden and clasped a reed.
> Gods and man, we are all deluded thus!
> —P. B. Shelley

RIDDLE ONE
The Summer of 2016
Lear, Goethe, Reik, Freud, Cogan

From the bookshelf of my beach-house host, Nathan Cogan, I randomly select a tantalizing title: *Pagan Rites in Judaism: From Sex Initiation, Magic, Moon-Cult, Tattooing, Mutilation, and Other Primitive Rituals to Family Loyalty and Solidarity* (1964). The psychoanalyst Reik dates his prologue "New York, October 1963." Reik was 75 years old, had published over twenty books, yet still wistfully admits in that prologue that his "technology" of "research into prehistoric Israel" was received by reviews "mostly negative."[1] My 80-year-old beach-house host, Nathan, inscribed this wistful volume "Nathan Cogan Berkeley May 1969" in a bold hand and red ink.

My eyes were immediately drawn to the epilogue. Reik reproduces a letter from his Viennese mentor Sigmund Freud, dated June 13, 1939, which the recipient reports to have been lost or forgotten. This recollection in turn reminds the nostalgic Reik of a conversation he had had with Freud in "1930 or 1931" concerning Goethe and King Lear. Reik's recollection leads him to re-create the precise scene of Freud pulling Goethe off his shelf. Reik formally reenacts the scene: "I get up from the chair (and I'm aware of making the same slow motions that Freud had then) and search for that volume of Goethe among my books: I find the lines: '*Ein alter Mann ist stets ein König Lear!*' An old man is always a King Lear!"[2] Reik's project, as it then turns out, was rooted in his own childhood King Lear, his grandfather. "It was my grandfather who first initiated me into the knowledge of Jewish rites ... and who showed me a sukkah in a Vienna Street, near a synagogue. I was perhaps eight years old then [i.e. 1896]."[3] Reik's sweet research into Jewish prehistory could only occur once he himself was an old man: "An old man is always a King Lear!"

Reoccupation is significance.[4] Cogan, Reik, Freud, Goethe, Shakespeare ... "*I get up from the chair (and I'm aware of making the same slow motions ...)."*

RIDDLE TWO
Seattle Visit
August 2016
Cruise, Trump, Puccini, Pavorotti, Dumézil
You have conquered!
Calaf to Turandot, *Turandot*, Act III

Relaxing after long research hours in the library, I watch Tom Cruise save Western Civilization in the Vienna Opera House. In *Rogue Nation* (2015) his CIA boss (Alec Baldwin) declares that "[Ethan] Hunt is the living manifestation of destiny." Hardly a King Lear, maybe not destiny, but Hunt is a winner. The viewer can make no mistake about it, since the Opera House scene climaxes with *I WILL WIN!* The victorious cry "*Vince rò!*" from Puccini's *Turandot* "*Nessun Dorma*" aria (Act III, Scene I).

And what is this victory? I quote some recent insights into mighty Turandot:[5]

Not only is Turandot an opulent, Orientalist fantasy set in imperial China by a composer who never set foot in Asia; Puccini also held a sympathetic spot in his heart for the fascist Italian dictator Benito Mussolini. The composer's late-career admiration for Mussolini's policies has prompted a new generation of historians to see his operas—especially Turandot—through a political lens ... In 2016 [Pavarotti's] signature recording of the aria "*Nessun Dorma*" began appearing regularly at Donald Trump's campaign events. In July, Pavarotti's family told Trump to stop playing the aria at rallies, saying the GOP nominee's values are "incompatible" with the singer's "values of brotherhood and solidarity."

The conjunction of Trump and Pavarotti led to Puccini himself, according to Brian Wise:

"*Mussolini was undoubtedly sent by God for the salvation of Italy*," [Puccini] wrote ... A few days after the dictator took power, Puccini sent Mussolini a congratulatory telegram. A year later, the composer was made an honorary member of the Fascist Party, and, soon after, a "Senator of the Realm."

How is it that Puccini's *Turandot* was perfect for orchestrating contemporary politics in operatically elaborate allegory? After all, *Turandot*'s core riddle would seem to transcend their historical moment: a princess who asks her suitors to answer three riddles and cuts off their heads if they are unable to answer correctly and a prince who will perish if people learn his name.

The first riddle is "What is born each night and dies at dawn?"
The Answer is hope.
The second riddle is "What flickers red and warm like a flame, yet is not fire?"

The answer is "blood."
The third riddle is "What is like ice yet burns?"
The answer is "Turandot."

These are ancient riddles. They form a kind of chain from Nizami's *Haft Paykar* (c. 1197),[6] to Schiller's 1801 *Turandot, Prinzessin von China* to Puccini to Trump and Cruise. In each Turandot we find a "Riddle-princess" or "suitor test,"[7] studied minutely in 1928 by Jan de Vries[8] and applied by Georges Dumézil, in his astonishing "Temps et mythes" of 1936. The motif of the three riddles was richly illuminated by Dumézil and de Vries. They re-appear in a study by Carl Hentze, in the first issue of *Antaios*, which Eliade edited with Ernst Jünger.[9]

> Ours is a century of cults. I have spoken at length about this with my friends Eliade and Jünger, and with Furio Jesi. Have you met [Jesi]? … It is a shame that he died so young. Perhaps because he doubted. *I instead made a pact with the Gods* [emphasis mine].[10]
> —Georges Dumézil, July 17. 1986 interview in *il Giornale*[11]

Dumézil died on October 11, 1986, a scant three months after making this confession. Dumézil's friends Eliade and Jünger co-published *Antaios*, which, as I said, featured Turandot's "Riddle Princess" in its first issue.

If you are interested in winning, Schiller, Puccini, Pavorotti, Dumézil, Cruise, Trump have just the riddles for you … But if you want to learn what *Vince Ro! I will win!* means in *Turandot*, is the correct answer Dumézil's "I have made a pact with the gods"?

RIDDLE THREE
The Appearance of the Stars, Paris 1942
Jünger [June 7, 1942] and Dunia Wasserstrom [July 1942]

In Paris, June 7, 1942, the most honored soldier in the occupying German army, the celebrated Ernst Jünger, lunched at Maxim's on Rue Royale.[12] We know this because, in his Paris diary, Jünger recorded what randomly happened after lunch. Jünger walked out onto the Rue Royale and saw three girls wearing the Jewish star.[13] According to this widely reproduced entry from the Paris diary, this was the first time—June 7, 1942—that Jünger beheld the yellow Star.[14]

> *Dans la rue Royale, j'ai rencontré, pour la première fois de ma vie, l'étoile jaune, portée par trois jeunes filles qui sont passées près de moi bras dessus, bras dessous […] Je considère cela comme une date qui marque profondément, même dans l'histoire personnelle.*

And years later Jünger claimed, "*J'ai toujours salué l'étoile, avouera-t-il plus tard.*" Even stronger versions persist: "*L'officier de la Wermacht salue militairement l'étoile jaune à chaque fois qu'il la croise.*"[15] Readers praise his gesture as a courageous salute.[16]

Others not so much so.[17] We might wonder about that. On March 30, 1942, barely a month before he famously saw those three girls strolling outside Maxim's, Jünger wrote the following in the same Paris diary:

> Claus Valentiner returned from Berlin. He reported about a horrible fellow, previously a drawing teacher, who supposedly boasted of having led a death squad in Lithuania and other borderlands, which slaughtered innumerable people. After rounding up the victims, one forces them to dig mass graves, then lie down inside them, and then they shoot them dead in layers from above. Before this they rob them of every last thing they have, down to the last shirt.[18]

In this polished anecdote the *novelist* Jünger quotes his *painter* friend Valentiner quoting a *drawing* teacher. Could these three artists not consider this slaughter beautiful? Does it surprise us that Jünger did? This was his reaction: "Grotesque images of the Athenian famine. Thus, at the climaxes of a great Wagner concerto the trombones decline because the weakened woodwinds cannot sustain the necessary breath."[19] *Trombones.*

Jünger's artistic young friend Klaus Valentiner, who reported this terrible anecdote, also happened to be a friend of Patrick Modiano's mother.[20] Patrick Modiano, you will recall, won the Nobel Prize for Literature in 2014. He came to fame in 1968 with *Place de l'étoile*. Modiano's joke epigraph for *Place de l'étoile* was set on the street, meeting passing Jews, precisely as in Jünger's Nazi-occupied Paris in June 1942:

> In the month of June 1942, a German officer approaches a young man and says, "Pardon, sir, where is the Place de l'Étoile?" The young man gestures to the left side of his chest.
>
> (Jewish story)[21]

The novelist underwrites this as "(Jewish story)," although it may read, to us, rather like a riddle.

Modiano puns on *place de l'Étoile* both as a location in Paris and as the blazing symbol of Nazi occupation; Modiano's pun re-occupies Jünger's widely repeated occupation diary incident.

The art teacher, the drawing student, the diarist soldier, Patrick Modiano's mother, a kind of sad contemporary caravanserai along the Rue Royale. Not quite the living embodiment of destiny. Writing these words that you are reading is a little Jewish Lear, a mere teacher of religion, himself a 68er, *aware that I am making the same slow motions*. Aware that I am repeating the sad punchline: "*The young man gestures to the left side of his chest.*"

RIDDLE FOUR
"*You don't make up this kind of detail, ladies and gentlemen.*"

April 18, 1964: Dunia Wasserstrom Arrives in Frankfurt; April 23, 1964: testifies against Stark, Dylewsky, Broad, and Boger.[22] On April 23, 1964, Dunia Wasserstrom, a

Jewish survivor of Auschwitz, gave the following testimony in the Frankfurt courtroom where a score of former members of the concentration camp staff were on trial:

> I remember a day on which Jewish children were brought to Auschwitz. They arrived in a truck that stopped a moment in front of the political department. A small boy, clasping an apple in his hands, jumped off the truck. Boger and another S.S. man by the name of Draser watched the scene from the door of the political department.
>
> I was standing at a window outside. The child stood by the truck fondling the apple in his hand and seemed to enjoy himself. Boger approached the boy grabbed him by his feet, and smashed him head first against the wall of the barracks. Unruffled, he then picked up the apple and Draser told me *to wash "that" off the wall*. About an hour later I was called to Boger to interpret an interrogation during which I saw him calmly munch the boy's apple.

Dunia told the story to a biographer before it become notorious around the world:[23] "Later in the day, Boger's wife and his small child came to visit him, and he took his own child on his lap and fondled it, and then reached into his desk drawer and took out the apple and gave it to his child."[24]

Another reporter observed: "In Auschwitz Dounia Ourisson-Wasserstrom was compelled to watch Boger pick up a small child by his legs and kill him by beating his head against the wall. Then she had to wash off the blood. 'Since then I haven't been able to look at a child without crying,' she says. When she became pregnant after the liberation, she had an abortion."[25]

> A most unusual group of survivors discovered by the state through the International Auschwitz Committee. This was a group of secretaries, transcribers, and translators who came to shed the most light on the activities of the Political Department of the Auschwitz I camp, where the brutal interrogation and torture of "political prisoners" took place. They are extraordinary because they were almost all Jewish, female, and privy to large amounts of information about the camp and its genocidal activities. Astoundingly, the large majority of them survived; of sixty-seven women, only six died in the camp. Nine of the survivors testified at the Auschwitz trial … The decision to put her on the stand was a wise one, for her recollections proved to be some of the most important and sensational in the entire trial.[26]

Indeed: "The story of the little boy has become part of a greater body of legendary tales of devastation, and makes up a crucial part of our historical imagination of the world of Auschwitz."[27]

Between 1945 and 1949, at least thirty-eight Auschwitz survivors publish memoirs and two collective memoirs are compiled: one of the very first, in 1946, was by the former Dounia Ourisson, our Dunia Wasserstrom.[28] Subsequently, the Holocaust denier Robert Faurisson cites Ourisson as "one of the best known" memoirs, in his landmark "Revisionist Chronicle. Impact and Future of Holocaust Revisionism."[29]

The internationally notorious holocaust denier David Irving appeared in Portland, Oregon, on October 16, 1992, precisely one year after Dunia's death. His "lecture" was attended by Ku Klux Klan members, Christian Identity believers, neo-Nazis, and one little Jewish professor. Verbatim from my testimony for the *Lipstadt* v. *Irving* trial in London:

> [Irving] described Adolf Eichmann's anguish on witnessing one such mass shooting. Eichmann had been standing so close to the event that the brains of a Jewish baby splattered on his greatcoat, which his chauffeur had to wipe off. After recounting this, Mr. Irving concluded by saying: "*You don't make up this kind of detail, ladies and gentlemen.*"

Writing to his friend Carl Schmitt on February 10, 1945, Ernst Jünger, far from denying the Holocaust, instead made it a myth. A myth of Jewish reoccupation.

> One would have to re-read Flavius Josephus; how extraordinary is the obstinacy of the Jews in the siege of Jerusalem. As proven by these experiences, loyalty to their [Jewish] forefathers obstructed a return to paganism. They had only the choice between the Old Testament and the New Testament—each attack on the New Testament benefits the Old Testament.
>
> This is one of the reasons for the monstrous propagation of Jewish ethics, apart from the fact that this ethics, precisely *by means of the extermination of the Jews to which it had been bound*, was now released and virulent. It is rather spooky, how the blind will conduct itself *ad absurdum*.[30]

Josephus, Jünger, Dunia, a nameless child with an apple, Boger "The Beast of Auschwitz," Adolf Eichmann's chauffeur, David Irving ...

In that piece in which Freud cites Goethe, Cordelia forces [her father King Lear] to "make friends with the necessity of dying."[31]

RIDDLE FIVE
"*I seemed to be acting in a movie.*"

We read the following in Dunia's autobiography:[32]

> A gentleman who had my same last name ... read the editorial page of the *New York Times* about my intervention in this trial. He added that they were six brothers and two sisters, for several generations born in the United States of America. We knew that with the same name was no one who was not of the same family or family tree ...

> He brought a lot of data on the family, [and] indeed, [our] ancestors came from the same village.

> —Very nice people ... "Tell them that we adopt as our cousins."
> *I had to laugh because it was like a movie.* We hugged and added:
> —From now on, you are our cousins.

—Enchanted-Lucien said. I am very happy because during World War II, I lost my whole family in the gas chambers, and I only had two cousins living in Israel. And so, just like that, we were admitted into a large clan of relatives in the U.S. A year later, they invited us to visit them. We went and when I saw so many cousins, brothers, sisters, nephews, nieces, all typical Americans, who marched in front of us, I was afraid. We were very different, but seeing that they so affectionately received us and adopted us as cousins, I was moved. They have a real ranch, with many cows, horses and land sown. All businesses have, warehouses, shops, transport, and belong, like the ranch, to the whole family together. Everyone works for everyone ...

Once we went with them to the wedding of a cousin. The ceremony was to take place in another city. We settled on several bus coaches, all with the inscription: "The family ... traveling to this city for the wedding ..."

During the trip I had fun, especially when we were accommodated in a hotel and in which two entire floors were rented for the whole family. *I seemed to be acting in a movie ...*

My testimony at the Frankfurt trial of Auschwitz perpetrators gave me the opportunity to find relatives of whom I have never dreamed.

Torture, a trial, an exile, a serendipitous discovery, a memorable bus caravan, by a woman who had long ago *"made friends with the necessity of dying."* Dunia Wasserstrom died on October 1, 1991.

RIDDLE SIX
Second Seattle Visit, June 2013
"The game has already been played."

In Seattle Hotel Deca, art deco digs and spring sun flooding through high Cascadian windows, time to think. So I browse bookshops; I serendipitously notice Dumézil's *The Riddle of Nostradamus* in the window of the Magus Bookshop. I am delighted to discover that this delicately arcane oddity was the last publication of the 86-year-old Georges Dumézil.

Dumézil (1898–1986) published *The Riddle of Nostradamus: A Critical Dialogue* (originally published as " ... *Le moyne noir en gris dedans Varennes*" in 1984) two years before his demise at age of 88. I am transfixed by the *apologia pro vita sua* that Dumézil left us in the form of riddle. A diverting if faintly repellent testament from a quirky sort of mandarin genius. I note for the moment that in *The Riddle of Nostradamus: A Critical Dialogue*, he asserts that *"a god is a necessity,"*[33] and he suggests Socrates making friends with the necessity of dying was like making a pact with the gods: "It is also about a course of action, a decision—and a decision that is imminent, whose urgency the two partners emphasize."[34]

This pact may have something to do with prophecy: Nostradamus "had access to the archives of the future, or was invaded by them."[35] Dumézil then gives several theories of prophecy.[36] A small circle of friends invents a prophecy, a future scenario—in other words, re-occupies Nostradamus.

Narrator writing to son of a friend about events with the friend fifty years before, then, invokes 1937,[37] when he fell asleep and saw the friend in a vision.[38] The two re-occupy Greek names and begin a dialogue concerning Socrates's last words. They assert "respect for philology" exclaiming "so much grammar in these few words!"[39] They then philologically deconstruct the mysterious Socratic sentence "I OWE A COCK TO AESCLEPIUS."

A dreamy retrospect nourished the 86-year-old philologian. He belonged nostalgically to Old Europe, loyal to the end to an anti-democratic elite, and they, his tiny intimate cohort, are what matters. They anciently precede and adamantly reject the French Revolution and are ultimately coexistent with the very Socrates himself. "The opinion of the majority, those who are ignorant, does not matter much," says his stand-in Socrates.[40] This apocryphon from his Part Two gives new depth to a sentence from Part One: "*De minimis non curat vates*" [the soothsayer pays no attention to the little people] (81). Socrates repeats that *only the opinion of the wise man matters* (109–10).

Tracking clues, whether by prophecy or philology, Georges Dumézil followed Nostradamus into the deep well of the past: From there, this old man cites the dream of another old man, Socrates's final dream, as he related it to Crito. "I thought I saw a beautiful and majestic woman all dressed in white came toward me, called me, and said '*Socrates, in three days you can arrive in fertile Phthia.*'"[41] The narrator then moves backward to the Homer echoed here by Socrates, when Achilles said to Ulysses, "*In three days I can be on the fertile soil of Phthia.*"[42]

In an early Eranos lecture, Eliade ended with an anecdote purportedly personally told to him by the Spanish man of letters Eugenio D'Ors.[43] D'Ors, according to Eliade's anecdote, burnt his favorite unpublished piece of the year on New Year's Eve. This ritual burning parallels the scenario in *The Riddle*, which opens with the aged Espopondie aided by the narrator in burning "several large envelopes still containing the ghosts of his life,"[44] which they ritually burnt one by one. Eliade of course himself "suffered" a fire of his papers.

I myself own a twice-burnt book. It was a gift made by Henry Corbin to Mircea, and it survived Eliade's office fire. A student I knew in Chicago retrieved it from the rubble and sent it to me. It then survived my own office fire.

I hope that this crisp relic makes the life experience of a working scholar and lifetime teacher of religion accessible to those interested in such things. Chips from my charred workshop.

Yes, I had a fire in my library. Shortly afterwards, I stumbled upon Walter Mehring's *The Lost Library*, which begins this way:

> The last place where I felt at home was Vienna. This was before Vienna fell and I was still surrounded by all the books of my father's library. I cannot remember how often since then the view outside my window has changed—a view more than once obstructed by wars. But in Vienna I still had my legacy of books: they had been salvaged thanks to the Czech Embassy in Berlin, and especially to the efforts of the Embassy attaché, Carroll Hoffmann, who was a lyric poet of the cabalistic-minded group, which numbered among its members Werfel, Meyrink, Kafka and Capek. Hoffmann was later burned alive in a crematorium.[45]

Mehring's *The Lost Library* lost memory itself ... but who can know how much memory has ever been lost? Alberto Manguel wrote "the version that haunts us is the other, the version of the library in ashes."[46] I still reach for lost books, some of which expressed a will to do the incinerating. Like Dumézil and Eliade, who themselves burned books.

The greatest scholars require the closest study,[47] to coin a phrase. Dumézil's philosophical summation[48] is satisfying and connects the dots set forth in the Nostradamus problem. By the way, in Berlin, in his November 15, 1942, entry, ironically recorded in his Paris diary, Jünger reflects both on Eliade and Nostradamus on the same day.[49] Heady days in occupied Paris. "The two weeks [Eliade] spent in Paris, in the autumn of 1943, in the company of Cioran, of Georges Dumézil, Paul Morand, and René Grousset, would substantially modify [his] inner alchemy."[50] On November 16, 1943, Eliade specifies he has just returned from fifteen days in Paris and returned with 200 books. Eliade wrote that he left Paris "heartsick. To have to stay in Portugal—when such a place as Paris exists! Surprised at the good situation of the Parisians. We didn't see anybody starving!"[51] Eliade thought 1943 Paris marvelous.

The Riddle of Nostradamus honors his old friends Eliade and Jünger; he cherishes his beloved philology; he confesses errors; he gives due both to Livy and to Socrates; he delights in making one last move in the great game, in "the great casino that is our world."[52] These are *his* dying words.

The greatest scholars of Paris found a way to keep prophecy alive while cultivating philology too.

A riddle it is: it has happened before. "The game has already been played."[53]

RIDDLE SEVEN
"God is Death"

Michel Foucault addressed Dumézil's death of Socrates almost as soon as it was conceived.

You will recall Dumézil on "I owe a cock to Aesclepius."

> Now this text, formulated in this way, referring to this kind of practice, has been interpreted in a fairly standard way which Dumézil amuses himself by synthesizing with some lines from a poem by Lamartine [*La mort de Socrate* (*"The Death of Socrates,"* 1823)]. Socrates, then, would have a debt to pay to Asclepius who had cured him. Of what, then, would Socrates have been cured, thus being in debt to Asclepius and having to thank him? What is this debt for? Well, with his death Socrates would have been cured of the illness of living ... Then, faced with this interpretation, Dumézil gets annoyed and says: Socrates has nothing in common with his colleague in sophistry, Sakyamuni. Socrates was not a Buddhist, and it is absolutely not a Greek idea, a Platonic, or a Socratic idea that life is an illness of which we are cured by death. So Dumézil symbolizes a whole interpretation with these lines from Lamartine. Actually this interpretation is neither Lamartinian nor Buddhist; it is a very traditional interpretation in the history of philosophy.[54]

Leo Strauss (1899–1973), an exact contemporary of Dumézil, offered an alternative interpretation to *Phaedo*'s "I owe a cock to Aesclepius." In his lecture on "Reason and Revelation," Strauss asserts that Aesclepius is a "hallucination," annotating the assertion: "Cf. also C. F. [Meyer], Heidegger: God is Death."[55] Here the Socrates of Strauss and the Socrates of Heidegger seem to agree that death is his divinity, and may indeed be a cure for life.

Socrates, Plato, Buddha, Lamartine, Strauss, Heidegger, Foucault. We schlepp in a philological line; we re-occupy the past. We approach Socrates but never arrive.

RIDDLE EIGHT
Conrad Ferdinand Meyer, Leo Strauss, Leo Perutz

As the tale goes, a European stranger wins the favor of the caliph of Cordova, ascends to the office of chief advisor and husband of the caliph's sister, Princess Sunshine. The nineteenth-century Swiss novelist Conrad Ferdinand Meyer, popular among certain sorts of Jews who were nostalgic for the days of the court Jew, writes:

> Sun and Moon, however, did not remain together longer than a year, as the birth of a little daughter cost the princess her life. Hereupon a hundred envious courtiers conspired secretly against the stranger, whose position they now considered less than secure. The wise young man exposed them, but magnanimously pleaded for their lives. One day, however, the caliph's slaves conducted ten mules laden with ten sacks each through the portals of the palace, and when attendants undid the sacks, the severed heads of his hundred enemies rolled out upon the marble pavement of the court. [One recalls the courtly beheading in Turandot.] The Prince immediately takes his daughter and escapes [Cordova]. With him departed forever the caliph's good fortune *and supremacy*.[56]

In Meyer's *Der Heilige* ("The Saint"; 1879), a historical novel about a real courtier, Thomas Becket, Becket is allegorized by Conrad Ferdinand Meyer in the figure of Prince Moonbeam, "as the citizens of Cordova called the stranger by reason of the soft pallor of his countenance."[57]

I turn to another parable about a foreign-born courtier, in this case, a court Jew. The Jewish Czech Israeli novelist Leo Perutz (1882–1957) published his final novel, *By Night Under the Stone Bridge*, in 1953.[58] *By Night Under the Stone Bridge* is a novel of finality, both personally and collectively. *By Night Under the Stone Bridge* does nothing less than confront the end-fate of the Jews of Prague. This decline occurred in three sharp phases. First in the seventeenth century, when Emperor Rudolf II exiled his chief financier Mordechai Meisl and other court Jews; again in 1893, when Prague's ancient Jewish ghetto was leveled; and finally, in the extermination of Czech Jewry at the hands of the Nazis.

One Berl Landfahrer, a schlemiel schlepper for the court Jew Meisl, is unjustly imprisoned, along with Meisl's poodle. In the dungeon, Berl Landfahrer experiences psychedelically kabbalistic visions, and then applies his kabbalistic secrets to acquire the understanding of his jail-mate poodle's dog language. Having acquired this occult insight, Berl Landfahrer learns that the poodle knows the location of Meisl's hidden fortune. Landfahrer lunges for the precious creature but the poodle runs off ... and Landfahrer goes mad.

> For many years after that he was to be seen in the ghetto and Old Town of Prague running after dogs, attracting and holding them and asking them whether they had seen a white poodle with black spots under one eye and over one ear, and telling them that if they met it they must tell it that he, Berl Landfahrer, had not been hanged, and that the poodle must take him to the Ufergasse, nothing would happen to it, it wouldn't be hanged, the fine had been paid for it too. The dogs would snap at him and struggle free, and Berl Landfahrer would run after them, and children would run after him, and grownups would shake their heads and say, "Poor Berl Landfahrer, that night in the prison cell he lost his human soul out of fright."[59]

Meisl's fate cuts the Prague Jews off from kabbalistic visions. "*He wanted to spend the whole night immersed in sacred matters, but the dogs wouldn't let him.*"[60]

In this gentle mockery, Leo Perutz simultaneously eulogized *and perpetuated* the wealth of Prague Jewry. In so far as that heritage was both spiritual and literal, in kabbalah as well as in Meisl's bags of gold ducats, the story itself achieves a kind of allegorical efficacy of its own. At the conclusion of *By Night Under the Stone Bridge*, the narrator is left literally holding nothing but fragments of Mordechai Meisl's will. *In continuity with the world of true riches, so the reader concludes, those fragments still suffice.*

No doubt at this point you are reminded of the parable with which I end *Religion after Religion*. It was the parable with which Scholem ended *Major Trends in Jewish Mysticism*. It was not a "traditional" tale, but rather an artwork devised by Shai Agnon.

> And the story-teller adds, the story which he told had the same effect as the [ritual magic] actions of the other three.[61]

And that too suffices. Now, Agnon suggests, we can only tell stories about a once-enchanted world. *But that too suffices.* "And the story-teller adds, the story which he told had the same effect as the actions of the other three."

Can the mere telling tales of kabbalah itself still *work*, can it still perpetuate kabbalah, as Scholem and Agnon seemed to believe? In fact, Scholem wrote privately, but repeatedly, throughout his life, that "nothing is left but fragments of Meisl's will?" *And that too suffices?*

Prince Moonbeam, Conrad Ferdinand Meyer, Leo Strauss, Leo Perutz, Baal Shem Tov, Mordechai Meisl, Berl Landfahrer, Agnon, and a poodle.

RIDDLE NINE
Yesterday

My aunt Miriam died yesterday at the age of 103.[62] Born in 1914, she was raised in the bleak coalfield villages of mountaintop West Virginia. From my brother I just learned yesterday the following:

On August 25, 1921, when Miriam was seven (and in Logan Elementary School), a huge conflict erupted between the miners and the coal companies (known for their cruel treatment of the miners). A family friend, Sheriff Don Chafin, was on the side of the coal companies and headed an "army" of local supporters when the miners marched to Blair Mountain, just outside Logan. Miriam remembered the event well because Ben, uncle Louis, Dave Freed and uncle Sam were recruited in the middle of the night (armed) to go to fight the miners. It was later named "The Battle of Blair Mountain" and received national attention as President Harding had to call in the National Guard to resolve the conflict. Books and movies have also been made about this event.

This battle was the biggest labor uprising in US history. It was not only large, but also well organized and one of the most heavily armed uprisings since the Civil War. For several days in summer of 1921, in Logan County, West Virginia, coal miners, estimated to number between 7,000 and 20,000, confronted government troops of several thousand men and strikebreakers, known as the Logan Defenders.[63] They included my uncles in their ranks. My aunt Miriam recalled staying up all night making coffee for the Logan Defenders.

At one time I had seventeen aunts and uncles; Miriam, the one who poured coffee for the Logan Defenders, was the last survivor. Like Dunia, Miriam was a kind of survivor. So, we cycle back to Reik's *Pagan Rites in Judaism: From Sex Initiation, Magic, Moon-Cult, Tattooing, Mutilation, and Other Primitive Rituals to Family Loyalty And Solidarity*.

As for solidarity, I share a final memory. In the momentous location of Jerusalem in the momentous year 2000, I attended the state funeral of Israel's national poet, Yehuda Amichai. One of his last great poems was titled "Jewish Travel: Change Is God and Death Is His Prophet." Amichai embraced change as "part of the cycle":

> Speak O my soul, Change is God.
> The cycle is all: the cycle of blood in the body, the cycle of water,
> of prayers for the holy days. Speak O my soul, sing
>   O my soul, to the God who is Himself part of the cycle
> of praise and lament, curse and blessing.
> Speak O my soul, sing O my soul, Change is God
> and death is His prophet.[64]

We scholars belong to "the cycle of praise and lament, curse and blessing" whose links for the WORK ON RELIGION must be datable, must have names, most belong to human action and human memory and human responsibility. In WORK ON RELIGION we live in real time, even the greatest scholars can only thrive in these constraints, the binds of human time and human space, only one at a time per body, even though "the game has already been played." Nevertheless, Reoccupation is significance itself: "*I get up from the chair and I'm aware of making the same slow motions*" as did Reik did for Freud who did for Goethe who did for Lear … It's part of the cycle, Work on Religion repeating itself, work on religion is repeating itself again, what choice do we have, King Lear leads us at the battle of Blair Mountain and all I got was this lousy riddle.

Enough. By now you bright pupils guessed the real meaning of the riddle. *I got you. You* reoccupy the Work on Religion! Take it from me, although you already know it is true, the game has already been played; this is a Vocation worth the work. So, *"get up from the chair and make the same slow motions."* In so doing if you are very, very lucky (as I have been), you can make *your* students *your* teachers.

Notes

Chapter 1

1. Steven M. Wasserstrom, "Nine Riddles," in this volume, §9.
2. Steven M. Wasserstrom, *Religion after Religion: Gershom Scholem, Mircea Eliade, and Henry Corbin at Eranos* (Princeton, NJ: Princeton University Press, 1999), x.
3. Steven M. Wasserstrom, "Nine Theses on the Study of Religion," in this volume, §5.
4. Personal communication between Wasserstrom and Wolfson (April 2, 1994), cited in Elliot R. Wolfson, "Anxiety, Lament, and the Language of Silence: Poetic Redemption and Gnostic Alienation," in this volume, 18.
5. Ibid., 37.
6. See Wasserstrom, *Religion after Religion*, 239–41.
7. Wasserstrom's "Nine Theses" riff off Lincoln's "Theses on Method," *Method & Theory in the Study of Religion* 17, no. 1 (2005): 8–10.
8. Wasserstrom, "Nine Theses," §6.
9. Steve Wasserstrom, Bruce Lincoln, and Elliot Wolfson, "Trialogue: Past, Present, and Future of the Study of Religion," accessed August 6, 2018, https://ensemble.reed.edu/hapi/v1/contents/permalinks/Mq79Kpw4/view.
10. Wasserstrom, "Nine Theses," §6.
11. Peter E. Gordon, "The Study of Religion in a Postmetaphysical Age: Philosophical and Political Reflections," in this volume, 44.
12. Anne Oravetz Albert, "On the Possibility of Jewish Politics in Our Time: Scholem, Exile, ad Early Modern Transformations," in this volume, 154.
13. Wasserstrom, "Nine Riddles," §1.
14. Ibid., § 4.
15. Wolfson, "Anxiety, Lament, and the Language of Silence," in this volume, 37.
16. Gordon, "Religion in a Postmetaphysical Age," in this volume, 40.
17. Wasserstrom, "Nine Theses," §5.
18. Gregory Given, "Nag Hammadi at Eranos: Rediscovering Gnosticism among the Historians of Religions," in this volume, 97.
19. Wasserstrom, "Nine Theses," §1.
20. Bruce Lincoln, *Theorizing Myth: Narrative, Ideology, and Scholarship* (Chicago, IL: University of Chicago Press, 1999), 208.

Chapter 2

1. Ralph Waldo Emerson, "The Scholar," in *The Complete Works of Ralph Waldo Emerson Lectures and Biographical Sketches* (Boston, MA: Houghton, Mifflin and Co., 1903), 262–3.
2. These theses are reflective and not analytic; they are provocations and not arguments.

3   Religious Studies is a science in the sense that linguistics is a science. Religious Studies is to religion as linguistics is to language.
4   Hans Blumenberg, *The Genesis of the Copernican World* (Cambridge, MA: MIT Press, 1987), 119.
5   Max Müller, *Introduction to the Science of Religion* (London: Longman, Green, and Co., 1873), 15–16.
6   Max Müller, *Chips from a German Workshop*, Vol. 1 (New York: Scribner, Armstrong, and Co., 1874), xxvii.
7   See the observations of Peter Szondi, *On Textual Understanding, and Other Essays* (Minneapolis: University of Minnesota Press, 1986), 13.
8   I was first stimulated to consider the centrality of contact by Charles Long, who announced that "I should like to see us develop a body of studies devoted to the religious situation of contact." See Charles H. Long, "A Look at the Chicago Tradition in the History of Religions: Retrospect and Future," in *The History of Religions Retrospect and Prospect*, ed. Joseph M. Kitagawa (New York: Macmillan Publishing Company, 1985), 102.
9   Or, as Adorno put it, *Kein Geist ist da*—there is no Spirit. See "Theses against Occultism," in Theodor W. Adorno, *The Stars Down to Earth: And Other Essays on the Irrational in Culture*, ed. Stephen Crook (New York: Routledge, 1995), 133.
10 For Steiner's views on philology as *cortesia*, see George Steiner, *Real Presences* (Chicago, IL: University of Chicago Press, 1989).
11 Vilem Flusser, "The Future of Writing," in *Writings*, ed. Flusser et al. (Minneapolis: University of Minnesota Press, 2002), 67, emphasis added.
12 Friedrich A. Kittler, *Literature, Media, Information Systems: Essays*, ed. and intro. Friedrich A. Kittler and John Johnston (Amsterdam: Overseas Publishers Association, 1997), 37, citing the interpretation of Friedrich Nietzsche.
13 Diane Rubenstein, *What's Left? The École Normale Supérieure and the Right* (Madison: University of Wisconsin Press, 1990), 130.
14 See my *Religion after Religion: Gershom Scholem, Mircea Eliade, and Henry Corbin at Eranos* (Princeton, NJ: Princeton University Press, 1999).
15 Gerardus Van der Leeuw, *Religion in Essence and Manifestation*, trans. J. E. Turner, fore. Ninian Smart (Princeton, NJ: Princeton University Press, 1986).
16 Theodor Adorno, *Minima Moralia: Reflections from Damaged Life*, trans. E. F. N. Jephcott (London: Verso, 2005), 132, on Carl Schmitt.
17 Which is the fatal flaw of Carl Schmitt.
18 Müller, *Introduction to the Science of Religion*.
19 See Wasserstrom, *Religion after Religion*, on the problem of "religious reality."
20 Like the enemy-brothers, Leo Strauss and Theodor Adorno.
21 Donald Wiebe, *Beyond Legitimation: Essays on the Problem of Religious Knowledge* (London: Macmillan, 1994) and "'Why the Academic Study of Religion?' Motive and Method in the Study of Religion," *Religious Studies* 24, no. 4 (1988): 403–13.
22 Robin Briggs, *Witches and Neighbors* (New York: Viking, 1996) and *Thinking with Demons* (New York: Oxford University Press, 1999).
23 See *Religion after Religion*, 305 n. 98, on "absolute" and "radical" empiricisms.
24 See Steven M. Wasserstrom, "The Challenge of Artificial Life: Medieval Jewish Responses from the Muslim World," "CCAR Symposium: Judaism and Islam," ed. Reuven Fireston, special issue, *CCAR Journal: A Reform Jewish Quarterly* (Fall 2000): 69–80; Tom Friedman, "The Parallel Universe," *New York Times*, New York City, May 12, 2000.

Chapter 3

1. Elliot R. Wolfson, "The Tree That Is All: Jewish-Christian Roots of a Kabbalistic Symbol in *Sefer ha-Bahir*," *Journal of Jewish Thought and Philosophy* 3 (1993): 31–76. A revised version of the essay appeared in Elliot R. Wolfson, *Along the Path: Studies in Kabbalistic Myth, Symbolism, and Hermeneutics* (Albany: State University of New York Press, 1995), 63–88.
2. I have explored this matter in Elliot R. Wolfson, *The Duplicity of Philosophy's Shadow: Heidegger, Nazism, and the Jewish Other* (New York: Columbia University Press, 2018).
3. Martin Heidegger, "Who Is Nietzsche's Zarathustra?" *Review of Metaphysics* 20 (1967): 426; *Vorträge und Aufsätze* [GA 7] (Frankfurt am Main: Vittorio Klostermann, 2000), 118.
4. Jürgen Habermas, "Martin Heidegger: On the Publication of the Lectures of 1935," in *The Heidegger Controversy: A Critical Reader*, ed. Richard Wolin (Cambridge, MA: MIT Press, 1993), 197. See Cristina Lafont, "World-Disclosure and Critique: Did Habermas Succeed in Thinking with Heidegger and against Heidegger," *Telos* 145 (2008): 161–76.
5. Martin Heidegger, *Introduction to Metaphysics*, trans. Gregory Fried and Richard Polt (New Haven, CT: Yale University Press, 2000), 182–3; *Einführung in die Metaphysik* [GA 40] (Frankfurt am Main: Vittorio Klostermann, 1983), 180.
6. Martin Heidegger, *Contributions to Philosophy (of the Event)*, trans. Richard Rojcewicz and Daniela Vallega-Neu (Bloomington: Indiana University Press, 2012), §13, p. 30; *Beiträge zur Philosophie (Vom Ereignis)* [GA 65] (Frankfurt am Main: Vittorio Klostermann, 1989), 36.
7. For a more detailed analysis, see Elliot R. Wolfson, "Heidegger's Apophaticism: Unsaying the Said and the Silence of the Last God," in *Contemporary Debates in Negative Theology and Philosophy*, ed. Nahum Brown and J. Aaron Simmons (New York: Palgrave, 2017), 185–216.
8. Martin Heidegger, *Identity and Difference*, trans. and with an intro. Joan Stambaugh (New York: Harper & Row, 1969), 73.
9. Ibid., 142. The translation appears in Robert Bernasconi, *The Question of Language in Heidegger's History of Being* (Atlantic Highlands: Humanities Press, 1985), 77, and see Elliot R. Wolfson, *Giving beyond the Gift: Apophasis and Overcoming Theomania* (New York: Fordham University Press, 2014), 13 and 283 n. 99.
10. Krzysztof Ziarek, *Language after Heidegger* (Bloomington: Indiana University Press, 2013), 64.
11. Martin Heidegger, *On the Way to Language*, trans. Peter D. Hertz (New York: Harper & Row, 1971), 41; *Unterwegs zur Sprache* [GA 12] (Frankfurt am Main: Vittorio Klostermann, 1985), 129.
12. Jean-Luc Nancy, *The Gravity of Thought*, trans. François Raffoul and Gregory Recco (Amherst: Humanity Books, 1997), 55.
13. Martin Heidegger, *Aus der Erfahrung des Denkens* [GA 13] (Frankfurt am Main: Vittorio Klostermann, 2002), 197.
14. Martin Heidegger, *Pathmarks*, ed. William McNeill (Cambridge: Cambridge University Press, 1998), 86; *Wegmarken* [GA 9] (Frankfurt am Main: Vittorio Klostermann, 1996), 108.
15. Heidegger, *Contributions*, §129, pp. 193–4; *Beiträge*, 246.
16. This theme is repeated on numerous occasions in Heidegger's work. See, for instance, the description of nature (*phusis*) as the presence (*Anwesens*) that "always withholds

itself at the same time in a concealedness [*Verborgenheit*]" in Martin Heidegger, *Poetry, Language, Thought*, trans. and intro. Albert Hofstadter (New York: Harper & Row, 1971), 53; *Holzwege* [GA 5] (Frankfurt am Main: Vittorio Klostermann, 1977), 40. On the unconcealment of being through its withdrawal, compare Martin Heidegger, *Off the Beaten Track*, ed. and trans. Julian Young and Kenneth Haynes (Cambridge: Cambridge University Press, 2002), 254; *Holzwege*, 337.

17 Jacques Derrida, *Writing and Difference*, trans., with an intro. and additional notes by Alan Bass (Chicago, IL: University of Chicago Press, 1978), 137, compared the passage from Heidegger's "Brief über den 'Humanismus'" (Heidegger, *Pathmarks*, 243; *Wegmarken*, 319) to the effect that one finds one's way into the nearness of being by learning to exist in the nameless (*Namenlosen*) to the kabbalistic conception of the "unnameable possibility of the Name." Concerning this passage, see Wolfson, *Giving*, 172, and the more recent analysis in Elliot R. Wolfson, "Heidegger's Seyn/Nichts and the Kabbalistic Ein Sof: A Study in Comparative Metaontology," in *Heidegger and Jewish Thought: Difficult Others*, ed. Micha Brumlik and Elad Lapidot (Lanham: Rowman & Littlefield, 2017), 177–8.

18 Heidegger, *Pathmarks*, 90; *Wegmarken*, 114.

19 Heidegger, *Pathmarks*, 86–8; *Wegmarken*, 109–11.

20 Compare the following account of the determined nothingness of the infinitesimal in the differential calculus of Hermann Cohen in Luc A. Anckaert, *A Critique of Infinity: Rosenzweig and Levinas* (Leuven: Peeters, 2006), 35 n. 37: "Nothingness, or the infinite within differential calculus is not a 'void' nothingness, but the 'nil' designates the something of nothingness. Within the differential, the properties of nothingness are linked to something. Nothingness envisaged is always the nothingness of something, a boundary concept of the indication of limit. Something is, as it were, latent in the womb of the limit or nothingness. The infinitely small contains, unarticulated, the characteristic of the finite quantity." See my comments on Cohen's idea of the nothing of the differential in Wolfson, *Giving*, 77–8, and references to other scholars cited on 344–5 nn. 322–3.

21 Martin Heidegger, *Being and Time*, trans. Joan Stambaugh, revised and with a forward by Dennis J. Schmidt (Albany: State University of New York Press, 2010), §40, pp. 182–3; *Sein und Zeit* (Tübingen: Max Niemeyer, 1993), 188–9. For an extensive discussion of this theme, see Katherine Withy, *Heidegger on Being Uncanny* (Cambridge, MA: Harvard University Press, 2015), 48–101.

22 For comparison of the Freudian *Unheimliche* as a psychological sentiment and Heidegger's *Unheimlichkeit* as an ontological dimension of Dasein, see Anneleen Masschelein, *The Unconcept: The Freudian Uncanny in Late-Twentieth-Century Theory* (Albany: State University of New York Press, 2011), 139–43.

23 According to the formulation in *Becoming Heidegger: On the Trail of His Early Occasional Writings, 1910-1927*, ed. Theodore Kisiel and Thomas Sheehan (Evanston: Northwestern University Press, 2007), 430, s.v. *Bekümmerung*. See ibid., 438, s.v. *Sorgen*; Gisbert Hoffmann, *Heideggers Phänomenologie: Bewusstsein—Reflexion—Selbst (Ich) und Zeit in Frühwerk* (Würzburg: Königshausen & Neumann, 2005), 39–43; Benjamin D. Crowe, *Heidegger's Religious Origins: Destruction and Authenticity* (Bloomington: Indiana University Press, 2006), 38, 57, 79, 172–174; Alexander S. Duff, *Heidegger and Politics: The Ontology of Radical Discontent* (Cambridge: Cambridge University Press, 2015), 33–4, 113, 182–3.

24 Heidegger, *Phenomenological Interpretations of Aristotle: Initiation into Phenomenological Research*, trans. Richard Rojcewicz (Bloomington: Indiana

University Press, 2001), 53; *Phänomenologische Interpretationen zu Aristoteles: Einführung in die Phänomenologische Forschung* [GA 61] (Frankfurt am Main: Vittorio Klostermann, 1994), 70.

25   Heidegger, *Pathmarks*, 88; *Wegmarken*, 111–12. See Bernasconi, *The Question of Language*, 54–7.

26   Martin Heidegger, *Ponderings II–VI: Black Notebooks 1931–1938*, trans. Richard Rojcewicz (Bloomington: Indiana University Press, 2016), 54; *Überlegungen II–VI (Schwarze Hefte 1931–1938)* [GA 94] (Frankfurt am Main: Vittorio Klostermann, 2014), 70–1.

27   Richard Reitzenstein, *Hellenistic Mystery-Religions: Their Basic Idea and Significance*, trans. John E. Steely (Pittsburgh: Pickwick Press, 1978), 354; Walter Schmithals, *Die Gnosis in Korinth: Eine Untersuchung zu den Korintherbriefen* (Göttingen: Vandenhoeck & Ruprecht, 1956), 82–134; Kurt Rudolph, *Gnosis: The Nature and History of Gnosticism*, translation edited by Robert McLachlan Wilson (San Francisco: Harper & Row, 1983), 121–2, 131–2.

28   Rudolf Bultmann, *Theology of the New Testament*, 2 vols., trans. Kendrick Grobel (Waco: Baylor University Press, 2007), 1:166–7, 175–7. See the pertinent comments in John Macquarrie, *An Existential Theology: A Comparison of Heidegger and Bultmann*, with a foreword by Rudolf Bultmann (London: SCM Press, 1955), 86–7, 173. For criticism of the appropriateness of the gnostic redeemer myth, see Wayne A. Meeks, *The Prophet-King: Moses Traditions and the Johannine Christology* (Leiden: Brill, 1967), 14–16.

29   Hans Jonas, *Gnosis und spätantiker Geist. Erster Teil: Die mythologische Gnosis* (Göttingen: Vandenhoeck & Ruprecht, 1988), 96–8; Hans Jonas, *The Gnostic Religion: The Message of the Alien God and the Beginnings of Christianity* (Boston: Beacon Press, 1963), 49–51, 75–80.

30   Heidegger, *Ponderings II–VI*, 54, emphasis original; *Überlegungen II–VI*, 71.

31   Bultmann, *Theology of the New Testament*, 1:165, emphasis original.

32   Jonas, *Gnosis und spätantiker Geist. Erster Teil*, 106–9, mentioned Heidegger in his discussion of the motif of thrownness (*Geworfensein*) in gnostic sources.

33   Heidegger, *Ponderings II–VI*, 54, emphasis original; *Überlegungen II–VI*, 71. Compare *Ponderings II–VI*, 160 (*Überlegungen II–VI*, 218): "A history of philosophy is to be presented as the history of the great isolation [*Vereinsammung*]."

34   Heidegger, *Pathmarks*, 89; *Wegmarken*, 112.

35   Heidegger, *Pathmarks*, 238; *Wegmarken*, 312.

36   Consider Scholem's poem "Amtliches Lehrgedicht der Philosophischen Fakultät der Haupt- und Staats-Universität Muri," dated December 5, 1927, and dedicated to Walter Benjamin, in Gershom Scholem, *The Fullness of Time: Poems*, ed. and intro. Steven M. Wasserstrom, trans. Richard Sieburth (Jerusalem: Ibis, 2003), 74–5: "Wer helig ist und hochmodern/Zugleich, hält es mit Husserl gern./Doch hört man ein Gerücht im Land/Daß Heidegger ihn nicht verstand" ("Whoever is ultramodern and ascetic/Will find Husserl most sympathetic./Though there is a rumor going through the land/He was someone Heidegger could never understand"). See also the entry from November 14, 1916, in Gershom Scholem, *Lamentations of Youth: The Diaries of Gershom Scholem, 1913–1919*, ed. and trans. Anthony David Skinner (Cambridge, MA: Harvard University Press, 2007), 148 (*Tagebücher nebst Aufsätzen und Entwürfen bis 1923, 1. Halbband 1913–1917*, ed. Karlfried Gründer and Friedrich Niewöhner, with the cooperation of Herbert Kopp-Oberstebrink [Frankfurt am Main: Jüdischer Verlag, 1995], 418): "Heidegger's essay on historical time is really quite ridiculous and

unphilosophical. Benjamin really got it right with his assessment of it." The reference is to Martin Heidegger, "Der Zeitbegriff in der Geschichtswissenschft," *Zeitschrift für Philosophie und philosophische Kritik* 161 (1916): 173–88, repr. Martin Heidegger, *Frühe Schriften* [GA 1] (Frankfurt am Main: Vittorio Klostermann, 1978), 415–33; an English translation by Harry S. Taylor and Hans W. Uffelmann was published as "The Concept of Time in the Science of History," *Journal of the British Society for Phenomenology* 9 (1978): 3–10, and reprinted with some revisions in Martin Heidegger, *Becoming Heidegger: On the Trail of His Early Occasional Writings, 1910–1927*, ed. Theodore Kisiel and Thomas Sheehan (Evanston: Northwestern University Press, 2007), 60–72. The criticism of Benjamin to which Scholem alludes is found in a letter to Scholem from November 11, 1916, in Benjamin, *The Correspondence of Walter Benjamin 1910-1940*, ed. Gershom Scholem and Theodor W. Adorno, trans. Manfred R. Jacobson and Evelyn M. Jacobson (Chicago, IL: University of Chicago Press, 1994), 82. See Peter Fenves, *The Messianic Reduction: Walter Benjamin and the Shape of Time* (Stanford: Stanford University Press, 2011), 118–22; and further discussion and reference to other scholarly analyses in Elliot R. Wolfson, "Not Yet Now: Speaking of the End and the End of Speaking," in *Elliot R. Wolfson: Poetic Thinking*, ed. Hava Tirosh-Samuelson and Aaron W. Hughes (Leiden: Brill, 2015), 159–60 n. 122. On Scholem's relationship to Heidegger, see Shaul Magid, "Gershom Scholem's Ambivalence toward Mystical Experience and His Critique of Martin Buber in Light of Hans Jonas and Martin Heidegger," *Journal of Jewish Thought and Philosophy* 4 (1995): 245–69. See also Steven Wasserstrom, *Religion after Religion: Gershom Scholem, Mircea Eliade, and Henry Corbin at Eranos* (Princeton, NJ: Princeton University Press, 1999), 136, 229, 310 n. 60.

37   Lina Barouch, "Lamenting Language Itself: Gershom Scholem on the Silent Language of Lamentation," *New German Critique* 37 (2010): 1–26, esp. 7–16. See also Daniel Weidner, *Gershom Scholem: Politisches, esoterisches und historiographisches Schreiben* (Munich: Wilhelm Fink Verlag, 2003), 191–6; Ilit Ferber, "A Language of the Border: On Scholem's Theory of Lament," *Journal of Jewish Thought and Philosophy* 21 (2013): 161–186, esp. 165–6, 175–6, 180–5; Daniel Weidner, "Lament and Pure Language: Scholem, Benjamin and Kant," *Jewish Studies Quarterly* 21 (2014): 42–54; Daniel Weidner, "'Incline Thine Ear Unto Me, and Hear My Speech': Scholem, Benjamin, and Cohen on Lament," in *Lament in Jewish Thought: Philosophical, Theological, and Literary Perspectives*, ed. Ilit Ferber and Paula Schwebel (Berlin: Walter de Gruyter, 2014), 111–30; Caroline Sauter, "The Ghost of the Poet: Lament in Walter Benjamin's Early Poetry, Theory, and Translation," in *Lament in Jewish Thought*, 205–20; Paula Schwebel, "Lament and the Shattered Expression of Mourning: Gershom Scholem and Walter Benjamin," *Jewish Studies Quarterly* 21 (2014): 27–41; Paula Schwebel, "The Tradition in Ruins: Walter Benjamin and Gershom Scholem on Language and Lament," in *Lament in Jewish Thought*, 277–301.

38   Gershom Scholem, "On Lament and Lamentation," in *Lament in Jewish Thought*, 313; *Tagebücher nebst Aufsätzen und Entwürfen bis 1923, 2. Halbband 1917–1923*, ed. Karlfried Gründer, Herbert Kopp-Oberstebrink, and Friedrich Niewöhner, with Karl E. Grözinger (Frankfurt am Main: Jüdischer Verlag, 2000), 128.

39   Gershom Scholem, "The Name of God and the Linguistic Theory of the Kabbala," *Diogenes* 80 (1972): 174, and compare ibid., 180, 193–4.

40   Heidegger, *Off the Beaten Track*, 46; *Holzwege*, 61–2. See Gerald L. Bruns, *Heidegger's Estrangements: Language, Truth, and Poetry in the Later Writings* (New Haven, CT: Yale University Press, 1989), 163–5. On Heidegger's conception of poetry as a

movement from wordlessness into language, see David Nowell Smith, *Sounding/Silence: Martin Heidegger at the Limits of Poetics* (New York: Fordham University Press, 2013). For a representative, and by no means exhaustive, list of other scholarly analyses of Heideggerian poetics, see Wolfson, *Giving*, 333–4 n. 261.

41 Scholem, "On Lament," 313; *Tagebücher*, 2:128.
42 Gershom Scholem, "Job's Lament," in *Lament in Jewish Thought*, 322; *Tagebücher*, 2:546.
43 Scholem, "On Lament," 316; *Tagebücher*, 2:130.
44 Lina Barouch, "The Erasure and Endurance of Lament: Gershom Scholem's Early Critique of Zionism and Its Language," *Jewish Studies Quarterly* 21 (2014): 15–16, and Lina Barouch, "Dancing on the Rope, Walking on the Boundary: Paradoxical Language and Modernistic Associations in Gershom Scholem's Treatise 'On Lament and Lamentation,'" in *Lamentations: Poetry and Thought in Gershom Scholem's World*, ed. Galili Shahar and Ilit Farber (Jerusalem: Carmel, 2016), 159 (Hebrew). Barouch relies on the understanding of apophasis as a linguistic expression that oscillates between the poles of saying and unsaying proffered by Michael A. Sells, *Mystical Languages of Unsaying* (Chicago, IL: University of Chicago Press, 1994). It appears that Barouch is unaware of my own discussion of the juxtaposition of the kataphatic and the apophatic in kabbalistic texts and other mystical traditions. I concur with Sells in marking apophasis as a verbal act, what I call speaking-not as opposed to not speaking, but I advance a more paradoxical understanding of the paradox by emphasizing that the saying itself is a verbal gesticulation of unsaying. See Elliot R. Wolfson, *Language, Eros, Being: Kabbalistic Hermeneutics and Poetic Imagination* (New York: Fordham University Press, 2005), 215, 217–19; 343; Elliot R. Wolfson, *Venturing Beyond: Law and Morality in Kabbalistic Mysticism*. Oxford: Oxford University Press, 2006), 246–8; Elliot R. Wolfson, "Nihilating Nonground and the Temporal Sway of Becoming: Kabbalistically Envisioning Nothing beyond Nothing," *Angelaki* 17 (2012): 38–9. Also pertinent here is the discussion in Elliot R. Wolfson, *Abraham Abulafia—Kabbalist and Prophet: Hermeneutics, Theosophy and Theurgy* (Los Angeles, CA: Cherub Press, 2001), 10–38, of Scholem's understanding of the nature of the secret and the authentic esoteric tradition that he culls from kabbalistic literature. The paradox of disclosing the secret by concealing it—every disclosure of the concealment is a concealment of the disclosure—corresponds to the demarcation of mystical language as a saying that is an unsaying. See ibid., 28–9, where I note the parallel between the inseparability of concealment and unconcealment in Heidegger's understanding of truth and Scholem's assumption that a secret can be revealed only to the extent that it remains hidden.
45 Scholem, "On Lament," 317; *Tagebücher*, 2:131. The similarity between the Heideggerian *Angst* and the Scholemian *Trauer* is mentioned by Agata Bielik-Robson, "The Unfallen Silence: *Kinah* and the Other Origin of Language," in *Lament in Jewish Thought*, 144. After noting the affinity, the author draws the following contrast: "But for Scholem being a symbol indicates something more than just a lack of literal objectivity. It is also evidence of a mythic knowledge of the world as a hermetic natural totality, one that is necessarily dark, vague, fluid, and half-concealed, for it lacks an external standpoint of judgment (precisely as in the famous saying of Heraclitus from Fragment 123, *physis kryptesthai philei*, 'nature loves to hide').While the language of revelation is literality itself—*das Aussprechlichste*, reserving no recess of darkness in its all-revealing light—the mythic knowledge of immanence rests in the silence of the symbol." Heidegger surely uses a different

terminology, but what is attributed to Scholem can be elicited from his thinking as well, including the interpretation linked to the Heraclitean dictum, which Heidegger uses to support his claim that the self-revealing of being is always also a self-concealing. See Martin Heidegger, *The Principle of Reason*, trans. Reginald Lilly (Bloomington: Indiana University Press, 1992), 70 (*Der Satz vom Grund* [GA 10] [Frankfurt am Main: Vittorio Klostermann, 1997], 104); Martin Heidegger, *The Metaphysical Foundations of Logic*, trans. Michael Heim (Bloomington: Indiana University Press, 1984), 217 (*Metaphysische Anfangsgründe der Logik im Ausgang von Leibniz* [GA 26] [Frankfurt am Main: Vittorio Klostermann, 1978], 281); Martin Heidegger, *The Fundamental Concepts of Metaphysics: World, Finitude, Solitude*, trans. William McNeill and Nicholas Walker (Bloomington: Indiana University Press, 1995), 27 (*Die Grundbegriffe der Metaphysik: Welt—Endlichkeit—Einsamkeit* [GA 29/30] [Frankfurt am Main: Vittorio Klostermann, 1983], 41); Martin Heidegger, *The Essence of Truth: On Plato's Cave Allegory and Theaetetus*, trans. Ted Sadler (New York: Continuum, 2002), 9–11 (*Vom Wesen der Wahrheit: Zu Platons Höhlengleichnis und Theätet* [GA 34] [Frankfurt am Main: Vittorio Klostermann, 1988], 13–15); Martin Heidegger, *Early Greek Thinking*, trans. David Farrell Krell and Frank A. Capuzzi (New York: Harper & Row, 1975), 113–14 (*Vorträge und Aufsätze*, 277–9); Heidegger, *Introduction to Metaphysics*, 120–1 (*Einführung in die Metaphysik*, 122); Heidegger, *Pathmarks*, 229–30 (*Wegmarken*, 300–1); Martin Heidegger, *Heraclitus: The Inception of Occidental Thinking and Logic: Heraclitus's Doctrine of the Logos*, trans. Julia Goesser Assaiante and S. Montgomery Ewegen (London: Bloomsbury Academic, 2018), 83–6, 90–1, 131–2; Martin Heidegger, *Heraklit* [GA 55] (Frankfurt am Main: Vittorio Klostermann, 1979), 109–14, 121–2, 175–7, 110, 121, 175. For discussion of Heidegger's interpretation of the Heraclitean saying and the self-concealing of nature, see Charles E. Scott, "Appearing to Remember Heraclitus," in *The Presocratics after Heidegger*, ed. David C. Jacobs (Albany: State University of New York Press, 1999), 249–61, esp. 252–7; Daniel O. Dahlstrom, "Being at the Beginning: Heidegger's Interpretation of Heraclitus," in *Interpreting Heidegger: Critical Essays*, ed. Daniel O. Dahlstrom (Cambridge: Cambridge University Press, 2011), 142–3, 150–1; Wolfson, *Giving*, 51–2, 316–17 n. 129. The interpretive history of the aphorism of Heraclitus is traced by Pierre Hadot, *The Veil of Isis: An Essay on the History of the Idea of Nature*, trans. Michael Chase (Cambridge, MA: Harvard University Press, 2006), 39–87. Heidegger's specific explication thereof is discussed on 303–7.

46 Heidegger, *Ponderings II-VI*, 55, emphasis original; *Überlegungen II-VI*, 72.
47 Heidegger, *Pathmarks*, 248–9; *Wegmarken*, 326.
48 Ludwig Wittgenstein, *Tractatus Logico-Philosophicus*, trans. Charles K. Ogden, intro. Bertrand Russell (London: Routledge, 1995), 27. See Wolfson, *Language*, 289–91; Timothy D. Knepper, "Ineffability Investigations: What the Later Wittgenstein Has to Offer to the Study of Ineffability," *International Journal for Philosophy of Religion* 65 (2009): 65–76. For comparative analyses of the topic of silence or the unsayable in the thought of Heidegger and Wittgenstein, see Peter J. McCormick, "Saying and Showing in Heidegger and Wittgenstein," *Journal of the British Society of Phenomenology* 3 (1972): 27–35; Peter J. McCormick, *Heidegger and the Language of the World: An Argumentative Reading of the Later Heidegger's Meditations on Language* (Ottawa: University of Ottawa Press, 1976), 157–71; Steven L. Bindeman, *Heidegger and Wittgenstein: The Poetics of Silence* (Lanham, MD: University Press of America, 1981), and Nikita Dhawan, *Impossible Speech: On the Politics of Silence and Violence* (Sankt Augustin: Academia, 2007), 122–97. On Heidegger and Wittgenstein,

see also Wolfson, *Language*, 15–16, and other studies cited on 410 nn. 128–9. See as well my remarks, ibid., 419 n. 211, and the slightly revised position in Elliot R. Wolfson, "Skepticism and the Philosopher's Keeping Faith," in *Jewish Philosophy for the Twenty-First Century: Personal Reflections*, ed. Hava Tirosh-Samuelson and Aaron W. Hughes (Leiden: Brill, 2014), 506–8. See also Herman Philipse, "Heidegger and Wittgenstein on External World Skepticism," in *Wittgenstein and Heidegger*, ed. David Egan, Stephen Reynolds, and Aaron James Wendland (New York: Routledge, 2013), 116–32.

49 Scholem, "On Lament," 314; *Tagebücher*, 2:129.
50 Ibid.
51 Bielik-Robson, "The Unfallen Silence," 142, refers to Scholem's understanding of lament as the "counter-revelation" based on its comportment as the *unsilenceable silence*, that is, the silence that is "on a par with the most pronounced, *ausprechlichst*, Word Divine. Silence as a tragic counter-revelation, rising up to meet 'revelation proper.'"
52 Scholem, "On Lament," 316; *Tagebücher*, 2:130–131.
53 Scholem, "On Lament," 316; *Tagebücher*, 2:130.
54 Martin Heidegger, *Hölderlin's Hymns "Germania" and "The Rhine"*, trans. William McNeill and Julia Ireland (Bloomington: Indiana University Press, 2014), 108; *Hölderlins Hymnen »Germanien« und »Der Rhein«* [GA 39] (Frankfurt am Main: Vittorio Klostermann, 1999), 119–20.
55 Scholem, "On Lament," 317; *Tagebücher*, 2:130–31. For a different assessment of Scholem's early writings on language and the mystical experience, related specifically to a critique of revelation as an ecstatic experience that must be translated into a poetic dictum, see David Biale, *Gershom Scholem: Kabbalah and Counter-History* (Cambridge, MA: Harvard University Press, 1979), 86–9. Also relevant is the poetic interpretation of some of Scholem's early writings on tradition and his later work on kabbalah and philology offered by Daniel Weidner, "Reading Gershom Scholem," *Jewish Quarterly Review* 96 (2006): 203–31.
56 Scholem, "On Lament," 318; *Tagebücher*, 2:132.
57 Scholem, "On Lament," 319; *Tagebücher*, 2:133.
58 Scholem, "Job's Lament," 323; *Tagebücher*, 2:57.
59 Scholem, "Job's Lament," 322; *Tagebücher*, 2:546.
60 Gershom Scholem, *On the Possibility of Jewish Mysticism in Our Time & Other Essays*, ed. with intro. Avraham Shapira, trans. Jonathan Chipman (Philadelphia: Jewish Publication Society of America, 1997), 28.
61 *The Correspondence of Walter Benjamin 1910–1940*, ed. Gershom Scholem and Theodor W. Adorno, trans. Manfred R. Jacobson and Evelyn M. Jacobson (Chicago, IL: University of Chicago Press, 1994), 142, emphasis original; *Walter Benjamin/Gershom Scholem: Briefwechsel*, ed. Gershom Scholem (Frankfurt am Main: Suhrkamp, 1980), 175. Regarding Scholem's "nothingness of revelation," see Wolfson, *Venturing Beyond*, 233 and reference to other scholars cited there in n. 166.
62 Gershom Scholem, *On the Mystical Shape of the Godhead: Basic Concepts in the Kabbalah*, trans. Joachim Neugroschel, ed. Jonathan Chipman, fore. Joseph Dan (New York: Schocken, 1991), 38; *Von der mystischen Gestalt der Gottheit: Studien zu Grundbegriffen der Kabbala* (Frankfurt am Main: Suhrkamp, 1995), 31. Compare the use of the term *Negation auf Negation* on the part of the kabbalists to refer to the unity of *Ein Sof* in Gershom Scholem, *Die Geheimnisse der Schöpfung: Ein Kapitel aus dem kabbalistischen Buche Sohar* (Frankfurt am main: Jüdischer Verlag, 1992),

33. See, however, Gershom Scholem, *Major Trends in Jewish Mysticism* (New York: Schocken, 1956), 11, where the Maimonidean view of God as the "negation of negation" is contrasted with the kabbalistic understanding of the conflict between the known and unknown aspects of God.

63 Scholem, *On the Mystical Shape*, 41–2; *Von der mystischen Gestalt*, 34. See David Kaufmann, "Imageless Refuge for All Images: Scholem in the Wake of Philosophy," *Modern Judaism* 20 (2000): 147–58, esp. 152–3; Wolfson, *Language*, 122–3.

64 Scholem, *Von der mystischen Gestalt*, 47. The English translation "a great modern thinker" in Scholem, *On the Mystical Shape*, 55, is based on the Hebrew translation *hogeh gadol mi-ḥakhmei dorenu*, in Gershom Scholem, *Elements of the Kabbalah and Its Symbolism*, trans. Joseph Ben-Shlomo (Jerusalem: Bialik Institute, 1976), 186 (Hebrew). The passage that Scholem paraphrases is from an essay of Benjamin published in *Neue schweizer Rundschau* in November 1929. See Walter Benjamin, *Selected Writings, Volume 2: 1927–1934*, ed. Michael W. Jennings, Howard Eiland, and Gary Smith (Cambridge, MA: Harvard University Press, 1999) (*Gesammelte Schriften*, 4.1, ed. Tillman Rexroth [Frankfurt am Main: Suhrkamp, 1991], 370): "The unprecedented yearning that had overcome me at the heart of what I had longed for was not the yearning that flies to the image from afar. It was the blissful yearning that has already crossed the threshold of image and possession, and knows only the power of the name—the power from which the loved one lives, is transformed, ages, rejuvenates itself, and imageless [*bildlos*], is the refuge of all images [*Zuflucht aller Bilder*]." See Kaufmann, "Imageless Refuge," 153; Wolfson, *Language*, 123. For Benjamin, the imageless is closely linked to his concept of the expressionless (*das Ausdruckslose*). See Winfried Menninghaus, "Walter Benjamin's Variations of Imagelessness," *Critical Horizons* 14 (2013): 407–28.

65 Scholem, *On the Mystical Shape*, 55; *Von der mystischen Gestalt*, 47.

66 Walter Benjamin, *Selected Writings, Volume 1: 1913–1926*, ed. Marcus Bullock and Michael W. Jennings (Cambridge, MA: Harvard University Press, 1996), 280. See analysis in Wolfson, "Not Yet Now," 168. On the critical assessment of the positive and negative dimensions attributed to the aesthetic role of the image in the different stages of Benjamin's thought, see Alison Ross, *Walter Benjamin's Concept of the Image* (London: Routledge, 2015). The author thus summarizes her argument: "Specifically, my hypothesis is that the main shifts and problems of Benjamin's thinking, including the gradual erosion of the system of oppositions that had characterised his early writing, can be grasped by an analysis of his writing on the topic of the image. Furthermore, this approach will be used to show that despite his attack on the 'demonic' expressivity of certain kinds of sensuous forms, Benjamin's major ideas also require and can be shown to avail themselves of an aesthetic mode of presentation in images."

67 Immanuel ben Abraham Ḥai Ricchi, *Mishnat Ḥasidim* (Jerusalem: Makhon Mishnat Ḥasidim, 2015), 507.

68 Gershom Scholem, "The Name of God and the Linguistic Theory of the Kabbala," *Diogenes* 79 (1972): 61. On the role of the symbol in Scholem's interpretation of the kabbalah, see Nathan Rotenstreich, "Symbolism and Transcendence: On Some Philosophical Aspects of Gershom Scholem's Opus," *Review of Metaphysics* 31 (1978): 604–14; Biale, *Gershom Scholem*, 89–92; Susan A. Handelman, *Fragments of Redemption: Jewish Thought and Literary Theory in Benjamin, Scholem, and Levinas* (Bloomington: Indiana University Press, 1991), 104–15; Moshe Idel, "Zur Funktion von Symbolen bei G. G. Scholem," in *Gershom Scholem: Literatur und Rhetorik*,

51–92, and the English version in Moshe Idel, *Old Worlds, New Mirrors: On Jewish Mysticism and Twentieth- Century Thought* (Philadelphia: University of Pennsylvania Press, 2010), 83–108; Weidner, *Gershom Scholem*, 174–96.

69 Sigrid Weigel, "Scholems Gedichte und seine Dichtungstheorie: Klage Adressierung, Gabe und das Problem einer biblischen Sprache in unserer Zeit," in *Gershom Scholem: Literatur und Rhetorik*, ed. Stéphane Mosès and Sigrid Weigel (Köln: Böhlau, 2000), 28–32, and Sigrid Weigel, "The Role of Lamentation for Scholem's Theory of Poetry and Language," in *Lament in Jewish Thought*, 192–6. According to Weigel, the earlier theory of Scholem centered on lament is an inversion of his later theory focused on the name of God and the linguistic theory of the kabbalah. Weigel acknowledges that the common denominator of the two texts is the addressing and extinction of the word, but she sees a shift from an emphatic theory of poetry, according to which the poem emerges from the transmission of an extinction of words, to a reflection on the potential task of poets alongside the kabbalists to serve as guardians of the knowledge of the name and the mystery of language.

70 Scholem, "The Name of God," 193–4.

71 Gershom Scholem, *On the Kabbalah and Its Symbolism*, trans. Ralph Manheim (New York: Schocken, 1965), 12–13, emphasis original.

72 Scholem, "The Name of God," 194.

73 Scholem, *Major Trends*, 27.

74 Handelman, *Fragments of Redemption*, 167.

75 Scholem, "The Name of God," 194. It is apposite to recall Scholem's comment in his address upon receiving the Bialik Prize in 1977 concerning the "tremendous poetic potential within Kabbalah, in its own unique language no less than in its poetry proper." See Scholem, *On the Possibility*, 48. See Wasserstrom, *Religion after Religion*, 108–9; Wolfson, *Language*, xi. For a more detailed discussion of the place occupied by poetry in Scholem's thinking, see Steven M. Wasserstrom, "The Fullness of Time: Some Thoughts on the Poetry on Gershom Scholem," in Scholem, *The Fullness of Time*, 13–41. See also Weigel, "Scholems Gedichte"; Weigel, "The Role of Lamentation"; Wolfson, *Language*, 421–2 n. 245.

76 See references cited above, n. 37. See also Biale, *Gershom Scholem*, 103–8; Handelman, *Fragments of Redemption*, 16–33, 90–2; Wolfson, *Language*, 26; Weidner, *Gershom Scholem*, 79–84; Weigel, "Scholems Gedichte," 28–38; Weigel, "The Role of Lamentation," 189–92.

77 Gershom Scholem, "Franz Rosenzweig and His Book *The Star of Redemption*," in *The Philosophy of Franz Rosenzweig*, ed. Paul Mendes-Flohr (Hanover: University Press of New England, 1988), 27–8.

78 Gershom Scholem, "Zionism—Dialectic of Continuity and Rebellion," in *Unease in Zion*, ed. Ehud Ben Ezer, fore. Robert Alter (New York: Quadrangle, 1974), 292.

79 Wasserstrom, *Religion after Religion*, 79. See also Ronny Miron, *The Angel of Jewish History: The Image of the Jewish Past in the Twentieth Century* (Boston: Academic Studies Press, 2014), 160. In n. 38 ad locum, Miron asserts that the concept of nothing implicit in Scholem's comment "is similar to that of Heidegger." On the matter of atheism, see Enrico Lucca, "Ateismo e profondità dell'essere. Un breve scambio epistolare tra Furio Jesi e Gershom Scholem," *Scienza & Politica* 26 (2013): 111–16.

80 Theodor W. Adorno, *Negative Dialectics*, trans. E. P. Ashton (New York: Seabury Press, 1973), 401.

81 Ibid., 401–2. Compare Max Horkheimer and Theodor W. Adorno, *Dialectic of Enlightenment: Philosophical Fragments*, ed. Gunzelin Schmid Noerr, trans. Edmund

Jephcott (Stanford: Stanford University Press, 2002), 17, and reference to scholarly analyses of Adorno's thought as an iconoclastic critique of idolatry and a false conceptual representation of the abstract cited in Wolfson, *Giving*, 264 n. 29.

82　Theodor W. Adorno, *Critical Models: Interventions and Catchwords*, trans. Henry W. Pickford, intro. Lydia Goehr (New York: Columbia University Press, 2005), 142. See Hent de Vries, *Minimal Theologies: Critiques of Secular Reason in Adorno and Levinas*, trans. Geoffrey Hale (Baltimore, MD: Johns Hopkins University Press, 2005), 607–8, and Christopher Craig Brittain, *Adorno and Theology* (London: T & T Clark International, 2010), 88–9.

83　Henri Atlan, *The Sparks of Randomness, vol. 2: The Atheism of Scripture*, trans. Lenn J. Schramm (Stanford: Stanford University Press, 2013), 346–7, emphasis added; passage previously cited in Wolfson, *Giving*, xvii.

84　For a fuller analysis of this theme, see Elliot R. Wolfson, "*Gottwesen* and the De-Divinization of the Last God: Heidegger's Meditation on the Strange and Incalculable," in *Heidegger's Black Notebooks and the Future of Theology*, ed. Mårten Björk and Jayne Svenungsson (New York: Palgrave Macmillan, 2017), 211–55. I have taken the liberty to repeat portions of that study here.

85　Heidegger, *Ponderings II–VI*, 222; *Überlegungen II–VI*, 303.

86　Compare Heidegger, *Ponderings II–VI*, 218 (*Überlegungen II–VI*, 297): "Are not the last death throes of the gods coming over the West? Only one who thinks out into this extreme possibility can fathom the plight concealed behind current history, wherein impotence and violence together seem to constitute the law of motion."

87　Heidegger, *Ponderings II–VI*, 183; *Überlegungen II–VI*, 250.

88　Heidegger, *Ponderings II–VI*, 242; *Überlegungen II–VI*, 333.

89　Martin Heidegger, *Ponderings VII–XI: Black Notebooks 1938–1939*, trans. Richard Rojcewicz (Bloomington: Indiana University Press, 2017), 57–8; *Überlegungen VII–XI (Schwarze Hefte 1938/39)*, [GA 95] (Frankfurt am Main: Vittorio Klostermann, 2014), 75–6.

90　Heidegger, *Ponderings II–VI*, 222; *Überlegungen II–VI*, 304.

91　Martin Heidegger, *The History of Beyng*, trans. William McNeill and Jeffrey Powell (Bloomington: Indiana University Press, 2015), 179; *Die Geschichte des Seyns* [GA 69] (Frankfurt am Main: Vittorio Klostermann, 1998), 211.

92　Heidegger, *Ponderings II–VI*, 68; *Überlegungen II–VI*, 90.

93　Heidegger, *Contributions*, §256, 325–6; *Beiträge*, 410–11.

94　Heidegger, *Contributions*, §256, 325, emphasis original; *Beiträge*, 410.

95　I have modified the term "anarchistic theology" used by Biale, *Gershom Scholem*, 94–100.

96　The bibliography of scholarly analyses of Scholem's Zionism is immense and I will here mention a modest sampling of the relevant studies: Biale, *Gershom Scholem*, 8–10, 53–72, 171–96, 207–10; David Biale, "Scholem und der moderne Nationalismus," in *Gershom Scholem: Zwischen den Disziplinen*, ed. Peter Schäfer and Gary Smith (Frankfurt am Main: Suhrkamp, 1995), 257–74; Nathan Rotenstreich, "Gershom Scholem's Conception of Jewish Nationalism," in *Gershom Scholem: The Man and His Work*, ed. Paul Mendes-Flohr (Albany: State University of New York, Press, 1994), 104–19; Weidner, *Gershom Scholem*, 40–54, 69–73, 91–103, 105–21; Amir Engel, *Gershom Scholem: An Intellectual Biography* (Chicago, IL: University of Chicago Press, 2017), 26–61, 94–123, 168–98; Noam Zadoff, *Gershom Scholem: From Berlin to Jerusalem and Back*, trans. Jeffrey Green (Waltham, MA: Brandeis University Press, 2018), 3–83.

97 The comparison is explored by Michael Fagenblat, "Of Dwelling Prophetically: On Heidegger and Jewish Political Theology," in *Heidegger and Jewish Thought: Difficult Others*, ed. Elad Lapidot and Micha Brumlik (London: Rowman& Littlefield, 2018), 245–67. For discussion of the larger cultural assumption regarding the potential of the German essence to heal the world, see Peter Staudenmaier, *Between Occultism and Nazism: Anthroposophy and the Politics of Race in the Fascist Era* (Leiden: Brill, 2014), 146–78.

98 The expression, which is the scriptural etymology for the name of the firstborn son of Moses and Zipporah, Gershom, *ger hayyiti be-ereṣ nokhriyyah* (Exodus 2:22), is appropriated from George Prochnik, *Stranger in a Strange Land: Searching for Gershom Scholem and Jerusalem* (New York: Other Press, 2016). Scholem's disappointment with Zionism and his sense of personal despair are documented by Engel, *Gershom Scholem*, 109–15, and Zadoff, *Gershom Scholem*, 83–94.

99 See my application of this term to Benjamin in Wolfson, "Not Yet Now," 169–70 n. 160.

100 Scholem, *Major Trends*, 260–4, 267–8, 269, 279–80, 286; Gershom Scholem, *Kabbalah* (Jerusalem: Keter, 1974), 143. See also Isaiah Tishby, "Gnostic Doctrines in Sixteenth-Century Jewish Mysticism," *Journal of Jewish Studies* 6 (1955): 146–52. The Sabbatian and Frankist heresies were also characterized by Scholem as gnostic on account of its nihilism, antinomianism, as well as its positing a dualism between the hidden God and the demiurgic potency. See Scholem, *Major Trends*, 297–9, 316, 322–3; Gershom Scholem, *The Messianic Idea and Other Essays on Jewish Spirituality* (New York: Schocken, 1971), 104–7; Gershom Scholem, *Sabbatai Ṣevi: The Mystical Messiah*, trans. R. J. Zwi Werblowsky (Princeton, NJ: Princeton University Press, 1973), 253, 312, 797. On the importance of Gnosticism in Scholem's historiography of Jewish mysticism, see Moshe Idel, "Subversive Catalysts: Gnosticism and Messianism in Gershom Scholem's View of Jewish Mysticism," in *The Jewish Past Revisited: Reflections on Modern Jewish Historians*, ed. David N. Myers and David B. Ruderman (New Haven, CT: Yale University Press, 1998), 39–76. See also Michael Brenner, "Gnosis and History: Polemics of German-Jewish Identity from Graetz to Scholem," *New German Critique* 77 (1999): 45–60. Kirsten J. Grimstad, *The Modern Revival of Gnosticism and Thomas Mann's Doktor Faustus* (Rochester, NY: Camden House, 2002), 63–79. For a different approach, see Agata Bielik-Robson, "The God of Luria, Hegel and Schelling: The Divine Contraction and the Modern Metaphysics of Finitude," in *Mystical Theology and Continental Philosophy: Interchange in the Wake of God*, ed. David Lewin, Simon D. Podmore, and Duane Williams (London: Routledge, 2017), 40–1.

101 Scholem, *The Messianic Idea*, 35.

102 See, for instance, the beginning of the poem "Traurige Erlösung," composed in 1926, in Scholem, *The Fullness of Time*, 68–9: "Der Glanz aus Zion scheinet vergangen/das Wirkliche hat sich gewährt./Wird nun sein Strahl, noch unversehrt/ ins Innere der Welt gelangen?," "The light of Zion is seen no more,/the real now has won the day./Will its still untarnished ray/attain the world's innermost core?" The poem ends with an ostensible glimmer of hope: "Nie konnte Gott dir näher sein,/ als wo Verzweiflung auch zerbirst:/in Zions selbstversunkenem Licht," "God never comes more close/than when despair bursts into shards:/in Zion's self-engulfing light." To my ear, even this image of despair bursting into shards, likely reflecting the language of Lurianic kabbalah, is ambiguous insofar as the hope itself is still framed calamitously in apocalyptic terms. Compare the concluding stanza of the poem "Begegnung mit Zion und der Welt (*Der Untergang*)," dated June 23, 1930, in

Scholem, *The Fullness of Time*, 88–9: "Was innen war, ist nach Außen/verwandelt, der Traum in Gewalt,/und wieder sind wir draußen/und Zion hat keine Gestalt," "What was within is now without,/the dream twists into violence,/and once again we stand outside/and Zion is without form or sense." And see the opening stanzas of the poem "Media in Vita," dated 1930/33, Scholem, *The Fullness of Time*, 94–5: "Ich habe den Glauben verloren/der mich hierher gebracht./Doch seit ich abgeschworen,/ist es um mich Nacht./Das Dunkel der Niederlage/zieht mich unheimlich an;/seit ich keine Fahne mehr trage,/bin ich ein ehrlicher Mann," "I have lost the faith/that brought me to this place./And in the wake of this forsaking,/ night is my surrounding space./I am uncannily attracted/by the darkness of this defeat;/since I no longer carry any banners,/I'm as honest a man you'll ever meet." My interpretation of Scholem coincides with Pawel Maciejko, "Gershom Scholem's Dialectic of Jewish History: The Case of Sabbatianism," *Journal of Modern Jewish Studies* 3 (2004): 207–20, esp. 216–19. For discussion of the German-Jewish background of Scholem's apocalyptic pessimism and the repudiation of the world, see Anson Rabinbach, "Between Enlightenment and Apocalypse: Benjamin, Bloch and Modern German Jewish Messianism," *New German Critique* 34 (1985): 78–124, esp. 80–2, and my own reflections on messianic time and historical disjointedness in Benjamin in Wolfson, "Not Yet Now," 156–80. See also the intriguing discussion of the Weimar paradox as it relates to understanding National Socialism as a form of Jewish heresy predicated on the annihilation of Israel and God in William H. F. Altmann, *The German Stranger: Leo Strauss and National Socialism*, fore. Michael Zank (Lanham, MD: Lexington Books, 2011), 281–300, esp. 283–7.

103 I have discussed this aspect of Scholem's understanding of the messianic element in Lurianic kabbalah and Sabbatianism in Elliot R. Wolfson, "The Engenderment of Messianic Politics: Symbolic Significance of Sabbatai Ṣevi's Coronation," in *Toward the Millennium: Messianic Expectations from the Bible to Waco*, ed. Peter Schäfer and Mark Cohen (Leiden: E. J. Brill, 1998), 204–6.

104 Scholem, *The Messianic Idea*, 35–6.

105 Rosenzweig, *The Star*, 263; *Der Stern*, 273.

106 Franz Rosenzweig, "Scripture and Luther," in Martin Buber and Franz Rosenzweig, *Scripture and Translation*, trans. Lawrence Rosenwald with Everett Fox (Bloomington: Indiana University Press, 1994), 56: "For the voice of the Bible is not to be enclosed in any space—not in the inner sanctum of a church, not in the linguistic sanctum of a people, not in the circle of heavenly images moving above a nation's sky. Rather this voice seeks again and again to resound from outside— from outside this church, this people, this heaven … If somewhere it has become a familiar, customary possession, it must again and anew, as a foreign and unfamiliar sound, stir up the complacent satedness of its alleged possessor from outside." See Leora Batnitzky, "Translation as Transcendence: A Glimpse into the Workshop of the Buber-Rosenzweig Bible Translation," *New German Critique* 70 (1997): 87–116, esp. 92 and 116; Klaus Reichert, "'It Is Time': The Buber-Rosenzweig Bible Translation in Context," in *The Translatability of Cultures: Figurations of the Space Between*, ed. Sanford Budick and Wolfgang Iser (Stanford: Stanford University Press, 1996), 169–85, esp. 174–6. There is clearly a structural similarity between Rosenzweig's approach to translation of the voice of the Hebrew Bible as that which cannot be restricted to any place and his rejection of Zionism. See Leora Batnitzky, *Idolatry and Representation: The Philosophy of Franz Rosenzweig Reconsidered* (Princeton, NJ: Princeton University Press, 2000), 141: "Rosenzweig's theory of

translation is consonant with his argument that Jews themselves must return to their strange, foreign pathos, both for their own sake and for the sake of redemption of the world. For Rosenzweig, this meant an embrace of a decidedly diaspora Judaism." On the messianic import of the act of translation according to Rosenzweig, see the comment cited by George Steiner, *After Babel: Aspects of Language and Translation*, third edition (Oxford: Oxford University Press, 1998), 257.

107 Barbara E. Galli, *Franz Rosenzweig and Jehuda Halevi: Translating, Translations, and Translators*, foreword by Paul Mendes-Flohr (Montreal: McGill-Queen's University Press, 1995), 177, cited and analyzed in Wolfson, *Giving*, 66–7. See also Wofson, *The Duplicity*, 74.

108 I have taken the liberty to restate the argument in Wolfson, *Giving*, 70–1. See also Agata Bielik-Robson, "Nihilism through the Looking Glass: Nietzsche, Rosenzweig, and Scholem on the Condition of Modern Disenchantment," *Revista de Estudos da Religião* (September 2007): 39–67, esp. 47–51.

109 Heidegger, *Hölderlin's Hymns*, 21–2; *Hölderlins Hymnen*, 20.

110 Heidegger, *Hölderlin's Hymn "The Ister,"* trans. William McNeill and Julia Davis (Bloomington: Indiana University Press, 1996), 49; *Hölderlins Hymne »Der Ister«* [GA 53] (Frankfurt am Main: Vittorio Klostermann, 1993), 60–1. See the discussion of the theme of homecoming through otherness in Fred Dallmayr, *The Other Heidegger* (Ithaca, NY: Cornell University Press, 1993), 149–80. See also Alejandro A. Vallega, *Heidegger and the Issue of Space: Thinking on Exilic Grounds* (University Park: Pennsylvania State University Press, 2003); Richard Capobianco, *Engaging Heidegger* (Toronto: University of Toronto Press, 2010), 52–69; Brendan O'Donoghue, *A Poetics of Homecoming: Heidegger, Homelessness and the Homecoming Venture* (Newcastle: Cambridge Scholars, 2011), 105–65; Jennifer Anna Gosetti-Ferencei, *Heidegger, Hölderlin, and the Subject of Poetic Language: Towards a New Poetics of Dasein* (New York: Fordham University Press, 2004), 125–8; Susanne Claxton, *Heidegger's Gods: An Ecofeminist Perspective* (London: Rowman & Littlefield, 2017), 43–79; Rafael Winkler, "Dwelling and Hospitality: Heidegger and Hölderlin," *Research in Phenomenology* 47 (2017): 378–80.

111 Martin Heidegger, *Nature, History, State 1933–1934*, trans. and ed. Gregory Fried and Richard Polt (London: Bloomsbury, 2013), 55.

112 Ibid., 56. See Wolfson, *The Duplicity*, 42–3.

113 Heidegger, *Hölderlin's Hymn*, 74; *Hölderlins Hymne*, 91. See Peter Warnek, "Translating *Innigkeit*: The Belonging Together of the Strange," in *Heidegger and the Greeks: Interpretive Essays*, ed. Drew A. Hyland and John Panteleimon Manoussakis (Bloomington: Indiana University Press, 2006), 63.

114 Heidegger, *Contributions*, §278, p. 399; *Beiträge*, 507.

115 Heidegger, *Contributions*, §144, p. 208; *Beiträge*, 264.

116 Heidegger, *Introduction to Metaphysics*, 60; *Einführung in die Metaphysik*, 61. It is of interest to recall the reaction in Martin Heidegger, *Schelling's Treatise on the Essence of Human Freedom*, trans. Joan Stambaugh (Athens: Ohio University Press, 1985), 90 (*Schelling: Vom Wesen der menschlichen Freiheit (1809)* [GA 42] [Frankfurt am Main: Vittorio Klostermann, 1988], 155–6) to Schelling's statement that a truly universal philosophy cannot be the property of a single nation, "Thus it was also truly German that Jacobi's appeals 'to the heart, the inner feelings and faith' did not prevail, but that the 'higher light of Idealism', that is, a more strict thinking, came about and gained control in that Idealism which is therefore called German—a higher kind of thinking which received essential inspiration from Leibniz and a

first true foundation in Kant." Even in this context Heidegger rejects the claim to a philosophical universalism and appeals to a nobler form of Idealism that is exclusively German in nature.
117 Heidegger, *Hölderlin's Hymns*, 107; *Hölderlins Hymnen*, 118.
118 Martin Heidegger, *Four Seminars: Le Thor 1966, 1968, 1969, Zähringen 1973*, trans. Andrew Mitchell and François Raffoul (Bloomington: Indiana University Press, 2003), 37; *Seminare* [GA 15] (Frankfurt am Main: Vittorio Klostermann, 2005), 330. In Heidegger's account of the conception of phenomenology in section 7 of *Sein und Zeit*, the emphasis is not on marking the historical trajectory of the philosophical school, which can be traced to Husserl, but rather on the Greek etymology of the words whence the German term is composed. See Stephen Mulhall, *Inheritance and Originality: Wittgenstein, Heidegger, Kierkegaard* (Oxford: Oxford University Press, 2001), 211–12. Many have discussed Heidegger's privileging of the Greeks and their special relation to the Germans. See the recently published analysis of Claxton, *Heidegger's Gods*, 7–41.
119 Martin Heidegger, *Elucidations of Hölderlin's Poetry*, trans. Keith Hoeller (Amherst, NY: Humanity Books, 2000), 171, emphasis original; *Erläuterungen zu Hölderlins Dichtung* [GA 4] (Frankfurt am Main: Vittorio Klostermann, 1996), 149–50. I have slightly modified the translation.
120 Philippe Lacoue-Labarthe, "Poetry's Courage," in *Walter Benjamin and Romanticism*, ed. Beatrice Hanssen and Andrew Benjamin (London: Continuum, 2002), 163–79, esp. 165 and 167. The essay appears in a different translation in Philippe Lacoue-Labarthe, *Heidegger and the Politics of Poetry*, trans. and intro. Jeff Fort (Urbana: University of Illinois Press, 2007), 60–81, and see esp. 63 and 66. See, however, 104, where the expression "theologico-poetic" is applied to Benjamin in contrast to the expression "theologico-political," which is applied to Heidegger.
121 Heidegger, *Elucidations*, 171; *Erläuterungen*, 150.
122 Heidegger, *Elucidations*, 160; *Erläuterungen*, 138.
123 Heidegger, *Hölderlin's Hymn*, 54; *Hölderlins Hymne*, 67. The point is repeated in Heidegger, *Hölderlin's Hymn*, 124; *Hölderlins Hymne*, 154. See James F. Ward, *Heidegger's Political Thinking* (Amherst, NY: University of Massachusetts Press, 1995), 221–2.
124 Heidegger, *Hölderlin's Hymn*, 54; *Hölderlins Hymne*, 67–8. See the detailed analysis of the themes of *Heimat, Heimkunft*, the holy, and poetic language in Arthur Anthony Grugan, "Thought and Poetry: Language as Man's Homecoming. A Study of Martin Heidegger's Question of Being and Its Ties to Friedrich Hölderlin's Experience of the Holy," PhD dissertation, Duquesne University, 1972, 100–56.
125 Heidegger, *Hölderlin's Hymn*, 55; *Hölderlins Hymne*, 69.
126 Heidegger, *Hölderlin's Hymn*, 62; *Hölderlins Hymne*, 75. For discussion of Heidegger's view of translation, see Miles Groth, *Translating Heidegger* (Amherst, NY: Humanity Books, 2004), 115–63. See also the exchange in Frank Schalow, "A Conversation with Parvis Emad on the Question of Translation in Heidegger," in *Heidegger, Translation, and the Task of Thinking: Essays in Honor of Parvis Emad*, ed. Frank Schalow (Dordrecht: Springer, 2011), 175–89, esp. 186–7; and in the same volume the essays by Julia A. Ireland, "Heidegger, Hölderlin, and Eccentric Translation," 253–67, and Frank Schalow, "Attunement and Translation," 291–311.
127 Heidegger, *Hölderlin's Hymn*, 66; *Hölderlins Hymne*, 81. With respect to this issue, Heidegger is heir to the romantic notion that the German people are the bearers of European culture through translation. See Pol Vandevelde, "Translation as a Mode

of Poetry: Heidegger's Reformulation of the Romantic Project," in *Phenomenology and Literature: Historical Perspectives and Systematic Accounts*, ed. Pol Vandevelde (Würzburg: Königshausen & Neumann, 2010), 93–113; Pol Vandevelde, *Heidegger and the Romantics: The Literary Invention of Meaning* (New York: Routledge, 2012), 42–3.

128   Warnek, "Translating *Innigkeit*," 59; Bret W. Davis, "Heidegger on the Way from Onto-Historical Ethnocentrism to East-West Dialogue," *Gatherings: The Heidegger Circle Annual* 6 (2016): 130–56.

129   Martin Heidegger, *Parmenides*, trans. André Schuwer and Richard Rojcewicz (Bloomington: Indiana University Press, 1992), 12; *Parmenides* [GA 54] (Frankfurt am Main: Vittorio Klostermann, 1992), 17. It is worth recalling the fictional exchange in Heidegger, *On the Way to Language*, 24 (*Unterwegs zur Sprache*, 109), between the Japanese scholar and the inquirer on the experience of translating German texts (including some of Heidegger's essays) into Japanese: "And while I was translating, I often felt as though I were wandering back and forth between two different language realities, such that at moments a radiance shone on me which let me sense that the wellspring of reality [*Wesensquell*] from which those two fundamentally different languages arise was the same." The response of Heidegger through the voice of the inquirer is telling: "You did not, then, seek for a general concept under which both the Europeans and the Eastasian languages could be subsumed." The Japanese scholar concurs, "Absolutely not." The exchange is significant because it affirms that there may be a common source that sustains the meaningfulness of both languages, a common source whose radiance is accessible through the act of translation, but this does not imply that there is a general concept under which the two disparate languages can be subsumed. This is another example of Heidegger's idea of the juxtaposition or belonging-together of the same that remains different.

130   *Novalis: Philosophical Writings*, trans. and ed. Margaret Mahony Stoljar (Albany: State University of New York Press, 1997), 135.

131   Wolfson, *The Duplicity*, 131–53.

132   Martin Heidegger, *What Is a Thing?* trans. W. B. Barton, Jr. and Vera Deutsch with an analysis by Eugene T. Gendlin (Chicago, IL: Henry Regnery Company, 1967), 150–1; *Die Frage Nach dem Ding: Zu Kants Lehre von den Transzendentalen Grundsätzen* [GA 41] (Frankfurt am Main: Vittorio Klostermann, 1984), 153–4. Describing the role of the philosopher to transform and to establish a new logic, which would entail constructing metaphysics upon the ground cleared by Kant's *Kritik der reinen Vernunft*, Heidegger surmises that this "did not lie within Kant's capacity, because such a task exceeds even the capacity of a great thinker. It demands nothing less than to jump over one's own shadow [*über den eigenen Schatten zu springen*] … Hegel alone apparently succeeded in jumping over this shadow, but only in such a way that he eliminated the shadow, i.e., the finiteness of man [*die Endlichkeit des Menschen*] and jumped into the sun itself. Hegel skipped over the shadow [*den Schatten übersprungen*], but he did not, because of that, surpass the shadow [*über den Schatten gesprungen*]. Nevertheless, every philosopher must want to do this. This 'must' is his vocation. The longer the shadow, the wider the jump [*Je länger der Schatten, um so weiter der Sprung*]."

133   Martin Heidegger, *Bremen and Freiburg Lectures: Insight into That Which Is and Basic Principles of Thinking*, trans. Andrew J. Mitchell (Bloomington: Indiana University Press, 2012), 102; *Bremer und Freiburger Vorträge* [GA79] (Frankfurt am Main: Vittorio Klostermann, 1994), 108–9.

134   Martin Heidegger, *Basic Writings*, rev. and exp., ed. and intro. David Farrell Krell, fore. Taylor Carman (London: Harper Perennial, 2008), 330; *Vorträge und Aufsätze*, 26.

Chapter 4

1. Yosef Hayim Yerushalmi, *Zakhor: Jewish History and Jewish Memory* (Seattle: University of Washington Press, 1982).
2. "Religion demands the greatest study of all: one that is required neither to privilege the transrational nor to submit to a supremacy beyond ethics. To stay within the limits of human knowledge, not to speak of the limits of human dignity, that is the difficult challenge. It remains almost impossible, finally, to imagine that we critical students of religion can meet that challenge by surrendering to theophany, theosophy, or event theology." Steven S. Wasserstrom, *Religion after Religion: Gershom Scholem, Mircea Eliade, and Henry Corbin at Eranos* (Princeton, NJ: Princeton University Press, 1999), 238.
3. Karl Jaspers, *Vom Ursprung und Ziel der Geschichte* (München: Piper Verlag, 1994).
4. For a comment on this famous image see Amos Funkenstein, *Perceptions of Jewish History* (Berkeley: University of California Press, 1993), 71.
5. Tomoko Masuzawa, *The Invention of World Religions, or, How European Universalism Was Preserved in the Language of Pluralism* (Chicago, IL: University of Chicago, 2005).
6. On this theme see especially Jürgen Habermas, *Glauben und Wissen. Friedenspreis des deutschen Buchhandels* (Frankfurt am Main: Suhrkamp Verlag, 2001); for commentary and criticism see Peter E. Gordon, "What Hope Remains? Habermas on Religion," *The New Republic*, December 14, 2012; and also Peter E. Gordon, "Kritische Theorie zwischen Sakralen und Profane," *WestEnd. Neue Zeitschrift für Sozialforschung* 1 (2016): 3–34.
7. Jürgen Habermas, *Postmetaphysical Thinking. Philosophical Essays* (Cambridge, MA: MIT Press, 1994).
8. Thorkild Jacobsen, "The Eridu Genesis," *Journal of Biblical Literature* 100, no. 4 (1981): 513–29; Samuel Noah Kramer, "The Sumerian Deluge Myth: Reviewed and Revised," *Anatolian Studies* 33 (1983): 115–21; and Miguel Civil, "The Sumerian Flood Story," in *Atra-ḫasis: The Babylonian Story of the Flood*, ed. W. G. Lambert and A. R. Millard (Warsaw, IN: Eisenbrauns, 1999).
9. Herbert Fingarette, *Confucius: The Secular as Sacred* (New York: Harper and Row, 1972).
10. Talal Asad, *Formations of the Secular: Christianity, Islam, Modernity* (Stanford, CA: Stanford University Press, 2003); Saba Mahmood, *Religious Difference in a Secular Age: A Minority Report* (Princeton, NJ: Princeton University Press, 2005).
11. Jürgen Habermas, "Notes on Post-Secular Society," *New Perspectives Quarterly* 25, no. 4 (Fall 2008): 17–29.
12. Steven M. Wasserstrom, *Between Muslim and Jew: The Problem of Symbiosis under Early Islam* (Princeton, NJ: Princeton University Press, 1995).

Chapter 5

1. Steven M. Wassserstrom, "Nine Theses on the Study of Religion," in this volume, §7. Wasserstrom describes "Religious Studies" as having a "miscegenated character" (§7) and earlier describes "the critical study of religion [as] a science of the human plural," which is to say the discipline seeks a "generalist perspective" (§1) of encounter, continuity, change, and negotiation (§§1 & 2).

2   Wasserstrom, "Nine Theses," §6: "Religious Studies not only compares religions but also reflects on that comparison [citing G. van der Leeuw, *Religion in Essence and Manifestation* (Princeton, NJ: Princeton University Press, 1986)]. It must compare historically and then reflect philosophically on the results of that comparison."
3   See n. 1, above.
4   Wasserstrom, "Nine Theses," §6, Wasserstrom states that "the new [meaning the 'religion after religion' academic study] Religious Studies must 'abjure such prescribed choices' between opposing revelations," citing Adorno, *Minima Moralia*. Such purportedly "opposing revelations" include emic/etic, truth/revelation, science/politics, empiricism/theology, and history/philosophy.
5   Ibid.
6   Steven M. Wasserstrom, *Religion after Religion: Gerschom Scholem, Mircea Eliade, and Henry Corbin at Eranos* (Princeton, NJ: Princeton University Press, 1999), 8, 46, 72, 142, 147, 207. See also the ways in which Wasserstrom's own approach in that monograph has been characterized as deploying Hermetic elements via the privileging of secrecy: Hugh B. Urban, "Review: Syndrome of the Secret: 'Esocentrism' and the Work of Steven M. Wasserstrom: Religion after Religion: Gershom Scholem, Mircea Eliade, and Henry Corbin at Eranos by Steven M. Wasserstrom," *Journal of the American Academy of Religion* 69, no.2 (2001): 437–47. Elsewhere, Wasserstrom explored the intersection of Hermeticism and Neoplatonism in the interconfessional circles of Christian, Jewish, and Islamic philosophers in the early medieval period, for example, around the *Theology of Aristotle* in Steven M. Wasserstrom, "The Islamic Social and Cultural Context," in *History of Jewish Philosophy*, ed. Daniel H. Frank and Oliver Leaman (New York: Routledge, 1997), 2–93. Consideration of the *Theology* must take account of Shlomo Pines, "La longue récension de la Théologie d'Aristote dans ses rapports avec la doctrine ismaélienne," *Revue des études Islamiques* 22 (1954): 7–20. Pines's main thrust addresses the potential authorship of the longer recension of the *Theology* via Ismailism.
7   The historical/philosophical dialectic is one of several broached in Wasserstrom's "Theses," just mentioned: emic/etic, truth/revelation, scientific/political, and empirical/theological. I focus on the historical/philosophical relationship, but any of the other dialectics could be substituted without much loss of force in my argument. Indeed, the reader will see that these various dialectics mutually implicate, and I reintroduce and engage with all of them in the course of my discussion.
8   Paul Robertson, *Paul's Letters and Contemporary Greco-Roman Literature: Theorizing a New Taxonomy* (Leiden: Brill, 2016).
9   J. Z. Smith, "Fences and Neighbors: Some Contours of Early Judaism," in *Imagining Religion: From Babylon to Jonestown*, ed. J. Z. Smith (Chicago, IL: Chicago University Press, 1982), 1–18 and chapter 7, "A Matter of Class: Taxonomies of Religion," in *Relating Religion: Essays in the Study of Religion*, ed. J. Z. Smith (Chicago, IL: University of Chicago Press, 2004). See further engagement with the notion of polythetism in A. P. Alston, "Religion," in *Encyclopedia of Philosophy* VII, ed. Paul Edwards (New York: Macmillan, 1967), 142; Rodney Needham, "Polythetic Classificaiton: Convergence and Consequences," *Man* 10 (1975): 349–69; Rem Edwards, *Reason and Religion: An Introduction to the Philosophy of Religion* (New York: Harcourt, 1972), 38.
10 An anthropology-based critique of the philosophically derived polytheism of scholars in the prior note can be found in Benson Saler, *Conceptualizing Religion: Immanent Anthropologists, Transcendent Natives, and Unbounded Categories* (Leiden:

Brill, 1993), where Saler forwards a "prototype" approach that he argues is more attentive to ethnographic differences than formal definitions.

11   Ludwig Wittgenstein, *Philosophical Investigations*, trans. Elizabeth Anscombe (Oxford: Blackwell, 1958 [1953]); see further R. W. Beardsmore, "The Theory of Family Resemblances," *Philosophical Investigations* 15, no. 2 (1992): 131–46.

12   Massimo Pigliucci, "Species as Family Resemblance Concepts: The (Dis-)Solution of the Species Problem," *BioEssays* 25, no. 6 (2003): 596–602.

13   For example, Paolo Vineis, "Definition and Classification of Cancer: Monothetic or Polythetic?," *Theoretical Medicine* 14, no. 3 (1993): 249–56; for biology, specifically plant communities, see Enrico Feoli, "A Criterion for Monothetic Classification of Phytosociological Entities on the Basis of Species Ordination," *Vegetatio* 33, no. 2/3 (1977): 147–52.

14   The so-called "Species Problem" in biology reflects in part the tension between monothetic and polythetic understandings: see Frank E. Zachos, *Species Concepts in Biology: Historical Development, Theoretical Foundations and Practical Relevance* (Basel: Springer, 2016).

15   §7: "There is virtually no religious situation that is not a situation of contact, and no Religious Studies that does not make sense of contact."

16   A few useful, more recent starting points that were instrumental in my own understanding of Hermeticism articulated in this paper: Florian Ebeling, *The Secret History of Hermes Trismegistus: Hermeticisim from Ancient to Modern Times*, trans. David Lorton (Ithaca, NY: Cornell University Press, 2007), n.b. the forward by Jan Assmann; Brian P. Copenhaver, *Hermetica: The Greek Corpus Hermeticum and the Latin Asclepius in a new English Translation, with Notes and Introduction* (Cambridge: Cambridge University Press, 1992); Garth Fowden, *The Egyptian Hermes: A Historical Approach to the Late Pagan Mind* (Cambridge: Cambridge University Press, 1986); Stanton J. Linden, *The Alchemy Reader: From Hermes Trismegistus to Isaac Newton* (Cambridge: Cambridge University Press, 2003); Roelof van Den Broek and Wouter J. Hanegraaff, *Gnosis and Hermeticism: From Antiquity to Modern Times* (Albany: State University of New York Press, 1998). Older, foundational work on Hermeticism should not be ignored, esp. Richard Reitzenstein, André Festugière, Jean-Pierre Mahé, Charles H. Dodd, and Frances A.Yates. Copenhaver's introduction gives a nice summary of scholarship on Hermeticism, ranging back hundreds of years.

17   This distinction is typical of older scholarship, and persists in general surveys today, for example, Michaela Pereira, "Alchemy and Hermeticism: An Introduction to This Issue," *Early Science and Medicine* 5, no. 2 (2000): 115–20. Notable is Fowden's insightful conclusion that these two categories of Hermetica, which he generally upholds as flawed but useful, should be read together: the former functions as the preparatory foundation for the latter, whereby the former is eventually discarded. In this view, the two were not understood as separate in the ancient world, but were part and parcel of a much wider body of literature whose constituent parts were variously read in different contexts but likely together.

18   Broek and Hanegraaff, *Gnosis and Hermeticism*, 5, notes this approach as a formally effective way to demarcate a body of literature that continues to manifest over time, but ultimately discards it.

19   Fowden and Copenhaver trend toward this more exhaustive approach, with different solutions as far as how to narrow or focus the evidential breadth: Fowden explores defined themes within which diversity manifested; Copenhaver takes the historical

approach in bounding "Hermetica" based on collections of texts from a certain time and sees "a blend of theology, cosmogony, anthropogony, ethics, soteriology and eschatology," *Hermetica*, xxxii–xxxiii.

20 Copenhaver, *Hermetica*, xli–xlii, outlines the argument that Byzantine editorial hands, such as Michael Psellos, artificially created collections such as the *Corpus Hermeticum*, wherein the Byzantine copyists' "abhorrence of magic" expressed in the manuscript margins was responsible for the comparative absence of astrology and magic, thereby artificially creating the "technical vs. philosophical" divide we see in Ficino's 1463 edition. Importantly, Copenhaver notes that this was not the creation of Hermetic collections per se: as the Vienna fragments show, collections were circulating by the second or third century CE.

21 Fowden, *Egyptian Hermes*, 73, for example, rejects the previous generations' proposals of "aphoristic wisdom literature" and "suitable for classroom" for these very reasons.

22 Recall the earlier discussion around my claim that taxonomy is epistemology.

23 For the importance of equal weighting in a taxonomy see Robert Sokal and Peter Sneath, *Principles of Numerical Taxonomy* (San Francisco and London: W.H. Freeman, 1963). The danger in non-equal weighting is that its relative subjectivity results in the taxonomist becoming increasingly subject to a weighting that confirms existing biases.

24 To reproduce a note from the very beginning of this paper: §6: "Religious Studies not only compares religions but also reflects on that comparison. It must compare historically and then reflect philosophically on the results of that comparison."

25 §4: Wasserstrom argues that Religious Studies must "mediate two powers centrally necessary for the functioning of the state, science and politics," taking what is empirically present in the past (science) and putting it into conversation with what is relevant (viz., entertaining) in our current era (politics) via a process whereby it "re-narrativizes our texts and our history" instead of merely "perpetuat[ing] ancient tales of legitimation." In other words, Wasserstrom argues that we *must* include "political hegemonies" as one of two organizing poles, for it is only thereby that we can mediate between the emic ("naturalistic explanation, from within") and the etic ("from without").

26 William James calls this "radical empiricism," which Wasserstrom includes as central to one of his "Theses" (§8), and concerns the reality of things that are derived from the relationships between things, such as the derivation and nature of value and meaning. Value and meaning are not naturalistic in the sense of basic phenomenology, namely the movement of basic atoms and physicalist sensations. Rather, they are naturalistic in the sense that the derivation of value and meaning is built on a phenomenological naturalism, but their ontology is at a second order above and beyond this type of naturalism: they can be located, understood, and seen to exist, but at a different qualitative level. We might take as example a dog as cultural object and the abstract understanding thereof.

27 Cf. Wasserstrom's discussion in §8, although Wasserstrom's reflections there extend to the nature of the most modern technology in changing conceptions of the self in always new ways. By including self-conscious meta-reflections as characteristics within our polythetic schema, however, we will hopefully be able to account for such changes. Polythetic characteristics that define a category will change based on the questions being asked, as well as the inherently shifting nature of data in a lived world. Including meta-reflexive principles in our polythetic schema will assure

that regardless of the nature of changing "human self-definition" and "miraculous remaking," our schema will be equipped to exchange previous self-understandings for new ones.

Chapter 6

1. Walter Benjamin, "Berlin Chronicle," in *Reflections: Essays, Aphorisms, Autobiographical Writings*, trans. Edmund Jephcott (New York: Schocken Books, 2007 [1978]).
2. This final question, which highlights the relationship between the "phenomenology" and history of cityscapes, has inspired much of my recent work, centered on the concepts of "disciplined historicity" and its later avatar, "textured historicity": for the former, see Jeremy F. Walton, "Geographies of Revival and Erasure: Neo-Ottoman Sites of Memory in Istanbul, Thessaloniki, and Budapest," *Die Welt Des Islams* 56 (2016): 510–32, 516; for the latter, Jeremy F. Walton, "Introduction: Textured Historicity and the Ambivalence of Imperial Legacies," *History and Anthropology* (under review).
3. Walter Benjamin, *The Arcades Project*, trans. Howard Eiland and Kevin McLaughlin (Cambridge, MA: The Belknap Press of Harvard University, 2002). Buck-Morss suggests that Berlin, Moscow, Naples, and Paris form the cardinal points on a sort of conceptual-aesthetic-ideological compass for Benjamin—see her diagram in *The Dialectics of Seeing: Walter Benjamin and the Arcades Project* (Cambridge, MA: The MIT Press, 1991), 25.
4. Martina Lauster, "Walter Benjamin's Myth of the 'Flâneur,'" *The Modern Language Review* 102, no. 1 (January 2007): 139–56.
5. See Bernd Witte, *Walter Benjamin: An Intellectual Biography* (New York: Verso, 1996).
6. Buck-Morss, *Dialectics of Seeing*.
7. See also David Harvey, *Paris, Capital of Modernity* (New York: Routledge, 2003); Walton, "Textured Historicity."
8. Susan J. Handelman, *Fragments of Redemption: Jewish Thought and Literary Theory in Benjamin, Scholem and Levinas* (Bloomington: Indiana University Press, 1991); cf. Judith Butler, "Critique, Coercion, and Sacred Life in Benjamin's 'Critique of Violence,'" in *Political Theologies: Public Religions in a Post-Secular World*, ed. Hent de Vries and Lawrence E. Sullivan (New York: Fordham University Press, 2006), 205.
9. Gershom Scholem, *Walter Benjamin: The Story of a Friendship* (New York: New York Review of Books, 1981); Walter Benjamin and Gershom Scholem, *The Correspondence of Walter Benjamin and Gershom Scholem, 1932–1940*, ed. Gershom Scholem, trans. Gary Smith et al. (Cambridge, MA: Harvard University Press, 1992); Buck-Morss, *Dialectics of Seeing*, 9 ff.; Eric Jacobson, *Metaphysics of the Profane: The Political Theology of Walter Benjamin and Gershom Scholem* (New York: Columbia University Press, 2010).
10. Steven M. Wasserstrom, *Religion after Religion: Gershom Scholem, Mircea Eliade, and Henri Corbin at Eranos* (Princeton, NJ: Princeton University Press, 1999). The Eranos discussion circle, which first convened in Ascona, Switzerland, in 1933, was (and continues to be) an annual assembly of scholars dedicated to research and debate surrounding themes of religion and spirituality, among other concerns. It was

initially inspired by the German philosopher of religion Rudolf Otto, founded by the Dutch scholar-theosophist Olga Fröbe-Kapteyn, and convened under the decisive influence of Carl Jung; see Wasserstrom, *Religion after Religion*, 36. For greater detail on the history of Eranos, see Hans Thomas Hakl, *Eranos: An Alternative Intellectual History of the Twentieth Century*, trans. Christopher McIntosh (New York: Routledge, 2013).

11 Judith Butler argues, however, that a conception of "divine violence" drawn from monotheistic traditions was crucial to Benjamin's critique of "law-founding and law-preserving violence": see Butler, "Critique, Coercion," 207 ff. on Benjamin's influential essay "Critique of Violence," in Benjamin, *Reflections*. Furthermore, Benjamin's notion of messianic time, developed in his "Theses on the Philosophy History," drew clearly on the prophetic traditions of Judaism and Christianity to contest the homogeneous, progressive time of modernity; see Benjamin, *Illuminations: Essays and Reflections*, trans. Harry Zohn (New York: Schocken, 1968).

12 Ibid., 80.
13 Svetlana Boym, *The Future of Nostalgia* (New York: Basic Books, 2001), xvi–xvii.
14 Benjamin, *Illuminations*, 258. This quotation is taken from Benjamin's famous passage on the Angel of History, inspired by Paul Klee's painting "Angelus Novus" (1968, 257–8). Scholem was equally fascinated by Klee's painting, it seems. Wasserstrom quotes the following poem on "Angelus Novus" written by Scholem: "I am an unsymbolic thing; My meaning is what I am; You turn the magic ring in vain; I have no sense"; see Wasserstrom, *Religion after Religion*, 86.
15 Wasserstrom, *Religion after Religion*, 67 ff.
16 Ibid., 80.
17 Ibid., 115 ff.
18 See Pierre Bourdieu, *The Political Ontology of Martin Heidegger*, trans. Peter Collier (Stanford, CA: Stanford University Press, 1991).
19 Wasserstrom, *Religion after Religion*, 75–7.
20 Buck-Morss, *Dialectics of Seeing*, 21.
21 Benjamin, *Reflections*, 165–6.
22 Le Corbusier, *Toward an Architecture*, trans. John Goodman (Los Angeles, CA: The Getty Research Institute, 2007 [1924]). Although Benjamin did not write about Le Corbusier directly to the best of my knowledge, his interrogation of the famous rebuilder of nineteenth-century Paris, Baron Haussmann, anticipates a critique of modernist urban planning and design that equally applies, *mutatis mutandis*, to Le Corbusier's vigorous ambition to reshape cities; see Benjamin, *Reflections*, 159–62.
23 Benjamin, *Reflections*, 166.
24 Ibid., 168.
25 Ibid., 169.
26 Ibid., 170.
27 Ibid., 171.
28 Ibid., 172.
29 Although urban porosity is the most striking and, in this context, pertinent instance of *coincidentia oppositorum* in Benjamin's work, one can detect "coinciding opposites" elsewhere in his oeuvre as well. His essay on Moscow—a fascinating companion piece to the essay on Naples—also gestures to porosity and the coincidence of the urban and the rural: Benjamin, *Reflections*, 125. More abstractly, Judith Butler argues that Benjamin's theory of political violence, as articulated in his "Critique of

Violence," constitutes a *coincidentia oppositorum*, "the paradoxical possibility of a nonviolent violence," in Butler, "Critique, Coercion," 202.
30 Wasserstrom, *Religion after Religion*, 191–3.
31 Ibid., 86 ff.
32 Ibid., 99, emphasis original.
33 Ibid., 86. The implicit antagonist of this Romantic theory of the symbol was almost certainly the "semiology" of Ferdinand de Saussure and early structuralist linguistics, which asserted the absolute "arbitrariness" of signs, understood as haphazard dyads of "signifiers" and "signifieds": Ferdinand de Saussure, *Course in General Linguistics*, trans. Roy Harris (Peru, IL: Open Court, 1986 [1916]). For Romantics and post-Romantics, including the Historians of Religion, signifier and signified necessarily determined and conditioned each other.
34 Benjamin, *Reflections*, 30, emphasis added.
35 Proust's famous passage on the involuntary memory triggered by the scent of a *petite madeleine* pastry is a clear precedent for Benjamin here: "The past is hidden somewhere outside the realm, beyond the reach of intellect, in some material object (in the sensation which that material object will give us) of which we have no inkling": Marcel Proust, *Remembrance of Things Past*, vol. 1, trans. C. K. Scott Moncrieff and Terence Kilmartin (New York: Vintage/Random House, 1981), 47–8.
36 Ibid., 8.
37 Drawing on Benjamin's work, archaeologist Shannon Dawdy has proposed the concept of "patina" to capture the palimpsestic manner in which objects and landscapes bear traces of the past in a manner that creates a unique, off-modern mode of historical value in the present; see Dawdy, *Patina: A Profane Archaeology* (Chicago, IL: University of Chicago Press, 2016).
38 Buck-Morss, *Dialectics of Seeing*, 4, emphasis original.
39 Ibid., 375 n. 6.
40 Benjamin, *Reflections*, 148.
41 Ibid.
42 Ibid., 162.
43 Cf. Reinhardt Kosseleck, *Futures Past: On the Semantics of Historical Time*, trans. Keith Tribe (New York: Columbia University Press, 2004).
44 See Walton, "Textured Historicity."
45 Wasserstrom, *Religion after Religion*, 159 ff.
46 Ibid., 144.
47 Ibid., 27.
48 Benjamin, *Illuminations*, 242.
49 Wasserstrom, *Religion after Religion*, 6.
50 The clearest biographical illustration of this uneasiness with nationalism was surely Benjamin's disinclination to emigrate to Palestine and join the Zionist project, despite the repeated overtures of his friend Scholem.
51 Wasserstrom highlights the stature of the *androgyne*, itself a *coincidentia oppositorum*, in "religion after religion"; he also mentions the appeal of this hermaphroditic figure to Benjamin in the context of Benjamin's brief fantasy, "Agesilaus Santander": Wasserstrom, *Religion after Religion*, 206–7.
52 William Mazzarella, "The Magic of Mass Publicity: Reading Ioan Couliano" (unpublished manuscript, courtesy of author), 7.
53 Steven M. Wasserstrom, "Nine Theses on the Study of Religion," in this volume, §6.
54 Ibid.

55 See also ibid., §6: "To know one [religion] is to know none," a paraphrase of Max Müller.

Chapter 7

1   Steven M. Wasserstrom, *Religion after Religion: Gershom Scholem, Mircea Eliade, and Henry Corbin at Eranos* (Princeton, NJ: Princeton University Press, 1999), 239.
2   Wasserstrom, *Religion after Religion*.
3   Steven M. Wasserstrom, "Response: Final Note to Significance Seekers," *Journal of the American Academy of Religion* 69, no. 2 (2001): 462.
4   Ibid., 461.
5   Wasserstrom, *Religion after Religion*, 247.
6   Gustavo Benavides, "*Afterreligion* after Religion," *Journal of the American Academy of Religion* 69, no. 2 (2001): 452–3.
7   *Religion after Religion*, 129–31; note the suggestion that a specifically Catholic form of German Romanticism informs Scholem's sensibilities. On a "counter-nationalism" in Scholem's thought, see David Biale, "Scholem und der moderne Nationalismus," in *Gershom Scholem: Zwischen den Disziplinen*, ed. Peter Schäfer and Gary Smith (Frankfurt am Main: Suhrkamp Verlag, 1995), 257–74.
8   Wasserstrom, "Response," 460–1.
9   Therefore, I take for granted that the predominantly anti-fascist character of Scholem's career has been duly stressed in scholarly representations; for example, David Biale, *Gershom Scholem: Kabbalah and Counter-History* (Cambridge, MA: Harvard University Press, 1982), 151; Noam Zadoff, *Gershom Scholem: From Berlin to Jerusalem and Back* (Waltham, MA: Brandeis University Press, 2018), 157–221.
10 I cite the first edition, Calchaquí, Salta, 1970. All English quotations below are my translations. *DCAP* has undergone two further Spanish editions (Buenos Aires: Epheta, 1994, and Segni: Verbo Incarnato, 2013), two Italian editions as *Influsso dello gnosticismo ebraico in ambiente Cristiano* (Rome: Sacra Fraternitas Aurigarum, 1988 & 1995), and one French edition as *De la cabale au progressisme* (Broché: Saint-Rémi, 2011).
11 David Berger and Jorgen Vijgen, eds. *Thomistenlexikon* (Bonn: Nova & Vetera, 2006), 447–53, s.n. "Meinvielle."
12 Jose María Medrano, *Los Iniciales "Cursos de Cultura Católica" de Buenos Aires* (Buenos Aires: Editorial Dunken, 2015), 32.
13 On this work, see Sandra McGee Deutsch, *Las Derechas: The Extreme Right in Argentina, Brazil, and Chile, 1890–1939* (Stanford, CA: Stanford University Press, 1999), 224–7.
14 See Alberto Spektorowski, "Los orígenes intelectuales del antisemitismo en la derecha nacionalista argentina: Los casos de J. Meinvielle, R. Doll y E. Osés," in *Ensayos sobre Judaismo Latinoamericano*, ed. Bernardo Blejmar and Ana Epelbaum de Weinstein (Buenos Aires: Editorial Milá, 1990), 200–26; Graciela Ben Dror, *The Catholic Church and the Jews in Argentina 1933–45* (Lincoln: University of Nebraska Press, 2008), 49–56; Federico Finchelstein, *Transatlantic Fascism: Ideology, Violence, and the Sacred in Argentina and Italy* (Durham, NC: Duke University Press, 2010), 118–38; Federico Finchelstein, *The Ideological Origins of the Dirty War: Fascism, Populism, and Dictatorship in Twentieth Century Argentina* (Oxford: Oxford University Press, 2014), 45–60.

15 Meinvielle apologists have characteristically soft-pedalled the antisemitic character of the priest's theological anti-Judaism. Use of this neo-Arendtian distinction between Christian religious anti-Judaism and modern antisemitism, however, is not intended to legitimate such apologetics, but to indicate the confluence of old and new factors. For such defenses, see, for example, *Thomistenlexikon*, 451–2, and Alberto Caturelli, *Historia de la filosofía en la Argentina, 1600–2000* (Buenos Aires: Ciudad Argentina, 2001), 859. On the neo-Arendtian distinction, see Robert Chazan, *Medieval Stereotypes and Modern Antisemitism* (Berkeley: University of California Press, 1997), 125–40. For an argument against this Arendtian framework, see David Nirenberg, "Epilogue: Drowning Intellectuals," in *Anti-Judaism: The Western Tradition* (New York: Norton, 2013).
16 Appraised of their reputation as a forgery, Meinvielle granted the explanatory value of the *Protocols*, without actually affirming their authenticity. See S. Deutsch, *Las Derechas*, 226. In private correspondence, Wasserstrom has shown me extensive documentation, which he has painstakingly gathered, demonstrating that such a position with respect to the *Protocols* was, in fact, a standard trope.
17 See note 44 below; on masonry, Eliade, and Corbin, see *Religion after Religion*, 38 and 48. On masonry, Martinism, and traditionalism, see Mark Sedgwick, *Against the Modern World: Traditionalism and the Secret Intellectual History of the Twentieth Century* (Oxford: Oxford University Press, 2004), 45–7.
18 See Patricia Alejandra Orbe, "La concepción política de Jacques Maritain, eje de una controversia católica," in *El pensamiento alternativo en la Argentina del siglo XX: Oberismo y justicia social (1930–1960)*, ed. Hugo Edgardo Biagini and Arturo Andrés Roig (Buenos Aires: Editorial Biblos, 2006), 157–72; see also Finchelstein, *Transatlantic Fascism*, 142–4.
19 On the Tacuara and Meinvielle's role, see Leonardo Senkman, "The Right and Civilian Regimes, 1955–1976," in *The Argentine Right*, ed. Sandra McGee Deutsch and Ronald Dolkart (Wilmington, DE: Scholarly Resources, 1993), 126–8; David Rock, *Authoritarian Argentina* (Berkeley: University of California Press, 1993), 205–9; Roberto Bardini, *Tacuara, la pólvora y la sangre* (Mexico City: Océano, 2002); Daniel Gutman, *Tacuara: Historia de la primera guerrilla urbana argentina* (Buenos Aires: Vergara, 2003)—I thank Nico Gutman for this reference; Raanan Rein, *Argentine Jews Or Jewish Argentines?: Essays on Ethnicity, Identity, and Diaspora* (Leiden: Brill, 2010), 174–7; and Mario Virgilio Santiago Jiménez, "Julio Meinvielle, Tacuaras, los Tecos y El Yunque contra la 'infiltración roja' en México y Argentina," *Cahiers des Amériques latines* 79 (2015): 1–18.
20 Finchelstein, *Ideological Origins*, 97–8.
21 Ibid., 110 and 192 n. 72.
22 Ibid.
23 "65 Arrests Made," *New York Times*, October 12, 1971: 7.
24 Sacheri, "R. P. Julio Meinvielle. In memoriam," *Cabildo* 5 (1973). My trans.
25 Héctor Hernández has published an elaborate biography of Sacheri, written in a hagiographic spirit: Héctor Hernández, *Sacheri: Predicar y Morir Por la Argentina* (Buenos Aires: Vórtice, 2007).
26 Edy Kaufman and Beatriz Cymberknopf, "La dimensión judía de la represión durante el gobierno militar (1976–1983)," in *Autoritarismo y antisemitismo: los judios durante la dictadura militar, 1976–1983*, ed. Leonardo Senkman (Buenos Aires: Centro Editor de América Latina, 1986), 236–75: "En febrero de 1979 el Ministerio de Educación y Cultura instrumenta un decreto por el cual se establece

la obligación de estudios confesionales católicos en la asignatura de Instrucción Moral y Cívica que afectó la libertad de cultos y el laicismo en la enseñanza. En la bibliografía recomendada se encontraban autores notoriamente antisemitas como el Rvdo. Julio Meinvielle y el profesor Bruno Genta"; cf. Finchelstein, *Ideological Origins*, 149.

27 C. M. Buela's brother, Alberto Buela Lamas, professor of gnoseology at Universidad de Patagonia, San Juan Bosco in Comodoro Rivadavia, was also a close disciple, whose speculative treatise on Thomist metaphysics—*El ente y los trascendentales* (Buenos Aires: Editorial Cruz y Fierro, 1972)—features a prologue written by Meinvielle, as well as the latter's equivocal note on the author's credibility.

28 Eric Voegelein, *The New Science of Politics: An Introduction* (Chicago, IL: University of Chicago Press, 1987), 126.

29 On Kelsen's critique, see Eckhart Arnold, *A New Science of Politics: Hans Kelsen's Reply to Eric Voegelin's "New Science of Politics": A Contribution to the Critique of Ideology* (Frankfurt: Ontos Verlag, 2004). On Voegelin's heresiological construction of Gnosticism, see Arthur Versluis, *The New Inquisitions: Heretic-Hunting and the Intellectual Origins of Modern Totalitarianism* (Oxford: Oxford University Press, 2006), 69–84, esp. 73 on Eliade's student Ioan Culianu's criticism. For an alternate approach to the Voegelinian problem of Gnosticism and modernity, see Hans Blumenberg, *The Legitimacy of the Modern Age*, trans. R. W. Wallace (Cambridge, MA: MIT Press, 1985), 125–37.

30 *DCAP*, 280–5.

31 Eric Voegelin, *Science, Politics, and Gnosticism: Two Essays* (Washington, DC: Regnery, 1997), 68.

32 The same basic charge of immanentism was alleged, in fact, against the earliest kabbalists by the Jewish *anti-Christian* polemicist Meir ben Simeon of Narbonne in the thirteenth century. See Alon Goshen-Gottstein, "The Triune and the Decaune God: Christianity and Kabbalah as Objects of Jewish Polemics," in *Religious Polemics in Context*, ed. Theo Hettema et al. (Leiden: Brill, 2005), 165–97.

33 Moreover, Voegelin, on the basis of Scholem's work, understood the golem as a Judaic affirmation of the death of God and a concomitant assertion of human self-divinization. See Voegelin, *Science, Politics, and Gnosticism*, 37–41, 51; on Scholem and Voegelin, see Moshe Idel, *Old Worlds, New Mirrors: On Jewish Mysticism and Twentieth-Century Thought* (Philadelphia: University of Pennsylvania Press, 2012), 31–51.

34 Bernardino Montejano, "La concepción política del Padre Julio Meinvielle," *Instituto de Filosofía Práctica*, May 21, 2013, http://www.infip.org.ar/wp-content/uploads/2012/06/Concepción-pol%C3%ADtica-del-Padre-J.Meinvielle1.doc (accessed March 31, 2018).

35 Voegelin, *Science, Politics, and Gnosticism*, 57; see the very first sentence of the "Forward to the American Edition," xix: "The more we come to know about the gnosis of antiquity, the more it becomes certain that modern movements of thought, such as progressivism, positivism, Hegelianism, and Marxism, are variants of gnosticism."

36 In fact, Meinvielle's disciples regarded his thoroughgoing opposition to progressivism, and Christian progressivism in particular, as the core of his political legacy. See, for example, Carlos M. Buela's preface to the posthumous edition of Julio Meinville, *El Progresismo Cristiano* (Buenos Aires: Cruz y Fierro Editores, 1983), i–vii. I thank Leonardo Senkman for graciously alerting me to the existence of this

volume, comprising mostly essays composed by Meinvielle during the 1960s, prior to the appearance of *DCAP*.

37 Gustavo Piemonte, "Notas sobre la creación de nihilo en Juan Escoto Eriugena," *Sapientia* 23, no. 87 (1968): 37–58, and *Sapientia* 23, no. 88 (1968): 115–32. Also see Piemonte, "Jean Scot et un opuscule hébreu pseudépigraphique du XIIIème siècle," in *Eriugena redivivus: Zur Wirkungsgeschichte seines Denkens im Mittelalter und im Übergang zur Neuzeit*, ed. Werner Beierwalters (Heidelberg: Universitätsverlag Winter, 1987), 279–310. See Scholem, *Origins of the Kabbalah*, trans. Arkush (Princeton, NJ: Princeton University Press, 1987), 270–2, 314, 318, 344, 375, 422–3.

38 *DCAP*, 178–82.

39 Ibid., 411–13. On this issue see pp. 72 below.

40 *DCAP*, 178–85, on Vajda, also see 185, whom Meinvielle cites to the effect that it is "legitimate to affirm that the kabbalistic doctrine is very ancient—as ancient as the penetration of gnosis into Judaism, but probably prior to Christianity by two or three generations."

41 *DCAP*, 49.

42 Meinvielle cites zoharic passages of interest for Christian theology from Drach's *La Cabale des Hébreux* (Rome: Imprimerie de la Propagande, 1864). On Drach, who, as a convert to Christianity, defended the kabbalah against Adolphe Franck's charges of pantheism, see Paul Fenton, "Qabbalah and Academia: The Critical Study of Jewish Mysticism in France," *Shofar: An Interdisciplinary Journal of Jewish Studies* 18, no. 2 (2000): 52–3.

43 Meinvielle calls this approach "*naturalista*" and "*universitaria*." See *DCAP*, 72–95.

44 He maintains that this traditional rabbinic approach extends to the masonic doctrines exposed in León Meurin, *Filosofía de la Masonería* (Madrid: Editorial Nos, 1957); the vitriolic epilogue to Meurin's book written by Spanish police officer and propagandist Mauricio Carlavilla (1896–1982, alias Karl), which equates kabbalah with satanism, similarly stimulated Meinvielle; although it cited Scholem minimally, this anti-kabbalistic polemic had not yet been refined via the latter's historiographic framework (Carlavilla also cited the history of Ernst Mueller). See especially Meurin, 258–69, and *DCAP*, 116–22. On Carlavilla, see Gonzalo Alvarez Chillida, *El antisemitismo en España: la imagen del judío, 1812–2002* (Madrid: Marcial Pons, 2002), 320–2, 428–36.

45 Also, on the issue of mystocentrism and kabbalah studies, see Boaz Huss, "The Mystification of Kabbalah and the Myth of Jewish Mysticism" (Hebrew), *Pe'amim* 110 (2007): 9–30; see also the fuller intervention in Huss, *The Question about the Existence of Jewish Mysticism: The Genealogy of Jewish Mysticism and the Theologies of Kabbalah Research* (Hebrew) (Jerusalem: Van Leer Institute, 2016).

46 *DCAP*, 78, 89, 170, 185, 415.

47 Ibid., 43–8.

48 Ibid., 77–80.

49 Ibid., 80–9.

50 Ibid., 90–5.

51 Ibid., 83–4.

52 See Joseph Ben Shlomo, "On Pantheism in Jewish Mysticism According to Gershom Scholem and His Critics" (Hebrew), *Da'at* 50–52 (2003): 461–82; Joseph Ben Shlomo, "Gershom Scholem on Pantheism in the Kabbala," in *Gershom Scholem: The Man and His Work*, ed. Paul Mendes-Flohr (Albany: State University of New York Press, 1993), 56–72. On eighteenth- and nineteenth-century debates concerning

the pantheistic character of kabbalah, see Wouter Hanegraaf, "The Beginnings of Occultist Kabbalah: Adolphe Franck and Eliphas Lévi," in *Kabbalah and Modernity: Interpretations, Transformations, Adaptations*, ed. Boaz Hus, Marco Pasi, and Kocku Von Stuckrad (Leiden: Brill, 2010), 107–28.

53 Gershom Scholem, *Major Trends in Jewish Mysticism* (New York: Schocken, 1941), 243.

54 *DCAP*, 89.

55 Wasserstrom, who admonished Scholem (among others) for his politically oblivious invocation of *coincidentia oppositorum*, actually approximates Meinvielle on this point, albeit within an alternate epistemic framework; see *Religion after Religion*, 70–1.

56 *DCAP*, 418–29.

57 This approach, of course, is informed by Wasserstrom's conviction that Religious Studies mediates between the scientific and the political.

58 "In this ancient account from Egypt, God comes out of the abyss, out of nothing, out of the indeterminate. And this god produces the other gods and the world sexually. From here, the Israelites could draw their kabbalistic conception. The conception of the kabbalah contains, therefore, five fundamental ideas. First, God, in the ultimate analysis, is nothing that comes from nothing; second, nothing, by evolution, becomes the world and man; third, God fabricates the world by sexual action; fourth, evil is in God and the evil of the world has a divine origin; fifth, the fully perfectly and fulfilled divinity culminates in the human, in humanity," *DCAP*, 413. One may compare Meinvielle's Scholem-informed assessment of kabbalah as nihilism to Baruch Kurzweill's view that Scholem's scholarship amounted to the same. See David Myers, "The Kurzweill-Scholem Debate and Modern Jewish Historiography," *Modern Judaism* 6, no. 3 (1986): 261–86.

59 Elliot Wolfson, *Language, Eros, Being: Kabbalistic Hermeneutics and Poetic Imagination* (New York: Fordham University Press, 2005), 182, 271–84.

60 For example, see Eveline Goodman-Thau, Gert Mattenklott, and Christoph Schulte, *Kabbala und die Literatur der Romantik* (Tübingen: Max Niemeyer Verlag, 1999); Wasserstrom, *Religion after Religion*, 38–41; Jonathan Garb, *Yearnings of the Soul: Psychological Thought in Modern Kabbalah* (Chicago, IL: University of Chicago Press, 2015), 130–5; Paul Franks, "'Nothing Comes from Nothing': Judaism, the Orient, and Kabbalah in Hegel's Reception of Spinoza," in *The Oxford Handbook of Spinoza*, ed. Michael Della Rocca (Oxford: Oxford University Press, 2017), 512–39.

61 On the Heideggerian dimensions of Wolfson's earlier work, see Steven M. Wasserstrom, "Melancholy Jouissance and the Study of Kabbalah: A Review Essay of Elliot Wolfson, *Alef, Mem, Tau*," *AJS Review* 32, no. 2 (2008): 389–96. Meinvielle's "kabbalized" interpretation of Heidegger coheres with the former's general repurposing of Voegelin's construction of Gnosticism. For Voegelin's reading of Heidegger as a gnostic, see Voegelin, *Science, Politics, and Gnosticism*, 32–4.

62 See my forthcoming bibliography on "Modern Kabbalah," in *Oxford Bibliographies in Jewish Studies*, ed. Naomi Seidman (New York: Oxford University Press, 2018).

63 Roni Weinstein, *Kabbalah and Jewish Modernity* (Portland, OR: Littman Library of Jewish Civilization, 2016); Jonathan Garb, *Modern Kabbalah as an Autonomous Domain of Research* (Hebrew) (Los Angeles, CA: Cherub Press, 2016); and see my review of Garb, "Yearnings of the Soul," *Aries: Journal for the Study of Western Esotericism* 18 (2018): 131–6.

64 I thank Jeremy Walton for suggesting this phrase.

65 Ironically, Dylan Burns, on page 127 of this volume, cites Wasserstrom arguing against ghettoizing approaches to the study of Gnosticism in Judaism and Christianity.
66 See *Religion after Religion*, 178–9. Also see Wasserstrom, "Response," 461, where the pregnant phrase attributed to Scholem by Hans Jonas becomes "metaphysical anti-Judaism [*sic*]."

Chapter 8

1 Inter alia, see: Ernst Feil, *Religio: Die Geschichte eines neuzeitlichen Grundbegriffs*, 4 vols. (Göttingen: Vandenhoeck & Ruprecht, 1986–2007); Michel Despland and Gérard Vallée, eds. *Religion in History: The Word, the Idea, the Reality* (Waterloo, Ontario: Wilfred Laurier University Press, 1992); Talal Asad, *Genealogies of Religion: Discipline and Reasons of Power in Christianity and Islam* (Baltimore, MD: Johns Hopkins University Press, 1993); William E. Arnal, "Definition," in *Guide to the Study of Religion*, ed. Willi Braun and Russell T. McCutcheon (London: Cassell, 2000), 21–34; Timothy Fitzgerald, *The Ideology of Religious Studies* (New York: Oxford University Press, 2000); Timothy Fitzgerald, *Discourse on Civility and Barbarity: A Critical History of Religion and Related Concepts* (New York: Oxford University Press, 2007); Daniel Dubuisson, *The Western Construction of Religion*, trans. William Sayers (Baltimore, MD: Johns Hopkins University Press, 2003 [French 1998]); Catherine Bell, "Paradigms Behind (and Before) the Modern Concept of Religion," *Method and Theory* 46 (2006): 27–46; Craig Martin, *Masking Hegemony: A Genealogy of Liberalism, Religion, and the Private Sphere* (London: Equinox, 2010); Russell McCutcheon, "Religion before 'Religion'?" in *Chasing Down Religion in the Sights of History and the Cognitive Sciences: Essays in Honor of Luther H. Martin*, ed. Panyotis Pachis and Donald Wiebe (Sheffield: Equinox, 2015), 285–301; Giovanni Casadio, "*Religio* versus Religion," in *Myths, Martyrs, and Modernity: Studies in the History of Religions in Honour of Jan Bremmer*, ed. Jitse Dijkstra et al. (Leiden: E.J. Brill, 2010), 301–26; Brent Nongbri, *Before Religion: A History of A Modern Concept* (New Haven, CT: Yale University Press, 2013); as well as the pioneering work of Wilfred Cantwell Smith, *The Meaning and End of Religion* (New York: MacMillan, 1963).
2 A point stressed, above all, by Jonathan Z. Smith: *Imagining Religion: From Babylon to Jonestown* (Chicago, IL: University of Chicago Press, 1982); Jonathan Z. Smith, "Religion, Religions, Religious," in *Critical Terms for Religious Studies*, ed. Mark C. Taylor (Chicago, IL: University of Chicago Press, 1998), 269–84, repr. Jonathan Z. Smith, *Relating Religion: Essays in the Study of Religion* (Chicago, IL: University of Chicago Press, 2002, 2013), 179–96.
3 Recent translators have offered the following definitions: "religion" (Enrico G. Raffaelli, *The Sīh-rōzag in Zoroastrianism: A Textual and Historico-Religious Analysis* (New York: Routledge, 2014), 256); "view/view-soul" (Helmut Humbach and Klaus Faiss, *Zarathushtra and his Antagonists. A Sociolinguistic Study with English and German Trabnslations of his Gāthās* (Wiesbaden: Ludwig Reichert, 2010), passim); "belief, vision, conception, religion" (Almut Hintze, *A Zoroastrian Liturgy. The Worship in Seven Chapters (Yasna 35–41)* (Wiesbaden: Harrassowitz, 2007), 337); "conscience religieuse; désigne tout à la fois la religion mazdéenne, déifiée comme fille de Mazdā, et la conscience religieuse d'un individu en particulier duquel c'est une part immortelle au même titre que l'âme" (Éric Pirart, *L'éloge mazdéen de l'ivresse*).

Édition, traduction et commentaire du Hōm Stōd (Paris: Harmattan, 2004), 291); "religiöse Anschauung" (Almut Hintze, *Der Zamyād-Yašt. Edition Übersetzung, Kommentar* (Wiesbaden: Ludwig Reichert, 1994), 432); "(religiöse) Anschauung, conscience" (Jean Kellens and Eric Pirart, *Les Textes vieil-avestiques* (Wiesbaden: L. Reichert Verlag, 1990), 252); "religious view, religion" (Helmut Humbach and Pallan R. Ichaporia, *Zamyād Yasht. Yasht 19 of the Younger Avesta: Text, Translation, Commentary* (Wiesbaden: Harrassowitz, 1998), 183); Andrea Piras, *Hadōxt Nask 2: Il racconto zoroastriano della sorte dell' anima. Edizione critica del testo avestico e pahlavi, traduzione e commento* (Rome: Istituto per l'Africa e l'Oriente, 2000) transliterates and leaves *daēnā* untranslated. The specialized studies devoted to this term are: Samuel Grant Oliphant, "Sanskrit *dhénā*, Avestan *daēnā*, Lithuanian *dainà*," *Journal of the American Oriental Society* 32 (1912): 393-413; Maurice Bloomfield, "On Vedic *Dhénā*, 'Prayer,' 'Song,'" *Journal of the American Oriental Society* 46 (1926): 303-8; J. H. Kramers, "The *Daēnā* in the Gathas," in *Oriental Studies in Honour of Curtseji Erachji Pavry* (London: Oxford University Press, 1933), 232-7; Marijan Molé, "*Daēnā*, le pont Činvat et l'initiation dans le Mazdéisme," *Revue de l'histoire des religions* 157 (1933); Boris Oguibenine, "Baltic Evidence and the Indo-Iranian Prayer," *Journal of Indo-European Studies* 2 (1974): 23-45; Boris Oguibenine, "Védique *dhénā*, avestique *daēnā*: examen des critiques de H.P. Schmidt," in *Lautgeschichte und Etymologie*, ed. Manfred Mayrhofer, Martin Peters, and Oskar E. Pfeiffer (Wiesbaden: Reichert, 1980), 293-316; Hans-Peter Schmidt, "Is Vedic *Dhénā* related to Avestan *Daēnā?*," in *Monumentum H.S. Nyberg*, vol. 2 (Leiden: E.J. Brill, 1975), 165-81; Carsten Colpe, "*Daēnā*, Lichtjungfrau, Zweite Gestalt. Verbindungen und Unterschiede zwischen zarathustrischer und manichäischer Selbst-Anschauung," in *Studies in Gnosticism and Hellenistic Religions Presented to Gilles Quispel* (Leiden: E.J. Brill, 1981), 58-77; Gherardo Gnoli, "Über die *Daēnā*: Haδōxt nask 2,7-9," in *Tradition und Translation: Zum Problem der interkulturellen Übersetzbarkeit religiöser Phänomene. Festschrift für Carsten Colpe*, ed. Christoph Elsass et al. (Berlin: de Gruyter, 1981), 292-8; Wojciech Skalmowski, "Some Remarks on Avestan *Daēnā*," in *Studia Paulo Naster Oblata*, ed. Jan Quaegebeur, vol. 2. Orientalia Antiqua (Leuven: Peeters, 1982), 223-9; Geo Widengren, "La rencontre avec la *Daēnā*, qui représente les actions de l'homme," *Orientalia Romana* 5 (1983): 41-79; Firouz-Thomas Lankarany, Daēnā *im Awesta, eine semantische Untersuchung* (Reinbek: Verlag für Orientalistische Fachpublikationen, 1985); Jean Kellens, "La fonction aurorale de Mithra et la Daēnā," in *Studies in Mithraism*, ed. John R. Hinnells (Rome: "L'Erma" di Bretschneider, 1994), 165-71; and Mansour Shaki, "Dēn," in *Encyclopaedia Iranica*, ed. Ehsan Yarshater (London: Routledge & Kegan Paul, 1994/2011), 7.279-81, available at http://www.iranicaonline.org/articles/den (original article 1994; last updated 2011).

Discussions of the concept are also included in most general works on Zoroastrianism: Herman Lommel, *Die religion Zarathustras nach dem Awesta dargestellt* (Tübingen: J.C.B. Mohr, 1930), 148-52; H. S. Nyberg, *Die Religionen des alten Iran*, trans. H. H. Schaeder (Leipzig: J.C. Hinrichs, 1938 [1937]), 114-20; Jacques Duchesne-Guillemin, *La religion de l'Iran ancien* (Paris: Presses Universitaires de France, 1962), 229-31; and Michael Stausberg, *Die Religion Zarathushtras. Vol. 1: Geschichte* (Stuttgart: W. Kohlhammer, 2002), 124-5, 146-9, 340. More recent and more detailed discussions include Andrea Piras, "Le concezioni dell' anima nell' Iran antico," *I Quaderni di Avallon* 29 (1992): 37-54, 45-8; Philippe Gignoux, *Man and Cosmos in Ancient Iran* (Rome: Istituto Italiano per l'Africa e l'Oriente, 2001), 12–16; and Éric Pirart, *Corps et âmes du Mazdéen. Le lexique zoroastrien de l'eschatologie individuelle* (Paris: L'Harmattan, 2012), 121–79.

4   Christian Bartholomae, *Altiransches Wörterbuch* (Strassburg: Karl J. Trübner, 1904), columns 662–65.

5   Visprad 5.3: *frā tē vərəne ahe daēnaiia ašāum ahura mazda mazdaiiasnō zaraθuštrīš vīdaēuuō.*

6   Yasna 8.7 (= Yasna 60.10): *haxšaiia azəmcit̰ yō zaraθuštrō
    fratəmą nmānanąmca vīsąmca zaṇtunąmca daxiiunąm
    aŋhå daēnaiiå anumataiiaēca anuxtaiiēca anuuarštaiiaēca yā āhūiriš zaraθuštriš.*

7   Vīdēvdāt 4.44: *narō hāmō.daēna.*

8   Vīdēvdāt 3.40: *āstūtō vā aiβisrauuanō vā daēnąm māzdaiiasnīm.*

9   On the position of priests within ancient Iranian society, see Duchesne-Guillemin, *La religion de l'Iran ancien*, 115–18; Molé, "Daēnā," 423–5; Geo Widengren, *Die Religionen Irans* (Stuttgart: W. Kohlhammer, 1965), 27–8; Mary Boyce, *A History of Zoroastrianism: the Early Period* (Leiden: Brill, 1996), 5–13.

10 Yasna 13.3: *mazištāiš vaēdiiāiš daēnaiiå māzdaiiasnōiš aθaurunō ratūm āmruiiē cašānąscā aēšąmcīt āmruiiē.*

11 Bruce Lincoln, *Holy Terrors: Thinking about Religion after September 11* (Chicago, IL: University of Chicago Press, 2003), 5–7. The crucial parts of the definition are these:

> A proper definition must be polythetic and flexible, allowing for wide variations and attending, at a minimum, to these four domains: 1) A discourse whose concerns transcend the human, temporal, and contingent, and that claims for itself a similarly transcendent status; 2) A set of practices whose goal is to produce a proper world and/or proper human subjects, as defined by a religious discourse to which these practices are connected; 3) A community whose members construct their identity with reference to a religious discourse and its attendant practices; 4) An institution that regulates religious discourse, practices, and community, reproducing them over time and modifying them as necessary, while asserting their eternal validity and transcendent value.

12 Bartholomae, *Altiransche Wörterbuch*, columns 665–7: "inneres Wesen, geistiges Ich, Individualität."

13 Thus, for instance, Pirart, *Corps et âmes du Mazdéen* or the concise account in Shaul Shaked, *Dualism in Transformation: Varieties of Religion in Sasanian Iran* (London: School of Oriental and African Studies, 1994), 36:

> The semantic ambiguity of *daēnā* is quite typical of the Iranian religious language, and should not have evoked so much scholarly consternation. It does incorporate within it the notions of "soul" as well as that of an outside manifestation of one's self; of "religion" in both its subjective sense, as the sum total of one's religous attitude and actions, and its objective sense, as the collective attitude of a whole community and also as a representation of that collective attitude.

14 Thus Lankarany, *Daēnā im Awesta*, 170: "den subjectiven Begriff Religiosität im Sinne einer individuellen vom Menschen gelebten und praktizierten Religion." Lankarany further maintains that the Older Avesta knows this sense only and that a model of religion as an objective rather than a subjective entity emerges only in the Younger Avesta. Given that many verses of the older stratum are quite ambiguous in their usage and remain open to multiple divergent interpretations, this part of his argument is less than fully convincing.

15 Yasna 44.9ab: *taṯ θβā pərəsā, ərəš mōi vaocā ahurā kaθā mōi yąm, yaoš daēnąm yaoždānē.*
For translation of the verb *yaoždā-* as "to perfect," rather than "to purify," see Bruce Lincoln, "Iūs e i suoi paralleli iranici. Dalla purezza alla giustizia," in *Giuristi nati. Antropologia e diritto romano*, ed. Aglaia McClintock (Bologna: Il Mulino, 2016), 9–25.

16 Yasna 48.4: *yə̄ dāṯ manō, vahiiō mazdā ašiiascā huuō daēnąm, šiiaoθanācā vacaŋhācā ahiiā zaošə̄ŋg, uštiš varənə̄ŋg hacaitē θβahmī ⁺xratāu, apə̄məm nanā aŋhaṯ.*

17 William James, *The Varieties of Religious Experience: A Study in Human Nature* (New York: Longmans, 1902); Rudolf Otto, *The Idea of the Holy: An Inquiry into the Non-Rational Factor in the Idea of the Divine and its Relation to the Rational*, trans. John W. Harvey (London: Oxford University Press, 1923 [1922]); Gerhardus van der Leeuw, *Religion in Essence and Manifestation: A Study in Phenomenology* (London: G. Allen & Unwin, 1938 [1933]); Joachim Wach, *The Comparative Study of Religions* (New York: Columbia University Press, 1958); Mircea Eliade, *The Sacred and the Profane: The Nature of Religion*, trans. Willard Trask (New York: Harcourt, Brace, 1959 [1958]).

18 The Wise Lord's creation of the "first" *daēnā* is mentioned at Yasna 31.11 and 46.6, but not narrated in any detail. Instruction by priests and others is at issue in Yasna 19.17, 46.7, 46.11; Vīdēvdāt 3.40-42, 9.2, 9.47-48, 9.52; Yašt 9.26, 11.14; and Visprad 12.3; self-cultivation at Yasna 9.31, 48.4, 49.5; Vīdēvdāt 5.21, 5.62; and Yašt 16.15, 17.46, 19.79, 19.84.

19 Yašt 9.26 (= 17.46): *dazdi.me vaŋuhi vəuuište … yaθa azəm hācaiiene vaŋuhīm āzātąm Hutaosąm anumatōe daēnaiiāi anūxtōe daēnaiiāi anu.varštōe daēnaiiāi yā.mē daēnąm māzdaiiasnīm zrasca dāṯ apica aotāṯ.*

20 Visprad 12.2-3: *cīšmaide … aršuxδanąmca vacaŋhąm srauuaŋhąmca zaraθuštrinąm huuaršt anąmca šiiaoθnanąm barəsmanąmca ašaiia frastarətanąm haomanąmca ašaiia hutanąm staotanąmca yesniianąm daēnaiiāsca māzdaiiasnōiš mąθβanąmca vaxəδβanąmca varštuuanąmca.*

21 References to "good religion" (*hu-daēnā*) and "bad religion" (*duž-daēnā*, also *drəguuatō daēnā*, "the religion of liars") are found at Yasna 37.5, 49.4, 49.11, 51.13, 53.1, 65.7; Yašt 4.9, 5.109, 9.31, 19.47, 49, and 95; Visprad 3.3; Pursišnīhā 33; Hādōxt Nask 2.11, 12, 18, and 36. The distinction is also pointedly asserted in one of the most celebrated verses attributed to Zarathuštra, Yasna 45.2.

> *I will proclaim the two first spirits of existence,*
> *The more beneficent of which could say to the one who is evil:*
> *"Neither our minds, nor our pronouncements, nor our intellects,*
> *Nor our choices, nor our utterances and deeds,*
> *Nor our religions, nor our souls are in agreement."*
>
> *at fravaxšiiā   aŋhə̄uš uš mainiiū paouruiiē*
> *yaiiå spaniiå   ūitī mrauuat yə̄m angrəm*
> *nōit nā manå   nōit sə̄ŋghā nōit xratauuō*
> *naēdā varanā   nōit uxā naēda šiiaoθanā*
> *nōit daēnå   nōit uruuaŋō hacaiṇtē.*

22 Zoroastrianism calls itself "the Good Religion" already in the Older Avesta: Yasna 51.17, 53.1, and 53.4.

The Younger Avesta usually expands the phrase and speaks of "the Good Mazdā-worshipping Religion" (*vaŋhvī daēnā māzdaiiasnī*): Vīdēvdāt 19.13; Visprad 6.1, 7.2, 11.5; Yasna 1.13, 2.13, 3.15, 4.18, 6.12, 7.15, 9.26, 15.1, 16.6, 17.13, 22.3, 22.15, 22.22, 22,25, 24.8, 25.325.6; Yašt 2.12, 13.94, 16.1; Nyayiš 1.8, et al.

23   The Younger Avesta contains variants of this narrative at Hādōxt Nask 2 and Vīdēvdāt 19.28-34. Pahlavi variants include the Pahlavi version of the Hādōxt Nask, as well as Arda Wirāz Nāmag 4.7-14, Mēnōg ī Xrad 2.123-57, Greater Bundahišn 30.8-34, Dādēstan ī Dēnīg 23-24, Selections of Zād Spram 30.42-52, and the much-discussed Sasanian inscription of Kirdīr at Naqš-ī Rustam. The relevant texts are conveniently assembled in Widengren, who recognized anticipatory aspects of the theme in the Older Avesta, particularly Yasna 51.13 and 17: Widengren, "La rencontre avec la Daēnā, qui représente les actions de l'homme," 41–79.

24   Hādōxt Nask, 2.2-8.

25   Hādōxt Nask, 2.9: *aŋhå dim vātaiiå frə̄rəṇta sadaiieiti yā hauua daēna kainīnō kəhrpa srīraiiå xšōiθniiå ⁺auruša.bāzuuō amaiiå huraoδaiiå uzarštaiiå bərəzaitiiå ərəduuafšniiå sraotanuuō āzātaiiå raēuuasciθraiiå paṇcadasaiiå raoδaēšuua kəhrpa auuauuatō sraiiå yaθa dāmąn sraēštāiš.*

26   Hādōxt Nask, 2.10: *cišca carāitiš ahi yąm it yauua carāitinąm kəhrpa sraēštąm dādarəsa.*

27   Hādōxt Nask, 2.11: *azəm bā tē ahmi yum humanō huuacō hušiiaoθana hudaēna yā hauua daēna xᵛaēpaiθe.tanuuō.*

28   Ardā Wirāz Nāmag, 4.11-14: *u-š passox dād ān ī xwēš dēn ud ān xwēš kunišn kū: man ēdōn kunišn ī tō ham ⁺juwān ī xūb-menišn ī xūb-gōwišn ī xūb-kunišn ī xūb-dēn kāmag ud kunišn ī tō rāy ka man ēdōn meh ud weh ud hubōy ud pērōzgar ud abē-bēš ham ciyōn tō sahist cē tō pad gētīg gāhān srūd u-t ī weh yašt u-t ātaxš pahrēxt u-t mard ī ahlaw šnāyēnīd kē az dūr frāz mad kē az nazdīk ka man frabīh būd ham u-t frabīhtar kard ham ud nēk būd ham u-t nēktar kard ham ud arzānīg būd ham u-t arzānīgtar kard ham ud ka pad gāh cašmagān nišast ham u-t cašmagāhtar nišāst ham ud ka burzišnīg būd ham u-t burzišnigtar kard ham pad humat ud hūxt ud huwaršt ī tō warzīd tō mard ī ahlaw.* Cf. Hādōxt Nask 2.11-14, Mēnōg ī Xrad 2.129-39, Greater Bundahišn 30.16, and Dādēstān ī Dēnīg 23.5. The last of these passages gives a much less thorough account than the others, but refers to the *dāenā*-maiden as "the guardian and treasurer of one's virtuous deeds" (*nigāhbed ud ganjwar ī kirbag*). Note that the kinds of actions the maiden singles out as particularly beneficial are all ritual, rather than ethical, as is true of the prime religious teachings listed in Visprad 12.2-3, quoted above.

29   Hādōxt Nask 2.15-18, Vīdēvdāt 19.30-32 and 34, Ardā Wirāz Nāmag 5.1-9, Mēnōg ī Xrad 2.145-57, Greater Bundahišn 30.22-23 and 26, Dādēstān ī Dēnīg 23.6, Selections of Zād Spram 30.52.

30   Hādōxt Nask 2.19-36, Vīdēvdāt 19.33, Mēnōg ī Xrad 2.158-94, Greater Bundahišn 30.27-34, Dādēstan ī Dēnīg 24. Selections of Zād Spram 30.44 challenge the view common to these other texts, suggesting that the soul (Pahlavi *ruwān* < Avestan *uruuan*) of an evil-doer is unaccompanied by his religion or any other spiritual aspect of the person. Rejected and abandoned, "it goes to hell repentantly, all by itself, just like one who is surprised and faces his enemies" (*ruwān ān ī tanīg ⁺pašēmānīhā ⁺ēwtāg be ō dušōx šawēd ōwōn ciyōn kē ⁺widimušt ēstēd dušmēnān*).

31   Eschatological rewards and punishments, dependent on the nature of one's religion, are already thematized in the Older Avesta: Yasna 31.20, 46.11, 48.4, 51.13, 53.1 and

53.4. Rewards of an unspecified nature are also mentioned at Yasna 34.13, 40.1, 49.9 and 54.1.

32 Yasna 9.5: *yimahe xšaθre auruuahe nōiṯ aotəm åŋha nōiṯ garəməm nōiṯ zauruua åŋha nōiṯ mərəθiiuš nōiṯ araskō daēuuō.dātō*. Other Avestan texts describing his golden age include Yašt 9.9-10, 15.16-17, 17.29-30, 19.32-33, and Vīdēvdāt 2.4-5; Pahlavi texts, Greater Bundahišn 32.10, Dēnkart 3.227, 3.229, and 7.1.23, Dādestān ī Dēnīg 38.19, and Mēnōg ī Xrad 27.24-26.

33 Vīdēvdāt 2.1-5: *pərəsat zaraθuštrō ahurəm mazdąm. ahura mazda mainiiō spəništa dātarə gaēθanąm astuuaitinąm ašāum kahmāi paoiriiō mašiiānąm apərəsa.tūm yō ahurō mazdå aniiō mana yat zaraθuštrāi. kahmāi fradaēsaiiō daēnąm yąm āhūirīm zaraθuštrīm. 2. āat mraot ahurō mazdå. Yimāi srīrāi huuąθβāi ašāum zaraθuštra ahmāi paoiriiō mašiiānąm apərəse azəm yō ahurō mazdå aniiō θβat yat zaraθuštrāt ahmāi fradaēsaēm daēnąm yąm āhūirīm zaraθuštrīm. 3. āat hē mraom zaraθuštra azəm yō ahurō mazdå vīsaŋha mē yima srīra vīuuaŋhana mərətō bərətaca daēnaiiāi. āat mē aēm paitiiaoxta Yimō srīrō zaraθuštra. nōit dātō ahmi nōit cistō mərətō bərətaca daēnaiiāi. 4. āat hē mraom zaraθuštra azəm yō ahurō mazdå yezi mē yima nōit vīuuīse mərətō bərətaca daēnaiiāi āat mē gaēθå frādaiia āat mē gaēθå varədaiia āat mē vīsāi gaēθanąm θrātāca harətāca aiβiiāxštaca. 5. āat mē aēm paitiiaoxta yimō srīrō zaraθuštra. azəm tē gaēθå frādaiieni azəm tē gaēθå varədaiieni azəm tē vīsāne gaēθanąm θrātāca harətāca aiβiiāxštaca. nōit mana xšaθre buuat aotō vātō nōit garəmō nōit axtīš nōit mahrkō*. Cf. Pahlavi Rivāyat accompanying the Dādestān ī Dēnīg 31c1-4, Dēnkart 3.12 and 3.129.

34 The Avestan sources (Yašt 9.10 and 17.30) report that Yima ruled for a millennium, while the Pahlavi sources (Greater Bundahišn 36.5, Mēnōg ī Xrad 27.25) reduce this to 616 years and 6 months.

35 The sources give slightly divergent accounts regarding the nature of Yima's lie, while agreeing on its consequences. Cf. Yašt 19.33-34, Dādestān ī Dēnīg 38.19-20, Pahlavi Rivāyat accompanying the Dādestān ī Dēnīg 31a10, 31c.5-6, and 47.8.

36 On Yima's fate and the loss of the golden age, see Yašt 19.34 and 19.46, Greater Bundahišn 18.6, 33.1, and 35.5, Selections of Zād Spram 35.46, Dādestān ī Dēnīg 38.19-20, Pahlavi Rivāyat accompanying the Dādestān ī Dēnīg 31a10, 31c.5-6, and 47.8. An absolutely classic treatment of all the major sources on Yima is Arthur Christensen, *Le premier homme et le premier roi dans l'histoire légendaire des iraniens. Ie partie: Gayōmard, Masjay et Masjānay, Hōšang et Taxmōrum* (Stockholm: P.A. Norstedt, 1918). More recently, see Helmut Humbach, "Yama/Yima/Jamšēd, King of Paradise of the Iranians," *Jerusalem Studies in Arabic and Islam* 26 (2002): 68-77; Samra Azarnouche and Céline Redard, eds. *Yama/Yima: Variations indo-iraniennes sur la geste mythique* (Paris, Collège de France: Boccard, 2012); and Audrey Tzatourian, *Yima: Structure de la pensée religieuse en Iran ancien* (Paris: L'Harmattan, 2012).

37 *abar ān ī Gannāg Mēnōg kōxšišn padiš škafttar az nigēz ī wehdēn hēd ān ī Gannāg Mēnōg koxšišn padiš skafttar ēk abar xwarrah ī xwadāyīh ud wehdēn pad ēk tan abardar zōrīhā ō ham madan abesīhišn ī-š az ēn hamīh rāy cē agar pad Yim abāz ān abardar zōrīhā xwarrah ī xwādāyīh abardar zōrīg-iz xwarrah ī wehdēn āyab pad Zarduxšt abāz abardar zōrīg ī xwarrah ī wehdēn xwarrah-iz ī abardar zōrīhā ciyōn pad Yim būd ō ham madan hē tēz Gannāg Mēnōg abesīhišn dām az ēbgat bōxtagīh ud frašgird pad kāmag andar axwān dahišn būd hē*.

38 Recently, Antonio Panaino has offered an ingenious and radical, but unconvincing, reinterpretation of this text, based on his sense "If Yima had really refused the

Mazdean religion, Ahura Mazdā would have surely annihilated him": Panaino, "Yima ed il 'rifiuto' della daēnā-. Ovvero dell' incestualità, della beatitudine e della morte tra ambigui ostacoli e seducenti trasparenze," in *Démons iraniens. Actes du colloque international ... à l'occasion des 65 ans de Jean Kellens*, ed. Philippe Swennen (Liège: Presses Universitaires de Liège, 2015), 97. Cantera has shown the philological problems in Panaino's attempt, while developing an alternative reinterpretation that stresses the importance of sacrifice as the essence of religious action and thus of religion: Alberto Cantera "Yima, son vara- et la daēnā mazdéenne," in *Yama/Yima*, ed. Azarnouche and Redard, 45-7. While the point is well taken and helps correct ethnocentric and anachronistic overemphasis on belief and interiority, the corrective is overstated. As the Hādōxt Nask and other texts make clear, *daēnā* includes all of one's thoughts, speech, and action, including not only ritual, but ethical and quotidian forms.

39 This etymology is accepted, inter alia, by Oliphant, "Sanskrit *dhénā*," 412; Bloomfield, "On Vedic *Dhénā*," 304-5, Lommel, *Die Yäšt's des Awesta*, 103; Nyberg, *Die Religionen des alten Iran*, 114-15; Kaj Barr, *Avesta* (Copenhagen: Gyldendal, 1954), 195-6; Humbach, "Rituelle termini," 76; Duchesne-Guillemin, *La religion de l'Iran ancien*, 139; Boyce, *A History*, 238; Schmidt, "Is Vedic *Dhénā related*"; Colpe, "*Daēnā*, Lichtjungfrau," 65; Lankarany, *Daēnā im Awesta*, 15-17 (with a list of its early adherents); Piras, "La concezioni," 45; Kellens, "La function aurorale," 71; Gignoux, *Man and Cosmos*, 12. On the verbal root, see Bartholomae, *Altiransches Wörterbuch*, 724-5; Johnny Cheung, *Etymological Dictionary of the Iranian Verb* (Leiden: Brill, 2007), 48-50.

40 Schmidt, "Is Vedic *Dhénā related*"; Gignoux, *Man and* Cosmos, 12-15.

41 Prods Oktor Skjærvø, *The Spirit of Zoroastrianism* (New Haven, CT: Yale University Press, 2012), 264; Prods Oktor Skjærvø, "Afterlife in Zoroastrianism," in *Jenseitsvorstellungen im Orient*, ed. Predrag Bukovec and Barbara Kolkmann-Klamt (Hamburg: Verlag Dr. Kovač, 2013), 317.

42 Stanley Insler, *The Gāthās of Zarathustra* (Leiden: E.J. Brill, 1975), passim.

43 Johanna Narten, *Der Yasna Haptaŋhāiti* (Wiesbaden: Ludwig Reichert, 1986), passim, *Gesinnung*.

44 Kellens and Pirart, *Les textes*, 252.

45 Boyce, *A History*, 238.

46 Barr, *Avesta*, 195: "Menneskets Betragtning af og Holdning over for Tilværelsens fundamentale Vilkaar."

47 Almut Hintze, "A Zoroastrian Vision," in *The Zoroastrian Flame: Exploring Religion, History and Tradition*, ed. Alan Williams, Sarah Stewart, and Almut Hintze (London: I.B. Tauris), 77.

48 The phrase is actually that of Cantera, "Yima," 47, summarizing Kellens's conclusions: "'la vision de l'au-delà obtenue à travers le sacrifice.'" Kellens's own explications of the idea are addressed to specialists and, as such, are much more technical and elaborate. See, for instance, Kellens, "Le jour se lève à la fin de la Gāthā Ahunauuaitī," *Journal asiatique* 301 (2013): 53-84, 78, where he distinguishes three interrelated forms of the dawn: (1) the material dawn, visible at sunrise, which is referred to as *ušah* in Avestan (a term cognate to Greek *eos* and Latin *aurora*); (2) the immaterial dawn, raised to the level of a divine entity under the name *daēnā*; (3) the interiorization of this immaterial dawn as the visionary experience of sacrificers. See also Jean Kellens, *Études avestiques et mazdéennes. Vol. 3. Le long préambule du sacrifice* (Paris: Collège

de France, 2010), 153, where he stresses the eschatological nature of the *daēnā* vision that reveals the path one will follow after death.

49 This interpretation emerged gradually in Kellens: 1994; 1995, 49–54; 2007; 2010, 149–55; 2013; 2016.

50 *yə̄ āiiat̰ ašauuanəm, diuuamnəm hōi aparəm xšiiō*
    darəgə̄m āiiū təmaŋhō, dušx"arəθəm auuaētās vacō
    tə̄m vå ahūm drəguuaṇtō, šiiaoθanāiš x"āiš daēnā naēšat̰.

51 Other verses showing a negative *daēnā* include Yasna 45.2, 46.11, 48.4, 49.4, 51.13; Vīdēvdāt 5.62, 18.8-9, and those passages where the term *duž.daēnā* ("s/he whose religion is bad") appears: Yasna 49.11, 65.7; Yašt 5.109, 9.31, 17.51, 19.47, 19.49, 19.87.

52 Jean Kellens, "La fonction aurorale de Mithra et la Daēnā," in *Studies in Mithraism*, ed. John R. Hinnells (Rome: L'Erma di Bretschneider, 1994), 165–71.

53 Bartholomae, *Altiranisches Wörterbuch*, 724: "'(das Rind, Akk.) hegen und pflegen, dafür sorgen, sich seiner sorgend annehmen bei.'" On ¹*dāy*- "'to suck, suckle, nourish,'" see Bartholomae, 724; Cheung, *Etymological Dictionary*, 47.

54 The chief advocates are Widengren, *Die Religionen*, 85; Widengren, "La rencontre," 65–72; Skalmowski, "Some Remarks"; Pirart, *Corps et âmes*, 129–48. Eilers, "Einige altiranische," 27–8, states no explicit opinion, but seems supportive of the idea, while Oguibenine, "Baltic Evidence," sought intermediate ground, imagining that both verbal roots were somehow active in the way Avestan *daēnā* and Vedic *dhénā* were used and understood. Kellens, *Études avestiques*, 151–5, was open to such a position, but three years later announced that he "abjured these hesitations": Kellens, "Le jour se lève à la fin de la Gāthā Ahunauuaitī," *Journal asiatique* 301 (2013): 53–84, 77 n. 24. The metric issue follows on recognition that *daēnā* was pronouced as trisyllabic (thus **dayanā*), which some experts believe favors, even demands, derivation from ¹*dāy*-, while others find this conclusion exaggerated. On this question, cf. the opinions of Kellens, *Études avestiques*, 154; and Pirart, *Corps et âmes*, 129–30.

55 Bartholomae, *Altiranisches Wörterbuch*, 724.

56 For this analysis, see Widengren, "La rencontre," 70–2; for further comparanda, see Hermann Grassmann, *Wörterbuch zum Rig-Veda* (Leipzig: F.A. Brockhaus, 1873), 675–6 and 695–6; Thomas V. Gamkrelidze and Vjačeslav V. Ivanov, *Indo-European and the Indo-Europeans*, trans. Johanna Nichols (Berlin: Mouton de Gruyter, 1995 [1984]), 487; Manfred Mayrhofer, *Etymologisches Wörterbuch des Altindoarischen*, vol. 1 (Heidelberg: Carl Winter, 1992), 775; and Cheung, *Etymological Dictionary*, 47.

57 Greater Bundahišn 7.10 describes how the Evil Spirit first afflicted Gayōmard with hunger. Only after this did the Wise Lord provide him with food; cf. Dēnkart 3.23, 3.80, 3.209, Dādestān ī Dēnīg 64.3-5. The best scholarly discussion of Gayōmard remains Christensen, *Le premier homme*, 7–105.

58 Greater Bundahišn 14.11-20. Zoroastrian cosmology treats plants, animals, and humans as original creations of the Wise Lord and theorizes them as pure, perfect, and not-to-be-injured-or-defiled by any moral subject. All aggressive action against them, which includes the cutting, tearing, uprooting, cooking, and eating of plants, originates with the Evil Spirit's primordial assault and partakes of the same Ahrimanian nature.

59 Cf. Greater Bundahišn 15.11. Cf. Vīdēvdāt 21.6-7, Dādestān ī Dēnīg 27.2, Dēnkart 3.374, Mēnōg ī Xrad 16.1-12. Also relevant, perhaps, is a tradition reported by Pliny: "They say that Zoroaster lived for thirty years in the desert on cheese prepared thus,

so that he felt no effects of old age," *Natural History* 11.102: *tradunt zoroastren in desertis caseo vixisse annis xx ita temperato, ut vetustatem non sentiret.*

60   Greater Bundahišn 14.21-24.

61   Greater Bundahišn 34.1-3. The passage is worth citing in its entirety:

> It says in the religion: "Just as when Mašya and Mašyānī emerged from the earth, they first consumed water, then plants, then milk, and then meat, so too people when they are dying first cease to eat meat, then milk, then bread and consume only water until they die." So too in the last millennium, the power of appetite decreases so that with one meal every three days and nights, a person continues to be satisfied. Then people cease from meat-consumption, consuming plants and the milk of beneficent animals. Then they cease from milk-consumption also and then they cease from plant-consumption and become exclusively water-consuming. For the ten years before Sōšyans [the eschatological hero and savior] comes they continue in non-consumption and they do not die. Then Sōšyans causes the dead to rise up.

> *gōwēd pad dēn kū az ān čiyōn Mašē ud Mašānē ka az zamīg abar rust hēnd nazdist āb ud pas urwar pas šīr ud pas gōšt xward hēnd mardōm-iz ka-šān murdan nazdist <az> gōšt ud šīr ud pas az nān xwardan-iz be estēnd ud ēwāz tā be murdan āb xwarēnd. 2. ēdōn-iz pad hazārag ī Ušēdarmāh nērōg ī āz ēdōn be kāhēd kū mardōm pad ēk pih-xwarišnīh se šab ud rōz pad sagrīh estēnd. 3. pas az ān az gōšt-xwarišnīh be estēnd ud urwar ud pēm ī gōspandān xwarēnd. pas az ān pēm-xwarišnīh-iz abāz estēnd ud pas az urwar-xwarišnīh-iz estēnd ud āb-xwarišn bawēnd. pēš pad dah sāl ka Sōšyans āyēd ō a-xwarišnīh estēnd ud nē mīrēnd. pas Sōšyans rist ul hangēzēnēd.*

> Cf. Selections of Zād Spram 34.34-43. Note also that the souls of the righteous who die before the Evil Spirit has been defeated receive milk or its purest form ("spring butter") upon their reception in heaven, food that will sustain them until the final Renovation (*frašgird*), when nutrition will no longer be necessary. Thus, Hādōxt Nask 2.18, Mēnōg ī Xrad 2.151-56, Dādestān ī Dēnīg 30.12-13, Pahlavi Rivāyat accompanying the Dādestan ī Dēnīg 23.17.

62   I have written about the nature of these poisons and the unique value attributed to milk on several occasions: Lincoln, *Religion, Empire, and Torture: The Case of Achaemenian Persia. With a Postscript on Abu Ghraib* (Chicago, IL: University of Chicago Press, 2007), 90–2 and 140; Lincoln, "Toward a more Materialist Ethics: Vermin and Poison in Zoroastrian Thought," *Studia Iranica* 44 (2015): 83–98; Lincoln, "Of Dirt, Diet, and Religious Others: A Theme in Zoroastrian Thought," *Dabir* 1 (2015): 44–52.

Chapter 9

1   Steven M. Wasserstrom, "Concubines and Puppies: Philologies of Esotericism in Jerusalem Between the World Wars," in *Adaptations and Innovations: Studies on the Interaction between Jewish and Islamic Thought and Literature from the Early Middle Ages to the Late Twentieth Century, Dedicated to Professor Joel L. Kraemer*, ed. Y. Tzvi Langermann and Josef Stern (Leuven: Peeters, 2007), 382 n. 4.

2   Steven M. Wasserstrom, *Religion after Religion: Gershom Scholem, Mircea Eliade, and Henry Corbin at Eranos* (Princeton, NJ: Princeton University Press, 1999), 3.
3   Perhaps this is a definitional debate that Wasserstrom does not want to join. See Wasserstrom, "Concubines and Puppies," 407; Steven M. Wasserstrom, *Between Muslim and Jew: The Problem of Symbiosis Under Early Islam* (Princeton, NJ: Princeton University Press, 1995), 8 n. 28.
4   Harold Bloom, *Genius: A Mosaic of One Hundred Exemplary Creative Minds* (New York: Warner, 2002). On the "only fair way to read Bloom," see Wasserstrom, *Religion after Religion*, 346 n. 14.
5   Tomoko Masuzawa, "Reflections on the Charmed Circle," *Journal of the American Academy of Religion* 69 (2001): 435: "This paradoxical success, finally, to my mind is the most interesting question that this book raises but leaves unanalyzed. As any reader would know, Wasserstrom repeats throughout the book, as a kind of morale-elevating slogan, the phrase 'the greatest scholars require the closest study.' Whatever its intended function was, I now see it also serving as a mantra warding off an unsettling and uncomfortable question, as a way of at once acknowledging and avoiding it by simply changing the subject. For behind the reality of the greatness of the Eranos Three's contributions and influences lies this exceedingly intriguing question: Why did they become so influential despite their eccentric orientation?"
6   Steven M. Wasserstrom, "Response: Final Note to Significance Seekers," *Journal of the American Academy of Religion* 69 (2001): 463.
7   Johannes van Oort, "Preface," in *Gnostica, Judaica, Catholica: Collected Essays of Gilles Quispel*, ed. Johannes van Oort (Leiden: Brill 2009), x.
8   Gilles Quispel, "Gnosis and Psychology," in *The School of Valentinus*, vol. 1 of *The Rediscovery of Gnosticism: Proceedings of the International Conference on Gnosticism at Yale, New Haven, Connecticut, March 28–31, 1978*, ed. Bentley Layton, Studies in the History of Religions 41 (Leiden: Brill, 1980), 17. Epigraph at the beginning of this section is from "Gnosis and Psychology," 19.
9   Gilles Quispel, "The Original Doctrine of Valentine," *Vigiliae Christianae* 1 (1947): 43–4.
10 Ibid.
11 Ibid., 46.
12 Ibid., 49: "This translation is intended to be not so much a literal reproduction of the Greek text as an interpretation of its meaning."
13 Ibid., 47.
14 Quispel, "Gnosis and Psychology," 17. See also Hans Thomas Hakl, *Eranos: An Alternative Intellectual History of the Twentieth Century*, trans. Christopher McIntosh (Montreal: McGill-Queen's University Press, 2013), 143.
15 On the significance of this particular Eranos meeting in the history of the circle and its relationship with the Bollingen Foundation, see William McGuire, *Bollingen: An Adventure in Collecting the Past* (Princeton, NJ: Princeton University Press, 1982), 138–9.
16 Gilles Quispel, "La Conception de l'Homme dans la Gnose Valentinienne," *Eranos-Jahrbuch* 15 (1947): 249–86; repr. in Quispel, *Gnostic Studies*, 2 vols. (Istanbul: Nederlands Historisch-Archaeologich Instituut in het Nabije Oosten, 1974), 1.37–57.
17 Only the first volume had been published at this point. Hans Jonas, *Gnosis und spätantiker Geist*, 2 vols. (Göttingen: Vandenhoek & Ruprecht, 1934–1954).
18 For a more recent critical overview of this era of defining Gnosticism, Karen L. King, *What Is Gnosticism?* (Cambridge, MA: Belknap Press of Harvard University Press, 2003), esp. 55–109.

19 Quispel, "Conception de l'Homme," 39: "cette conception que l'homme est un étranger dans un monde démoniaque." All translations are my own unless otherwise noted.
20 Quispel, "Conception de l'Homme," 39–40.
21 Ibid., 40: "Dans ces circonstances il est plus prudent de ne pas discuter la conception l'homme dans le gnosticism en général, mais de se limiter à l'anthropologie d'un seul gnostique."
22 According to Quispel, at least: "Of course I lectured about my Valentinus, Jung said a few words of appreciation and then everybody liked me," "Gnosis and Psychology," 17.
23 van Oort, "Preface," x–xi.
24 Gilles Quispel, "L'Homme gnostique (La doctrine de Basilide)," *Eranos-Jahrbuch* 16 (1948): 89–140.
25 Quispel, "Conception de l'Homme," 57: "Elle est, en effet, un christianiasme tragique."
26 See Robert A. Segal, *The Gnostic Jung* (Princeton, NJ: Princeton University Press, 1992), 103–6. Here Segal publishes the preface that Jung wrote for Quispel's volume, but he does not explain why *Tragic Christianity* never made it to print. I have found no further information about this book elsewhere.
27 Puech was appointed in 1929 to a chair in Christian Literature and the History of the Church at l'École practique des Haute Études at only 27 years of age. Paul Lévy and Etienne Woolf, "Avant-propos," in *Mélanges d'Histoire des Religions offerts à Henri-Charles Puech*, ed. Antoine Guillaumont and Ernst-Marie Laperrousaz (Paris: Presses Universitaires de France, 1974), 5–6. He was first invited to lecture on Gnosticism at Eranos in 1936; see Hakl, *Eranos*, 105.
28 Letter from Doresse to Puech, October 4, 1947, text and translation in James M. Robinson, *The Nag Hammadi Story*, 2 vols. Nag Hammadi and Manichaean Studies 86 (Leiden and Boston: Brill, 2014), 1.185–6.
29 Letter from Daumas to James Robinson, November 29, 1977, text and translation in Robinson, *Nag Hammadi Story*, 1.178.
30 Robinson ponders the extent to which this early meeting with Daumas and Corbin may have informed what Mina later reported were his "first" impressions of the codex and its significance: *Nag Hammadi Story*, 1.179.
31 Letter from Puech to Doresse, October 8, 1947, text and translation in Robinson, *Nag Hammadi Story*, 1.186–7.
32 Robinson, *Nag Hammadi Story*, 1.183–5.
33 Based on these descriptions, it is clear that Doresse was viewing the two codices now known (respectively) as Nag Hammadi Codex VII and Codex II. Letter from Doresse to Puech, December 14, 1947, text and translation in Robinson, *Nag Hammadi Story*, 1.1 n. 2 and 1.127. Doresse mentions the account of Schwartz in his letter, and it is then repeated with a bit greater detail in Henri-Charles Puech and Jean Doresse, "Nouveaux écrits gnostiques découverts en Égypte," *Comptes rendus des séances de l'Académie des Inscriptions et Belles-Lettres* 92, no. 1 (1948): 89.
34 The most complete accounting of the evidence for the find is that of James M. Robinson, published piecemeal in various forms over the course of the past half-century but collected in the archival compendium, *The Nag Hammadi Story*. The accuracy of the find story has recently been called into question, both on account of its shades of Orientalist sensationalism and inconsistencies across various retellings of the story. See Maia Kotrosits, "Romance and Danger at Nag Hammadi," *The Bible and*

Critical Theory 8, no. 1 (2012): 39–52; Nicola Denzey Lewis and Justine Ariel Blount, "Rethinking the Origins of the Nag Hammadi Codices," *Journal of Biblical Literature* 133 (2014): 399–419; and Mark Goodacre, "How Reliable is the Story of the Nag Hammadi Discovery?" *Journal for the Study of the New Testament* 35 (2013): 303–22. On the occasion of the 70th anniversary of the Nag Hammadi find, the *Bulletin for the Study of Religion* devoted an entire issue to pondering the implications of these challenges to the find story: see *Bulletin for the Study of Religion* 45, no. 2 (2016), esp. Dylan Burns, "Telling Nag Hammadi's Egyptian Stories," *Bulletin for the Study of Religion* 45, no. 2 (2016): 5–11. Hugo Lundhaug and Lance Jenott have also responded to these challenges, presenting previously unpublished photographs and maps of the find area in a fresh assessment of the discovery narrative. Hugo Lundhaug and Lance Jenott, *The Monastic Origins of the Nag Hammadi Codices*, Studien und Texte zu Antike und Christentum 97 (Tübingen: Mohr Siebeck, 2015), 11–21.

35 Puech and Doresse, "Nouveaux écrits gnostiques." Puech also issued a similar announcement (curiously, without Doresse listed as a co-author) in *Revue de l'histoire des religions*, of which he was the editor. Puech, "Nouveaux écrits gnostiques découverts à Nag Hammadi," *Revue de l'histoire des religions* 134 (1948): 244–8.

36 Togo Mina, "Le Papyrus gnostique du Musee Copte," *Vigiliae Christianae* 2 (1948): 129–36; Jean Doresse, "Trois livres gnostiques inédits: Évangile des Égyptiens.—Épître d'Eugnoste.—Sagesse de Jésus Christ," *Vigiliae Christianae* 2 (1948): 137–60. On the institutional context of the Coptic Museum at this time, see Donald Malcolm Reed, *Contesting Antiquity in Egypt: Archaeologies, Museums, and the Struggle for Identities from World War I to Nasser* (Cairo and New York: American University in Cairo Press, 2015), 197–228.

37 This text was subsequently identified as the *Prayer of the Apostle Paul*.

38 Puech and Doresse, "Nouveaux écrits," 89: "Mais la personne qui le détient actuellement n'autorise à donner sur lui que quelques détails. Il s'agit d'un codex de 150 pages environ, assez bien conservé et qui, comme le montre sa reliure, faisait partie du même fonds. Le format est très allongé; les pages comportent de 39 à 41 lignes écrites sur toute la largeur. L'écriture, extrêmement maladroite et même inculte, paraît dater du IVe siècle. Nous sommes cette fois en présence de textes rédigés dans un dialecte subachmimique présentant quelques particularités nouvelles. Trois ouvrages au moins composent le volume: une *Apocalypse de Jacques*, à sujet moral; un *Évangile du vérité* (est-ce le *Veritatis Evangelium* des Valentiniens, signalé par saint Irénée?) et une *Prière de l'apôtre Pierre,* tous deux traités d'un genre abstrait."

39 Jean Doresse and Togo Mina, "Nouveaux Textes Gnostiques Coptes découverts en Haute-Egypte: La Bibliotheque de Chenoboskion," *Vigiliae Christianae* 3 (1949): 129–41.

40 For a detailed account of Doresse's investigations, see Robinson, *Nag Hammadi Story*, 3–20.

41 Doresse and Mina, "Nouveaux Textes," 130.

42 Henri-Charles Puech, "Les Nouveaux écrits gnostiques découverts en Haute-Égypte (Premier inventaire et essai d'identification)," in *Coptic Studies in Honor of Walter Ewing Crum*, ed. Michel Malinine (Boston: The Byzantine Institute, 1950), 91–154. It is not at all clear to me that Puech had personally examined the codices at this time; he may well have been working solely off of his student's transcriptions.

43 The "Nag Hammadi Archive" at the Claremont Graduate University's Institute for Antiquity and Christianity holds Gilles Quispel's membership card for the 21st Congrès International des Orientalistes, in Paris, July 23rd–31st, 1948. Written on

44 Gilles Quispel, "The Jung Codex and Its Significance," in *The Jung Codex: A Newly Recovered Gnostic Papyrus*, ed. F. L. Cross (London: Mowbray, 1955). All of what follows is drawing upon the remarkable tick-tock compiled by James Robinson, "The Jung Codex: Rise and Fall of a Monopoly," *Religious Studies Review* 3 (1977): 17–30, esp. here 19–20.
45 Robinson, "Jung Codex," 20–2.
46 While it is unclear who initiated the invitation, Johannes van Oort implies that the lectures were an attempt by Quispel to gin up interest about the Nag Hammadi find among Jung and his circle ("Preface," xiii).
47 Hakl, *Eranos*, 143.
48 Gilles Quispel, *Gnosis als Weltreligion* (Zürich: Origo, 1951), 1: "Eine Weltreligion ist neu entdeckt."
49 Tertullian, *Adversus Valentinianos*, §4, in Jean Claude Fredouille, ed., *Tertullien Contre les valentiniens*, Sources chrétiennes 280–281 (Paris: Cerf, 1980–1981).
50 Quispel, *Gnosis als Weltreligion*, 71: "Ein Gnostiker als Papst von Rom. Und sogar der bedeutendste aller Gnostiker! Soweit wäre es wirklich einmal beinahe gekommen."
51 van Oort, "Preface," xii.
52 Gilles Quispel, "Gnosis and the Future of Christian Religion," in *Gnostica, Judaica, Catholica*, 831. This lecture was delivered by Quispel in 2000, when Ratzinger was Cardinal and Prefect of the Sacred Congregation for the Doctrine of Faith.
53 Hakl, *Eranos*, 154, 169.
54 In fact, it was the subject of a silent documentary film, an excerpt of which is still viewable on the Eranos foundation website: http://www.eranosfoundation.org/bas_stray_pages/trailer1951_b.htm
55 Henri-Charles Puech, "La Gnose et le temps," *Eranos-Jahrbuch* 20 (1951): 57–114; repr. in Puech, *En quête de la Gnose*, 2 vols. (Paris: Gallimard, 1978), 1.215–70; Gilles Quispel, "Zeit und Geschichte im antiken Christentum," *Eranos-Jahrbuch* 20 (1951): 115–40. These and other papers from the 1951 meeting were published in English translation in Joseph Campbell, ed. *Man and Time: Papers from the Eranos Yearbooks*, Bollingen Series 30.3 (Princeton, NJ: Princeton University Press, 1957).
56 Quispel, "Jung Codex and Its Significance," 42; Hakl, *Eranos*, 331 n. 112.
57 Robinson, "Jung Codex," 21.
58 Gilles Quispel, "Note on an Unknown Gnostic Codex," *Vigiliae Christianae* 7 (1953): 193.
59 Perhaps needless to say, this identification was soon contested, and remains so.
60 Quispel, "Note," 193. This claim that the *Gospel of Truth*, as of 1953, is the "only heretical gospel known up till now" is a curious one, since Quispel himself mentions other gospels among the Nag Hammadi Codices (*Gospel of Thomas*, the so-called *Gospel of the Egyptians*) in *Gnosis als Weltreligion* (1951). Perhaps he did not consider these gospels "heretical"?
61 Puech and Quispel's addresses were published in 1955 as Henri-Charles Puech, "The Jung Codex and other Gnostic Documents from Nag Hammadi," in *Jung Codex*, 11–34; and Quispel, "Jung Codex and Its Significance." Jung's address is published in his *Collected Works* as well as in Segal, *The Gnostic Jung*, 98–101.
62 Puech, "Jung Codex and the other Gnostic Documents," 18.
63 Quispel, "Jung Codex and Its Significance," 38–9.

(the back of this card—in whose hand is unclear (perhaps Robinson's?)—is the note, "During this congress Puech and Q. made their plans.")

64 Henri-Charles Puech and Gilles Quispel, "Les Écrits Gnostiques du Codex Jung," *Vigiliae Christianae* 8 (1954): 1–51.
65 Henri-Charles Puech and Gilles Quispel, "La Quatrième Écrit Gnostique du Codex Jung," *Vigiliae Christianae* 9 (1955): 65–102.
66 Michel Malinine, Henri-Charles Puech, and Gilles Quispel, eds. *Evangelium Veritatis: Codex Jung f.VIII^r–XVI^v (p. 16-32) / f.XIX^r–XXII^r (p. 37-43)*, Studien aus dem C. G. Jung-Institut 6 (Zürich: Rascher, 1956). This volume carries the dedication, "C. G. Jung Octogenario 26. VII. MCMLV."
67 Henri-Charles Puech, "Une collection de paroles de Jésus récemment retrouvée: L'Évangile selon Thomas," *Comptes rendus de l'Académie des Inscriptiones et Belles-Lettres* 101, no. 2 (1957): 146–67; repr. in Puech, *En quête de la Gnose*, 2.33–57, see esp. 42–5. Puech notes that he had previously presented the material at lectures and conferences in 1956 (33 n. 1).
68 Antoine Guillaumont, Henri-Charles Puech, Gilles Quispel, Walter Till, and Yassah 'Abd al Masih, eds. *L'Évangile selon Thomas* (Leiden: Brill; Paris: Presses Univeritaires de France, 1959). On the role of Puech and Quispel in setting the course for scholarship on the *Gospel of Thomas*, see my article "'Finding' the *Gospel of Thomas* in Edessa," *Journal of Early Christian Studies* 25 (2017): 501–30, esp. 507–16.
69 A publication pace sharply criticized by Robinson ("Jung Codex"), among others.
70 Robinson, "Jung Codex," 18.
71 Quotation from the letter of Doresse to Puech dated October 4, 1947; text and translation in Robinson, *Nag Hammadi Story*, 1.185–6. Puech not only worked against the wishes of Doresse, his student and advisee, he also colluded with Quispel in actively seeking to prevent him from working on the materials. As a condition for the sale, Quispel demanded that Doresse hand over the photographs that he had made of the codex in 1947: Robinson, "Jung Codex," 21; Quispel, "Jung Codex and Its Significance," 44.
72 Once acquired through the Jung Institute, Puech and Quispel monopolized the codex and its contents, allowing access only to a small circle of philologists who aided them in preparing editions of the four texts contained within it, a process that took two decades (for the full story of this monopolization, see Robinson, "Jung Codex"). They even went so far as to leverage their control over the Jung Codex (and implicit power to withhold its eventual repatriation) to secure Puech a seat on the Committee working on the other codices in Cairo: Robinson, "Jung Codex," 23.
73 A generation of critical reassessment was inaugurated by Michael Allen Williams, *Rethinking "Gnosticism": An Argument for Dismantling a Dubious Category* (Princeton, NJ: Princeton University Press, 1996) and King, *What Is Gnosticism?* More recently, closer attention is being paid to the historical context of the physical manuscripts, substantially inspired by Lundhaug and Jenott, *Monastic Origins*.
74 Eva Mroczek makes just such a point about the frequent tendency of contemporary scholars to assume moral superiority over previous generations in our treatment of ancient texts: "By such accounts we are alienated not only from the orientalized subjects of our find stories but also from the scholars a generation or two before us. We are the only ones with the proper relationship to our ancient texts, with evolved practices that, uniquely, can preserve a fragile past. Of course, in reality this is not so simple." Mroczek, "True Stories and the Poetics of Discovery," *Bulletin for the Study of Religion* 45, no. 2 (2016): 28. Similar postures of secrecy, control, and a suspension of the ethical in relation to ancient manuscripts can be seen, for example, in the current involvement of scholars with the Green Scholars Initiative and the Museum of the

Bible, as now documented in Candida Moss and Joel Baden, *Bible Nation: The United States of Hobby Lobby* (Princeton, NJ: Princeton University Press, 2017).
75. Steven M. Wasserstrom, "Nine Theses on the Study of Religion," in this volume, §2 and §3, emphasis mine.

Chapter 10

1. Maurice Blanchot, trans. Susan Hanson, "Affirmation (Desire, Affliction)," in *The Infinite Conversation* (Minneapolis: University of Minnesota Press, 1993), 111. French edition: "L'Affirmation (le désir, le malheur)," in *L'Entretien Infini* (Paris: Gallimard, 1969), 160. Originally published in "Simone Weil et la certitude," *La Nouvelle Revue française* 55 (July 1957): 103–14.
2. Maurice Blanchot, trans. Elizabeth Rottenberg, "Traces," in *Friendship* (Stanford, CA: Stanford University Press, 1997), 223. Originally published as the second half of "L'Interruption," in *La Nouvelle Revue française* 137 (May 1964): 869–81. Republished as part of "Traces," in *L'Amitié* (Paris: Gallimard, 1971), 252. Rupture is the key term in Blanchot's essay on Jabès, and a key to Blanchot's own understanding of the relationship between language and Judaism, which this essay will explore at length.
3. Seven M. Wasserstrom, "Nine Theses on the Study of Religion," in this volume, §1, emphasis in original.
4. Ibid.
5. Ibid.
6. Steven M. Wasserstrom, *Religion after Religion: Gerschom Scholem, Mircea Eliade, and Henry Corbin at Eranos* (Princeton, NJ: Princeton University Press, 1999); Ibid., *Between Muslim and Jew: The Problem of Symbiosis under Early Islam* (Princeton, NJ: Princeton University Press, 1995).
7. See Sarah Hammerschlag, *The Figural Jew: Politics and Identity in French Post-War Thought* (Chicago, IL: University of Chicago Press, 2010).
8. Wasserstrom, "Nine Theses," §7.
9. Leslie Hill gives an account of Blanchot's work for *Combat* and *L'Insurgé*, two extremely nationalist, anti-capitalist, anti-communist, and, on occasion, anti-Semitic papers. Blanchot's articles were virulently anti-democratic, and carried anti-Semitic undertones: in "Le Terrorisme, méthode de salut public," published in *Combat* in July 1936, Blanchot argued for violent opposition to Léon Blum's government, which he characterized in anti-Semitic terms, while in "Après la coup de force germanique," published in *Combat* in April 1936, he attacks the calls for immediate action against Hitler by claiming they are promulgated by "unbridled Jews" (*"des Juifs déchaînés"*). Leslie Hill, "An intellectual itinerary," in *Maurice Blanchot: Extreme Contemporary* (London: Routledge, 1997), 37. Hill interprets these statements as Blanchot slipping into a rhetoric common within his political milieu, rather than expressing agreement with any explicitly anti-Jewish opinions. For a more critical discussion of Blanchot's articles for *Combat*, one which calls into question the revolutionary possibility of Blanchot's later work, see: Jeffrey Mehlman "Blanchot at Combat: Of Literature and Terror," in *Legacies of Antisemitism in France* (Minneapolis: University of Minnesota Press, 1983), 6–22.
10. Wasserstrom, *Religion after Religion*, 238.

11 Maurice Blanchot, "Literature and the Right to Death," in *The Work of Fire*, trans. Charlotte Mandell (Stanford, CA: University of California Press, 1995), 319. French edition: "La littérature et la droit à la mort," in *La part du feu* (Paris: Gallimard, 1949), 309. Originally published as two separate essays: "Le Règne animal de l'esprit," *Critique* 18 (November 1947): 387–405; and "La Littérature et la droit à la mort," *Critique* 20 (January 1948): 30–47.
12 Ibid., 321/311.
13 Ibid., 322/311.
14 Ibid., 323/312.
15 Eric Hoppenot, *Maurice Blanchot et la tradition juive* (Paris: Kimé, 2014), 195–6.
16 Maurice Blanchot, "Prophetic Speech," trans. Charlotte Mandell, in *The Book to Come* (Stanford, CA: Stanford University Press, 2003), 79. French edition: "La parole prophétique," in *Le livre à venir* (Paris: Gallimard, 1959), 109. Originally published as "La Parole prophétique," *La Nouvelle Revue française* 49 (January 1957): 101–10.
17 Ibid., 81/112.
18 Ibid., 82/113.
19 Ibid., 83/114.
20 Ibid., 85/118.
21 Maurice Blanchot, "The Indestructible: Being Jewish," trans. Susan Hanson, in *The Infinite Conversation*, 125. French edition: "L'indestructible: Être juif," in *L'entretien infini*, 183. Originally published as two essays: "Être juif" (I), *La Nouvelle Revue française* 116 (August 1962): 279–85; and "Être juif" (II), *La Nouvelle Revue française* 117 (September 1962): 471–6.
22 Ibid., 127/186.
23 Ibid., 127/187.
24 Ibid., emphasis mine.
25 Ibid., 128/187.
26 Georg W. F. Hegel, "The Spirit of Christianity and Its Fate," in *Early Theological Writings*, trans. T. M. Knox (Chicago, IL: University of Chicago Press, 1948), 206. That Blanchot considers Hegel's negative conception of Judaism an exemplary religion implicitly contests the views of Mircea Eliade and Henri Corbin as traced by Wasserstrom, insofar as their *coincidentia oppositorum* accords with the Hegelian notion of Christianity that Blachot rejects in favor of its opposite.
27 Blanchot, *Infinite Conversation/Entretien Infini*, 128/187.
28 But rather than privileging the *coincidentia oppositorum*, he argues that the opposition or distance between god and man never finds a point of union, and instead must be navigated by a speech that avoids synthesis.
29 Neher, in *L'Existence juive,* and Levinas, in "Être Juif," focus on the relationship between God and Israel one of love. Love, in Hegel's "The Spirit of Judaism," is absent from Judaism and can only be found in Christianity, where it unifies the binaries of real and ideal. Blanchot follows Hegel in this regard: there is no possibility of God "loving" anything human, since the concept of God is incommensurable with the human scale of love. He rejects love in favor of the less intimate speech, discussed in "Prophetic Speech," which does not erase the distance between real and ideal, but preserves their distance while still crossing from one to the other. See Levinas, "Etre juif," *Confluences* 15–17 (1947): 253–64, trans. as Emmanuel Levinas, "Being Jewish," translated by Mary Beth Mader, *Continental Philosophy Review* 40 (2007): 205–10. See also: André Neher, *L'existence juive: solitudes et affrontements* (Paris: Seuil, 1962).

30 On the unpopularity of making reference to Judaism, see Steven Jaron, *Edmond Jabès: The Hazard of Exile* (Oxford: Europeans Humanities Research Centre of the University of Oxford, 2003), 65–6. Jabès identified strongly as a Franco-Egyptian poet, and his investment in French culture and the absence of not only Judaism, but Islam or the Arabic language, from his work, at times put him in conflict with Arabic-speaking Egyptian writers who considered his poetry too French; see exchange with "Seiffoula" in *La semaine égyptienne* (1932), in Jaron, *Hazard of Exile*, 53–6. His commitment to French cultural and political values became especially notable after the Second World War, in his work with organization *Groupement des amitiés françaises*, founded in 1944 to strengthen ties between France and Egypt by propounding universality of French values through literary readings and lectures; see Jaron, *Hazard of Exile*, 76–7.
31 Ruchama Johnston-Bloom, "Abrahamic Encounters in the Weimar Wüste."
32 Edmond Jabès, *The Book of Questions, Volume I* [*The Book of Questions, The Book of Yukel, The Return to the Book*] (Middletown, CT: Wesleyan University Press, 1977), 149. Originally appearing in Edmond Jabès, *Le livre des questions* (Paris: Gallimard, 1963), 164.
33 Jean Starobinski, "Out of This Violated Mineral Night …," in *Edmond Jabès: The Sin of the Book* (Lincoln: University of Nebraska Press, 1985), 42.
34 In French, this "wearing out" (*usure*) is the key word in the phrase: "Je vous ai parlé de la difficulté d'être Juif qui se confonde avec la difficulté d'écrire, car le judaïsme et l'écriture ne sont qu'une même attente, un même espoir, une même usure," in Jabès, *Livre des questions*, 132. The word *usure* indicates both the wearing down of an object through use, and usury. Jabès uses it here to connect the writing to and the figures of Judaism with which he plays throughout the text—words as sand, as remains of the Tablets of Law, and as the stigmatizing name "Juif" through which Jewish identity is marked and effaced. Jacques Derrida centers this term in his explanation of metaphor: as *usure* refers both to effacement and to the charging of excessive interest, so a metaphor attempts to efface the image it describes in order to present the meaning at which it aims but in so doing produces an excess of signification (the image) that does not collapse into meaning. While Derrida does not, in "White Mythologies," explicate the associations between the word *usure* and Judaism, his use of the term to discuss how metaphor functions in language helps us clarify how Blanchot draws on Jabès for his use of Judaism as a metaphor for the function of metaphor. Jacques Derrida, "White Mythology: Metaphor in the Text of Philosophy," in *Margins of Philosophy*, trans. Alan Bass (Chicago, IL: University of Chicago Press, 1982), 215–16.
35 Jabès, *Book of Questions/Livre des questions*, 100/109.
36 Ibid., 157/174.
37 Ibid., 19/18.
38 Ibid., 19/17.
39 Ibid., 61/64.
40 Ibid.
41 Ibid. Translation modified.
42 Ibid.
43 Regarding the first form of interruption, Blanchot writes: "Let us take the most steady conversation … even if its discourse is coherent, it must always fragment itself by changing protagonists. Moving from one to the other interlocutor, it interrupts itself

… Interrupting for the sake of understanding, understanding in order to speak," in Blanchot, *Infinite Conversation/Entretien infini* 75-6/107. This form of interruption is subordinated to the goal of understanding, "the affirmation of a unitary truth," in ibid., 76/108. In contrast, the second form of interruption rests on the alterity of each individual: it "measures the distance between two interlocutors … an irreducible distance" (Ibid.) that cannot be erased by subsuming both under the unitary truth posited as the goal of ordinary conversation. See Maurice Blanchot, "Interruption (as on a Riemann Surface)," in *The Infinite Conversation*, 75-6. Originally appears in Blanchot "L'Interruption (comme sur une surface de Riemann)," in *L'Entretien Infini*, 107-8.
44 Jaron, *Hazard of Exile*, 153.
45 Blanchot, *Friendship/L'Amitié*, 222-3/252. Translation my own, with reference to Elizabeth Rottenberg's translation.
46 Ibid., 223/252.
47 Ibid.
48 Ibid., 223/253.
49 Ibid. Translation modified.
50 Ibid., 224/254.
51 Ibid.
52 Jabès, *The Book of Questions*, 122.
53 Blanchot, *Friendship/L'Amitié*, 224/254.
54 Rosemarie Waldrop, *Lavish Absence: Recalling and Rereading Edmond Jabès* (Middletown: Wesleyan University Press, 2002), 11.
55 Ibid.
56 Maurice Blanchot, "A Plural Speech," trans. Susan Hanson, in *The Infinite Conversation*, 81. Originally appearing in Blanchot, "Une parole plurielle," in *L'entretien infini*, 114.
57 Blanchot, *Friendship/Amitié*, 223/252. Translation modified.
58 See also Hoppenot, *Maurice Blanchot et la tradition Juive*, 33. Hoppenot argues that the concept of fragmentary writing that Blanchot develops and practices to mark the rupture at the center of speech is theoretically premised on the Breaking of the Tablets. Blanchot's discussion of Hegel, Mallarmé, and the Bible in "The Absence of the Book" supports this: Blanchot, *Infinite Conversation/Entretien infini*, 427-8/627-8.
59 Blanchot, *Infinite Conversation/Entretien infini*, 75/106.

Chapter 11

1 Steven M. Wasserstrom, *Religion after Religion: Gershom Scholem, Mircea Eliade, and Henry Corbin at Eranos* (Princeton, NJ: Princeton University Press, 1999), 234.
2 Reuven Firestone, "Abraham and Authenticity," in *The Oxford Handbook of the Abrahamic Religions*, ed. Adam J. Silverstein and Guy G. Stroumsa (Oxford: Oxford University Press, 2015), 3-21, esp. 4. Firestone also argues that Abraham was subsequently "'Christianized,' 'Islamized,' and 'Judaized' because of his importance as *homo religiosus* in popular religious discourse" (19).
3 Wasserstrom, *Religion after Religion*, 225-6. See also the essays in *Interpreting Abraham: Journeys to Moriah*, ed. Bradley Beach and Matthew T. Powell (Augsburg: Fortress Publishers, 2014).
4 According to Bove, "Levinas's interpretation emphasizes the key feature of the Akedah as the ability of Abraham to listen to the second voice of the angel, drop

the knife, and unbind Isaac. This choice of nonviolence was, in Levinasian terms, a return to the ethical." Laurence Bove, "Unbinding the Other: Levinas, the Akedah, and Going beyond the Subject," in *Interpreting Abraham*, 169–86, 170–1.

5   Steven M. Wasserstrom, "Nine Theses on the Study of Religion," in this volume, §5.
6   Wasserstrom, *Religion after Religion*, 239–41.
7   Xavier de Planhol, "Deserts," in *Encyclopedia of Religion*, ed. Lindsay Jones, 2nd ed., vol. 4 (New York: Macmillan Reference USA, 2005), 2300–2303.
8   Ernest Renan, *Histoire générale et système comparé des langues sémitiques* (Paris: Michel Lévy Frères, 1855).
9   de Planhol, "Deserts," 2302.
10 Accessed September 24, 2017, http://isrlc.org/?p=384.
11 The conference was held in Glasgow and also invited "discussion of the Celtic tradition's relocation of desert spirituality to these islands." Ibid.
12 Darlene L. Bird, *Theology and Religious Studies in Higher Education: Global Perspectives* (London and New York: Continuum, 2009), 22. The International Society for Religion, Culture and Literature, originally the Society for Religion and Literature, was founded at the University of Durham. See http://isrlc.org/. When discussing the future of the study of religion, one might therefore ask, where? And by whom?
13 Steven M. Wasserstrom, *Between Muslim and Jew: The Problem of Symbiosis under Early Islam* (Princeton, NJ: Princeton University Press, 1995).
14 See *Orientalism and the Jews*, ed. Ivan Davidson Kalmar and Derek J. Penslar (Waltham, MA and Hanover, NH: Brandeis University Press and University Press of New England, 2005).
15 Steven M. Wasserstrom, "Apology for S. D. Goitein: An Essay," in *A Faithful Sea: The Religious Cultures of the Mediterranean, 1200–1700*, ed. Adnan A. Husain and K. E. Fleming (Oxford: Oneworld, 2007), 176.
16 Gil Eyal, *The Disenchantment of the Orient: Expertise in Arab Affairs and the Israeli State* (Stanford, CA: Stanford University Press, 2006).
17 Renan, *Histoire générale*, 6.
18 Tomoko Masuzawa, *The Invention of World Religions, or, How European Universalism Was Preserved in the Language of Pluralism* (Chicago, IL: University of Chicago Press, 2005), 25. Said argued that, for Renan, Semites could never "outdistance the organizing claims on him of his origins … No Semite could ever shake loose the pastoral, desert environment of his tent and tribe." Edward Said, *Orientalism* (New York: Pantheon Books, 1978), 234.
19 Masuzawa, *Invention*, 25. See also Marchand on Renan's philology: Suzanne L. Marchand, "German Orientalism and the Decline of the West," *Proceedings of the American Philosophical Society* 145, no. 4 (December 2001): 466–7.
20 Suzanne L. Marchand, *German Orientalism in the Age of Empire: Religion, Race, and Scholarship* (Washington, DC and New York: German Historical Institute and Cambridge University Press, 2009), 285–6.
21 Gil Anidjar, *The Jew, the Arab: A History of the Enemy* (Stanford, CA: Stanford University Press, 2003), xi.
22 See Sayyid Jamal al-Din al-Afghani, "Answer to Renan," in Nikki R. Keddie, *An Islamic Response to Imperialism: Political and Religious Writings of Sayyid Jamal ad-Din al-Afghani* (Berkeley: University of California Press, 1968).
23 Ibid., 84–92.
24 Ignác Goldziher, *Mythology among the Hebrews and Its Historical Development*, trans. Russell Martineau (London: Longmans, Green and Co., 1877). For this work as a

refutation of Renan, see Lawrence I. Conrad, "Ignaz Goldziher on Ernest Renan: From Orientalist Philology to the Study of Islam," in *The Jewish Discovery of Islam*, ed. Martin Kramer (Tel Aviv: Tel Aviv University, 1999), 137–80, 143–5.

25 Goldziher, *Mythology*, xvi. This conviction that Jews and Muslims can lay claim to mythology presages Scholem's approach, as detailed by Wasserstrom in *Religion after Religion*.

26 Shulamit Volkov, *Germans, Jews, and Antisemites: Trials in Emancipation* (Cambridge: Cambridge University Press, 2006), 261.

27 See Susannah Heschel, "Abraham Geiger and the Emergence of Jewish Philoislamism," in *"Im vollen Licht der Geschichte": die Wissenschaft des Judentums und die Anfänge der kritischen Koranforschung*, ed. Dirk Hartwig, Walter Homolka, Michael J. Marx, and Angelika Neuwirth (Würzburg: Ergon, 2008), 65–86; Ruchama Johnston-Bloom, "Jews, Muslims and *Bildung*: The German-Jewish Orientalist Gustav Weil in Egypt," *Religion Compass* 8, no. 2 (2014): 49–59.

28 Michael Brenner, *The Renaissance of Jewish Culture in Weimar Germany* (New Haven, CT: Yale University Press, 1996).

29 The address was later published in Martin Buber, *Vom Geist des Judentums: Reden und Geleitworte* (Leipzig: K. Wolff Verlag, 1916). An English translation is included in *On Judaism*, ed. Nahum N. Glatzer (New York: Schocken Books, 1967).

30 Buber, *On Judaism*, 75.

31 Stefan Vogt, "The Postcolonial Buber: Orientalism, Subalternity, and Identity Politics in Martin Buber's Political Thought," *Jewish Social Studies: History, Culture, Society* 22, no. 1 (2016): 161–86, 164.

32 Buber, *On Judaism*, 56.

33 Paul Mendes-Flohr, "Werner Sombart's: The Jews and Modern Capitalism; An Analysis of its Ideological Premises," *Leo Baeck Institute Year Book* 20 (January 1976): 87–107, 100. Capitalism, according to Sombart, had turned the modern city into a desert.

34 Ritchie Robertson, "*Urheimat Asien*: The Re-Orientation of German and Austrian Jews, 1900–1925," *German Life and Letters* 49, no. 2 (1996): 182–92, 186. Franz Oppenheimer also referred to ancient Israelites as a "gallant, warrior-like people" who "burst out the desert to conquer the Promised Land." Qtd. in ibid., 186.

35 See Eyal, *Disenchantment of the Orient*.

36 Sander L. Gilman, *Jewish Self-Hatred: Anti-Semitism and the Hidden Language of the Jews* (Baltimore, MD: Johns Hopkins University Press, 1986).

37 Eyal, *Disenchantment of the Orient*, 45.

38 Oz Almog, *The Sabra: The Creation of the New Jew* (Berkeley: University of California Press, 2000), 185–208.

39 For more on Essad Bey see Tom Reiss, *The Orientalist: Solving the Mystery of a Strange and a Dangerous Life* (New York: Random House, 2005).

40 Both Nussimbuam and Asad were involved with Berlin's Islamic Society in the 1920s, where Asad converted; see Günther Windhager, *Leopold Weiss alias Muhammad Asad: von Galizien nach Arabien 1900–1927* (Wien: Böhlau, 2002), 177–9, and Reiss, *The Orientalist*, 200–2.

41 For more on Asad see Windhager, *Leopold Weiss alias Muhammad Asad*; Martin Kramer, "The Road from Mecca: Muhammad Asad (born Leopold Weiss)," in *Jewish Discovery of Islam*, 225–47; Abraham Rubin, "Muhammad Asad's Conversion to Islam as a Case Study in Jewish Self-Orientalization," *Jewish Social Studies: History, Culture, Society* 22, no. 1 (2016): 1–28; Dominik Schlosser, *Lebensgesetz und*

Vergemeinschaftungsform: Muḥammad Asad (1900–1992) und sein Islamverständnis (Berlin: EBVerlag, 2015).

42   Kurban Said, *Ali and Nino: A Love Story* (New York: Anchor Books/Random House, 2000), 51.
43   For more on geographical determinism in the work of Essad Bey, see Ruchama Johnston-Bloom, "Ali and Nino and Jewish Questions," in *Approaches to Kurban Said's "Ali and Nino": Love, Identity, and Intercultural Conflict*, ed. Carl Niekerk and Cori Crane (Rochester, NY: Camden House, 2017), 210–26.
44   Essad Bey, *Mohammed: A Biography*, trans. Helmut L. Ripperger (New York and Toronto: Longmans, Green and Co., 1936), 20.
45   Just as Nussimbaum's books were written for a non-Muslim, European audience, Muhammad Asad's autobiography was written and published in New York. However, he also structures the work as a *rihla*, embedding his reflections about his life in a narrative of traversing Arabia toward Mecca with his faithful Bedouin companion. At the outset he informs the reader "it is told in the context and, it should be kept in mind, on the time level of my last desert journey from the interior of Arabia to Mecca in the late summer of 1932: for it was during those twenty-three days that the pattern of my life became fully apparent to myself." Muhammad Asad, *The Road to Mecca* (New York: Simon and Schuster, 1954), 9.
46   Ibid., 144–5.
47   Ibid., 91.
48   Ibid., 49–50.
49   See Kramer, "Road from Mecca," and Rubin, "Muhammad Asad's Conversion to Islam," for the former, as well as Dan Diner, *Lost in the Sacred: Why the Muslim World Stood Still*, trans. Steven Rendall (Princeton, NJ: Princeton University Press, 2009), 173.
50   "It seems to me evident that this notion of an Islamic politics draws one away from the modern project of an Islamic state that cannot be different in essence from any modern state. I believe that this is also the view implicit in my father's life and writing, and therefore the most important part of his legacy." Talal Asad, "Muhammad Asad: Between Religion and Politics," *Islam & Science* 10, no. 1 (2012): 77–88, 87–8.
51   Muhammad Asad, *This Law of Ours and Other Essays* (Gibraltar: Dar al-Andalus, 1987).
52   Muhammad Asad, *The Message of the Quran* (Gibraltar: Dar al-Andalus, 1980).
53   Gil Anidjar makes this case quite strongly when he writes, "the affirmation of the 'Judeo-Christian,' a post-genocidal concession of Faustian proportions, which functions in each and every single case as a negation of both Jews and Muslims, must be recognized as meaningless." Gil Anidjar, "The Issue Between Judaism and Islam," *AJS Perspectives* (Spring 2012): 49. See also Santiago Slabodsky, *Decolonial Judaism: Triumphal Failures of Barbaric Thinking* (New York: Palgrave Macmillan, 2014).
54   For the history of the use of "Abrahamic" see Mark Silk, "The Abrahamic Religions as a Modern Concept," in *The Oxford Handbook of the Abrahamic Religions*, 71–87. See also the contribution of Dylan Burns in this volume regarding whether or not Sethian Gnosticism can meaningfully be categorized an Abrahamic religion.
55   Aaron Hughes, *Abrahamic Religions on the Uses and Abuses of History* (New York: Oxford University Press, 2012), 119. Hughes, like Wasserstrom, calls for us to focus on boundaries, as opposed to essences, ibid., 114.

56 Jon Douglas Levenson, *Inheriting Abraham: The Legacy of the Patriarch in Judaism, Christianity, and Islam* (Princeton, NJ: Princeton University Press, 2012). See also Rémi Brague, "The Concept of the Abrahamic Religions, Problems and Pitfalls," in *The Oxford Handbook of the Abrahamic Religions*, 88–108.
57 Wasserstrom, "Nine Theses," §2.
58 Ibid., §1.
59 Ibid.

Chapter 12

1 I speak only of fore*fathers* because Asad makes no mention of his matrilineal forbearers in the work.
2 He is sometimes remembered as the father of the influential anthropologist of Islam and the Middle East, Talal Asad. A more complete biography and bibliography for Asad can be found in Ruchama Johnston-Bloom's compelling chapter in this volume, "Abrahamic Encounters in the Weimar Wüste."
3 James Porter, "Erich Auerbach and the Judaizing of Philology," *Critical Inquiry* 35, no. 1 (Autumn 2008): 115.
4 Steven M. Wasserstrom, *Religion after Religion: Gershom Scholem, Mircea Eliade, and Henry Corbin at Eranos* (Princeton, NJ: Princeton University Press, 1999), 242.
5 Wasserstrom, *Religion after Religion*, 242.
6 Steven M. Wasserstrom, "Nine Theses on the Study of Religion," in this volume, §1.
7 Wasserstrom notes that both Auerbach and Scholem had a friend in Walter Benjamin. Wasserstrom, *Religion after Religion*, 6.
8 As Johnston-Bloom notes above (p. 116), the term "Abrahamic" has rightly come under attack for the homogeneity, harmonious filiation, and exclusiveness it presupposes to exist between Judaism, Christianity, and Islam. I use the term for three reasons: it is a way to name the religions that Auerbach and Asad most commonly consider; this chapter focuses on the figure of Abraham himself; and, my use of the term is not intended to convey harmony. On the contrary, I intend to underscore the plurality of contradictory interpretations that exist within and between these religions. See further, Aaron Hughes, *Abrahamic Religions: On the Uses and Abuses of History* (New York: Oxford University Press, 2012).
9 In *Religion after Religion*, Wasserstrom asks readers to compare Auerbach's statement on exile with Theodor Adorno's. In his essay, "Philology and *Weltliteratur*," Auerbach says that a philologist can be effective only after he transcends his own nation and culture. By contrast, Adorno says that he acquired a perspective "outside" of culture while in America. Wasserstrom says that Auerbach's project was one of trying to achieve "universality" and Adorno's one of "deprovincialization": *Religion after Religion*, 258 n. 10.
10 Muhammad Asad, *The Road to Mecca* (New York: Simon and Schuster, 1954), 53.
11 Wasserstrom, "Nine Theses," §2.
12 Ibid.
13 Asad, *The Road to Mecca*, 60–1.
14 Muhammad Asad, *Islam at the Crossroads* (New Delhi: Goodword Books, 2001), 3.
15 See, for example, Asad, *The Road to Mecca*, 64–5.
16 Ibid., 51.

17 This observation runs the risk of rebelling against Talal Asad's warning to avoid seeing his father as "a bridge between Islam and the West." According to the younger Asad, such a move would deracinate his father from the complex tradition of Islam that he wholly embraced because it would make "Westerner" stand for at least half of Muhammad Asad's identity. This view, Talal Asad states, is sometimes marshaled when the argument is made that Muhammad Asad attempted to liberalize Islam; see Talal Asad, "Muhammad Asad, Between Religion and Politics," *Islam & Science* 10, no. 1 (Summer 2012): 77–8. Professor Asad's warning ought to, in the main, be heeded. Muhammad Asad did not set out to liberalize Islam by importing a stream of European thought. In his works, *Principles of State and Government in Islam* and *Islam at a Crossroads*, which were written for a primarily Muslim audience, he most often looks for solutions to the challenges faced by Islam from sources within the tradition as he understands and defines it. Any reading of his autobiography—in which he once again addressed himself mostly (though not totally) to a non-Muslim audience—would also have to stretch to argue that he saw himself as a bridge figure or as a hyphenated European-Muslim. "The West" in this text most often stands on the other side of a vast, indeed nearly unbridgeable, chasm from Islam. Muhammad Asad writes, "Certainly [I do not long for] the intellectual interests of Europe. I have left them behind me. I do not miss them": Asad, *The Road to Mecca*, 52. Without disregarding this statement or Talal Asad's warning, I argue that ignoring the complex role of Europe and European identity—and even the intellectual concerns of his youth—in Muhammad Asad's autobiographical text would be a mistake. Even if Asad's description of his pre-conversion self as a somewhat normal, disaffected European youth is meant only as a rhetorical strategy to draw in similar readers (and perhaps to persuade them of the validity of Islam), we should not ignore Asad's own vacillations in the way he calls on or recalls his European identity.

18 Asad, *The Road to Mecca*, 50.

19 Quoted in Kader Konuk, *East-West Mimesis: Auerbach in Turkey* (Stanford, CA: Stanford University Press, 2010), 92.

20 Ibid., 156.

21 Ibid., 158.

22 It might be objected that the Abrahamic story is a non-European one. But Auerbach's emphasis is on the text's impact on European literature; and, as Porter argues ("Erich Auerbach," 143), even the biblical figures appear as heroes of Western literature in Auerbach.

23 Erich Auerbach, *Mimesis: The Representation of Reality in Western Literature*, trans. Willard R. Trask (Princeton, NJ: Princeton University Press, 2003), 552.

24 Ibid.

25 Ibid.

26 Ibid., 225–50.

27 Edward Said, "Erich Auerbach, Critic of the Earthly World," *boundary 2* 31, no. 2 (Summer 2004): 24.

28 Porter, "Erich Auerbach," 115–47.

29 My argument here is fully reliant on Porter. It should be noted that, to the degree that Auerbach's philological method was Jewish, it was a Judaism that was informed by a reading of texts and not necessarily by the lived experience of Jews. For this reason, Porter's (and my) observations about Auerbach's Judaism risk re-inscribing Jews and Judaism as merely figures.

30 Wasserstrom, "Nine Theses," §7.

31. For example, Asad thought that the Islamic legal allowance for polygamy stemmed from Islam's realism with respect to man's natural sexual needs: Asad, *The Road to Mecca*, 284. Auerbach, as we have already seen, reveals his central concern at the end of *Mimesis* to be living with human difference: Auerbach, *Mimesis*, 552.
32. Wasserstrom, *Religion after Religion*, 235, emphasis in original.
33. Auerbach, *Mimesis*, 3.
34. Wasserstrom remarked on a possible reading of Auerbach that has, to my knowledge, gone otherwise unacknowledged in the scholarship: Odysseus's scar must be read in relationship to the scar of circumcision. Personal communication, October 28, 2017.
35. Auerbach, *Mimesis*, 7.
36. Ibid., 11–2.
37. Porter, "Erich Auerbach," 117–21.
38. Ibid., 126.
39. Auerbach, *Mimesis*, 20.
40. Wasserstrom, *Religion after Religion*, 234.
41. Ibid., 231, emphasis added.
42. Ibid.
43. Ibid., 234.
44. Auerbach, *Mimesis*, 10.
45. Ibid., 75–6.
46. Wasserstrom, *Religion after Religion*, 243.
47. Konuk, *East-West Mimesis*, 159.
48. Johnston-Bloom also notes the significance of Abraham for Asad in her chapter "Abrahamic Encounters in the Weimar *Wüste*," in this volume.
49. Asad, *The Road to Mecca*, 277–8.
50. Ibid.
51. See, for example, his commentary on Qur'an 3:96–7, which apparently discusses the pre-Islamic history of the Ka'ba: Asad, *The Message of the Qur'ān: The Full Account of the Revealed Arabic Text Accompanied by Parallel Transliteration*, trans. Muhammad Asad (London: Book Foundation, 2012), 112.
52. Wasserstrom, "Nine Theses," §7.
53. Auerbach, *Mimesis*, 549.
54. Asad, *The Road to Mecca*, 50.

Chapter 13

1. Hans-Martin Schenke initially recognized the complex of features shared across a wide range of Nag Hammadi texts and some heresiological witnesses, chief among them veneration of Seth, third son of Adam and Eve, as revealer and/or savior; see e.g. Hans-Martin Schenke, "The Phenomenon and Significance of Gnostic Sethianism," trans. Bentley Layton, in *The Rediscovery of Gnosticism: Proceedings of the International Conference on Gnosticism*, ed. Bentley Layton, 2 vols. (Leiden: Brill, 1981), 588–616, and John D. Turner, *Sethian Gnosticism and the Platonic Tradition*. Bibliothèque Copte de Nag Hammadi, section "études" 6 (Québec and Louvain: Les presses de l'université Laval and Peeters, 2001). Important caveats are discussed in the final section of this paper. The present study takes "Gnosticism" to refer to the ancient "school of thought" professed by self-described *Gnostikoi*, per the discussion

of David Brakke, *The Gnostics: Myth, Ritual, and Diversity in Early Christianity* (Cambridge, MA: Harvard University Press, 2010), a majority of whose extant scriptures are the "Sethian" texts so denoted by Schenke. For an argument against use of the term "Gnosticism," see Michael Allen Williams, *Rethinking "Gnosticism": Arguments for Dismantling a Dubious Category* (Princeton, NJ: Princeton University Press, 1996).

2 For *Forschungsgeschichte*, see Michael Allen Williams, "Sethianism," in *Companion to Second-Century "Heretics*," ed. A. Marjanen and P. Luomanen (Leiden: Brill, 2005), 32–63; Dylan M. Burns, *Apocalypse of the Alien God: Platonism and the Exile of Sethian Gnosticism. Divinations* (Philadelphia: University of Pennsylvania, 2014), 49–50, 141–5, 154–7.

3 For Sethianism as an initially "pre-Christian"/Jewish movement, see Schenke, "Phenomenon," 607; for its eventual "Paganization," see Turner, *Sethian Gnosticism*, esp. 179–82, 293; for "Sethian Christianity," see Williams, "Sethianism," and Lance Jenott, "Emissaries of Truth and Justice: The Seed of Seth as Agents of Divine Providence," in *Gnosticism, Platonism, and the Late Ancient World: Essays in Honour of John D. Turner*, ed. Kevin Corrigan and Tuomas Rasimus et al., Nag Hammadi and Manichaean Studies 82 (Leiden and Boston: Brill, 2013), 43–62, 43 n. 1. For Sethianism as recalling "Jewish-Christian" baptismal movements fond of apocalypses, see Burns, *Apocalypse*, 141–7.

4 It was a bit over fourteen years ago. Thirteen plus one.

5 Steven M. Wasserstrom, "Nine Theses on the Study of Religion," in this volume, §§ 1, 6, 7 respectively.

6 Quoted in Steven M. Wasserstrom, *Religion After Religion: Gershom Scholem, Mircea Eliade, and Henry Corbin at Eranos* (Princeton, NJ: Princeton University Press, 1999), 179.

7 Hughes charges that the term "Abrahamic religions" is only valid as a category in interfaith theology: Aaron W. Hughes, *Abrahamic Religions: On the Uses and Abuses of History* (Oxford: Oxford University Press, 2012); Stroumsa responds that "it is rather convenient for referring to what one used to call 'the monotheistic religions,' as it highlights the genetic link between these families of religions": Guy G. Stroumsa, *The Making of the Abrahamic Religions in Late Antiquity*. Oxford Studies in the Abrahamic Religions 1 (Oxford: Oxford University Press, 2015), 7. On the pedigree of the "seal of the prophets" (Qur'an 33.40) in Manichaeism, see Stroumsa, *Making*, 99; on the importance of Jewish-Christian as well as "dualist" currents (such as Gnosticism and Manichaeism) in the formation of Islam, see ibid., 158, 148, respectively. On the category "Abrahamic religion," see further the contribution of Johnston-Bloom, in this volume.

8 Steven M. Wasserstrom, "The Moving Finger Writes: Mughīra ibn Saʿīd's Islamic Gnosis and the Myths of its Rejection," *History of Religions* 25, no. 1 (1985): 1–29; on the *ghulat* and Gnosticism, see recently Mushegh Asatryan and Dylan M. Burns, "Is Ghulat Religion Islamic Gnosticism? Religious Transitions in Late Antiquity," in *Esotérisme shi'ite: ses racines et ses prolongements*, ed. Mohammad Ali Amir-Moezzi. Bibliothèque de l'École des Hautes Études 177 (Paris: Bibliothèque de l'École des Hautes Études and London: Institute of Ismaili Studies, 2016), 55–86.

9 Cf. Wasserstrom's notion of religion as taking place in "cultural encounters" between different traditions.

10 "So gehen etwa die Schriften des Sethianismus auf die Patriarchenüberlieferung entweder gar nicht oder nur im Zusammenhang mit den Ereignissen von Sodom

und Gomorra ein und haben an der Gestalt Abrahams kein Interesse": Jaan Lahe, *Gnosis und Judentum: Alttestamentliche und jüdische Motive in der gnostischen Literatur und das Ursprungsproblem der Gnosis*. Nag Hammadi and Manichaean Studies 75 (Leiden and Boston: Brill, 2012), 313, in turn following Hans-Gebhard Bethge, "Die Ambivalenz alttestamentlicher Geschichtstraditionen in der Gnosis," in *Altes Testament, Frühjudentum, Gnosis: Neue Studien zu "Gnosis und Bibel,"* ed. Karl-Wolfgang Tröger (Berlin: Evangelische Verlagsanstalt, 1980), 89–109, esp. 98–9.

11 On the genre of the text, see Birger A. Pearson, "Jewish Sources in Gnostic Literature," in *The Literature of the Jewish People in the Period of the Second Temple*, ed. Michael E. Stone. Compendia Rerum Iudaicarum ad Novum Testamentum 2.2 (Leiden: Brill, 1984), 443–81, 470; Burns, *Apocalypse*, 79–80.

12 For Adam and Eve as Saklas's slaves, see *Apoc. Adam* NHC V 65.16. All Nag Hammadi texts quoted in this essay I have translated myself, with reference to the CGL editions (Brill).

13 Ibid., [71].1–8.

14 Ibid., [72].15–23.

15 Ibid., [73].14–28, [74].7–24.

16 Ibid., [75].9–16; i.e., the heavenly bodies (luminaries = planets and stars) will go dark, and the generations (of men) will not see them.

17 With Guy G. Stroumsa, *Another Seed: Studies in Gnostic Mythology*. Nag Hammadi Studies 24 (Leiden: Brill, 1984), 106.

18 *Apoc. Adam*, [76].4–17.

19 For a *terminus post quem* of the mid–late second century CE, given the polemic against the "thirteenth kingdom," likely the Christians, see Stroumsa, *Another Seed*, 97–103; Turner, *Sethian Gnosticism*, 155, 749–50; cf. Pearson, "Jewish Sources," 473. On the "fourteenth kingdom," cf. above, n. 4.

20 *Apoc. Adam*, [82].10–22.

21 Ibid., [85].10–14.

22 Thus Pearson, "Jewish Sources," 470, 472–3, noting objections at ibid., 472 n. 189; see also Schenke, "Phenomenon," 607; Charles W. Hedrick, *The Apocalypse of Adam: A Literary and Source Analysis. Ancient Texts and Translations* (Eugene, OR: Wipf & Stock, 2005), 214–15.

23 On the celestial Seth, see Burns, *Apocalypse*, 80–6.

24 Lit. "place of pasture."

25 NHC III 69.9–26.

26 Ibid., 68.1–69.4.

27 Schenke, "Phenomenon," 607, followed by Pearson, "Jewish Sources," 469.

28 NHC III 60.25–6[2].24.

29 Ibid., 63.4–64.5.

30 Ibid., 66.8–68.1; Burns, *Apocalypse*, 132–4.

31 See Dylan M. Burns, "Gnosis Undomesticated: Archon-Seduction, Demon Sex, and Sodomites in the *Paraphrase of Shem* (NHC VII, 1)," *Gnosis: Journal of Gnostic Studies* 1–2 (2016): 149–50.

32 See recently *Sodom's Sin: Genesis 18–19 and its Interpretations*, ed. Ed Noort and Eibert Tigchelaar (Leiden/Boston: Brill, 2004).

33 Surveyed in James L. Kugel, ed. *Traditions of the Bible: A Guide to the Bible as it was at the Start of the Common Era* (Cambridge, MA and London: Harvard University Press, 1998), 331–3.

34 Surveyed in ibid., 333–5; see further Judith H. Newman, "Lot in Sodom: The Post-Mortem of a City and the Afterlife of a Biblical Text," in *The Function of Scripture*

in Early Jewish and Christian Tradition, ed. Craig A. Evans and James A. Sanders. Journal for the Study of the New Testament Supplement Series 154 / Studies in Scripture in Early Judaism and Christianity 6 (Sheffield: Sheffield Academic Press, 1998), 34–44.

35 Burns, "Gnosis Undomesticated," 132–56 regarding *Paraph. Shem* NHC VII 28.31–29.1, 29.12–31.
36 Jenott, "Emissaries," 58, with reference to Themis's birthing of Eunomia, Dike, and Eirene in Hesiod's *Theogony*, 901–6.
37 NHC V [31].14.
38 On the importance and meaning of this pericope, see Ronald Hendel, *Remembering Abraham: Culture, Memory, and History in the Hebrew Bible* (Oxford: Oxford University Press, 2005), 38–40.
39 For a survey, see recently Denise Kimber Buell, *Why This New Race? Ethnic Reasoning in Early Christianity* (New York: Columbia University Press, 2005); for discussion and further citations, Burns, *Apocalypse*, 86–8.
40 See Reuven Firestone, "Abraham and Authenticity," in *The Oxford Handbook of the Abrahamic Religions*, ed. Adam J. Silverstein and Guy G. Stroumsa, assoc. ed. Moshe Blidstein (Oxford: Oxford University Press, 2015), 3–21, 10; esp. Jeffery S. Siker, *Disinheriting the Jews: Abraham in Early Christian Controversy* (Louisville, KY: Westminister/John Knox Press, 1991), 28–76.
41 *Dial. Tryph.* 11.5, 43.1; similarly, Euseb. *Eccl. Hist.* 1.4.5–14. For discussion and further passages, see Siker, *Disinheriting*, 163–84; Buell, *Why This New Race?*, 103–14; Stroumsa, *Making*, 193–5.
42 See Burns, *Apocalypse*, 102–5; more widely, Benjamin H. Dunning, *Aliens and Sojourners: Self as Other in Early Christianity* (Philadelphia: University of Pennsylvania Press, 2009).
43 Burns, *Apocalypse*, 103–4.
44 E.g. Gen. 15.4, 23.4; Exod. 2.22, 18.3; Deut. 14.21, 23.8; Pss. 39.13, 119.19; Jer. 14.8; 2 Sam. 1.13; for further references, see Burns, *Apocalypse*, 223 n. 48.
45 For discussion, see Dunning, *Aliens and Sojourners*, 53 *et passim*.
46 Michael Allen Williams, *The Immovable Race: A Gnostic Designation and the Theme of Stability in Late Antiquity*. Nag Hammadi Studies 29 (Leiden: Brill, 1985), 158–85; see also Burns, *Apocalypse*, 88–9.
47 On Marcion's treatment of Abraham in Luke, see *Pan.* 42.56–57; for Marcion's treatment of Abraham, see further *Haer.* 1.27.3, 4.8.1; Siker, *Disinheriting*, 155; Heikki Räisänen, "Marcion," in *Companion to Second-Century Christian "Heretics,"* ed. Antti Marjanen and Petri Luomanen. Vigiliae Christianae Supplements 76 (Leiden: Brill, 2005), 100–24, 114 n. 39. On the *Antitheses*, see Judith Lieu, *Marcion and the Making of a Heretic: God and Scripture in the Second Century* (New York: Cambridge University Press, 2015), 285–8.
48 The Manichaean teacher Secundius, for instance, mocked the story of Sarah's infertility and eventual pregnancy in a letter to Augustine, dated ca. 405/6 CE (in Iain Gardner and Samuel Lieu, eds. *Manichaean Texts from the Roman Empire* (Cambridge: Cambridge University Press, 2004), 139). For inventory on Manichaean rejection of the Old Testament, see Byard Bennett, "Didymus the Blind's Knowledge of Manichaeism," in *The Light and the Darkness: Studies in Manichaeism and its World*, ed. Paul Mirecki and Jason BeDuhn. Nag Hammadi and Manichaean Studies 50 (Leiden: Brill, 2001), 38–67, 46–7.
49 Lieu, *Marcion*, 346 on Philo, *Abr.* 45 and Just. Mart. *Tryph.* 56; see also Siker, *Disinheriting*, 179–81.

50 *Ref.* 6.34.4, 6.36.2; similarly Basilides (ibid., 7.25.4).
51 Epiph. *Pan.* 33.3.7, 34.16.8, respectively. Meanwhile, Heracleon took the children of Abraham to be "animates," the intermediate grade of humanity (cit. Siker, *Disinheriting*, 154).
52 *Ref.* 5.20.1; Jaan Lahe, *Gnosis*, 312 takes this to mean that "Sethians" had diverse approaches to the Patriarchs, perhaps unaware that the system the anonymous author describes is completely different than that of the "Sethians" *sensu* Schenke.
53 Ir. *Haer.* 1.30.10.
54 Rightly Lahe, *Gnosis*, 313, 324, 328 on Gen. 13:18–20. Epiphanius claimed that a group he calls "Gnostics" blasphemed Abraham, Moses, Elijah, and their God (*Pan.* 26.11.12).
55 *GR* 43.22, 46.10 (Lidzbarski), cit. Lahe, *Gnosis*, 313.
56 Its title notwithstanding, the treatise does not contain any of the mythologoumena shared between *Eg. Gos.*, *Apoc. Adam*, and other texts called "Sethian" by scholars today.
57 *Treat. Seth* NHC VII 62.27–63.27.
58 Ibid., 64.1–4; this passage recalls the account of Simon Magus's teaching in *Ref.* 6.19.6–8.
59 Stroumsa, *Making*, 180.
60 *Princ.* 2.5.3; similarly, Ter. *Marc* 2.14.3–4, per Lieu, *Marcion*, 346.
61 *Ref.* 10.30–31.
62 *Pan.* 1.3.1, 1.3.9, 4.1.1–4. See also his treatment of Satornilos, invoking John 8:56 and Matt. 8:11 on Abraham, in *Pan.* 23.6.1, 6.3, respectively. Epiphanius argued against the Manichaeans that if they truly believed the Jews to be sons of the devil (John 8:39–41), they must think the same of all the children of Abraham (*Pan.* 66.63.3–6).
63 In Gardner and Lieu, *Manichaean Texts*, 120.
64 *Gos. Phil.* NHC II 82.26–29; see Lahe, *Gnosis*, 313, and esp. Hugo Lundhaug, *Images of Rebirth: Cognitive Poetics and Transformational Soteriology in the Gospel of Philip and the Exegesis on the Soul*. Nag Hammadi and Manichaean Studies 73 (Leiden and Boston: Brill, 2010), 181, 220, 262, 392; cf. Siker, *Disinheriting*, 153–5. See also *Ex. Soul* NHC II 133.29–31, on Gen. 12:1.
65 *Pistis Sophia* 230.16, cit. Lahe, *Gnosis*, 313.
66 This fact lends some appeal to M.A. Williams' suggestion of the otherwise awkward term "Biblical Demiurgical" to describe sources others might call "Gnostic": Williams, *Rethinking "Gnosticism,"* 51–2. Cf. also the title of Smagina's article on Manichaean use of Jewish lore: Eugenia Smagina, "The Manichaean Cosmogonical Myth as a 'Re-Written Bible,'" In *"In Search of Truth": Augustine, Manichaeism, and other Gnosticism: Studies for Johannes van Oort at Sixty*, ed. Jacob Albert van Den Berg et al. Nag Hammadi and Manichaean Studies 74 (Leiden: Brill, 2011), 201–16; this piece takes the sense of the term "rewritten Bible" to be self-evident.
67 If these works did not find the Bible authoritative, it would not be worth criticizing. Or: transgression is an integral aspect of the dynamic of sacred negation, petitioning the boundaries and barriers of what is holy to "erupt into being" by crossing them: Michael Taussig, "Transgression," in *Critical Terms for Religious Studies*, ed. Mark C. Taylor (Chicago, IL: University of Chicago Press, 1998), 349–64, 350. To the transgressor, the "boundaries of the holy" are *second only to the holy itself* in importance.
68 On *m. San.* 10.1, see Annette Yoshiko Reed, "Apocrypha, 'Outside Books,' and Pseudepigrapha: Ancient Categories and Modern Perceptions of Parabiblical

Literature," 2002. Published online at http://ccat.sas.upenn.edu/psco/year40/areed1.html. The term was coined by Emmanuel Tov, to denote Qumran texts from Cave Four which span "rewritten Bible" and "apocrypha"; see Florentino García Martínez, "Apocryphal, Pseudepigraphal, and Para-Biblical Texts from Qumran," *Revue de Qumrân* 21, no. 3 (2004): 365–77, esp. 369–71. See further Hindy Najman, *Seconding Sinai: The Development of Mosaic Discourse in Second Temple Judaism*. Supplements to the Journal for the Study of Judaism 77 (Leiden and Boston: Brill, 2003), 7–9, and Stephen Shoemaker, "Early Christian Apocryphal Literature," in *The Oxford Handbook of Early Christian Studies*, ed. Susan Ashbrook Harvey and David G. Hunter (Oxford: Oxford University Press, 2008), 521–48. Cf. Najman's term "Mosaic discourse" (on which see *Seconding Sinai*, esp. 16–17), although in the texts under examination in this study, the figure and authority of Moses is as problematic as those of Abraham: see recently e.g. Grant Adamson, "'Turned Away Away from the Temple': Sethian Counterculture in the Apocryphon of John," *Gnosis: Journal of Gnostic Studies* 1 (2016): 36–55; also Jonathan Cahana, "None of Them Knew Me or My Brothers: Gnostic Antitraditionalism and Gnosticism as a Cultural Phenomenon," *The Journal of Religion* 94, no. 1 (2014): 49–73, 60–2. On the other hand, cf. the previous note: transgression of the Abrahamic and the Mosaic certainly implicates the self in the Abrahamic and the Mosaic. On the problem of constructing tradition with regard to the case of Islam, see the contribution of Brown, in this volume.

69 Cf. Wasserstrom's point in the "Nine Theses" that "all religion is inter-religion," and that all religion is inherently constituted by historical-conceptual contact.

70 The upshot of Frederik Wisse, "Stalking Those Elusive Sethians," in *The Rediscovery of Gnosticism: Proceedings of the International Conference on Gnosticism*, ed. Bentley Layton, 2 vols. Numen Book Series (Leiden: Brill, 1981), 563–76; further Williams, "Sethianism," 33, 56–7.

71 Shoemaker, "Early Christian," 533–5; Hugo Lundhaug and Lance Jenott, *The Monastic Origins of the Nag Hammadi Codices*. Studien und Texte zu Antike und Christentum 97 (Tübingen: Mohr Siebeck, 2015), esp. 263–8, although I do not share their beliefs regarding the usefulness of the term "Gnosticism."

72 Alan B. Scott, "Churches or Books? Sethian Social Organization," *Journal of Early Christian Studies* 3, no. 2 (1995): 109–22; cf. recently Michael Kaler, "The Cultic Milieu, the Nag Hammadi Collectors and Gnosticism," *Religious Studies* 38 (2009): 427–44.

73 Dylan M. Burns, "Is the *Apocalypse of Paul* a Valentinian Apocalypse? Pseudepigraphy and Group Definition in NHC V,2," in *Die Nag-Hammadi-Schriften in der Literatur- und Theologiegeschichte des frühen Christentums*, ed. Jens Schröter and Konrad Schwarz. Studien und Texte zu Antike und Christentum 106 (Tübingen: Mohr Siebeck, 2017), 97–112.

74 On this *koinē*, cf. Stroumsa, *Making*, 43, 105, 121. Notably, Celsus criticized the invocation of Abraham in magical formulas by individuals who were neither Jewish nor Christian, a practice acknowledged by Origen (*Cels.* 1.22, 4.33, cit. Siker, *Disinheriting*, 159).

75 See e.g. the Gnostic heroine Norea at the Cairo Genizah: Reimund Leicht, "Gnostic Myth in Jewish Garb: Niriyah (Norea), Noah's Bride," *Journal of Jewish Studies* 51 (2000): 133–40; Wasserstrom tackled the religious milieu of "the first Gnostic of Islam," Mughīra ibn Sa`īd, through analysis of his thought vis-à-vis Aramaic incantation bowls, in "The Moving Finger Writes," 5–7.

76 Jorunn Jacobsen Buckley, *The Mandaeans: Ancient Texts and Modern People*. AAR The Religions (Oxford: Oxford University Press, 2002), 27; also quoted in Nathaniel Deutsch, *Guardians of the Gate: Angelic Vice Regency in Late Antiquity*. Brill's Series in Jewish Studies 22 (Leiden, Boston and Köln: Brill, 1999), 4–5.

77 Cf. the correlate of the first of Wasserstrom's "Nine Theses" (italics his): "*All religion susceptible of our study is in a situation of contact*. There is no religion in the singular and the study of religion must suspect every assertion for the unique, the autonomous, the untouched, the monad, the alone. Inter-relational complexity constitutes our subject."

Chapter 14

1 A. S. Samahat, الساحر التائب حامد ادم موسى كيف كنا نعلم الغيب, *YouTube*, February 12, 2013, accessed July 24, 2018, https://www.youtube.com/watch?v=UqZ4rVI414U; Ibid., الساحر التائب حامد ادم موسى خطورة العين, *YouTube*, February 12, 2013, accessed July 24, 2018, https://www.youtube.com/watch?v=c51nzPMRTls; Ibid., الساحر التائب حامد ادم موسى من علامات الساحر, *YouTube*, February 12, 2013, accessed July 24, 2018, https://www.youtube.com/watch?v=B9xYP2tD3W8.

2 This chapter was composed in October 2017 and based on data I collected for my dissertation (University of Chicago, 2010) and subsequent conference papers in the intervening years. As it turns out, late 2017 and 2018 witnessed a plethora of pathbreaking work on Islamic esoterica, the *jinn*, magic, and qur'anic medicine. Among them are Alireza Doostdar's *The Iranian Metaphysicals: Explorations in Science, Islam and the Uncanny* (Princeton, NJ: Princeton University Press, 2018), Stefania Pandolfo's *Knot of the Soul: Madness, Psychoanalysis, Islam* (Chicago, IL: University of Chicago Press, 2018), and Anand Vivek Taneja's *Jinnealogy: Time, Islam and Ecological Thought in the Medieval Ruins of Delhi* (Stanford, CA: Stanford University Press, 2017), as well as the forthcoming work of Ana Maria Vinea. After much consideration, I decided not to revise this chapter so as to take into account these subsequent publications, even though each of them weighs on the topic at hand in important ways, as I did not want to distract focus from my engagement with Wasserstrom's field-changing interventaions. I discuss the implications of these recent works, however, in an essay I wrote for the *Immanent Frame* entitled "New Inquiries in Science and Islam: An Introduction." (https://tif.ssrc.org/2018/09/27/science-and-the-soul-introduction/).

3 For example, Muhammad Asad, *The Message of the Qur'an* (Gibralter: Dar al-Andalus, 1984), 987.

4 See, for example, the descriptions in Amira El-Zein, *Islam, Arabs and the Intelligent World of the Jinn* (Syracuse, NY: Syracuse University Press, 2009).

5 Personal interview, 2007.

6 "So Religious Studies cannot decide if witches fly; but can explicate friendships between spell-casters and hex-makers—it can locate witches as neighbors." Steven M. Wasserstrom, "Nine Theses on the Study of Religion," in this volume, §7.

7 Steven M. Wasserstrom, *Between Muslim and Jew: The Problem of Symbiosis under Early Islam* (Princeton, NJ: Princeton University Press, 1995), 167f.

8 *Khalwa* is a common Sufi practice in which physical seclusion and constant worship are prescribed as a means of drawing closer to God. Sudanese Qur'an schools are

also called by this name (*khalwa*, pl. *khalawi*) due to both their origins in the Sufi orders and their demands (at least in their traditional arrangement) that the student be separated from his family in order to embark on the educational experience therein.

9 For example, Elizabeth Sirriyeh, *Sufis and Anti-Sufis: The Defence, Rethinking and Rejection of Sufism in the Modern World* (New York: Curzon, 1999); M. Brett Wilson, "The Twilight of Ottoman Sufism: Antiquity, Immorality, and Nation in Yakup Kadri Karaosmanoğlu's Nur Baba," *International Journal of Middle East Studies* 49, no. 2 (2017): 233–53.

10 Note that Naveeda Khan observes a similar phenomenon in her study of the presence of *jinn* in the lives of a family with whom she conducts research. There, it is the social conditions of everyday life that are deemed "illusory" by her informant who turns to consulting what is, in his mind, the rather stable world of *jinn* as he strives to become a better Muslim. Naveeda Khan, *Muslim Becoming: Aspiration and Skepticism in Pakistan* (Durham, NC: Duke University Press, 2012), 139.

11 Noah Salomon, *In the Shadow of Salvation: Sufis, Salafis, and the Project of Late Islamism in Contemporary Sudan* (PhD Dissertation, University of Chicago. Ann Arbor: ProQuest/UMI, 2010); Ibid., "Evidence, Secrets Truth: Debating Islamic Knowledge in Contemporary Sudan," *Journal of the American Academy of Religion* 81, no. 3 (2013): 820–51.

12 Noah Salomon, "Rethinking Scripturalism: Ethics, Knowledge and Textual Practice in Contemporary Sudanese Salafism," in *The Transformation of Islamic Knowledge in Africa: Media, Agents and Institutions*, ed. Britta Frede, Noah Salomon, and Rüdiger Seesemann, manuscript awaiting submission.

13 Rüdiger Seesemann, "Islam in Africa or African Islam? Evidence from Kenya," in *The Global Worlds of the Swahili: Interfaces of Islam, Identity and Space in 19th and 20th Century East Africa*, ed. Rüdiger Seesemann and Roman Loimeier (Berlin: Lit Verlag, 2006).

14 Cf. Rudolph Ware, *The Walking Qur'an: Islamic Education, Embodied Knowledge and History in West Africa* (Chapel Hill: University of North Carolina Press, 2014).

15 One exception can be found in Eleanor Abdella Duomato, *Getting God's Ear: Women, Islam and Healing in Saudi Arabia and the Gulf* (New York: Columbia University Press, 2000).

16 As Mayanthi Fernando has observed, while the topic of the agency of non-human actors has had growing purchase in the recent post-humanist turn in anthropology, these trends have been preoccupied with the natural world, giving insufficient attention to the supernatural and its agencies. She raises the possibility instead of a more capacious posthumanism that offers "onto-epistemic horizons beyond the material," and in so doing suggests a study of supernatural relations in which the nonmaterial might be imagined as "constitut[ing] both themselves and an entangled set of agencies" with the outside world. Shaykh Hamid's *jinn*—relying at once on the particularity of his biography and an identity shaped through a long history that exceeds it—might productively be thought of in this sense (https://tif.ssrc.org/2017/12/11/supernatureculture/).

17 El-Zein, *Islam, Arabs*, 131.

18 Ibid. For a parallel discussion of non-human agency in the Islamic tradition, see also Amira Mittermaier's *Dreams that Matter: Egyptian Landscapes of the Imagination* (Berkeley: University of California Press, 2010) that discusses a co-inhabited universe in which the actors of waking life share agency with those of the dreamworld.

19 Wasserstrom, *Between Muslim and Jew*, 220.
20 Ibid., 172.
21 Wasserstrom himself offers one solution in the final lines of *Between Muslim and Jew*, 237: "Only in historical change can we properly seek the *concordia mundi*, the rational harmony hidden maddeningly inside a radically pluralistic world. 'The reassurance is / that through change / continuities sinuously work.'" I am, however, admittedly still not sure what to make of these complicated lines (irony, perhaps, or hope, in the context of a bleak world?) particularly in light of his later work which would seem to destabilize any attempts at finding such a universal harmony; cf. Steven M. Wasserstrom, *Religion after Religion: Gershom Scholem, Mircea Eliade, and Henri Corbin at Eranos* (Princeton, NJ: Princeton University Press, 1999).
22 J. Andrew Bush. "An offer of pleasure: Islam, poetry, and the ethics of religious difference in a Kurdish home" *American Ethnologist*, 44, no. 3 (2017): 516-27.
23 J. Andrew Bush, "Islamism and Intimacy Workshop Introduction," 2015, unpublished.
24 Ibid.
25 E.g., Roel Meijer, ed. *Global Salafism: Islam's New Religious Movement* (New York: Columbia University Press, 2009); Stéphane Lacroix, *Awakening Islam: The Politics of Religious Dissent in Contemporary Saudi Arabia* (Cambridge, MA: Harvard University Press, 2011).
26 *Between Muslim and Jew*, 11.

Chapter 15

1 The great Jewish historians of the twentieth century treated Jewish self-government and interactions with non-Jewish authorities, as well as less governmentally oriented politics like power relations between rabbis and lay leaders or between Jews of different national and economic background, largely as "social" history. See, for example, Salo Baron, *Social and Religious History of the Jews* (New York: Columbia University Press, 1937); Yitzhak Baer, *A History of the Jews in Christian Spain*, trans. L. Schoffman, 2 vols. (Philadelphia, PA: Jewish Publication Society of America, 1961–1966 [1929–1936]), and *Galut* (New York: Schocken, 1947); Jacob Katz, *Out of the Ghetto: The Social Background of Jewish Emancipation, 1770–1870* (Cambridge, MA: Harvard University Press, 1973), and *Tradition and Crisis: Jewish Society at the End of the Middle Ages* (New York: New York University Press, 1963 [1958]); Cecil Roth, *A History of the Jews in England* (Oxford: Oxford University Press, 1941).
2 The field of Jewish political thought is an increasingly visible presence in the academy. Daniel Elazar and Daniel Frank were pioneers, and have been followed by the likes of Julie E. Cooper, David N. Myers, Amnon Raz-Krakotzkin, and of course Michael Walzer. The 2016–2017 fellowship theme at the University of Pennsylvania's Katz Center for Advanced Judaic Studies was devoted to the topic, and a decade earlier, *AJS Perspectives: The Magazine of the Association for Jewish Studies* devoted an issue (Fall 2006) to Jewish political studies. As this essay goes to print, a proposal is under consideration to add Jewish politics as a new subject area within the Association for Jewish Studies. Still, few historians take this approach, examining spheres of Jewish intellectual or practical activity through a political lens. Menachem Lorberbaum's *Politics and the Limits of Law: Secularizing the Political*

in Medieval Jewish Thought (Stanford, CA: Stanford University Press, 2001) and Claude Stuczynski's numerous studies of *converso* politics ("Harmonizing Identities: The Problem of the Integration of the Portuguese Conversos in Early Modern Iberian Corporate Polities," *Jewish History* 25, no. 2 (2011): 229–57 and "Portuguese Conversos and the Manueline Imperial Idea—A Preliminary Study," *Anais de Historia de Alem-Mar* 14 (2013): 45–61 are just two examples) are exceptions.

3   Michael Walzer, "Introduction," in *The Jewish Political Tradition, Volume 1: Authority*, ed. M. Walzer, M. Lorberbaum, N. Zohar, and Y. Lorberbaum (New Haven, CT: Yale University Press, 2003), xxii.
4   Gershom Scholem, "On the Possibility of Jewish Mysticism in Our Time," in Scholem, *On the Possibility of Jewish Mysticism in Our Time & Other Essays*, ed. A. Shapira, trans. J. Chipman (Philadelphia, PA: Jewish Publication Society, 1997), 15.
5   Gershom Scholem, "Isaac Luria and His School," in *Major Trends in Jewish Mysticism* (New York: Schocken, 1946 [1941]), 244. The "crisis" in these comments is explicitly precipitated by the exile from Spain—a rare claim of external historical causality for Scholem, and indeed, one that is not widely accepted.
6   Scholem, "Isaac Luria and His School," 246.
7   Ibid., 249.
8   Ibid., 275.
9   Gershom Scholem, *Sabbatai Sevi: The Mystical Messiah*, trans. R. J. Zwi Werblowsky (Princeton, NJ: Princeton University Press, 1973).
10 See Benjamin Lazier, *God Interrupted: Heresy and the European Imagination between the World Wars* (Princeton, NJ: Princeton University Press, 2012), 162–4.
11 For example, Scholem writes that "beneath the superficial peculiarities of Hasidic life there subsists a stratum of positive values, which were all too easily overlooked in the furious struggle between rationalistic 'enlightenment' and mysticism during the nineteenth century ... The writings of the Hasidim contained more fruitful and original ideas than those of those of their rationalistic opponents, the *Maskilim*," Scholem, "Hasidism: The Latest Phase," in *Major Trends*, 326.
12 Scholem, "Hasidism," 329.
13 His essay "Toward an Understanding of the Messianic Idea in Judaism" begins by explaining that Judaism, in contrast to Christianity, "has always maintained a concept of redemption as an event which takes place publicly, on the stage of history and within the community. It is an occurrence which takes place in the visible world and which cannot be conceived apart from such a visible appearance." Written for an Eranos conference in 1959 and published in English in *The Messianic Idea in Judaism and Other Essays on Jewish Spirituality* (New York: Schocken, 1971), 1.
14 Scholem, "On the Possibility," 9.
15 Ibid.
16 Joseph Dan, *Gershom Scholem and the Mystical Dimension of Jewish History* (New York: New York University Press, 1987), 288. Dan also points out the alignment between Scholem's chronology of Jewish history and the periodization of European history, indicating that Scholem saw the Sabbatian aftermath as the beginning of Jewish modernity, 287.
17 Scholem, "On the Possibility," 11.
18 Gershom Scholem, "Exile Today Is Devoid of the Seeds of Redemption," in *On the Possibility*, 30–4.
19 See Noam Zadoff, "'Zion's Self-Engulfing Light': On Gershom Scholem's Disillusionment with Zionism," *Modern Judaism* 31, no. 3 (2011): 272–84; Amir Engel,

Gershom Scholem: An Intellectual Biography (Chicago, IL: University of Chicago Press, 2017), especially ch. 4, "When a Dream Comes True: Zionist Politics in Palestine, 1923–1931," 94–123; David Biale, *Gershom Scholem: Kabbalah and Counter-History*, 2nd ed. (Cambridge, MA: Harvard University Press, 1982, especially ch. 5, "The Politics of Historiography," 94–111; and Maor Zohar, "Scholem and Rosenzweig: Redemption and (Anti-)Zionism," *Modern Judaism* 37, no. 1 (2017): 1–23.

20 For a general treatment of de Barrios's life and works, see Kenneth Scholberg, "Miguel de Barrios and the Amsterdam Sephardic Community," *The Jewish Quarterly Review* 53, no. 2 (1962): 120–59. Two monographs have also been devoted to de Barrios: Julia Rebollo Lieberman, *El teatro alegórico de Miguel (Daniel Leví) de Barrios* (Newark, DE: Juan de la Cuesta, 1996); Wilhelmina C. Pieterse, *Daniel Levi de Barrios als Geschiedschrijver van de Portugees-Israelietische Gemeente te Amsterdam in Zijn "Triumpho del Govierno Popular"* (Amsterdam: Scheltema & Holkema, 1968).

21 Yirmiyahu Yovel, *The Other Within. The Marranos: Split Identity and Emerging Modernity* (Princeton, NJ: Princeton University Press, 2009) and *Spinoza and Other Heretics, vol. 1, The Marrano of Reason* (Princeton, NJ: Princeton University Press, 1989); José Faur, *In the Shadow of History: Jews and Conversos at the Dawn of Modernity* (Albany: State University of New York Press, 1992); J. A. van Praag, "Almas En Litigio," *Clavileño* I (1950): 14–26; Henry Méchoulan, *Hispanidad y judaismo en tiempos de Espinoza: Estudio y edicion anotada de* La certeza del camino de Abraham Pereyra, Amsterdam 1666 (Salamanca: Universidad de Salamanca, 1987), esp. 31ff. on the "double attitude" of hatred and loyalty; and finally, stretching backwards and forwards from the seventeenth century, problematizing the narrative, David A. Wacks, *Double Diaspora in Sephardic Literature: Jewish Cultural Production before and after 1492* (Bloomington: Indiana University Press, 2015) and Daniel B. Schwartz, *The First Modern Jew: Spinoza and the History of an Image* (Princeton, NJ: Princeton University Press, 2012).

22 See David B. Ruderman, *Early Modern Jewry* (Princeton, NJ: Princeton University Press, 2010).

23 Scholem, *Sabbatai Sevi*, 894.

24 At least, he gave up on openly supporting the movement around Shabbetai Tsvi. Whether his ideas as discussed below suggest an ongoing form of Sabbatian belief may be debated.

25 A *parnas* (plural, *parnassim*) is a lay leader, a single member of the *Mahamad*.

26 The gabbai is the particular parnas designated to serve as treasurer or secretary. De Barrios dedicates his work to a *Mahamad* in which the gabbai is named Joseph.

27 The comparison is elaborated in Section 6 of the work, "On the three worlds, angelic, spherical, and elemental, created in six days, which the six illustrious Parnassim represent, and the seventh, the very noble Gabbai of the Amsterdam Kahal Kadosh in this year of 5443." See Daniel Levi de Barrios, *Triumpho del govierno popular y de la antiguedad Holandesa* (Amsterdam, 1683), 50–1.

28 De Barrios, *Triumpho*, 2, but note that there are multiple, inconsistent and sometimes overlapping pagination systems within this edition. The numbers listed here are the ones given as part of the printed page, and not the ones marked in by hand.

29 De Barrios, *Triumpho*, 28–9 (Glosa III S. IV): "Tuvo tres populares, ô inferiores/ Goviernos Israel, uno entre Egypcios/Dynastia se llamò de los Pastores,/otro entre Babilonios, y Phenizios:/es el tercero de Sustentadores/o Parnasim, con tales frontispicios,/en varios templos entre gentes varias, que en ellos tiene Dios sus luminarias."

30 De Barrios, *Triumpho*, 31.
31 De Barrios, "Govierno Popular Judayco," in *Triumpho*, 46. See Ex. 24:10.
32 De Barrios, *Triumpho*, 8.
33 Ibid., 19.
34 De Barrios, "Historia de la monarchia y origen de Ioctan," in *Triumpho*, 9–18, for example.
35 When "the Hebrews irritated the Infinite Emperor in their aristocracy and monarchy," they were punished with expulsion, but in place of that rule, "popular governments were established … in the places to which they were expelled" according to the subtitle of gloss V, section IV. De Barrios, *Triumpho*, 28.
36 This nine part scheme is echoed in Wasserstrom's "Nine Theses" and "Nine Riddles" in this volume.
37 Gershom Scholem, "On the Historical Development of Jewish Mysticism," in *On the Possibility*, 152, quoted by Steven M. Wasserstrom in *Religion after Religion: Gershom Scholem, Mircea Eliade, and Henry Corbin at Eranos* (Princeton, NJ: Princeton University Press, 1999), 7.
38 See Méchoulan, *Hispanidad y Judaismo en tiempos de Espinoza*.
39 Anne O. Albert, "'A Civil Death': Sovereignty and the Jewish Republic in an Early Modern Treatment of Genesis 49:10," in *Jewish Culture in Early Modern Europe: Essays in Honor of David B. Ruderman*, ed. R. I. Cohen, N. B. Dohrmann, A. Shear, and E. Reiner (Cincinnati, OH: Hebrew Union College Press, 2014), 63–72.
40 See Anne O. Albert, "The Rabbi and the Rebels: A Pamphlet on the *Herem* by Rabbi Isaac Aboab da Fonseca," *The Jewish Quarterly Review* 104, no. 2 (Spring 2014): 171–91.
41 Wasserstrom, *Religion after Religion*, 238.
42 "All religion susceptible of our study is in a situation of contact"; and "There is no reducibly essential religion any more than there is such a person. Religion is a function of folks meeting other folks—*contact*—and folks maintaining their old ways—*continuity*." Steven M. Wasserstrom, "Nine Theses on the Study of Religion," in this volume, §§ 1–2.
43 Scholem, "On the Possibility," 17–18.
44 Scholem, "A Lecture about Israel," in *On the Possibility*, 36.

Chapter 16

1 Steven M. Wasserstrom, "Nine Theses on the Study of Religion," in this volume, §1.
2 Keith Thomas, *The Ends of Life: Roads to Fulfillment in Early Modern England* (Oxford: Oxford University Press, 2009).
3 Wasserstrom, "Nine Theses," §1.
4 Ibid., §9.
5 These ideas may be traced back to Menéndez y Pelayo, Llorente, and Ranke, respectively.
6 Most recently see Cedric Cohen Skalli, *Don Isaac Abarbanel* (Hebrew) (Jerusalem: Salman Shazar, 2017).
7 Benzion Netanyahu, *Don Isaac Abravanel: Statesman & Philosopher* (Philadelphia, PA: Jewish Publication Society, 1953), 63.
8 Ibid., 25.
9 Elia Capsali, cited in H. H. Ben Sasson, "The Generation of the Spanish Exiles on Its Fate" (Hebrew), *Zion* (1961): 23–64, 32.

10 Yom Tov Assis, "Social Unrest and Class Tension in Spanish Jewish Communities before the Expulsion" (Hebrew), in *Tarbut ve-Historia*, ed. Yosef Dan (Jerusalem: Misgav Yerushalayim, 1987), 121–45, 122–23.
11 Eleazar Gutwirth, "Towards Expulsion: 1391–1492," in *Spain and the Jews: The Sephardi Experience 1492 and After*, ed. Elie Kedourie (London: Thames and Hudson, 1992), 51–73, 68.
12 Eleazar Gutwirth, "Abraham Seneor: Social Tensions and the Court-Jew," *Michael: On the History of Jews in the Diaspora* 11 (1989): 169–229, 190.
13 Luis Felip de Peñalosa, "Juan Bravo y la familia Coronel," *Estudios Segovianos* 1 (1949): 73–109, Appendix II.
14 Netanyahu, *Abravanel*, 55.
15 Elia Capsali, *Seder Eliyahu Zuta*, ed. A. Shmuelevitz, S. Simonson, and M. Benayahu, 3 vols. (Jerusalem: Ben Zvi Institute, 1975), 2:209.
16 Meir Benayahu, "Teudah min ha-Dor ha-Rishon shel Megorashey Sefarad bi-Sefat," in *Sefer Assaf*, ed. M. D. Cassuto, J. Klausner, and J. Gutman (Jerusalem: Mosad HaRav Kook, 1953), 109–25, 118 n. 63.
17 Samuel G. Armistead and Joseph H. Silverman, "A New Collection of Judeo-Spanish Songs," *Jahrbuch für Volksliederforschung* 19 (1974): 154–66.
18 Juan Piqueras Haba, "Los judíos y el vino en España: siglos XI-XV, una geografía histórica," *Cuadernos de Geografía* 75 (2004): 17–41, 20.
19 See Andrés Bernáldez, *Memorias del Reinado de los Reyes Católicos*, ed. J. de Mata Carriazo and M. Gomez-Moreno (Madrid: Real Academia de la Historia, 1962), 98. This translation from John Edwards, *The Jews in Western Europe: 1400–1600* (Manchester: Manchester University Press, 1994), 75.
20 Isaac Abravanel, *Perush al ha-Torah, Bereshit* (Jerusalem: Benei Arabel, 1964), 125.
21 Angus MacKay, "Popular Movements and Pogroms in Fifteenth-Century Castile," *Past and Present* 55 (May 1972): 33–67.
22 Ibid., 41.
23 Yitzhak Baer, *A History of the Jews in Christian Spain*, trans. Louis Schoffman (Philadelphia, PA: Jewish Publication Society, 1961 [1888]), 2:250–1.
24 Mackay, "Popular Movements," 44.
25 Ibid., 61.
26 J. N. Hillgarth, *The Spanish Kingdoms 1250–1516* (Oxford: Oxford University Press, 1978), 2:453.
27 Ibid., 2:133.
28 On Saba see Abraham Gross, *Iberian Jewry from Twilight to Dawn: The World of Rabbi Abraham Saba* (Leiden: Brill, 1995).
29 Cited in Gross, *Iberian Jewry from Twilight to Dawn*, 101.
30 Ibid.
31 Abraham Saba, *Zeror ha-Mor* (Warsaw: Walden, 1879); Leviticus 32a.
32 Solomon Alami, *Iggeret ha-Mussar*, ed. Abraham M. Habermann (Jerusalem: Mosad HaRav Kook, 1946), 39.
33 Exodus 16:3, all translations from the English Standard Version.
34 Ibid., 16:4.
35 Exodus 16:3–20.
36 On Venice's tolerance of Jews see Benjamin Ravid, *Studies on the Jews of Venice, 1382–1797* (Aldershot: Ashgate, 2003), passim.
37 Abravanel, *Perush al ha-Torah*, 340.
38 Ibid.
39 Ibid.

40 Ibid.
41 Ibid., 341.
42 Exodus 32.
43 Abravanel, *Perush al ha-Torah*, 312.
44 Ibid.
45 Ibid.
46 Ibid.
47 Ibid.
48 Ibid.
49 Ibid.
50 Isaac Abravanel, *Naḥalat avot* (Ashkelon: Oren Golan, 2013), 1.
51 Isaac Abravanel, *She'elot le-heḥakham Sha'ul ha-Kohen* (Jerusalem: s.n., 1966 [1574]), 7v.
52 Ibid.
53 Ibid.
54 Abravanel, *Naḥalat avot*, 45.
55 Proverbs 27:24.
56 Abravanel, *Naḥalat avot*, 45.
57 Ibid.
58 Joseph Hacker, "New Chronicles on the Expulsion of the Jews from Spain, Its Causes and Results" (Hebrew), *Zion* 44 (1979): 201–28, 207.
59 Ibid.
60 Saba, *Zeror ha-Mor*; cf. Deuteronomy 59v.
61 Quoted in L. P. Harvey, *Islamic Spain, 1250–1500* (Chicago, IL: University of Chicago Press, 1990), 58. Al-Wansharisi's name is mistakenly spelled as Wansharashi in this volume, a mistake that Harvey corrects in the subsequent volume *Islamic Spain, 1500–1614* (Chicago, IL: University of Chicago Press, 2005).
62 Ibid.
63 Wasserstrom, "Nine Theses," §3.
64 Poggio Bracciolini, "On Avarice," trans. Benjamin G. Kohl and Elizabeth B. Welles in *The Earthly Republic: Italian Humanists on Government and Society*, ed. Benjamin G. Kohl and Ronald G. Witt (Philadelphia: University of Pennsylvania Press, 1978), 241–89. For the complete Latin text with an Italian translation and critical notes see Giuseppe Germano, ed., *Poggio Bracciolini, De avaritia (Dialogus contra avaritiam)* (Belforte: Livorno, 1994).
65 Bracciolini, "On Avarice," 251.
66 Ibid., 283, 288.
67 Isaac Abravanel, *Perush ha-Nevi'im, Sefer Melakhim* (Jerusalem: Horev, 2009), 1; cf. Exodus 18:4.
68 Deborah Shuger, *The Renaissance Bible: Scholarship, Sacrifice, and Subjectivity* (Berkeley: University of California Press, 1994), 4.
69 Wasserstrom, "Nine Theses," §1.

Chapter 17

1 Deborah Feldman, *Unorthodox: The Scandalous Rejection of My Hasidic Roots* (New York: Simon & Schuster, 2012), 40.
2 Steven M. Wasserstrom, "Nine Theses on the Study of Religion," in this volume, §2.

3 For this term, see George Kranzler, *Williamsburg: A Jewish Community in Transition* (New York: Feldheim, 1961), 14.
4 As Barry Chiswick has shown, from 1950 to 1970, the number of American Jews with blue-collar jobs steeply declined. See Chiswick, "The Postwar Economy of American Jews," in *A New Jewry? America since the Second World War*, ed. Peter Y. Medding (Oxford: Oxford University Press, 1992), 93.
5 For a recent overview of this topic, see *Chosen Capital: The Jewish Encounter with American Capitalism*, ed. Rebecca Kobrin (New Brunswick, NJ: Rutgers University Press, 2012), and within it, Ira Katznelson, "Two Exceptionalisms: Points of Departure for Studies of Capitalism and Jews in the United States," 12–27.
6 For example, from 1950 to 1951, the percentage of American homes with a television jumped from 9 percent to 23.5 percent; by 1961, the number was almost 90 percent. See Cobbett S. Steinberg, *TV Facts* (New York: Facts on File, Inc., 1980), 142.
7 Israel Rubin, *Satmar: An Island in the City* (Chicago, IL: Quadrangle Books, 1972), 224.
8 Kranzler, *Williamsburg*, 74.
9 David Biale, "Jewish Consumer Culture in Historical and Contemporary Perspective," in *Longing, Belonging, and the Making of Jewish Consumer Culture*, ed. Gideon Reuveni and Nils Roemer (Leiden: Brill, 2010), 25–6.
10 Kranzler, *Williamsburg*, 56.
11 See for example Bernhard Wachstein, "Di Prager takones fun 1767 kegn luksus," *YIVO bleter* 1, no. 4 (April 1931) and Avraham Rechtman, *Yidishe etnografye un folklor* (Buenos Aires: YIVO, 1958), 212–14. I thank Nathaniel Deutsch for the latter reference.
12 Max Weber, *The Protestant Ethic and the Spirit of Capitalism*, trans. Talcott Parsons (New York: Scribner, 1958).
13 Werner Sombart, *The Jews and Modern Capitalism*, trans. Mordechai Epstein (Kitchener: Batoche Books, 2001), 22.
14 See Vasile Puşcaş, "Modernizing Process in Romania in the Interwar Period," *Revue Roumaine des Sciences Sociales: Serie des sciences économiques* 32, no. 2 (1988): 123, and Răzvan Pârâianu, "Semitism as a Metaphor for Modernity," *Studia Hebraica* V (2006): 51 n. 113.
15 See Z. Brender et al., "Geschichte der J.N.A.V 'Zephirah' in Czernowitz," in *Geschichte der Juden in der Bukowina*, vol. 2, ed. Hugo Gold (Tel Aviv: Olamenu, 1962), 157.
16 Rebecca Kobrin, "The Chosen People in the Chosen Land: The Jewish Encounter with American Capitalism," in *Chosen Capital*, 8.
17 On the Satmar philosophy against change, see Nathaniel Deutsch, "The Forbidden Fork, the Cell Phone Holocaust, and Other Haredi Encounters with Technology," *Contemporary Jewry* 29 (2009): 3–4.
18 Avraham D. Gluck, ed. *Seyfer Zakhor Tsadik Levrokhe*, vol. 1 (Kiryas Joel, NY: Mazel, 2002), 421–2. All translations here and following are my own unless otherwise noted.
19 See Ramban's commentary on Leviticus 19:2. I thank Andrew Berns for this reference.
20 Hertz Frankel, *The Satmar Rebbe and His English Principal* (Brooklyn, NY: Menucha Publishers, 2015), 26.
21 As quoted in Chaim Stauber, *The Satmar Rebbe* (New York: Feldheim, 2011), 158 n. 188.

22   As cited in Dovid Meisels, *The Rebbe* (New York: Israel Book Shop Publications, 2010), 224.
23   Ibid., 227.
24   Frankel, *The Satmar Rebbe*, 110–11.
25   A. S. D., "Groyser koved shemayim bay dem kinus klali fun yehidus," *Der Yid*, June 9, 1961, 4.
26   Meisels, *The Rebbe*, 373.
27   Ibid., 232–3. See also Stauber, *The Satmar Rebbe*, 188 n. 226.
28   A. S. D. "Groyser koved shemayim," 5. For a history of this martial rhetoric see David N. Myers, "'Commanded War': Three Chapters in the 'Military' History of Satmar Hasidism," *Journal of the American Academy of Religion* 81, no. 2 (June 2013).
29   Solomon Poll, *The Hasidic Community of Williamsburg* (New York: Free Press of Glencoe, 1962), 49.
30   Ibid., x.
31   Michael Cohn, ed. *The Hasidic Community of Williamsburg, Brooklyn*, Occasional Papers in Cultural History, no. 4 (New York: Brooklyn Children's Museum, 1963), 21 and also 25.
32   On the *badkhn* and Hasidism, see David Biale et al., eds. *Hasidism: A New History* (Princeton, NJ: Princeton University Press, 2018), 72. On the figure of the *badkhn* generally, see most recently Ariela Krasney, *Ha-badchan* (Ramat Gan: Bar-Ilan University Press, 1998) and Zehavit Stern, "From Jester to Gesture: Eastern European Jewish Culture and the Re-Imagination of Folk Performance" (PhD dissertation, University of California, Berkeley, 2011). On the fate of the *badkhn*, see James Loeffler, "*A Gilgul Fun a Nigun*: Jewish Musicians in New York, 1881–1945," in *Harvard Judaica Collection Student Research Papers*, no. 3 (Cambridge, MA: Harvard College Library, 1997), 20 n. 43, 51; and Yaakov Mazor, "The *Badkhn* in Contemporary Hasidic Society: Social, Historical, and Musical Observations," *Polin: Studies in Polish Jewry* 16 (2003).
33   See *Oytseres hanigunim*, vol. 1 (Jerusalem: 5764 [2003–2004]), 151. I rely on *Oytseres hanigunim*, a two-volume compendium of transcriptions of Ehrlich's audio recordings. As Ariela Krasney has demonstrated in a study of the genre of the "*badkhones* booklet," *badkhones* transitioned in the mid-nineteenth century from an oral performance to a written literature, and the two traditions of performance and print have since coexisted. See Ariela Krasney, "The *Badkhn*: From Wedding Stage to Writing Desk," *Polin: Studies in Polish Jewry* 16 (2003): 8.
34   For biographical information, I synthesize the unpaginated author's note in *Oytseres hanigunim*, vol. 1 and Ehrlich's obituary in *Der Yid*, July 27, 1990, 26.
35   In *Oytseres hanigunim*, vol. 1, 324–5.
36   On the figure of the *badkhn*, see, most recently, Krasney, *Ha-badchan*; and Stern, "From Jester to Gesture." On the fate of the *badkhn*, see Loeffler, "*A Gilgul fun a Nigun*," 20 n. 43, 51; Mazor, "The *Badkhn* in Contemporary Hasidic Society"; and Hankus Netsky, "American Klezmer: A Brief History," in *American Klezmer: Its Roots and Offshoots*, ed. Mark Slobin (Berkeley: University of California Press, 2002).
37   For critical treatment of Ehrlich as a musician, see Henry Sapoznik, *Klezmer! Jewish Music from Old World to Our World* (New York: Schirmer Books, 1999), 161; Ester-Basya (Asya) Vaisman, "'She Who Seeks Shall Find': The Role of Song in a Hasid Woman's Life Cycle," *Journal of Synagogue Music* 35 (Fall 2010): 169; Mark Kligman, "Contemporary Jewish Music in America," *American Jewish Yearbook* 101 (2001):

115; and Peter Sokolow, "Mazel Tov! Klezmer Music and Simchas in Brooklyn, 1910 to Present," in *Jews of Brooklyn*, ed. Ilana Abramovitch and Seán Galvin (Waltham, MA: Brandeis University Press, 2001), 181.
38 Kranzler, *Williamsburg*, 54.
39 Ibid., 55.
40 Ibid., 56.
41 Perhaps Yisroel Elimelech Moskowitz, the Zborover Rebbe, who passed away in 1958.
42 See George Kranzler, *Hasidic Williamsburg: A Contemporary American Hasidic Community* (Northvale, NJ: Jason Aronson, 1995), 129 and Jerome Mintz, *Hasidic People: A Place in the New World* (Cambridge, MA: Harvard University Press, 1992), 365.
43 Sholom Kalib, *The Musical Tradition of the Eastern European Synagogue*, vol. 1 (Syracuse, NY: Syracuse University Press, 2002), 245.
44 George Kranzler, *The Face of Faith: An American Hassidic Community* (Baltimore, MD: Baltimore Hebrew College Press, 1972), 65, 114.
45 Herbert Gans, "The 'Yinglish' Music of Mickey Katz," *American Quarterly* 5, no. 3 (Autumn 1953): 215, 218.
46 Stauber, *The Satmar Rebbe*, 255 and Weisshaus, *The Rebbe*, 161, 163.
47 For memories on the Rebbe's humor, see, for example, Mintz, *Hasidic People*, 29 and Frankel, *The Satmar Rebbe*, 149.
48 As cited in Meisels, *The Rebbe Speaks*, 155. For more on the Rebbe's position on television, see *Seyfer Zakhor Tsadik Levrokhe*, vol. 1, 425-7 and Meisels, *The Rebbe*, 368-71. For a pun about destructive books, see Meisels, *The Rebbe Speaks*, 158.
49 *Oytseres hanigunim*, vol. 1, 155-6.
50 Ibid., 170.
51 See "Luksus" Part 1, *Oytseres hanigunim*, vol. 1, 300.
52 Ibid., 301.
53 See Exodus 12: 35-36 and Midrash Tanhuma Yashan 16.
54 *Oytseres hanigunim*, vol. 1, 308.
55 Ibid., 324.
56 Ibid., 316.
57 Ibid., 364.
58 Ibid., 364-8.
59 Reprinted as "The Hasidic Poor in New York City," in *Poor Jews: An American Awakening*, ed. Naomi Levine and Martin Hochbaum (New Brunswick, NJ: Transaction Books, 1974), 59.
60 R. Elchanan Yosef Hertzman, "Golus Amerike," *Der Yid*, July 25, 1969, [page illegible].
61 *Kuntres nachpesu drucheni* (Brooklyn, NY: Nachpesu drucheni, 1975-6), 12-15.
62 Kranzler, *Hasidic Williamsburg*, 83.
63 Joseph Berger, "God Said Multiply, and Did She Ever," *New York Times*, February 19, 2010, MB7.
64 Feldman, *Unorthodox*, 238, 247.
65 As cited by George Kranzler, "The Women of Williamsburg: A Contemporary Hasidic Community in Brooklyn, New York," in *Ethnic Women: A Multiple Status Reality*, ed. Vasilikie Demos and Marcia Texler Segal (Dix Hills, NY: General Hall, 1994), 77.

Epilogue

1. Theodore Reik, *Pagan Rites in Judaism: From Sex Initiation, Magic, Moon-Cult, Tattooing, Mutilation, and Other Primitive Rituals to Family Loyalty and Solidarity* (New York: The Noonday Press, 1964), vii.
2. Ibid., 181–2.
3. Ibid., 3.
4. "*For men of this sort … truth is found not in nature but in the confrontation of texts.*" From a 1610 letter of Galileo to Kepler, cited in Hans Blumenberg, *Die Lesbarkeit der Welt* (Frankfurt: Suhrkamp, 1981), 72.
5. B. Wise, "I Will Win! Trump *Loves* Puccini—and New Research Is Showing How Facism Infused the Composer's Work," *Slate*, August 1, 2016. Available online: http://www.slate.com/articles/arts/culturebox/2016/08/donald_trump_s_favorite_aria_by_puccini_nessun_dorma_is_sort_of_fascist.html (accessed July 17, 2018).
6. A. M. Piemontese and J. C. Bürgel, "Turandot- von Nizami bis Puccini: Alessandro/ Dhû l-Qarnayn in viaggio tra i due mari," *Quaderni di Studi Indo-Mediterranei* 1 (2008): 347–64.
7. Christine Goldberg, Preface in *Turandot's Sisters: A Study of the Folktale AT 851* (New York: Garland Publishing Inc, 1993), ix.
8. Jan de Vries, *Die Märchen von klugen Rätsellösern, eine Vergleichende Untersuchung* (Helsinki: Suomalainen Tiedeakatemia, Academia Scientiarum Fennica, 1928).
9. Carl Hentze, "Religiöse und mythische Hintergründe zu Turandot," *Antaios* 1 (1959/60): 21–41. See also Carl Hentze, "Die Gottin mit dem Haus auf dem Kopf," *Antaios* 7 (1965): 47–67.
10. See Bruce Lincoln, *Theorizing Myth: Narrative, Ideology, and Scholarship* (Chicago, IL: University of Chicago Press, 1999), 135.For the idea of "pact with the gods," see George Dumézil, *Myth et dieux des Germains: Essai d'interprétation comparative* (Paris: E. Leroux, 1939).
11. Andrea Cavalletti, "Introduction," in Furio Jesi, *Spartakus: The Symbology of Revolt*, trans. Alberto Toscano (London: Seagull Books, 2014), 7 n. 13.
12. Ernst Jünger, *Strahlungen* (Tubinggen: Heliopolis-Verlag, 1949), 101.
13. It was only in May 1942 that this was imposed on the Jews of France.
14. "Reinhard Heydrich, chief of the Reich Main Security Office, first recommended that Jews should wear identifying badges following the Kristallnacht pogrom of November 9 and 10, 1938. Shortly after the invasion of Poland in September 1939, local German authorities began introducing mandatory wearing of badges. By the end of 1939, all Jews in the newly acquired Polish territories were required to wear badges. Upon invading the Soviet Union in June 1941, the Germans again applied this requirement to newly conquered lands. Throughout the rest of 1941 and 1942, Germany, its satellite states and western occupied territories adopted regulations stipulating that Jews wear identifying badges." From "Holocaust Badges," *Holocaust Memorial Center Zekelman Family Campus*, n.d., accessed July 27, 2018, https://www.holocaustcenter.org/holocaust-badges.
15. F. Hadjadj, "La victoire de l'écrivain soldat," *Le Figaro*, Februrary 21, 2008. Available online: http://www.lefigaro.fr/livres/2008/02/21/03005-20080221ARTFIG00195-la-victoire-de-l-ecrivain-soldat.php (accessed July 27, 2018).
16. Andrei Oișteanu praises this gesture as Jünger courageously saluting the girls: Andrei Oișteanu, *Inventing the Jew: Antisemitic Stereotypes in Romanian and Other Central-East European Cultures*, trans. Mirela Adascalitei (Lincoln: University of

Nebraska Press, 2009), 112. For other discussions, see Julien Hervier, *Ernst Jünger: Dans les tempêtes du siècle* (Paris: Fayard, 2014), chapter 3. For examples of German soldiers saluting Jews wearing the star, see, for example, Philippe Barthelet, *Ernst Jünger* (Lausanne: Age d'homme, 2001), 18. See also F. Dufay, "Ernst Jünger—Un occupant si korrekt," *l'Express*, February 14, 2008. Available online: http://www.lexpress.fr/informations/ernst-junger-un-occupant-si-korrekt_721403.html (accessed July 27, 2018): *"Il s'attriste quand la femme du pharmacien juif « si serviable » dont il fréquente l'officine rue La Pérouse est déportée, se dit « gêné » de se trouver en uniforme quand, le 7 juin 1942, il croise, au sortir de chez Maxim's, trois jeunes filles porteuses de l'étoile jaune. Pour marquer sa désapprobation, il rend hommage, d'un claquement de talons, aux juifs qu'il rencontre sur son chemin. Cinquante-quatre ans plus tard, uncertain Dr Sée, découvrant que l'officier qui l'a salué au sortir d'une librairie n'était autre qu'Ernst Jünger, dira, dans un texte intitulé Le Salut à l'étoile, sa reconnaissance émue."*

17 "Those that he observes resisting, seem to him fools. Describing the French youths who wear yellow stars on their lapels bearing such words as 'Idealist,' he cynically records: 'These are the types who do not yet know that the times of discussion are over.'" Laura Honsberger, "A Difference of Degrees: Ernst Jünger, The National Socialists, and a New Europe" (PhD dissertation, History Department, Boston College, Boston, 2006), 90. Honsberger here is citing Jünger, *Strahlungen*, 58 and 153. "*Das sind Naturen, die noch nicht wissen, daß die Zeiten der Diskussion vorüber sind.*" Jünger, *Strahlungen*, 126.

18 "*Paris, 30. März 1942: Claus Valentiner kehrte aus Berlin zurück. Er erzählte von einem schauerlichen Burschen, früherem Zeichenlehrer, der sich gerühmt hatte, in Litauen und anderen Randgebieten ein Mordkommando geführt zu haben, das zahllose Menschen schlachtete. Man läßt die Opfer, nachdem sie zusammengetrieben sind, zuerst die Massengräber ausheben, dann sich hineinlegen und schießt sie von oben in Schichten tot. Zuvor beraubt man sie des Letzten, der Lumpen, die sie am Leibe tragen, bis auf das Hemd. Groteske Bilder der Athener Hungersnot. So fielen an den Höhepunkten eines großen Wagnerkonzerts die Posaunen aus, weil die geschwächten Bläser mit dem Atem nicht mitkamen.*" Jünger, *Strahlungen*, 113. This is reproduced and translated at http://holocaustcontroversies.blogspot.com/2017/06/ernst-jungers-march-1942-diary-entry-on.html. I use here the translation in Eli Nathans, *Peter von Zahn's Cold War Broadcasts to West Germany: Assessing America* (New York: Palgrave Macmillan, 2017), 33.

19 "*Groteske Bilder der Athener Hungersnot. So fielen an den Höhepunkten eines großen Wagnerkonzerts die Posaunen aus, weil die geschwächten Bläser mit dem Atem nicht mitkamen.*" Jünger, *Strahlungen*, 113.

20 Patrick Modiano, *Pedigree: A Memoir*, trans. Mark Polizzotti (New Haven, CT: Yale University Press, 2015), 4.

21 Patrick Modiano, *La place de l'étoile* (Paris: Gallimard, 1968), 11.

22 See especially, Devin O. Pendas, "'I Didn't Know What Auschwitz Was': The Frankfurt Auschwitz Trial and the German Press, 1963–1965," *Yale Journal of Law & the Humanities* 12, no. 2 (2000): 397–446.

23 From Nancy H. Kobrin, "Holocaust Literature in Judeo-Spanish, Portuguese, and Spanish," *Tradition: A Journal of Orthodox Jewish Thought* 18, no. 3 (1980): 288–94. According to Kobrin, 194 n. 16, Albert Maltz's novel, *A Tale of One January*, is a "transcription of Dunia Wasserstrom's flight." "*A Tale of One January* was published in England and has never been printed in the United States; chronicling the escape

of two women from Auschwitz, its narrative centers on one woman's rediscovery of her sense of self, her womanhood, and her relationship to the larger world." G. Miller, "Albert Maltz," in *The Heath Anthology of American Literature*, 5th ed., ed. Paul Lauter, accessed July 31, 2018, https://college.cengage.com/english/lauter/heath/4e/students/author_pages/modern/maltz_al.html. See also Bernard F. Dick, *Radical Innocence: A Critical Study of the Hollywood Ten* (Lexington: The University Press of Kentucky, 2009), 82–103.

24   Albert Maltz et al., *The Citizen Writer in Retrospect* (Los Angeles: Oral History Program, University of California, 1983), 996, accessed 31 July 2018, https://archive.org/details/citizenwriterinr02malt.

25   Dounia Wasserstrom, testimony from the Auschwitz Trial, April 23, 1964, in Hermann Langbein, *Der Auschwitz-Prozess, Eine Dokumentation*, 2 vols. (Frankfurt am Main: Verlag Neue Kritik, 1995), 481.

26   Rebecca E. Wittmann, "Telling the Story: Survivor Testimony and the Narration of the Frankfurt Auschwitz Trial," *German Historical Institute Bulletin* 32 (2003): 99.

27   Ibid., 100.

28   Dounia Ourisson, *Les secrets du bureau politique d'Auschwitz* (Paris: Ed. de l'Amicale des déportés d'Auschwitz, 1946).

29   R. Faurisson, "Revisionist Chronicle. Impact and Future of Holocaust Revisionism," *The Journal of Historical Review* 19, no. 1 (2000): 2–31. For his mention of Ourisson, see n. 32 of the article.

30   "*PS Man müßte jetzt auch wieder im Flavius Josephus lesen; die Hartnäckigkeit [stubbornness] der Juden bei der Belagerung von Jerusalem ist außerordentlich. Zu den Erfahrungen dieser Zeit, gehört, daß es eine Rückkehr zum Heidentum, zur vorväterbindung nicht gibt. Es gibt nur die Wahl zwischen dem Alten und dem Neuen Testament—jeder Angriff auf das Neue kommt dem Alten zugute.*
Dies ist einer der Gründe für die ungeheure Ausbreitung der jüdischen Moral, abgesehen davon, daß diese Moral durch die Exterminierung der Juden, an die sie gebunden war, nun frei und virulent geworden ist. Es hat etwas Gespenstisches, wie der blinde Wille sich ad absurdum führt," emphasis added, in Ingeborg Villinger and Alexander Jaser, *Briefwechsel Gretha Jünger und Carl Schmitt 1934-1953* (Berlin: Walter de Gruyter, 2007), 95.

31   Sigmund Freud, "The Theme of the Three Caskets," in *Collected Papers*, vol. 4 (London: Hogarth Press, 1925), 256.

32   Dunia Wasserstrom, *Never Again*, new ed. (n.p., n.d.), 152–3. Originally published in Spanish, available in multiple editions under the title *Nunca Jamás … !* and attributed to Dunia Wasserstrom or Dunya Vasershtrom.

33   Georges Dumézil, *The Riddle of Nostradamus: A Critical Dialogue*, trans. Betsy Wing (Baltimore: Johns Hopkins University Press, 1999), 70.

34   Ibid., 112.

35   Ibid., 64; cf. Philip K. Dick, *The Divine Invasion* (New York: Vintage Books, 1991 [1981]).

36   Ibid., 63–7.

37   Ibid., 98.

38   Ibid., 99.

39   Ibid., 102.

40   Ibid., 109.

41   Ibid., 118.

42   Ibid., 119.

43 I learn after writing this that Eliade had used this anecdote much earlier in Rumanian.
44 Ibid., 5.
45 Walter Mehring, *The Lost Library*, trans. Richard and Cara Winston (London: Secker & Warburg, 1951), 11. To a certain extent, this is the trace of excessive bookishness of an identifiable sort. "The Warburg library is almost by definition the most Jewish of creations, a maze of volumes in which one title led to another and the whole to a comprehensive vision of man defining himself in words, pictures, beliefs." Peter Gay cited in Amos Elon, *The Pity of It All* (New York: Metropolitan Books, 2002), 279.
46 Alberto Manguel, *The Library at Night* (New Haven, CT: Yale University Press, 2006), 247.
47 Steven M. Wasserstrom, *Religion after Religion: Gershom Scholem, Mircea Eliade, and Henry Corbin at Eranos* (Princeton, NJ: Princeton University Press, 1999), 223.
48 Dumézil, *The Riddle*, 120.
49 "*Berlin, 15. November 1942, Lektüre der Zeitschrift Zalmoxis, die sich nach einem von Herodot erwähnten skythischen Herakles benennt. Ich las darin zwei Aufsätze, einen über die Bräuche, unter denen die Wurzel der Mandragora ausgegraben und verwendet wird, und einen zweiten über den »Symbolisme Aquatique«, der die Beziehungen zwischen dem Monde, den Frauen und dem Meere bespricht. Beide von Mircea Eliade, dem Herausgeber, über den, sowie über seinen Meister René Guennon, C. S. mir Näheres berichtete. Aufschlußreich besonders die etymologischen Beziehungen zwischen den Muscheln und den weiblichen Genitalien, wie sie sich im lateinischen Conca und im dänischen Kudefisk für Muschel andeuten, wobei Kude gleichbedeutend mit Vulva ist ... Abends Spaziergang durch das verdunkelte Dahlem; wir sprachen dabei über die Herrnhuter Tageslosungen, die Quatrains von Nostradamus, über Jesaja und Prophezeiungen überhaupt. Daß Prophezeiungen zutreffen, und zwar für die verschiedensten Zeiträume, ist eben ein Prognostikon, an dem man die eigentlich prophetische Kraft der Vision erkennt. Im Ablauf der Zeiten wiederholt sich kaleidoskopisch, was der Seher in den Elementen schaut. Sein Blick ruht nicht auf der Historie, sondern auf der Substanz, nicht auf der Zukunft, sondern auf dem Gesetz. Mit Recht gilt daher die bloße Kenntnis zukünftiger Daten und Konstellationen als Zeichen krankhafter Einsicht oder niederer Magie*," from Jünger, *Strahlungen*, 199–200.
50 Sergiu Miculescu, "Mircea Eliade's Journal—As an Attempt at Developing a Personal Soteriology," *Analele Universității Ovidius Din Constanța. Seria Filologie*, XXIII 2 (2012): 104–11.
51 Mircea Eliade, *The Portugal Journal*. SUNY Series, Issues in the Study of Religion (Albany: State University of New York Press, 2010), 97.
52 Dumézil, *The Riddle*, 120.
53 Ibid.
54 Michel Foucault, *The Courage of the Truth (The Governmnet of Self and Others II): Lectures at the Collège de France, 1983–1984* (London: Palgrave Macmillan Limited, 2011), 97.
55 Heinrich Meier, *Death as God: A Note on Martin Heidegger* (Cambridge: Cambridge University Press, 2006), 45.
56 Conrad Ferdinand Meyer, *Der Heilige* (Leipzig: H. Haefel Berlag, 1909), 28–9. Conrad Ferdinand Meyer, *The Saint: A Fictional Biography of Thomas Becket*, trans. W. F. Twaddell (Providence, RI: Brown University Press, 1977), 18.
57 Meyer, *Heilige*, 28.

58 *Nachts unter der steinernen Brücke. Ein Roman aus dem alten Prag* (Frankfurt: Frankfurter Verlagsanstalt, 1953).
59 Leo Perutz, *By Night Under the Stone Bridge*, trans. Eric Mosbacher (New York: Arcade Publishing, 1989, 1990), 31–2.
60 Ibid., 27.
61 Gershom Scholem, *Major Trends in Jewish Mysticism* (New York: Schocken Books, 1954), 350.
62 Wasserstrom gave this lecture to students, colleagues, and friends to close out the conference that was held in his honor at Reed College. It was delivered on October 29, 2017. [Editors]
63 Robert Shogan, *The Battle of Blair Mountain: The Story of America's Largest Labor Uprising* (Boulder, CO: Westview Press, 2004); Kenneth R. Bailey, "Battle of Blair Mountain," *e-WV: The West Virginia Encyclopedia*, June 29, 2018, (accessed August 11, 2018).
64 Yehuda Amichai, *Open Close Open: Poems* (New York: Houghton Mifflin Harcourt, 2006), 122.

Publications of Steven M. Wasserstrom

Books

Between Muslim and Jew: The Problem of Symbiosis under Early Islam. Princeton, NJ: Princeton University Press, 1995.
Religion after Religion: Gershom Scholem, Mircea Eliade, and Henry Corbin at Eranos. Princeton, NJ: Princeton University Press, 1999. Portuguese translation, *Religião além da Religião, A Diálogos entre Gershom Scholem, Mircea Eliade e Henry Corbin*, trans. Dimas David. São Paulo: TRIOM, 2003.

Volumes Edited and Introduced

Fourteen Hundred Years of Shared Values. Portland, OR: Institute for Judaic Studies in the Pacific Northwest, 1991.
"The Fullness of Time": Poems by Gershom Scholem, translated by Richard Sieburth. Jerusalem: Ibis Editions, 2003. Reissued by Archipelago Books in 2017 as *Greetings from Angelus: Poems by Gershom Scholem*.

Articles, Chapters, and Essays

"The Delay of Maghrib: A Study in Comparative Polemics." In *Logos Islamikos: Studia Islamica in Honorem Georgii Michaelis Wickens*, edited by Roger M. Savory and Dionisius A. Agius, 269–86. Toronto: Pontifical Institute of Mediaeval Studies, 1984.
"The Moving Finger Writes: Mughīra b. Saʿīd's Islamic Gnosis and the Myths of Its Rejection." *History of Religions* 25, no. 1 (1985): 1–29.
"Islamicate History of Religions?" [A Review Essay]. *History of Religions* 27, no. 4 (1988): 405–11.
"Recent Works on the 'Creative Symbiosis' of Judaism and Islam." *Religious Studies Review* 16, no. 1 (1990): 43–7.
"Mutual Acknowledgements: Modes of Recognition between Muslim and Jew." In *Islam and Judaism: 1400 Years of Shared Values*, edited by Steven M. Wasserstrom, 56–75. Portland, OR: Institute for Judaic Studies in the Pacific Northwest, 1991.
"Jewish Pluralism in the Gaonic Period: The Case of the 'Jewish-Christians.'" *Journal of the Society of Rabbis in Academia* 1 (1991): 75–9.
"Who Were the Jewish Sects under Early Islam?" In *Jewish Sects, Religious Movements and Political Parties*, edited by Menahem Mor, 101–12. Omaha: Creighton University Press, 1992.
"The ʿĪsāwiyya Revisited." *Studia Islamica* 75 (1992): 57–80.

"A Response to Gordon D. Newby's *A History of the Jews of Arabia* and *Making of the Last Prophet*." *Religious Studies Review* 18, no. 3 (1992): 185–6.

"The Magical Texts in the Cairo Genizah." In *Genizah Research after Ninety Years: The Case of Judaeo-Arabic*, edited by Joshua Blau and Stefan Reif, 160–6. Cambridge: Cambridge University Press, 1992.

"*Sefer Yeṣira* and Early Islam: A Reappraisal." *Journal of Jewish Thought and Philosophy* 3 (1993): 1–30.

"Scriptures in Comparison" [A Review Essay]. *Religious Studies Review* 19, no. 1 (1993): 3–7.

"Jewish Pseudepigrapha in Muslim Literature: A Bibliographical and Methodological Sketch." In *Tracing the Threads: Studies in the Vitality of Jewish Pseudepigrapha*, edited by John C. Reeves, 87–114. Atlanta, GA: Scholars Press, 1994.

"'The Šīʿīs are the Jews of Our Community': An Interreligious Comparison within Sunnī Thought." In *Concepts of the Other in Near Eastern Religions*, edited by Ilai Alon, Ithamar Gruenwald, and Itamar Singer, special issue, *Israel Oriental Studies* 14 (1994): 297–324.

"The Lives of Baron Evola." *Alphabet City* 4, no. 5 (1995): 84–90.

"Moses (Arab. *Musa*)" and "Ibn al-Rewandi." In *HarperCollins Dictionary of Religion*, edited by Jonathan Z. Smith et al. San Francisco, CA: HarperSanFrancisco, 1995.

"Reflections on Holocaust Denial: Response to Jeffrey A. Ross." In *Conspiracies: Real Grievances, Paranoia, and Mass Movements*, edited by Eric Ward, 145–52. Seattle, WA: Peanut Butter Publishing, 1996.

"Šahrastānī on the Maġāriyya." In *Dhimmis and Others: Jews and Christians and the World of Classical Islam*, edited by Uri Rubin and David Wasserstein, special issue, *Israel Oriental Studies* 17 (1997): 127–54.

"Marilyn Robinson Waldman." *History of Religions* 37, no. 1 (1997): 1–2.

"Defeating Evil from Within: Comparative Perspectives [on Gershom Scholem's 'Redemption through Sin'." *Journal of Jewish Thought and Philosophy* 6 (1997): 37–57.

"The Islamic Social and Cultural Context." In *The Routledge History of Jewish Philosophy*, edited by Daniel H. Frank and Oliver Leaman, 72–90. London: Routledge, 1997.

"A Rustling in the Wood: The Turn to Myth in Weimar Jewish Thought." In *The Seductiveness of Jewish Myth: Challenge or Response?* edited by S. Daniel Breslauer, 97–122. Albany, NY: State University of New York Press, 1997.

"Uses of the Androgyne in the History of Religions." *Studies in Religion/Sciences Religieuses* 27, no. 4 (1998): 437–53.

"The Compunctious Philosopher? [Recent Studies on Judah HaLevi's *Kuzari*: A Review Essay]." *Medieval Encounters* 4, no. 2 (1998): 161–73.

"Jewish-Muslim Relations in the Context of Andalusian Emigration." In *Christians, Muslims, and Jews in Medieval and Early Modern Spain: Interaction and Cultural Change*, edited by Mark D. Meyerson and Edward D. English, 69–90. Notre Dame, IN: University of Notre Dame Press, 1999.

"Heresiography of the Jews in the Mamluk Times." In *Muslim Perceptions of Other Religions: Historical Survey*, edited by Jacques Waardenburg, 160–80. New York: Oxford University Press, 1999.

"Sense and Senselessness in Religion: Reflections on [Walter Burkert's] *Creation of the Sacred*." *Religion* 30 (2000): 273–81.

"Jewish Pseudepigrapha and *Qiṣaṣ al-Anbiyā*." In *Judaism and Islam: Boundaries, Communication and Interaction: Essays in Honor of William M. Brinner*, edited by Benjamin H. Hary, John L. Hayes, and Fred Astren, 237–56. Leiden: Brill, 2000.

"The Challenge of Artificial Life: Medieval Jewish Responses from the Muslim World." In *CCAR Symposium: Judaism and Islam*, edited by Reuven Firestone, special issue, *CCAR Journal: A Reform Jewish Quarterly* (Fall 2000): 69–80.

"The Unwritten Chapter: Notes towards a Social and Religious History of Geniza Magic." In *Officina Magica: Essays on the Practice of Magic in Antiquity*, edited by Shaul Shaked, 269–94. Leiden: Brill, 2005. Hebrew translation, "Ha-Perek She-Terem Nikhtav. Haarot Historia Hevratit ve-Datit shel Ha-Magia Ha-Musmachi Genizat Kahir," *Pe'amin* 85 (2000): 43–61.

"Jewish Sectarianism in the Near East: A Muslim's Account." In *Judaism in Practice: From the Middle Ages through the Early Modern Period*, edited by Lawrence Fine, 229–36. Princeton, NJ: Princeton University Press, 2001.

"Response: Final Note to Significance Seekers." *Journal of the American Academy of Religion* 69, no. 2 (2001): 459–64.

"Further Thoughts on the Origins of *Sefer Yeṣirah*." *Aleph* 2 (2002): 201–21.

"'Udj" [A revision of Bernhard Heller's article on 'Udj in *Encyclopaedia of Islam*, 1st ed.]. In *Encyclopaedia of Islam*, 2nd ed., edited by P. Bearman et al. Leiden: Brill, 2008 print and 2012 online.

"Concubines and Puppies: Philologies of Esotericism in Jerusalem between the World Wars." In *Adaptations and Innovations: Studies on the Interaction between Jewish and Islamic Thought and Literature from the Early Middle Ages to the Late Twentieth Century, Dedicated to Professor Joel L. Kraemer*, edited by Y. Tzvi Langermann and Josef Stern, 381–413. Paris: Peeters, 2007.

"An Apology for S. D. Goitein: An Essay." In *A Faithful Sea: The Religious Cultures of the Mediterranean, 1200–1700*, edited by Adnan A. Husain and Katherine E. Fleming, 173–98. Oxford: Oneworld, 2007.

"Adorno's Kabbalah: Some Preliminary Observations." In *Polemical Encounters: Esoteric Discourse and Its Others*, edited by Olav Hammer and Kocku von Stuckrad, 55–80. Leiden: Brill, 2007.

"Melancholy Jouissance and the Study of Kabbalah: Review Essay of Elliot R. Wolfson, *Alef, Mem, Tau*." *Association for Jewish Studies Review* 32 (2008): 389–96.

"The Medium of the Divine." In *Experientia, Volume 1: Inquiry into Religious Experience in Early Judaism and Christianity*, edited by Frances Flannery, Colleen Shantz, Rodney A. Werline, 75–82. Atlanta, GA: Society for Biblical Literature, 2008.

"Hans Jonas at Marburg, 1928." In *The Legacy of Hans Jonas: Judaism and the Phenomenon of Life*, edited by Hava Tirosh-Samuelson and Christian Wiese, 39–72. Leiden: Brill, 2008.

"'Abd Allāh ibn Salām." In *Encyclopedia of Jews in the Islamic World*, edited by Norman A. Stillman et al. Leiden: Brill, 2010.

"Maghāriyya, al- (The Cave Sect)." In *Encyclopedia of Jews in the Islamic World*, edited by Norman A. Stillman et al. Leiden: Brill, 2010.

"'Abd Allāh ibn Saba." In *Encyclopedia of Jews in the Islamic World*, edited by Norman A. Stillman et al. Leiden: Brill, 2010.

"Sharing Secrets: Inter-Confessional Philosophy as Dialogical Practice." In *New Directions in Jewish Philosophy*, edited by Elliot R. Wolfson and Aaron Hughes, 205–28. Bloomington: Indiana University Press, 2010.

"The Master-Interpreter: Notes on the German Career of Joachim Wach (1922–1935)." In *Hermeneutics, Politics, and the History of Religions: The Contested Legacies of Joachim Wach and Mircea Eliade*, edited by Christian K. Wedemeyer and Wendy Doniger, 21–50. New York: Oxford University Press, 2010.

"'The Great Goal of the Political Will Is Leviathan': Ernst Jünger and the Cabala of Enmity." In *Kabbalah and Modernity: Interpretations, Transformations, Adaptations*, edited by Boaz Huss, Marco Pasi, and Kocku von Stuckrad, 327–56. Leiden: Brill, 2010.

"Sefer Yetzira (Jewish Mystical Text)." In *Encyclopedia of Ancient History*, edited by Roger S. Bagnall et al. Malden, MA: Wiley-Blackwell, 2012.

"'The True Dreams of Mankind': Mircea Eliade's Transhumanist Fiction and the History of Religions." In *Building Better Humans? Refocusing the Debate on Transhumanism*, edited by Hava Tirosh-Samuelson and Kenneth L. Mossman. Frankfurt am Main: Peter Lang, 2012.

Bibliography

Abravanel, Isaac. *Naḥalat avot*. Ashkelon: Oren Golan, 2013.
Abravanel, Isaac. *Perush ha-Nevi'im, Sefer Melakhim*. Jerusalem: Ḥorev, 2009.
Abravanel, Isaac. *She'elot le-heḥakham Sha'ul ha-Kohen*. Jerusalem: n.p., 1966.
Abravanel, Isaac. *Perush al ha-Torah, Bereshit*. Jerusalem: Benei Arabel, 1964.
Adamson, Grant. "'I Turned Away from the Temple': Sethian Counterculture in the Apocryphon of John." *Gnosis: Journal of Gnostic Studies* 1 (2016): 36–55.
Adorno, Theodor W. *Minima Moralia: Reflections from Damaged Life*, translated by E. F. N. Jephcott. London: Verso, 2005.
Adorno, Theodor W. *Critical Models: Interventions and Catchwords*, translated by Henry W. Pickford, introduction by Lydia Goehr. New York: Columbia University Press, 2005.
Adorno, Theodor W. "Theses against Occultism." In *The Stars Down to Earth: And Other Essays on the Irrational in Culture*, edited by Stephen Crook, 172–80. New York: Routledge, 1995.
Adorno, Theodor W. *Negative Dialectics*, translated by E. P. Ashton. New York: Seabury Press, 1973.
Alami, Solomon. *Iggeret ha-Mussar*, edited by Abraham M. Habermann. Jerusalem: n.p., 1946.
Albert, Anne O. "The Rabbi and the Rebels: A Pamphlet on the *Herem* by Rabbi Isaac Aboab da Fonseca." *The Jewish Quarterly Review* 104, no. 2 (Spring 2014): 171–91.
Albert, Anne O. "'A Civil Death': Sovereignty and the Jewish Republic in an Early Modern Treatment of Genesis 49:10." In *Jewish Culture in Early Modern Europe: Essays in Honor of David B. Ruderman*, edited by R. I. Cohen, N. B. Dohrmann, A. Shear, and E. Reiner, 63–72. Cincinnati, OH: Hebrew Union College Press, 2014.
Almog, Oz. *The Sabra: The Creation of the New Jew*. Berkeley: University of California Press, 2000.
Alston, A. P. "Religion." In *Encyclopedia of Philosophy*, edited by Paul Edwards. New York: Macmillan, 1967.
Altmann, William H. F. *The German Stranger: Leo Strauss and National Socialism*. Lanham, MD: Lexington Books, 2011.
Amichai, Yehuda. *Open Close Open: Poems*. New York: Houghton Mifflin Harcourt, 2006.
Anckaert, Luc A. *A Critique of Infinity: Rosenzweig and Levinas*. Leuven: Peeters, 2006.
Anidjar, Gil. *The Jew, the Arab: A History of the Enemy*. Stanford, CA: Stanford University Press, 2003.
Armistead, Samuel G., and Joseph H. Silverman. "A New Collection of Judeo-Spanish Songs." *Jahrbuch für Volksliederforschung* 19 (1974): 154–66.
Arnal, William E. "Definition." In *Guide to the Study of Religion*, edited by Willi Braun and Russell T. McCutcheon, 21–34. London: Cassell, 2000.
Asad, Muhammad. *Islam at the Crossroads*. New Delhi: Goodword Books, 2001.
Asad, Muhammad. *This Law of Ours and Other Essays*. Gibraltar: Dar al-Andalus, 1987.
Asad, Muhammad. *The Message of the Quran*. Gibraltar: Dar al-Andalus, 1980.

Asad, Muhammad. *The Road to Mecca*. New York: Simon and Schuster, 1954.
Asad, Talal. "Muhammad Asad: Between Religion and Politics." *Islam & Science* 10, no. 1 (2012): 77–88.
Asad, Talal. *Formation of the Secular: Christianity, Islam, Modernity*. Stanford, CA: Stanford University Press, 2003.
Asad, Talal. *Genealogies of Religion: Discipline and Reasons of Power in Christianity and Islam*. Baltimore, MD: Johns Hopkins University Press, 1993.
Asatryan, Mushegh and Dylan M. Burns. "Is Ghulat Religion Islamic Gnosticism? Religious Transitions in Late Antiquity." In *Esotérisme shi'ite: ses racines et ses prolongements*, edited by Mohammad Ali Amir-Moezzi, 55–86. Paris: Bibliothèque de l'École des Hautes Études; London: Institute of Ismaili Studies, 2016.
Atlan, Henri. *The Sparks of Randomness, Vol. 2: The Atheism of Scripture*, translated by Lenn J. Schramm. Stanford, CA: Stanford University Press, 2013.
Auerbach, Erich. *Mimesis: The Representation of Reality in Western Literature*, translated by Willard R. Trask. Princeton, NJ: Princeton University Press, 2003.
Azarnouche, Samra and Céline Redard, eds. *Yama/Yima: Variations indo-iraniennes sur la geste mythique*. Paris: Collège de France; Boccard, 2012.
Baer, Yitzhak. *A History of the Jews in Christian Spain*, 2 vols., translated by L. Schoffman. Philadelphia, PA: Jewish Publication Society of America, 1961–1966.
Baer, Yitzhak. *Galut*. New York: Schocken, 1947.
Barnouw, Erik. *The Magician and the Cinema*. New York: Oxford University Press, 1981.
Baron, Salo. *Social and Religious History of the Jews*. New York: Columbia University Press, 1937.
Barouch, Lina. "The Erasure and Endurance of Lament: Gershom Scholem's Early Critique of Zionism and Its Language." *Jewish Studies Quarterly* 21 (2014): 13–26.
Barouch, Lina. "Lamenting Language Itself: Gershom Scholem on the Silent Language of Lamentation." *New German Critique* 37 (2010): 1–26.
Barrios, Daniel Levi de. *Triumpho del govierno popular y de la antiguedad Holandesa*. Amsterdam: n.p., 1683.
Barthelet, Philippe. *Ernst Jünger*. Lausanne: Age d'homme, 2001.
Bartholomae, Christian. *Altiranisches Wörterbuch*. Strassburg: Karl J. Trübner, 1904.
Batnitzky, Leora. *Idolatry and Representation: The Philosophy of Franz Rosenzweig Reconsidered*. Princeton, NJ: Princeton University Press, 2000.
Batnitzky, Leora. "Translation as Transcendence: A Glimpse into the Workshop of the Buber-Rosenzweig Bible Translation." *New German Critique* 70 (1997): 87–116.
Beach, Bradley, and Matthew T. Powell, eds. *Interpreting Abraham: Journeys to Moriah*. Augsburg: Fortress Publishers, 2014.
Beardsmore, R. W. "The Theory of Family Resemblances." *Philosophical Investigations* 15, no. 2 (1992): 131–46.
Bell, Catherine. "Paradigms behind (and before) the Modern Concept of Religion." *Method and Theory* 46 (2006): 27–46.
Benavides, Gustavo. "*Afterreligion* after Religion." *Journal of the American Academy of Religion* 69, no. 2 (2001): 449–57.
Ben Dror, Graciela. *The Catholic Church and the Jews in Argentina 1933–45*. Lincoln: University of Nebraska Press, 2008.
Benjamin, Walter. "Berlin Chronicle." In *Reflections: Essays, Aphorisms, Autobiographical Writings*, 1978, translated by Edmund Jephcott. New York: Schocken Books, 2007.
Benjamin, Walter. *The Arcades Project*, translated by Howard Eiland and Kevin McLaughlin. Cambridge, MA: The Belknap Press of Harvard University, 2002.

Benjamin, Walter. *Selected Writings, Vol. 2: 1927–1934*, edited by Michael W. Jennings, Howard Eiland, and Gary Smith. Cambridge, MA: Harvard University Press, 1999.

Benjamin, Walter. *Selected Writings, Vol. 1: 1913–1926*, edited by Marcus Bullock and Michael W. Jennings. Cambridge, MA: Harvard University Press, 1996.

Benjamin, Walter. *The Correspondence of Walter Benjamin 1910–1940*, edited by Gershom Scholem and Theodor W. Adorno, translated by Manfred R. Jacobson and Evelyn M. Jacobson. Chicago, IL: University of Chicago Press, 1994.

Benjamin, Walter. *Gesammelte Schriften* 4.1, edited by Tillman Rexroth. Frankfurt am Main: Suhrkamp, 1991.

Benjamin, Walter. *Walter Benjamin/Gershom Scholem: Briefwechsel*, edited by Gershom Scholem. Frankfurt am Main: Suhrkamp, 1980.

Benjamin, Walter. *Illuminations: Essays and Reflections*, translated by Harry Zohn. New York: Schocken, 1968.

Benjamin, Walter, and Gershom Scholem. *The Correspondence of Walter Benjamin and Gershom Scholem, 1932–1940*, edited by Gershom Scholem, translated by Gary Smith et al. Cambridge, MA: Harvard University Press, 1992.

Bennett, Byard. "Didymus the Blind's Knowledge of Manichaeism." In *The Light and the Darkness: Studies in Manichaeism and Its World*, edited by Paul Mirecki and Jason BeDuhn, 38–67. Leiden: Brill, 2001.

Berger, David, and Jorgen Vijgen, eds. *Thomistenlexikon*. Bonn: Nova & Vetera, 2006.

Bernáldez, Andrés. *Memorias del Reinado de los Reyes Católicos*, edited by J. de Mata Carriazo and M. Gomez-Moreno. Madrid: Real Academia de la Historia, 1962.

Bernasconi, Robert. *The Question of Language in Heidegger's History of Being*. Atlantic Highlands: Humanities Press, 1985.

Bethge, Hans-Gebhard. "Die Ambivalenz alttestamentlicher Geschichtstraditionen in der Gnosis." In *Altes Testament, Frühjudentum, Gnosis: Neue Studien zu "Gnosis und Bibel,"* edited by Karl-Wolfgang Tröger, 89–109. Berlin: Evangelische Verlagsanstalt, 1980.

Bey, Essad. *Mohammed: A Biography*, translated by Helmut L. Ripperger. New York: Longmans, 1936.

Biale, David. "Jewish Consumer Culture in Historical and Contemporary Perspective." In *Longing, Belonging, and the Making of Jewish Consumer Culture*, edited by Gideon Reuveni and Nils Roemer, 23–38. Leiden: Brill, 2010.

Biale, David. "Scholem und der moderne Nationalismus." In *Gershom Scholem: Zwischen den Disziplinen*, edited by Peter Schäfer and Gary Smith, 257–74. Frankfurt am Main: Suhrkamp Verlag, 1995.

Biale, David. *Gershom Scholem: Kabbalah and Counter-History*, 2nd ed. Cambridge, MA: Harvard University Press, 1982.

Bielik-Robson, Agata. "The God of Luria, Hegel and Schelling: The Divine Contraction and the Modern Metaphysics of Finitude." In *Mystical Theology and Continental Philosophy: Interchange in the Wake of God*, edited by David Lewin, Simon D. Podmore, and Duane Williams, 32–50. London: Routledge, 2017.

Bindeman, Steven L. *Heidegger and Wittgenstein: The Poetics of Silence*. Lanham, MD: University Press of America, 1981.

Bird, Darlene L. *Theology and Religious Studies in Higher Education: Global Perspectives*. London: Continuum, 2009.

Blanchot, Maurice. *The Book to Come*, translated by Charlotte Mandell. Stanford, CA: Stanford University Press, 2003.

Blanchot, Maurice. *Friendship*, translated by Elizabeth Rottenberg. Stanford, CA: Stanford University Press, 1997.

Blanchot, Maurice. *The Work of Fire*, translated by Charlotte Mandell. Stanford, CA: Stanford University Press, 1995.
Blanchot, Maurice. *The Infinite Conversation*, translated by Susan Hanson. Minneapolis: University of Minnesota Press, 1993.
Blanchot, Maurice. *L'Amitié*. Paris: Gallimard, 1971.
Blanchot, Maurice. *L'Entretien Infini*. Paris: Gallimard, 1969.
Blanchot, Maurice. "L'Interruption." *La Nouvelle Revue française* 137 (May 1964): 869–81.
Blanchot, Maurice. "Être juif" (II). *La Nouvelle Revue française* 117 (September 1962): 471–6.
Blanchot, Maurice. "Être juif" (I). *La Nouvelle Revue française* 116 (August 1962): 279–85.
Blanchot, Maurice. "Simone Weil et la certitude." *La Nouvelle Revue française* 55 (July 1957): 103–14.
Blanchot, Maurice. "La Parole prophétique." *La Nouvelle Revue française* 49 (January 1957): 101–10.
Blanchot, Maurice. "La Littérature et la droit à la mort." *Critique* 20 (January 1948): 30–47.
Blanchot, Maurice. "Le Règne animal de l'esprit." *Critique* 18 (November 1947): 387–405.
Bloom, Harold. *Genius: A Mosaic of One Hundred Exemplary Creative Minds*. New York: Warner, 2002.
Bloomdfield, Maurice. "On Vedic *Dhénā*, 'Prayer,' 'Song.'" *Journal of the American Oriental Society* 46 (1926): 303–8.
Blumenberg, Hans. *The Genesis of the Copernican World*. Cambridge, MA: MIT Press, 1987.
Blumenberg, Hans. *Die Lesbarkeit der Welt*. Frankfurt: Suhrkamp, 1981.
Bourdieu, Pierre. *The Political Ontology of Martin Heidegger*, translated by Peter Collier. Stanford, CA: Stanford University Press, 1991.
Bove, Laurence. "Unbinding the Other: Levinas, the Akedah, and Going beyond the Subject." In *Interpreting Abraham: Journeys to Moriah*, edited by Bradley Beach and Matthew T. Powell, 169–86. Augsburg: Fortress Publishers, 2014.
Boyce, Mary. *A History of Zoroastrianism: The Early Period*. Leiden: Brill, 1996.
Boym, Svetlana. *The Future of Nostalgia*. New York: Basic Books, 2001.
Bracciolini, Poggio. "On Avarice." In *The Earthly Republic: Italian Humanists on Government and Society*, edited by Benjamin G. Kohl and Ronald G. Witt, translated by Benjamin G. Kohl and Elizabeth B. Welles, 241–89. Philadelphia: University of Pennsylvania Press, 1978.
Brakke, David. *The Gnostics: Myth, Ritual, and Diversity in Early Christianity*. Cambridge, MA: Harvard University Press, 2010.
Brenner, Michael. "Gnosis and History: Polemics of German-Jewish Identity from Graetz to Scholem." *New German Critique* 77 (1999): 45–60.
Brenner, Michael. *The Renaissance of Jewish Culture in Weimar Germany*. New Haven, CT: Yale University Press, 1996.
Briggs, Robin. *Thinking with Demons*. New York: Oxford University Press, 1999.
Briggs, Robin. *Witches and Neighbors*. New York: Viking, 1996.
Brittain, Christopher C. *Adorno and Theology*. London: T & T Clark International, 2010.
Brown, Daniel. *Rethinking Tradition in Modern Islamic Thought*. Cambridge: Cambridge University Press, 1999.
Brown, Jeremy. "Review of Jonathan Garb's Yearnings of the Soul: Psychological Thought in Modern Kabbalah." *Aries: Journal for the Study of Western Esotericism* 18 (2018): 131–6.

Bruns, Gerald L. *Heidegger's Estrangements: Language, Truth, and Poetry in the Later Writings*. New Haven, CT: Yale University Press, 1989.
Buber, Martin. *On Judaism*, edited by Nahum N. Glatzer. New York: Schocken Books, 1967.
Buber, Martin. *Vom Geist des Judentums: Reden und Geleitworte*. Leipzig: K. Wolff Verlag, 1916.
Buckley, Jorunn J. *The Mandaeans: Ancient Texts and Modern People*. Oxford: Oxford University Press, 2002.
Buck-Morss, Susan. *The Dialectics of Seeing: Walter Benjamin and the Arcades Project*. Cambridge, MA: MIT Press, 1991.
Buell, Denise Kimber. *Why This New Race? Ethnic Reasoning in Early Christianity*. New York: Columbia University Press, 2005.
Bultmann, Rudolf. *Theology of the New Testament*, 2 vols., translated by Kendrick Grobel. Waco: Baylor University Press, 2007.
Burns, Dylan. "Telling Nag Hammadi's Egyptian Stories." *Bulletin for the Study of Religion* 45, no. 2 (2016), 5–11.
Burns, Dylan M. "Is the *Apocalypse of Paul* a Valentinian Apocalypse? Pseudepigraphy and Group Definition in NHC V, 2." In *Die Nag-Hammadi-Schriften in der Literatur- und Theologiegeschichte des frühen Christentums*, edited by Jens Schröter and Konrad Schwarz, 97–112. Tübingen: Mohr Siebeck, 2017.
Burns, Dylan M. "Telling Nag Hammadi's Egyptian Stories." *Bulletin for the Study of Religion* 45, no. 2 (2016), 5–11.
Burns, Dylan M. "Gnosis Undomesticated: Archon-Seduction, Demon Sex, and Sodomites in the *Paraphrase of Shem* (NHC VII,1)." *Gnosis: Journal of Gnostic Studies* 1–2 (2016): 132–56.
Burns, Dylan M. *Apocalypse of the Alien God: Platonism and the Exile of Sethian Gnosticism*. Divinations. Philadelphia: University of Pennsylvania, 2014.
Butler, Judith. "Critique, Coercion, and Sacred Life in Benjamin's 'Critique of Violence.'" In *Political Theologies: Public Religions in a Post-Secular World*, edited by Hent de Vries and Lawrence E. Sullivan, 201–19. New York: Fordham University Press, 2006.
Cahana, Jonathan. "None of Them Knew Me or My Brothers: Gnostic Antitraditionalism and Gnosticism as a Cultural Phenomenon." *The Journal of Religion* 94, no. 1 (2014): 49–73.
Campbell, Joseph, ed. *Man and Time: Papers from the Eranos Yearbooks*. Princeton, NJ: Princeton University Press, 1957.
Capobianco, Richard. *Engaging Heidegger*. Toronto: University of Toronto Press, 2010.
Capsali, Elia. *Seder Eliyahu Zuta*, edited by A. Shmuelevitz, S. Simonson, and M. Benayahu, 3 vols. Jerusalem: Ben Zvi Institute, 1975.
Casadio, Giovanni. "*Religio* versus Religion." In *Myths, Martyrs, and Modernity: Studies in the History of Religions in Honour of Jan Bremmer*, edited by Jitse Dijkstra et al. Leiden: Brill, 2010.
Cavalletti, Andrea. "Introduction." In *Spartakus: The Symbology of Revolt*, edited by Furio Jesi, translated by Alberto Toscano. London: Seagull Books, 2014.
Cheung, Johnny. *Etymological Dictionary of the Iranian Verb*. Leiden: Brill, 2007.
Chiswick, Barry. "The Postwar Economy of American Jews." In *A New Jewry? America since the Second World War*, edited by Peter Y. Medding, 85–101. Oxford: Oxford University Press, 1992.
Christensen, Arthur. *Le premier homme et le premier roi dans l'histoire légendaire des iraniens. Ie partie: Gayōmard, Masjay et Masjānay, Hōšang et Taxmōrum*. Stockholm: P.A. Norstedt, 1918.

Civil, Miguel. "The Sumerian Flood Story." In *Atra-ḫasis: The Babylonian Story of the Flood*, edited by W. G. Lambert and A. R. Millard. Warsaw: Eisenbrauns, 1999.

Claxton, Susanne. *Heidegger's Gods: An Ecofeminist Perspective*. London: Rowman & Littlefield, 2017.

Cohn, Michael, ed. *The Hasidic Community of Williamsburg, Brooklyn*, Occasional Papers in Cultural History, no. 4. New York: Brooklyn Children's Museum, 1963.

Colpe, Carsten. "*Daēnā*, Lichtjungfrau, Zweite Gestalt. Verbindungen und Unterschiede zwischen zarathustrischer und manichäischer Selbst-Anschauung." In *Studies in Gnosticism and Hellenistic Religions Presented to Gilles Quispel*, edited by M. J. Vermaseren and Roel B. van Den Broek, 58–77. Leiden: E.J. Brill, 1981.

Conrad, Lawrence I. "Ignaz Goldziher on Ernest Renan: From Orientalist Philology to the Study of Islam." In *The Jewish Discovery of Islam*, edited by Martin Kramer, 137–80. Tel Aviv: Tel Aviv University, 1999.

Copenhaver, Brian P. *Hermetica: The Greek Corpus Hermeticum and the Latin Asclepius in a New English Translation, with Notes and Introduction*. Cambridge: Cambridge University Press, 1992.

Crowe, Benjamin D. *Heidegger's Religious Origins: Destruction and Authenticity*. Bloomington: Indiana University Press, 2006.

Dahlstrom, Daniel O. "Being at the Beginning: Heidegger's Interpretation of Heraclitus." In *Interpreting Heidegger: Critical Essays*, edited by Daniel O. Dahlstrom, 135–55. Cambridge: Cambridge University Press, 2011.

Dallmayr, Fred. *The Other Heidegger*. Ithaca, NY: Cornell University Press, 1993.

Dan, Joseph. *Gershom Scholem and the Mystical Dimension of Jewish History*. New York: New York University Press, 1987.

Davis, Bret W. "Heidegger on the Way from Onto-Historical Ethnocentrism to East-West Dialogue." *Gatherings: The Heidegger Circle Annual* 6 (2016): 130–56.

Dawdy, Shannon L. *Patina: A Profane Archaeology*. Chicago, IL: University of Chicago Press, 2016.

Derrida, Jacques. *Margins of Philosophy*, translated by Alan Bass. Chicago, IL: University of Chicago Press, 1982.

Derrida, Jacques. *Writing and Difference*, translated and introduced by Alan Bass. Chicago, IL: University of Chicago Press, 1978.

Despland, Michel, and Gérard Vallée, eds. *Religion in History: The Word, the Idea, the Reality*. Waterloo: Wilfred Laurier University Press, 1992.

Deutsch, Nathaniel. "The Forbidden Fork, the Cell Phone Holocaust, and Other Haredi Encounters with Technology." *Contemporary Jewry* 29 (2009): 3–19.

Deutsch, Nathaniel. *Guardians of the Gate: Angelic Vice Regency in Late Antiquity*. Leiden: Brill, 1999.

Deutsch, Sandra M. *Las Derechas: The Extreme Right in Argentina, Brazil, and Chile, 1890–1939*. Stanford, CA: Stanford University Press, 1999.

Dhawan, Nikita. *Impossible Speech: On the Politics of Silence and Violence*. Sankt Augustin: Academia, 2007.

Dick, Bernard F. *Radical Innocence: A Critical Study of the Hollywood Ten*. Lexington: University Press of Kentucky, 2009.

Dick, Philip K. *The Divine Invasion*. New York: Vintage Books, 1991.

Diner, Dan. *Lost in the Sacred: Why the Muslim World Stood Still*, translated by Steven Rendall. Princeton, NJ: Princeton University Press, 2009.

Dodd, Charles, H. *The Interpretation of the Fourth Gospel*. Cambridge: Cambridge University Press, 1992.

Dodd, Charles, H. *The Bible and the Greeks*. London: Hodder and Stoughton, 1964.

Doostdar, Alireza. *The Iranian Metaphysicals: Explorations in Science, Islam and the Uncanny*. Princeton, NJ: Princeton University Press, 2018.
Doresse, Jean. "Trois livres gnostiques inédits: Évangile des Égyptiens.—Épître d'Eugnoste.—Sagesse de Jésus Christ." *Vigiliae Christianae* 2 (1948): 137–60.
Doresse, Jean, and Togo Mina. "Nouveaux Textes Gnostiques Coptes découverts en Haute-Egypte: La Bibliotheque de Chenoboskion." *Vigiliae Christianae* 3 (1949): 129–41.
Dubuisson, Daniel. *The Western Construction of Religion*, translated by William Sayers. Baltimore, MD: Johns Hopkins University Press, 2003.
Duchesne-Guillemin, Jacques. *La religion de l'Iran ancient*. Paris: Presses Universitaires de France, 1962.
Duff, Alexander S. *Heidegger and Politics: The Ontology of Radical Discontent*. Cambridge: Cambridge University Press, 2015.
Dumézil, Georges. *The Riddle of Nostradamus: A Critical Dialogue*, translated by Betsy Wing. Baltimore, MD: Johns Hopkins University Press, 1999.
Dumézil, Georges. *Myth et dieux des Germains: Essai d'interprétation comparative*. Paris: E. Leroux, 1939.
Dunning, Benjamin H. *Aliens and Sojourners: Self as Other in Early Christianity*. Philadelphia: University of Pennsylvania Press, 2009.
Duomato, Eleanor Abdella. *Getting God's Ear: Women, Islam and Healing in Saudi Arabia and the Gulf*. New York: Columbia University Press, 2000.
Ebeling, Florian. *The Secret History of Hermes Trismegistus: Hermeticisim from Ancient to Modern Times*, translated by David Lorton. Ithaca, NY: Cornell University Press, 2007.
Edwards, John. *The Jews in Western Europe: 1400–1600*. Manchester: Manchester University Press, 1994.
Edwards, Rem. *Reason and Religion: An Introduction to the Philosophy of Religion*. New York: Harcourt, 1972.
Eliade, Mircea. *The Portugal Journal*. Albany: State University of New York Press, 2010.
Eliade, Mircea. *The Sacred and the Profane: The Nature of Religion*, translated by Willard Trask. New York: Harcourt, Brace, 1959.
Elon, Amos. *The Pity of It All*. New York: Metropolitan Books, 2002.
El-Zein, Amira. *Islam, Arabs and the Intelligent World of the Jinn*. Syracuse: Syracuse University Press, 2009.
Emerson, Ralph Waldo. "The Scholar." In *The Complete Works of Ralph Waldo Emerson: Lectures and Biographical Sketches*, 261–89. Boston: Houghton, Mifflin and Co., 1903.
Engel, Amir. *Gershom Scholem: An Intellectual Biography*. Chicago, IL: University of Chicago Press, 2017.
Eyal, Gil. *The Disenchantment of the Orient: Expertise in Arab Affairs and the Israeli State*. Stanford, CA: Stanford University Press, 2006.
Fagenblat, Michael. "Of Dwelling Prophetically: On Heidegger and Jewish Political Theology." In *Heidegger and Jewish Thought: Difficult Others*, edited by Elad Lapidot and Micha Brumlik, 245–67. London: Rowman & Littlefield, 2018.
Faur, José. *In the Shadow of History: Jews and Conversos at the Dawn of Modernity*. Albany: State University of New York Press, 1992.
Feil, Ernst. *Religio: Die Geschichte eines neuzeitlichen Grundbegriffs*, 4 vols. Göttingen: Vandenhoeck & Ruprecht, 1986–2007.
Feldman, Deborah. *Unorthodox: The Scandalous Rejection of My Hasidic Roots*. New York: Simon & Schuster, 2012.

Fenves, Peter. *The Messianic Reduction: Walter Benjamin and the Shape of Time*. Stanford, CA: Stanford University Press, 2011.
Feoli, Enrico. "A Criterion for Monothetic Classification of Phytosociological Entities on the Basis of Species Ordination." *Vegetatio* 33, no. 2/3 (1977): 147–52.
Ferber, Ilit. "Lament and Pure Language: Scholem, Benjamin and Kant." *Jewish Studies Quarterly* 21 (2014): 42–54.
Ferber, Ilit. "'Incline Thine Ear unto Me, and Hear My Speech': Scholem, Benjamin, and Cohen on Lament." In *Lament in Jewish Thought: Philosophical, Theological, and Literary Perspectives*, edited by Ilit Ferber and Paula Schwebel, 111–30. Berlin: Walter de Gruyter, 2014.
Ferber, Ilit. "A Language of the Border: On Scholem's Theory of Lament." *Journal of Jewish Thought and Philosophy* 21 (2013): 161–86.
Festugière, André Marie Jean. *La révélation d'Hermès Trismégiste*, 4 vols. Paris: Belles Lettres, 1990.
Festugière, André Marie Jean, and Arthur Darby Nock, eds. *Corpus Hermeticum*, 4 vols. Paris: Belles Lettres, 2002.
Finchelstein, Federico. *The Ideological Origins of the Dirty War: Fascism, Populism, and Dictatorship in Twentieth Century Argentina*. Oxford: Oxford University Press, 2014.
Finchelstein, Federico. *Transatlantic Fascism: Ideology, Violence, and the Sacred in Argentina and Italy*. Durham, NC: Duke University Press, 2010.
Fingarette, Herbert. *Confucius: The Secular as Sacred*. New York: Harper and Row, 1972.
Fitzgerald, Timothy. *Discourse on Civility and Barbarity: A Critical History of Religion and Related Concepts*. New York: Oxford University Press, 2007.
Fitzgerald, Timothy. *The Ideology of Religious Studies*. New York: Oxford University Press, 2000.
Flusser, Vilem. "The Future of Writing." In *Writings*, edited by Andreas Ströhl, translated by Erik Eisel. Minneapolis: University of Minnesota Press, 2002.
Foucault, Michel. *The Courage of the Truth (The Government of Self and Others II): Lectures at the Collège de France, 1983–1984*, edited by Frédéric Gros, translated by Graham Burchell. New York: Palgrave Macmillan, 2011.
Fowden, Garth. *The Egyptian Hermes: A Historical Approach to the Late Pagan Mind*. Cambridge: Cambridge University Press, 1986.
Franck, Phyllis. "The Hasidic Poor in New York City." In *Poor Jews: An American Awakening*, edited by Naomi Levine and Martin Hochbaum. New Brunswick: Transaction Books, 1974.
Frankel, Hertz. *The Satmar Rebbe and His English Principal*. New York: Menucha Publishers, 2015.
Freud, Sigmund. "The Theme of the Three Caskets." In Sigmund Freud, *Collected Papers*, vol. 4, translated by Joan Riviere, London: Hogarth Press, 1925.
Funkenstein, Amos. *Perceptions of Jewish History*. Berkeley: University of California Press, 1993.
Galli, Barbara E. *Franz Rosenzweig and Jehuda Halevi: Translating, Translations, and Translators*. Montreal: McGill-Queen's University Press, 1995.
Gamkrelidze, Thomas V., and Vjačeslav V. Ivanov. *Indo-European and the Indo-Europeans*, translated by Johanna Nichols. Berlin: Mouton de Gruyter, 1995.
Gans, Herbert. "The 'Yinglish' Music of Mickey Katz." *American Quarterly* 5, no. 3 (Autumn, 1953): 213–18.
Garb, Jonathan. *Modern Kabbalah as an Autonomous Domain of Research*. Los Angeles, CA: Cherub Press, 2016.

Germano, Giuseppe, ed. *Poggio Bracciolini, De avaritia (Dialogus contra avaritiam)*. Belforte: Livorno, 1994.
Gignoux, Philippe. *Man and Cosmos in Ancient Iran*. Rome: Istituto Italiano per l'Africa e l'Oriente, 2001.
Given, J. Gregory. "'Finding' the *Gospel of Thomas* in Edessa." *Journal of Early Christian Studies* 25 (2017): 501–30.
Gluck, Avraham D., ed. *Seyfer Zakhor Tsadik Levrokhe*, vol. 1. Kiryas Joel. New York: Mazel, 2002.
Gnoli, Gherardo. "Über die *Daēnā*: Haδōxt nask 2,7-9." In *Tradition und Translation: Zum Problem der interkulturellen Überstetzbarkeit religiöser Phänomene. Festschrift für Carsten Colpe*, edited by Christoph Elsass et al., 292–8. Berlin: de Gruyter, 1981.
Goldberg, Christine. *Turandot's Sisters: A Study of the Folktale AT 851*. New York: Garland Publishing, 1993.
Goldziher, Ignác. *Mythology among the Hebrews and Its Historical Development*, translated by Russell Martineau. London: Longmans, Green, and Co., 1877.
Goodacre, Mark. "How Reliable Is the Story of the Nag Hammadi Discovery?" *Journal for the Study of the New Testament* 35 (2013): 303–22.
Gordon, Peter E. "Kritische Theorie zwischen Sakralen und Profane." *WestEnd: Neue Zeitschrift für Sozialforschung* 1 (2016): 3–34.
Gordon, Peter E. "What Hope Remains? Habermas on Religion." *The New Republic*, December 14, 2012.
Gosetti-Ferencei, Jennifer A. *Heidegger, Hölderlin, and the Subject of Poetic Language: Towards a New Poetics of Dasein*. New York: Fordham University Press, 2004.
Grassmann, Hermann. *Wörterbuch zum Rig-Veda*. Leipzig: F. A. Brockhaus, 1873.
Gross, Abraham. *Iberian Jewry from Twilight to Dawn: The World of Rabbi Abraham Saba*. Leiden: Brill, 1995.
Groth, Miles. *Translating Heidegger*. Amherst, NY: Humanity Books, 2004.
Grugan, Arthur Anthony. "Thought and Poetry: Language as Man's Homecoming. A Study of Martin Heidegger's Question of Being and Its Ties to Friedrich Hölderlin's Experience of the Holy." PhD dissertation, Duquesne University, 1972.
Guillaumont, Antoine, Henri-Charles Puech, Gilles Quispel, Wlater Till, and Yassah 'Abd Al Masih, eds. *L'Évangile selon Thomas*. Leiden: Brill; Paris: Presses Univeritaires de France, 1959.
Gutwirth, Eleazar. "Towards Expulsion: 1391–1492." In *Spain and the Jews: The Sephardi Experience 1492 and After*, edited by Elie Kedourie, 51–73. London: Thames and Hudson, 1992.
Gutwirth, Eleazar. "Abraham Seneor: Social Tensions and the Court-Jew." *Michael: On the History of Jews in the Diaspora* 11 (1989): 169–229.
Haba, Juan Piqueras. "Los judíos y el vino en España: siglos XI–XV, una geografía histórica." *Cuadernos de Geografía* 75 (2004): 17–41.
Habermas, Jürgen. "Notes on Post-Secular Society." *New Perspectives Quarterly* 25, no. 4 (Fall, 2008): 17–29.
Habermas, Jürgen. *Glauben und Wissen: Friedenspreis des deutschen Buchhandels*. N.p.: Suhrkamp Verlag, 2001.
Habermas, Jürgen. *Postmetaphysical Thinking: Philosophical Essays*. Cambridge, MA: MIT Press, 1994.
Habermas, Jürgen. "Martin Heidegger: On the Publication of the Lectures of 1935." In *The Heidegger Controversy: A Critical Reader*, edited by Richard Wolin, 190–7. Cambridge, MA: MIT Press, 1993.

Hacker, Joseph. "New Chronicles on the Expulsion of the Jews from Spain, Its Causes and Results." *Zion* 44 (1979): 201–28.
Hadot, Pierre. *The Veil of Isis: An Essay on the History of the Idea of Nature*, translated by Michael Chase. Cambridge, MA: Harvard University Press, 2006.
Hakl, Hans Thomas. *Eranos: An Alternative Intellectual History of the Twentieth Century*, translated by Christopher McIntosh. Montreal: McGill-Queen's University Press, 2013.
Hammerschlag, Sarah. *The Figural Jew: Politics and Identity in French Post-War Thought*. Chicago, IL: University of Chicago Press, 2010.
Handelman, Susan A. *Fragments of Redemption: Jewish Thought and Literary Theory in Benjamin, Scholem, and Levinas*. Bloomington: Indiana University Press, 1991.
Harvey, David. *Paris, Capital of Modernity*. New York: Routledge, 2003.
Harvey, L. P. *Islamic Spain, 1500–1614*. Chicago, IL: University of Chicago Press, 2005.
Harvey, L. P. *Islamic Spain, 1250–1500*. Chicago, IL: University of Chicago Press, 1990.
Hedrick, Charles W. *The Apocalypse of Adam: A Literary and Source Analysis*. Eugene, OR: Wipf & Stock, 2005.
Hegel, Georg W. F. *Early Theological Writings*, translated by T. M. Knox. Chicago, IL: University of Chicago Press, 1948.
Heidegger, Martin. *Ponderings VII–XI: Black Notebooks 1938–1939*, translated by Richard Rojcewicz. Bloomington: Indiana University Press, 2017.
Heidegger, Martin. *Ponderings II–VI: Black Notebooks 1931–1938*, translated by Richard Rojcewicz. Bloomington: Indiana University Press, 2016.
Heidegger, Martin. *The History of Beyng*, translated by William McNeill and Jeffrey Powell. Bloomington: Indiana University Press, 2015.
Heidegger, Martin. *Hölderlin's Hymns "Germania" and "The Rhine"*, translated by William McNeill and Julia Ireland. Bloomington: Indiana University Press, 2014.
Heidegger, Martin. *Überlegungen II–VI (Schwarze Hefte 1931–1938)*. Frankfurt am Main: Vittorio Klostermann, 2014.
Heidegger, Martin. *Überlegungen VII–XI (Schwarze Hefte 1938/39)*. Frankfurt am Main: Vittorio Klostermann, 2014.
Heidegger, Martin. *Nature, History, State 1933–1934*, translated and edited by Gregory Fried and Richard Polt. London: Bloomsbury, 2013.
Heidegger, Martin. *Bremen and Freiburg Lectures: Insight into That Which Is and Basic Principles of Thinking*, translated by Gregory Andrew J. Mitchell. Bloomington: Indiana University Press, 2012.
Heidegger, Martin. *Contributions to Philosophy (of the Event)*, translated by Richard Rojcewicz and Daniela Vallega-Neu. Bloomington: Indiana University Press, 2012.
Heidegger, Martin. *Being and Time*, translated by Joan Stambaugh, revised by Dennis J. Schmidt. Albany: State University of New York Press, 2010.
Heidegger, Martin. *Basic Writings*, rev. and exp. Ed., edited and introduced by David Farrell Krell. London: Harper Perennial, 2008.
Heidegger, Martin. *Becoming Heidegger: On the Trail of His Early Occasional Writings, 1910–1927*, edited by Theodore Kisiel and Thomas Sheehan. Evanston, IL: Northwestern University Press, 2007.
Heidegger, Martin. *Seminare*. Frankfurt am Main: Vittorio Klostermann, 2005.
Heidegger, Martin. *Four Seminars: Le Thor 1966, 1968, 1969, Zähringen 1973*, translated by Andrew Mitchell and François Raffoul. Bloomington: Indiana University Press, 2003.
Heidegger, Martin. *Aus der Erfahrung des Denkens*. Frankfurt am Main: Vittorio Klostermann, 2002.

Heidegger, Martin. *Off the Beaten Track*, edited and translated by Julian Young and Kenneth Haynes. Cambridge: Cambridge University Press, 2002.

Heidegger, Martin. *The Essence of Truth: On Plato's Cave Allegory and Theaetetus*, translated by Ted Sadler. New York: Continuum, 2002.

Heidegger, Martin. *Phenomenological Interpretations of Aristotle: Initiation into Phenomenological Research*, translated by Richard Rojcewicz. Bloomington: Indiana University Press, 2001.

Heidegger, Martin. *Elucidations of Hölderlin's Poetry*, translated by Keith Hoeller. Amherst, NY: Humanity Books, 2000.

Heidegger, Martin. *Introduction to Metaphysics*, translated by Gregory Fried and Richard Polt. New Haven, CT: Yale University Press, 2000.

Heidegger, Martin. *Vorträge und Aufsätze*. Frankfurt am Main: Vittorio Klostermann, 2000.

Heidegger, Martin. *Hölderlins Hymnen "Germanien" und "Der Rhein"*. Frankfurt am Main: Vittorio Klostermann, 1999.

Heidegger, Martin. *Die Geschichte des Seyns*. Frankfurt am Main: Vittorio Klostermann, 1998.

Heidegger, Martin. *Pathmarks*, edited by William McNeill. Cambridge: Cambridge University Press, 1998.

Heidegger, Martin. *Der Satz vom Grund*. Frankfurt am Main: Vittorio Klostermann, 1997.

Heidegger, Martin. *Erläuterungen zu Hölderlins Dichtung*. Frankfurt am Main: Vittorio Klostermann, 1996.

Heidegger, Martin. *Hölderlin's Hymn "The Ister,"* translated by William McNeill and Julia Davis. Bloomington: Indiana University Press, 1996.

Heidegger, Martin. *Wegmarken*. Frankfurt am Main: Vittorio Klostermann, 1996.

Heidegger, Martin. *The Fundamental Concepts of Metaphysics: World, Finitude, Solitude*, translated by William McNeill and Nicholas Walker. Bloomington: Indiana University Press, 1995.

Heidegger, Martin. *Bremer und Freiburger Vorträge*. Frankfurt am Main: Vittorio Klostermann, 1994.

Heidegger, Martin. *Phänomenologische Interpretationen zu Aristoteles: Einführung in die Phänomenologische Forschung*. Frankfurt am Main: Vittorio Klostermann, 1994.

Heidegger, Martin. *Hölderlins Hymne "Der Ister."* Frankfurt am Main: Vittorio Klostermann, 1993.

Heidegger, Martin. *Sein und Zeit*. Tübingen: Max Niemeyer, 1993.

Heidegger, Martin. *Parmenides*, translated by André Schuwer and Richard Rojcewicz. Bloomington: Indiana University Press, 1992.

Heidegger, Martin. *The Principle of Reason*, translated by Reginald Lilly. Bloomington: Indiana University Press, 1992.

Heidegger, Martin. *Beiträge zur Philosophie (Vom Ereignis)*. Frankfurt am Main: Vittorio Klostermann, 1989.

Heidegger, Martin. *Schelling: Vom Wesen der menschlichen Freiheit (1809)*. Frankfurt am Main: Vittorio Klostermann, 1988.

Heidegger, Martin. *Vom Wesen der Wahrheit: Zu Platons Höhlengleichnis und Theätet*. Frankfurt am Main: Vittorio Klostermann, 1988.

Heidegger, Martin. *Schelling's Treatise on the Essence of Human Freedom*, translated by Joan Stambaugh. Athens: Ohio University Press, 1985.

Heidegger, Martin. *Unterwegs zur Sprache*. Frankfurt am Main: Vittorio Klostermann, 1985.

Heidegger, Martin. *Die Frage Nach dem Ding: Zu Kants Lehre von den Transzendentalen Grundsätzen*. Frankfurt am Main: Vittorio Klostermann, 1984.
Heidegger, Martin. *The Metaphysical Foundations of Logic*, translated by Michael Heim. Bloomington: Indiana University Press, 1984.
Heidegger, Martin. *Die Grundbegriffe der Metaphysik: Welt—Endlichkeit—Einsamkeit*. Frankfurt am Main: Vittorio Klostermann, 1983.
Heidegger, Martin. *Einführung in die Metaphysik*. Frankfurt am Main: Vittorio Klostermann, 1983.
Heidegger, Martin. *Heraklit*. Frankfurt am Main: Vittorio Klostermann, 1979.
Heidegger, Martin. *Frühe Schriften*. Frankfurt am Main: Vittorio Klostermann, 1978.
Heidegger, Martin. *Metaphysische Anfangsgründe der Logik im Ausgang von Leibniz*. Frankfurt am Main: Vittorio Klostermann, 1978.
Heidegger, Martin. *Holzwege*. Frankfurt am Main: Vittorio Klostermann, 1977.
Heidegger, Martin. *Early Greek Thinking*, translated by David Farrell Krell and Frank A. Capuzzi. New York: Harper & Row, 1975.
Heidegger, Martin. *On the Way to Language*, translated by Peter D. Hertz. New York: Harper & Row, 1971.
Heidegger, Martin. *Poetry, Language, Thought*, translated and introduced by Albert Hofstadter. New York: Harper & Row, 1971.
Heidegger, Martin. *Identity and Difference*, translated and introduced by Joan Stambaugh. New York: Harper & Row, 1969.
Heidegger, Martin. *What Is a Thing?*, translated by W. B. Barton, Jr., and Vera Deutsch with an analysis by Eugene T. Gendlin. Chicago, IL: Henry Regnery Company, 1967.
Heidegger, Martin. "Who Is Nietzsche's Zarathustra?" *Review of Metaphysics* 20 (1967): 411–31.
Hendel, Ronald. *Remembering Abraham: Culture, Memory, and History in the Hebrew Bible*. Oxford: Oxford University Press, 2005.
Hentze, Carl. "Die Gottin mit dem Haus auf dem Kopf." *Antaios* 7 (1965): 47–67.
Hentze, Carl. "Religiöse und mythische Hintergründe zu Turandot." *Antaios* 1 (1959/60): 21–41.
Hervier, Julien. *Ernst Jünger: Dans les tempêtes du siècle*. Paris: Fayard, 2014.
Heschel, Susannah. "Abraham Geiger and the Emergence of Jewish Philoislamism." In *"Im vollen Licht der Geschichte": die Wissenschaft des Judentums und die Anfänge der kritischen Koranforschung*, edited by Dirk Hartwig, Walter Homolka, Michael J. Marx, and Angelika Neuwirth. Würzburg: Ergon, 2008.
Hill, Leslie. "An intellectual itinerary." In *Maurice Blanchot: Extreme Contemporary*. London: Routledge, 1997.
Hillgarth, J. N. *The Spanish Kingdoms 1250–1516*. Oxford: Oxford University Press, 1978.
Hintze, Almut. "A Zoroastrian Vision." In *The Zoroastrian Flame: Exploring Religion, History and Tradition*, edited by Alan Williams, Sarah Stewart, and Almut Hintze, 77–96. London: I.B. Tauris, 2016.
Hintze, Almut. *A Zoroastrian Liturgy: The Worship in Seven Chapters (Yasna 35–41)*. Wiesbaden: Harrassowitz, 2007.
Hintze, Almut. *Der Zamyād-Yašt: Edition, Übersetzung, Kommentar*. Wiesbaden: L. Reichert Verlag, 1994.
Hoffmann, Gisbert. *Heideggers Phänomenologie: Bewusstsein—Reflexion—Selbst (Ich) und Zeit in Frühwerk*. Würzburg: Königshausen & Neumann, 2005.
Honsberger, Laura. "A Difference of Degrees: Ernst Jünger, The National Socialists, and a New Europe." PhD dissertation, History Department, Boston College, Boston, 2006.

Horkheimer, Max, and Theodor W. Adorno. *Dialectic of Enlightenment: Philosophical Fragments*, edited by Gunzelin Schmid Noerr, translated by Edmund Jephcott. Stanford, CA: Stanford University Press, 2002.

Hughes, Aaron. *Abrahamic Religions: On the Uses and Abuses of History*. New York: Oxford University Press, 2012.

Humbach, Helmut. "Yama/Yima/Jamšēd, King of Paradise of the Iranians." *Jerusalem Studies in Arabic and Islam* 26 (2002): 68–77.

Humbach, Helmut, and K. Faiss. *Zarathushtra and His Antagonists: A Sociolinguistic Study with English and German Translations of His Gāthās*. Wiesbaden: Reichert, 2010.

Humbach, Helmut, and Pallan R. Ichaporia. *Zamyād Yasht: Yasht 19 of the Younger Avesta; Text, Translation, Commentary*. Wiesbaden: Harrassowitz, 1998.

Idel, Moshe. *Old Worlds, New Mirrors: On Jewish Mysticism and Twentieth-Century Thought*. Philadelphia: University of Pennsylvania Press, 2010.

Idel, Moshe. "Subversive Catalysts: Gnosticism and Messianism in Gershom Scholem's View of Jewish Mysticism." In *The Jewish Past Revisited: Reflections on Modern Jewish Historians*, edited by David N. Myers and David B. Ruderman, 39–76. New Haven, CT: Yale University Press, 1998.

Insler, Stanley. *The Gāthās of Zarathustra*. Leiden: E.J. Brill, 1975.

Ireland, Julia A. Heidegger, Hölderlin, and Eccentric Translation. In *Heidegger, Translation, and the Task of Thinking*, edited by Frank Schalow, 253–67. Dordrecht: Springer, 2011.

Jabès, Edmond. *The Book of Questions*, vol. 1, translated by Rosmarie Waldrop. Middletown, CT: Wesleyan University Press, 1977.

Jabès, Edmond. *Le livre des questions*. Paris: Gallimard, 1963.

Jacobsen, Thorkild. "The Eridu Genesis." *Journal of Biblical Literature* 100, no. 4 (1981): 513–29.

Jacobson, Eric. *Metaphysics of the Profane: The Political Theology of Walter Benjamin and Gershom Scholem*. New York: Columbia University Press, 2010.

James, William. *The Varieties of Religious Experience: A Study in Human Nature*. New York: Longmans, 1902.

Jaron, Steven. *Edmond Jabès: The Hazard of Exile*. Oxford: Europeans Humanities Research Centre of the University of Oxford, 2003.

Jaspers, Karl. *Vom Ursprung und Ziel der Geschichte*. Munich: Piper Verlag, 1994.

Jenott, Lance. "Emissaries of Truth and Justice: The Seed of Seth as Agents of Divine Providence." In *Gnosticism, Platonism, and the Late Ancient World: Essays in Honour of John D. Turner*, edited by Kevin Corrigan and Tuomas Rasimus, 43–62. Leiden; Boston: Brill, 2013.

Johnston-Bloom, Ruchama. "Ali and Nino and Jewish Questions." In *Approaches to Kurban Said's 'Ali and Nino': Love, Identity, and Intercultural Conflict*, edited by Carl Niekerk and Cori Crane, 210–26. Rochester, NY: Camden House, 2017.

Johnston-Bloom, Ruchama. "Jews, Muslims and *Bildung*: the German-Jewish Orientalist Gustav Weil in Egypt." *Religion Compass* 8, no. 2 (2014): 49–59.

Jonas, Hans. *The Gnostic Religion: The Message of the Alien God and the Beginnings of Christianity*. Boston: Beacon Press, 1963.

Jonas, Hans. *Gnosis und spätantiker Geist*, 2 vols. Göttingen: Vandenhoek & Ruprecht, 1934–1954.

Jünger, Ernst. *Strahlungen*. Tubinggen: Heliopolis-Verlag, 1949.

Kaler, Michael. "The Cultic Milieu, the Nag Hammadi Collectors and Gnosticism." *Religious Studies* 38 (2009): 427–44.

Kalib, Sholom. *The Musical Tradition of the Eastern European Synagogue*, vol. 1. Syracuse, NY: Syracuse University Press, 2002.
Katz, Jacob. *Out of the Ghetto: The Social Background of Jewish Emancipation, 1770–1870*. Cambridge, MA: Harvard University Press, 1973.
Katz, Jacob. *Tradition and Crisis: Jewish Society at the End of the Middle Ages*. New York: New York University Press, 1963.
Kaufmann, David. "Imageless Refuge for All Images: Scholem in the Wake of Philosophy." *Modern Judaism* 20 (2000): 147–58.
Kellens, Jean. "Le jour se lève à la fin de la Gāthā Ahunauuaitī." *Journal asiatique* 301 (2013): 53–84.
Kellens, Jean. *Études avestiques et mazdéennes*. Vol. 3. *Le long préambule du sacrifice*. Paris: Collège de France, 2010.
Kellens, Jean. "La fonction aurorale de Mithra et la Daēnā." In *Studies in Mithraism*, edited by John R. Hinnells, 165–71. Rome: "L'Erma" di Bretschneider, 1994.
Kellens, Jean, and Eric Pirart. *Les Textes vieil-avestiques*. Wiesbaden: L. Reichert Verlag, 1990.
Khan, Naveeda. *Muslim Becoming: Aspiration and Skepticism in Pakistan*. Durham, NC: Duke University Press, 2012.
King, Karen L. *What Is Gnosticism?* Cambridge, MA: Belknap Press of Harvard University Press, 2003.
Kittler, Friedrich A. *Literature, Media, Information Systems: Essays*, edited and introduced by John Johnston. Amsterdam: Overseas Publishers Association, 1997.
Kligman, Mark. "Contemporary Jewish Music in America." *American Jewish Yearbook* 101 (2001): 88–141.
Knepper, Timothy D. "Ineffability Investigations: What the Later Wittgenstein Has to Offer to the Study of Ineffability." *International Journal for Philosophy of Religion* 65 (2009): 65–76.
Kobrin, Rebecca, ed. *Chosen Capital: The Jewish Encounter with American Capitalism*. New Brunswick: Rutgers University Press, 2012.
Konuk, Kader. *East-West Mimesis: Auerbach in Turkey*. Stanford, CA: Stanford University Press, 2010.
Kosseleck, Reinhardt. *Futures Past: On the Semantics of Historical Time*, translated by Keith Tribe. New York: Columbia University Press, 2004.
Kotrosits, Maia. "Romance and Danger at Nag Hammadi." *The Bible and Critical Theory* 8, no. 1 (2012): 39–52.
Kramer, Samuel N. "The Sumerian Deluge Myth: Reviewed and Revised." *Anatolian Studies* 33 (1983): 115–21.
Kramers, J. H. "The *Daēnā* in the Gathas." In *Oriental Studies in Honour of Curtseji Erachji Pavry*. London: Oxford University Press, 1933.
Kranzler, George. *Hasidic Williamsburg: A Contemporary American Hasidic Community*. Northvale, NJ: Jason Aronson, 1995.
Kranzler, George. "The Women of Williamsburg: A Contemporary Hasidic Community in Brooklyn, New York." In *Ethnic Women: A Multiple Status Reality*, edited by Vasilikie Demos and Marcia Texler Segal, 69–81. Dix Hills, NY: General Hall, 1994.
Kranzler, George. *The Face of Faith: An American Hassidic Community*. Baltimore, MD: Baltimore Hebrew College Press, 1972.
Kranzler, George. *Williamsburg: A Jewish Community in Transition*. New York: Feldheim, 1961.
Krasney, Ariela. "The *Badkhn*: From Wedding Stage to Writing Desk." *Polin: Studies in Polish Jewry* 16 (2003): 7–28.

Krasney, Ariela. *Ha-badchan*. Ramat Gan: Bar-Ilan University Press, 1998.
Lacoue-Labarthe, Philippe. *Heidegger and the Politics of Poetry*, translated and introduced by Jeff Fort. Urbana: University of Illinois Press, 2007.
Lacoue-Labarthe, Philippe. "Poetry's Courage." In *Walter Benjamin and Romanticism*, edited by Beatrice Hanssen and Andrew Benjamin, 163–79. London: Continuum, 2002.
Lacroix, Stéphane. *Awakening Islam: The Politics of Religious Dissent in Contemporary Saudi Arabia*. Cambridge, MA: Harvard University Press, 2011.
Lafont, Cristina. "World-Disclosure and Critique: Did Habermas Succeed in Thinking with Heidegger and against Heidegger." *Telos* 145 (2008): 161–76.
Lahe, Jaan. *Gnosis und Judentum: Alttestamentliche und jüdische Motive in der gnostischen Literatur und das Ursprungsproblem der Gnosis*. Leiden; Boston: Brill, 2012.
Langbein, Hermann. *Der Auschwitz-Prozess, Eine Dokumentation*, 2 vols. Frankfurm am Main: Verlag Neue Kritik, 1995.
Lankarany, Firouz-Thomas. *Daēnā im Awesta, eine semantische Untersuchung*. Reinbek: Verlag für Orientalistische Fachpublikationen, 1985.
Lauster, Martina. "Walter Benjamin's Myth of the 'Flâneur.'" *The Modern Language Review* 102, no. 1 (January 2007): 139–56.
Lazier, Benjamin. *God Interrupted: Heresy and the European Imagination between the World Wars*. Princeton, NJ: Princeton University Press, 2012.
Le Corbusier. *Toward an Architecture*, translated by John Goodman. Los Angeles, CA: The Getty Research Institute, 2007.
Leicht, Reimund. "Gnostic Myth in Jewish Garb: Niriyah (Norea), Noah's Bride." *Journal of Jewish Studies* 51 (2000): 133–40.
Levenson, Jon D. *Inheriting Abraham: The Legacy of the Patriarch in Judaism, Christianity, and Islam*. Princeton, NJ: Princeton University Press, 2012.
Levinas, Emmanuel. "Being Jewish," translated by Mary Beth Mader. *Continental Philosophy Review* 40 (2007): 205–10.
Levinas, Emmanuel. "Être juif." *Confluences* 15–17 (1947): 253–64.
Lévy, Paul, and Etienne Woolf. "Avant-propos." In *Mélanges d'Histoire des Religions offerts à Henri-Charles Puech*, edited by Antoine Guillaumont and Ernst-Marie Laperrousaz. Paris: Presses Universitaires de France, 1974.
Lewis, Nicola D., and Justine Ariel Blount. "Rethinking the Origins of the Nag Hammadi Codices." *Journal of Biblical Literature* 133 (2014): 399–419.
Lieberman, Julia R. *El teatro alegórico de Miguel (Daniel Leví) de Barrios*. Newark, DE: Juan de la Cuesta, 1996.
Lieu, Judith. *Marcion and the Making of a Heretic: God and Scripture in the Second Century*. New York: Cambridge University Press, 2015.
Lincoln, Bruce. "Iūs e i suoi paralleli iranici. Dalla purezza alla giustizia." In *Giuristi nati. Antropologia e diritto romano*, edited by Aglaia McClintock. Bologna: Il Mulino, 2016.
Lincoln, Bruce. "Of Dirt, Diet, and Religious Others: A Theme in Zoroastrian Thought." *Dabir* 1 (2015): 44–52.
Lincoln, Bruce. "Toward a More Materialist Ethics: Vermin and Poison in Zoroastrian Thought." *Studia Iranica* 44 (2015): 83–98.
Lincoln, Bruce. *Religion, Empire, and Torture: The Case of Achaemenian Persia. With a Postscript on Abu Ghraib*. Chicago, IL: University of Chicago Press, 2007.
Lincoln, Bruce. "Theses on Method." *Method & Theory in the Study of Religion* 17, no. 1 (2005): 8–10.
Lincoln, Bruce. *Holy Terrors: Thinking about Religion after September 11*. Chicago, IL: University of Chicago Press, 2003.

Lincoln, Bruce. *Theorizing Myth: Narrative, Ideology, and Scholarship*. Chicago, IL: University of Chicago Press, 1999.
Linden, Stanton J. *The Alchemy Reader: From Hermes Trismegistus to Isaac Newton*. Cambridge: Cambridge University Press, 2003.
Loeffler, James. "A Gilgul Fun a Nigun: Jewish Musicians in New York, 1881–1945." *Harvard Judaica Collection Student Research Papers*, no. 3. Cambridge, MA: Harvard College Library, 1997.
Lommel, Herman. *Die religion Zarathustras nach dem Awesta dargestellt*. Tübingen: J. C. B. Mohr, 1930.
Long, Charles H. "A Look at the Chicago Tradition in the History of Religions: Retrospect and Future." In *The History of Religions Retrospect and Prospect*, edited by Joseph M. Kitagawa. New York: Macmillan Publishing Company, 1985.
Lorberbaum, Menachem. *Politics and the Limits of Law: Secularizing the Political in Medieval Jewish Thought*. Stanford, CA: Stanford University Press, 2001.
Lucca, Enrico. "Ateismo e profondità dell'essere. Un breve scambio epistolare tra Furio Jesi e Gershom Scholem." *Scienza & Politica* 26 (2013): 111–16.
Lundhaug, Hugo. *Images of Rebirth: Cognitive Poetics and Transformational Soteriology in the Gospel of Philip and the Exegesis on the Soul*. Leiden; Boston: Brill, 2010.
Lundhaug, Hugo, and Lance Jenott. *The Monastic Origins of the Nag Hammadi Codices*. Tübingen: Mohr Siebeck, 2015.
MacKay, Angus. "Popular Movements and Pogroms in Fifteenth-Century Castile." *Past and Present* 55 (May 1972): 33–67.
Macquarrie, John. *An Existential Theology: A Comparison of Heidegger and Bultmann*. London: SCM Press, 1955.
Magid, Shaul. "Gershom Scholem's Ambivalence toward Mystical Experience and His Critique of Martin Buber in Light of Hans Jonas and Martin Heidegger." *Journal of Jewish Thought and Philosophy* 4 (1995): 245–69.
Mahé, Jean-Pierre. *Hermès en Haute-Égypte, Tome II: Le fragment du discours parfait et les définitions Hermétiques Arméniennes*. Québec: Les Presses de l'Université Laval, 1982.
Mahmood, Saba. *Religious Difference in a Secular Age: A Minority Report*. Princeton, NJ: Princeton University Press, 2005.
Malinine, Michel, Henri-Charles Puech, and Gilles Quispel, eds. *Evangelium Veritatis: Codex Jung f. VIII^v–XVI^v (p. 16–32)/f.XIX^r–XXII^r (p. 37–43)*. Zürich: Rascher, 1956.
Maltz, Albert et al. *The Citizen Writer in Retrospect*. Los Angeles: Oral History Program, University of California, 1983.
Manguel, Alberto. *The Library at Night*. New Haven, CT: Yale University Press, 2006.
Marchand, Suzanne L. *German Orientalism in the Age of Empire: Religion, Race, and Scholarship*. New York: Cambridge University Press, 2009.
Marchand, Suzanne L. "German Orientalism and the Decline of the West." *Proceedings of the American Philosophical Society* 145, no. 4 (December 2001): 466–7.
Martin, Craig. *Masking Hegemony: A Genealogy of Liberalism, Religion, and the Private Sphere*. London: Equinox, 2010.
Martínez, Florentino García. "Apocryphal, Pseudepigraphal, and Para-Biblical Texts from Qumran." *Revue de Qumrân* 21, no. 3 (2004): 365–77.
Masschelein, Anneleen. *The Unconcept: The Freudian Uncanny in Late-Twentieth-Century Theory*. Albany: State University of New York Press, 2011.
Masuzawa, Tomoko. *The Invention of World Religions, or, How European Universalism Was Preserved in the Language of Pluralism*. Chicago, IL: University of Chicago Press, 2005.

Masuzawa, Tomoko. "Reflections on the Charmed Circle." *Journal of the American Academy of Religion* 69 (2001): 429–36.
Mayrhofer, Manfred. *Etymologisches Wörterbuch des Altindoarischen*, vol. 1. Heidelberg: Carl Winter, 1992.
Mazor, Yaakov. "The *Badkhn* in Contemporary Hasidic Society: Social, Historical, and Musical Observations." *Polin: Studies in Polish Jewry* 16 (2003): 279–96.
McCormick, Peter J. *Heidegger and the Language of the World: An Argumentative Reading of the Later Heidegger's Meditations on Language*. Ottawa: University of Ottawa Press, 1976.
McCormick, Peter J. "Saying and Showing in Heidegger and Wittgenstein." *Journal of the British Society of Phenomenology* 3 (1972): 27–35.
McCutcheon, Russell. "Religion before 'Religion'?" In *Chasing Down Religion in the Sights of History and the Cognitie Sciences*, edited by Panayotis Pachis and Donald Wiebe, 285–301. Sheffield: Equinox, 2015.
Medrano, Jose María. *Los Iniciales "Cursos de Cultura Católica" de Buenos Aires*. Buenos Aires: Editorial Dunken, 2015.
Meeks, Wayne A. *The Prophet-King: Moses Traditions and the Johannine Christology*. Leiden: Brill, 1967.
Mehlman, Jeffrey. *Legacies of Antisemitism in France*. Minneapolis: University of Minnesota Press, 1983.
Mehring, Walter. *The Lost Library*, translated by Richard and Cara Winston. London: Secker & Warburg, 1951.
Meier, Heinrich. *Death as God: A Note on Martin Heidegger*. Cambridge: Cambridge University Press, 2006.
Meijer, Roel, ed. *Global Salafism: Islam's New Religious Movement*. New York: Columbia University Press, 2009.
Meinvielle, Julio. *Influsso dello gnosticismo ebraico in ambiente Cristiano*. Rome: Sacra Fraternitas Aurigarum in Urbe, 1988.
Meinvielle, Julio. *De la Cábala al Progresismo*. Salta: Editora Calchaquí, 1970.
Meisels, Dovid. *The Rebbe*. New York: Israel Book Shop Publications, 2010.
Mendes-Flohr, Paul. "Werner Sombart's: The Jews and Modern Capitalism; An Analysis of its Ideological Premises." *Leo Baeck Institute Year Book* 20 (January 1976): 87–107.
Menninghaus, Winfried. "Walter Benjamin's Variations of Imagelessness." *Critical Horizons* 14 (2013): 407–28.
Meyer, Conrad F. *The Saint: A Fictional Biography of Thomas Becket*, translated by W. F. Twaddell. Providence, RI: Brown University Press, 1977.
Meyer, Conrad F. *Der Heilige*. Leipzig: H. Haefel Berlag, 1909.
Miculescu, Sergiu. "Mircea Eliade's Journal–As an Attempt at Developing a Personal Soteriology." *Analele Universității Ovidius Din Constanța. Seria Filologie* 23, no. 2 (2012): 104–11.
Miller, G. "Albert Maltz." In *The Heath Anthology of American Literature*, 5th ed., edited by Paul Lauter. Boston, MA: Houghton Mifflin Company, 2006.
Mina, Togo. "Le Papyrus gnostique du Musee Copte." *Vigiliae Christianae* 2 (1948): 129–36.
Mintz, Jerome. *Hasidic People: A Place in the New World*. Cambridge, MA: Harvard University Press, 1992.
Miron, Ronny. *The Angel of Jewish History: The Image of the Jewish Past in the Twentieth Century*. Boston: Academic Studies Press, 2014.
Modiano, Patrick. *Pedigree: A Memoir*, translated by Mark Polizzotti. New Haven, CT: Yale University Press, 2015.
Modiano, Patrick. *La place de l'étoile*. Paris: Gallimard, 1968.

Molé, Marijan. "*Daēnā*, le pont Činvat et l'initiation dans le Mazdéisme." *Revue de l'histoire des religions* 157 (1933): 155–85.
Moss, Candida, and Joel Baden. *Bible Nation: The United States of Hobby Lobby*. Princeton, NJ: Princeton University Press, 2017.
Mroczek, Eva."True Stories and the Poetics of Discovery." *Bulletin for the Study of Religion* 45, no. 2 (2016): 21–31.
Mulhall, Stephen. *Inheritance and Originality: Wittgenstein, Heidegger, Kierkegaard*. Oxford: Oxford University Press, 2001.
Müller, Max. *Chips from a German Workshop*, vol. 1. New York: Scribner, Armstrong, and Co., 1874.
Müller, Max. *Introduction to the Science of Religion*. London: Longman, Green, and Co., 1873
Myers, David N. "'Commanded War': Three Chapters in the 'Military' History of Satmar Hasidism." *Journal of the American Academy of Religion* 81, no. 2 (June, 2013): 311–56.
Najman, Hindy. *Seconding Sinai: The Development of Mosaic Discourse in Second Temple Judaism*. Leiden: Brill, 2003.
Nancy, Jean-Luc. *The Gravity of Thought*, translated by François Raffoul and Gregory Recco. Amherst, NY: Humanity Books, 1997.
Narten, Johanna. *Der Yasna Haptaŋhāiti*. Wiesbaden: Ludwig Reichert, 1986.
Nathans, Eli. *Peter von Zahn's Cold War Broadcasts to West Germany: Assessing America*. New York: Palgrave Macmillan, 2017.
Needham, Rodney. "Polythetic Classificaiton: Convergence and Consequences." *Man* 10 (1975): 349–69.
Neher, André. *L'éxistence juive: solitudes et affrontements*. Paris: Seuil, 1962.
Netanyahu, Benzion. *Don Isaac Abravanel: Statesman & Philosopher*. Philadelphia, PA: Jewish Publication Society, 1953.
Netsky, Hankus. "American Klezmer: A Brief History." In *American Klezmer: Its Roots and Offshoots*, edited by Mark Slobin, 13–23. Berkeley: University of California Press, 2002.
Nongbri, Brent. *Before Religion: A History of a Modern Concept*. New Haven, CT: Yale University Press, 2013.
Novalis. *Novalis: Philosophical Writings*, translated and edited by Margaret Mahony Stoljar. Albany: State University of New York Press, 1997.
Nyberg, H. S. *Die Religionen des alten Iran*, 1937, translated by H. H. Schaeder. Leipzig: J.C. Hinrichs, 1938.
Nyberg, H. S. "Védique *dhénā*, avestique *daēnā*: examen des critiques de H. P. Schmidt." In *Lautgeschichte und Etymologie*, edited by Manfred Mayrhofer, Martin Peters and Oskar E. Pfeiffer, 293–316. Wiesbaden: Reichert, 1980.
O'Donoghue, Brendan. *A Poetics of Homecoming: Heidegger, Homelessness and the Homecoming Venture*. Newcastle: Cambridge Scholars, 2011.
Oguibenine, Boris. "Baltic Evidence and the Indo-Iranian Prayer." *Journal of Indo-European Studies* 2 (1974): 23–45.
Oişteanu, Andrei. *Inventing the Jew: Antisemitic Stereotypes in Romanian and Other Central-East European Cultures*, translated by Mirela Adascalitei. Lincoln: University of Nebraska Press, 2009.
Oliphant, Samuel Grant. "Sanskrit *dhénā*, Avestan *daēnā*, Lithuanian *dainà*." *Journal of the American Oriental Society* 32 (1912): 393–413.
Oort, Johannes van. "Preface." In *Gnostica, Judaica, Catholica: Collected Essays of Gilles Quispel*, edited by Johannes van Oort, ix–xiv. Leiden: Brill, 2009.

Otto, Rudolf. *The Idea of the Holy: An Inquiry into the Non-Rational Factor in the Idea of the Divine and Its Relation to the Rational*, translated by John W. Harvey. London: Oxford University Press, 1923.

Panaino, Antonio. *Démons iraniens: Actes du colloque international ... à l'occasion des 65 ans de Jean Kellens*, edited by Philippe Swennen. Liège: Presses Universitaires de Liège, 2015.

Pandolfo, Stefania. *Knot of the Soul: Madness, Psychoanalysis, Islam*. Chicago, IL: University of Chicago Press, 2018.

Pârâianu, Răzvan. "Semitism as a Metaphor for Modernity." *Studia Hebraica* 5 (2006): 23–68.

Pearson, Birger A. "Jewish Sources in Gnostic Literature." In *The Literature of the Jewish People in the Period of the Second Temple*, edited by Michael E. Stone, 443–81. Leiden: Brill, 1984.

Peñalosa, Luis Felip de. "Juan Bravo y la familia Coronel." *Estudios Segovianos* 1 (1949): 73–109.

Pendas, Devin O. "'I Didn't Know What Auschwitz Was': The Frankfurt Auschwitz Trial and the German Press, 1963–1965." *Yale Journal of Law & the Humanities* 12, no. 2 (2000): 397–446.

Pereira, Michaela. "Alchemy and Hermeticism: An Introduction to This Issue." *Early Science and Medicine* 5, no. 2 (2000): 115–20.

Perutz, Leo. *By Night under the Stone Bridge*, translated by Eric Mosbacher. New York: Arcade Publishing, 1990.

Perutz, Leo. *Nachts unter der steinernen Brücke. Ein Roman aus dem alten Prag*. Frankfurt: Frankfurter Verlagsanstalt, 1953.

Philipse, Herman. "Heidegger and Wittgenstein on External World Skepticism." In *Wittgenstein and Heidegger*, edited by David Egan, Stephen Reynolds, and Aaron James Wendland, 116–32. New York: Routledge, 2013.

Piemontese, A. M., and J. C. Bürgel. "Turandot- von Nizami bis Puccini: *Alessandro/Dhû l-Qarnayn in viaggio tra i due mari*." *Quaderni di Studi Indo-Mediterranei* no. 1 (2008): 347–64.

Pieterse, Wilhelmina C. *Daniel Levi de Barrios als Geschiedschrijver van de Portugees-Israelietische Gemeente te Amsterdam in Zijn 'Triumpho del Govierno Popular'*. Amsterdam: Scheltema & Holkema, 1968.

Pigliucci, Massimo. "Species as Family Resemblance Concepts: The (Dis-)Solution of the Species Problem." *BioEssays* 25, no .6 (2003): 596–602.

Pines, Shlomo. "La longue récension de la Théologie d'Aristote dans ses rapports avec la doctrine ismaélienne." *Revue des études Islamiques* 22 (1954): 7–20.

Pirart, Éric. *Corps et âmes du Mazdéen: Le lexique zoroastrien de l'eschatologie individuelle*. Paris: L'Harmattan. 2012.

Pirart, Éric. *L'éloge mazdéen de l'ivresse: édition, traduction et commentaire du Hom Stod*. Paris: L'Harmattan, 2004.

Piras, Andrea. "Le concezioni dell' anima nell' Iran antico." *I Quaderni di Avallon* 29 (1992): 37–54.

Poll, Solomon. *The Hasidic Community of Williamsburg*. New York: Free Press of Glencoe, 1962.

Porter, James. "Erich Auerbach and the Judaizing of Philology." *Critical Inquiry* 35, no. 1 (Autumn 2008): 115–47.

Praag, Jonas Andries van. "Almas En Litigio." *Clavileño* 1 (1950): 14–26.

Prochnik, George. *Stranger in a Strange Land: Searching for Gershom Scholem and Jerusalem*. New York: Other Press, 2016.

Proust, Marcel. *Remembrance of Things Past*, vol. 1, translated by C. K. Scott Moncrieff and Terence Kilmartin. New York: Vintage/Random House, 1981.
Puech, Henri-Charles. *En quête de la Gnose*, 2 vols. Paris: Gallimard, 1978.
Puech, Henri-Charles. "Une collection de paroles de Jésus récemment retrouvée: L'Évangile selon Thomas." *Comptes rendus de l'Académie des Inscriptiones et Belles-Lettres* 101, no. 2 (1957): 146–67.
Puech, Henri-Charles. "Les Écrits Gnostiques du Codex Jung." *Vigiliae Christianae* 8 (1954): 1–51.
Puech, Henri-Charles. "La Gnose et le temps." *Eranos-Jahrbuch* 20 (1951): 57–114.
Puech, Henri-Charles. "Nouveaux écrits gnostiques découverts en Haute-Égypte (Premier inventaire et essai d'identification)." In *Coptic Studies in Honor of Walter Ewing Crum*, edited by Michel Malinine, 91–154. Boston: Byzantine Institute, 1950.
Puech, Henri-Charles. "Nouveaux écrits gnostiques découverts à Nag Hammadi." *Revue de l'histoire des religions* 134 (1948): 244–8.
Puech, Henri-Charles, and Gilles Quispel. "La Quatrième Écrit Gnostique du Codex Jung." *Vigiliae Christianae* 9 (1955): 65–102.
Puech, Henri-Charles. "Les Écrits Gnostiques du Codex Jung." *Vigiliae Christianae* 8 (1954): 1–51.
Puşcaş, Vasile. "Modernizing Process in Romania in the Interwar Period." *Revue Roumaine des Sciences Sociales: Serie des sciences économiques* 32, no. 2 (1988): 117–26.
Quispel, Gilles. "Gnosis and Psychology." In *The Rediscovery of Gnosticism: Proceedings of the International Conference on Gnosticism at Yale, New Haven, Connecticut, March 28–31, 1978, Vol. 1, The School of Valentinus*, edited by Bentley Layton, 17–31. Leiden: Brill, 1980.
Quispel, Gilles. *Gnostic Studies*, 2 vols. Istanbul: Nederlands Historisch-Archaeologich Instituut in het Nabije Oosten, 1974.
Quispel, Gilles. "The Jung Codex and Its Significance." In *The Jung Codex: A Newly Recovered Gnostic Papyrus*, translated and edited by Frank L. Cross, 37–78. London: Mowbray, 1955.
Quispel, Gilles. *Gnosis als Weltreligion*. Zürich: Origo, 1951.
Quispel, Gilles. "Zeit und Geschichte im antiken Christentum." *Eranos-Jahrbuch* 20 (1951): 115–40.
Quispel, Gilles. "L'Homme gnostique (La doctrine de Basilide)." *Eranos-Jahrbuch* 16 (1948): 89–140.
Quispel, Gilles. "La Conception de l'Homme dans la Gnose Valentinienne." *Eranos-Jahrbuch* 15 (1947): 249–86.
Quispel, Gilles. "The Original Doctrine of Valentine." *Vigiliae Christianae* 1 (1947): 43–73.
Rabinbach, Anson. "Between Enlightenment and Apocalypse: Benjamin, Bloch and Modern German Jewish Messianism." *New German Critique* 34 (1985): 78–124.
Raffaelli, Enrico. *The Sīh-rōzag in Zoroastrianism: A Textual and Historico-Religious Analysis*. London: Routledge, 2014.
Räisänen, Heikki. "Marcion." In *Companion to Second-Century Christian "Heretics,"* edited by Antti Marjanen and Petri Luomanen, 100–24. Leiden: Brill, 2005.
Ravid, Benjamin. *Studies on the Jews of Venice, 1382–1797*. Aldershot: Ashgate, 2003.
Rechtman, Avraham. *Yidishe etnografye un folklor*. Buenos Aires: YIVO, 1958.
Reed, Donald Malcolm. *Contesting Antiquity in Egypt: Archaeologies, Museums, and the Struggle for Identities from World War I to Nasser*. Cairo: American University in Cairo Press, 2015.

Reichert, Klaus. "'It Is Time': The Buber-Rosenzweig Bible Translation in Context." In *The Translatability of Cultures: Figurations of the Space Between*, edited by Sanford Budick and Wolfgang Iser, 169–85. Stanford, CA: Stanford University Press, 1996.

Reik, Theodore. *Pagan Rites in Judaism: From Sex Initiation, Magic, Moon-Cult, Tattooing, Mutilation, and Other Primitive Rituals to Family Loyalty and Solidarity*. New York: The Noonday Press, 1964.

Reiss, Tom. *The Orientalist: Solving the Mystery of a Strange and a Dangerous Life*. New York: Random House, 2005.

Reitzenstein, Richard. *Poimandres: Studien zur grieschisch-ägyptischen und frühchristlichen literatur*. Darmstadt: Wissenschaftliche Buchgesellschaft, 1996.

Reitzenstein, Richard. *Hellenistic Mystery-Religions: Their Basic Idea and Significance*, translated by John E. Steely. Pittsburgh, PA: Pickwick Press, 1978.

Ricchi, Immanuel ben Abraham Ḥai. *Mishnat Ḥasidim*. Jerusalem: Makhon Mishnat Ḥasidim, 2015.

Robertson, Paul. *Paul's Letters and Contemporary Greco-Roman Literature: Theorizing a New Taxonomy*. Leiden: Brill, 2016.

Robertson, Ritchie. "*Urheimat Asien*: the Re-Orientation of German and Austrian Jews, 1900–1925." *German Life and Letters* 49, no. 2 (1996): 182–92.

Robinson, James M. *The Nag Hammadi Story*, 2 vols. Nag Hammadi and Manichaean Studies 86. Leiden and Boston: Brill, 2014.

Robinson, James M. "The Jung Codex: Rise and Fall of a Monopoly." *Religious Studies Review* 3 (1977): 17–30.

Rosenzweig, Franz. "Scripture and Luther." In Martin Buber and Franz Rosenzweig, *Scripture and Translation*, translated by Lawrence Rosenwald with Everett Fox, 47–69. Bloomington: Indiana University Press, 1994.

Ross, Alison. *Walter Benjamin's Concept of the Image*. London: Routledge, 2015.

Rotenstreich, Nathan. "Gershom Scholem's Conception of Jewish Nationalism." In *Gershom Scholem: The Man and His Work*, edited by Paul Mendes-Flohr, 104–19. Albany: State University of New York Press, 1994.

Rotenstreich, Nathan. "Symbolism and Transcendence: On Some Philosophical Aspects of Gershom Scholem's Opus." *Review of Metaphysics* 31 (1978): 604–14.

Roth, Cecil. *A History of the Jews in England*. Oxford: Oxford University Press, 1941.

Rubenstein, Diane. *What's Left? The École Normale Supérieure and the Right*. Madison: University of Wisconsin Press, 1990.

Rubin, Abraham. "Muhammad Asad's Conversion to Islam as a Case Study in Jewish Self-Orientalization." *Jewish Social Studies: History, Culture, Society* 22, no. 1 (2016): 1–28.

Rubin, Israel. *Satmar: An Island in the City*. Chicago, IL: Quadrangle Books, 1972.

Ruderman, David B. *Early Modern Jewry*. Princeton, NJ: Princeton University Press, 2010.

Rudolph, Kurt. *Gnosis: The Nature and History of Gnosticism*, translated and edited by Robert McLachlan Wilson. San Francisco, CA: Harper & Row, 1983.

Saba, Abraham. *Ẓeror ha-Mor*. Warsaw: Walden, 1879.

Said, Edward. "Erich Auerbach, Critic of the Earthly World." *boundary 2* 31, no. 2 (Summer 2004): 11–34.

Said, Edward. *Orientalism*. New York: Pantheon Books, 1978.

Said, Kurban. *Ali and Nino: A Love Story*. New York: Anchor Books/Random House, 2000.

Saler, Benson. *Conceptualizing Religion: Immanent Anthropologists, Transcendent Natives, and Unbounded Categories*. Leiden: Brill, 1993.

Salomon, Noah. "Evidence, Secrets Truth: Debating Islamic Knowledge in Contemporary Sudan." *Journal of the American Academy of Religion* 81, no. 3 (2013): 820–51.

Salomon, Noah. "In the Shadow of Salvation: Sufis, Salafis, and the Project of Late Islamism in Contemporary Sudan." PhD dissertation, University of Chicago Divinity School, 2010.

Sapoznik, Henry. *Klezmer! Jewish Music from Old World to Our World*. New York: Schirmer Books, 1999.

Saussure, Ferdinand de. *Course in General Linguistics*, translated by Roy Harris. Peru, IL: Open Court, 1986.

Schalow, Frank "A Conversation with Parvis Emad on the Question of Translation in Heidegger." In *Heidegger, Translation, and the Task of Thinking: Essays in Honor of Parvis Emad*, edited by Frank Schalow, 175–89. Dordrecht: Springer, 2011.

Schenke, Hans-Martin. "The Phenomenon and Significance of Gnostic Sethianism." In *The Rediscovery of Gnosticism: Proceedings of the International Conference on Gnosticism*, edited by Bentley Layton, translated by Bentley Layton, 2 vols., 588–616. Leiden: Brill, 1981.

Schlosser, Dominik. *Lebensgesetz und Vergemeinschaftungsform: Muḥammad Asad (1900–1992) und sein Islamverständnis*. Berlin: EBVerlag, 2015.

Schmidt, Hans-Peter. "Is Vedic *Dhénā* Related to Avestan *Daēnā*?" *Monumentum H. S. Nyberg*, vol. 2, 165–81. Leiden: Brill, 1975.

Schmithals, Walter. *Die Gnosis in Korinth: Eine Untersuchung zu den Korintherbriefen*. Göttingen: Vandenhoeck & Ruprecht, 1956.

Scholberg, Kenneth. "Miguel de Barrios and the Amsterdam Sephardic Community." *The Jewish Quarterly Review* 53, no. 2 (1962): 120–59.

Scholem, Gershom. *Lamentations of Youth: The Diaries of Gershom Scholem, 1913–1919*, edited and translated by Anthony David Skinner. Cambridge, MA: Harvard University Press, 2007.

Scholem, Gershom. *The Fullness of Time: Poems*, edited and introduced by Steven M. Wasserstrom, translated by Richard Sieburth. Jerusalem: Ibis, 2003.

Scholem, Gershom. *On the Possibility of Jewish Mysticism in Our Time & Other Essays*, edited and introduced by Avraham Shapira, translated by Jonathan Chipman. Philadelphia, PA: Jewish Publication Society of America, 1997.

Scholem, Gershom. *Tagebücher nebst Aufsätzen und Entwürfen bis 1923, 1. Halbband 1913–1917*, edited by Karlfried Gründer and Friedrich Niewöhner, with the cooperation of Herbert Kopp-Oberstebrink. Frankfurt am Main: Jüdischer Verlag, 1995.

Scholem, Gershom. *Von der mystischen Gestalt der Gottheit: Studien zu Grundbegriffen der Kabbala*. Frankfurt am Main: Suhrkamp, 1995.

Scholem, Gershom. *Die Geheimnisse der Schöpfung: Ein Kapitel aus dem kabbalistischen Buche Sohar*. Frankfurt am main: Jüdischer Verlag, 1992.

Scholem, Gershom. *On the Mystical Shape of the Godhead: Basic Concepts in the Kabbalah*, edited by Jonathan Chipman, translated by Joachim Neugroschel. New York: Schocken, 1991.

Scholem, Gershom. "Franz Rosenzweig and His Book *The Star of Redemption*." In *The Philosophy of Franz Rosenzweig*, edited by Paul Mendes-Flohr, 20–41. Hanover: University Press of New England, 1988.

Scholem, Gershom. *Walter Benjamin: The Story of a Friendship*. New York: New York Review of Books Classics, 1981.

Scholem, Gershom. *Elements of the Kabbalah and Its Symbolism*, translated by Joseph Ben-Shlomo. Jerusalem: Bialik Institute, 1976.
Scholem, Gershom. *Kabbalah*. Jerusalem: Keter, 1974.
Scholem, Gershom. "Zionism – Dialectic of Continuity and Rebellion." In *Unease in Zion*, edited by Ehud Ben Ezer, 263–96. New York: Quadrangle, 1974.
Scholem, Gershom. *Sabbatai Ṣevi: The Mystical Messiah*, translated by R. J. Zwi Werblowsky. Princeton, NJ: Princeton University Press, 1973.
Scholem, Gershom. "The Name of God and the Linguistic Theory of the Kabbala." *Diogenes* 80 (1972): 59–194.
Scholem, Gershom. *The Messianic Idea and Other Essays on Jewish Spirituality*. New York: Schocken, 1971.
Scholem, Gershom. *On the Kabbalah and Its Symbolism*, translated by Ralph Manheim. New York: Schocken, 1965.
Scholem, Gershom. *Major Trends in Jewish Mysticism*. New York: Schocken, 1956.
Schwartz, Daniel B. *The First Modern Jew: Spinoza and the History of an Image*. Princeton, NJ: Princeton University Press, 2012.
Schwebel, Paula. "Lament and the Shattered Expression of Mourning: Gershom Scholem and Walter Benjamin." *Jewish Studies Quarterly* 21 (2014): 27–41.
Schwebel, Paula. "The Tradition in Ruins: Walter Benjamin and Gershom Scholem on Language and Lament." In *Lament in Jewish Thought: Philosophical, Theological, and Literary Perspectives*, edited by Ilit Ferber and Paula Schwebel, 277–301. Berlin: Walter de Gruyter, 2014.
Scott, Alan B. "Churches or Books? Sethian Social Organization." *Journal of Early Christian Studies* 3, no. 2 (1995): 109–22.
Scott, Charles E. "Appearing to Remember Heraclitus." In *The Presocratics after Heidegger*, edited by David C. Jacobs. Albany: State University of New York Press, 1999.
Seesemann, Rüdiger. "Islam in Africa or African Islam? Evidence from Kenya." In *The Global Worlds of the Swahili: Interfaces of Islam, Identity and Space in 19th and 20th Century East Africa*, edited by Rüdiger Seesemann and Roman Loimeier. Berlin: Lit Verlag, 2006.
Segal, Robert A. *The Gnostic Jung*. Princeton, NJ: Princeton University Press, 1992.
Sells, Michael A. *Mystical Languages of Unsaying*. Chicago, IL: University of Chicago Press, 1994.
Shaked, Shaul. *Dualism in Transformation: Varieties of Religion in Sasanian Iran*. London: School of Oriental and African Studies, 1994.
Shoemaker, Stephen. "Early Christian Apocryphal Literature." In *The Oxford Handbook of Early Christian Studies*, edited by Susan A. Harvey and David G. Hunter, 521–48. Oxford: Oxford University Press, 2008.
Shogan, Robert. *The Battle of Blair Mountain: The Story of America's Largest Labor Uprising*. Boulder: Westview Press, 2004.
Shuger, Deborah. *The Renaissance Bible: Scholarship, Sacrifice, and Subjectivity*. Berkeley: University of California Press, 1994.
Siker, Jeffery S. *Disinheriting the Jews: Abraham in Early Christian Controversy*. Louisville, KY: Westminister/John Knox Press, 1991.
Sirriyeh, Elizabeth. *Sufis and Anti-Sufis: The Defence, Rethinking and Rejection of Sufism in the Modern World*. New York: Curzon, 1999.
Skalli, Cedric C. *Don Isaac Abarbanel*. Jerusalem: Salman Shazar, 2017.
Skalmowski, Wojciech. "Some Remarks on Avestan *Daēnā*." In *Studia Paulo Naster Oblata*, edited by Jan Quaegebeur, 223–9. Leuven: Peeters, 1982.

Skjærvø, Prods Oktor. "Afterlife in Zoroastrianism." In *Jenseitsvorstellungen im Orient: Kongreßakten der 2. Tagung der RVO (3./4. Juni 2011, Tübingen)*, edited by Predrag Bukovec and Barbara Kolkmann-Klamt, 311–50. Hamburg: Verlag Dr. Kovač, 2013.
Skjærvø, Prods Oktor. *The Spirit of Zoroastrianism*. New Haven, CT: Yale University Press, 2012.
Slabodsky, Santiago. *Decolonial Judaism: Triumphal Failures of Barbaric Thinking*. New York: Palgrave Macmillan, 2014.
Smagina, Eugenia. "The Manichaean Cosmogonical Myth as a 'Re-Written Bible.'" In *'In Search of Truth': Augustine, Manichaeism, and Other Gnosticism: Studies for Johannes van Oort at Sixty*, edited by Jacob Albert van Den Berg et al., 199–216. Leiden: Brill, 2011.
Smith, David N. *Sounding/Silence: Martin Heidegger at the Limits of Poetics*. New York: Fordham University Press, 2013.
Smith, Jonathan Z. *Relating Religion: Essays in the Study of Religion*, 2002. Chicago, IL: University of Chicago Press, 2013.
Smith, Jonathan Z. "Religion, Religions, Religious." In *Critical Terms for Religious Studies*, edited by Mark C. Taylor, 269–84. Chicago, IL: University of Chicago Press, 1998.
Smith, Jonathan Z. *Imagining Religion: From Babylon to Jonestown*. Chicago, IL: University of Chicago Press, 1982.
Smith, Wilfred Cantwell. *The Meaning and End of Religion*. New York: MacMillan, 1963.
Sokal, Robert, and Peter Sneath. *Principles of Numerical Taxonomy*. San Francisco, CA: W.H. Freeman, 1963.
Sokolow, Peter. "Mazel Tov! Klezmer Music and Simchas in Brooklyn, 1910 to Present." In *Jews of Brooklyn*, edited by Ilana Abramovitch and Seán Galvin. Waltham, MA: Brandeis University Press, 2001.
Sombart, Werner. *The Jews and Modern Capitalism*, translated by Mordechai Epstein. Kitchener: Batoche Books, 2001.
Spektorowski, Alberto. "Los orígenes intelectuales del antisemitismo en la derecha nacionalista argentina: Los casos de J. Meinvielle, R. Doll y E. Osés." In *Ensayos sobre Judaismo Latinoamericano*, edited by Bernardo Blejmar and Ana Epelbaum de Weinstein, 200–26. Buenos Aires: Editorial Milá, 1990.
Starobinski, Jean. *Edmond Jabès: The Sin of the Book*. Lincoln: University of Nebraska Press, 1985.
Stauber, Chaim. *The Satmar Rebbe*. New York: Feldheim, 2011.
Staudenmaier, Peter. *Between Occultism and Nazism: Anthroposophy and the Politics of Race in the Fascist Era*. Leiden: Brill, 2014.
Stausberg, Michael. *Die Religion Zarathushtras. Vol. 1: Geschichte*. Stuttgart: W. Kohlhammer, 2002.
Steinberg, Cobbett S. *TV Facts*. New York: Facts on File, Inc., 1980.
Steiner, George. *After Babel: Aspects of Language and Translation*, 3rd edn. Oxford: Oxford University Press, 1998.
Steiner, George. *Real Presences*. Chicago, IL: University of Chicago Press, 1989.
Steiner, George. *Another Seed: Studies in Gnostic Mythology*. Leiden: Brill, 1984.
Stern, Zehavit. "From Jester to Gesture: Eastern European Jewish Culture and the Re-Imagination of Folk Performance." PhD dissertation, Jewish Studies, Graduate Theological Union and University of California Berkeley, 2011.
Stroumsa, Guy G. *The Making of the Abrahamic Religions in Late Antiquity*. Oxford: Oxford University Press, 2015.
Stuczynski, Claude. "Portuguese Conversos and the Manueline Imperial Idea—A Preliminary Study." *Anais de Historia de Alem-Mar* 14 (2013): 45–6.

Stuczynski, Claude. "Harmonizing Identities: The Problem of the Integration of the Portuguese Conversos in Early Modern Iberian Corporate Polities." *Jewish History* 25, no. 2 (2011): 229–57.

Szondi, Peter. *On Textual Understanding, and Other Essays*. Minneapolis: University of Minnesota Press, 1986.

Taneja, Anand V. *Jinnealogy: Time, Islam and Ecological Thought in the Medieval Ruins of Delhi*. Stanford, CA: Stanford University Press, 2017.

Taussig, Michael. "Transgression." In *Critical Terms for Religious Studies*, edited by Mark C. Taylor, 349–64. Chicago, IL: University of Chicago Press, 1998.

Taylor, Harry S., and Hans W. Uffelmann "The Concept of Time in the Science of History." *Journal of the British Society for Phenomenology* 9 (1978): 3–10.

Thomas, Keith. *The Ends of Life: Roads to Fulfillment in Early Modern England*. Oxford: Oxford University Press, 2009.

Tishby, Isaiah. "Gnostic Doctrines in Sixteenth-Century Jewish Mysticism." *Journal of Jewish Studies* 6 (1955): 146–52.

Turner, John D. *Sethian Gnosticism and the Platonic Tradition*. Québec; Louvain: Les presses de l'université Laval; Peeters, 2001.

Tzatourian, Audrey. *Yima: Structure de la pensée religieuse en Iran ancien*. Paris: L'Harmattan, 2012.

Urban, Hugh B. "Review: Syndrome of the Secret: 'Esocentrism' and the Work of Steven M. Wasserstrom: *Religion after Religion: Gershom Scholem, Mircea Eliade, and Henry Corbin at Eranos by Steven M. Wasserstrom*." *Journal of the American Academy of Religion* 69, no. 2 (2001): 437–47.

Vaisman, Ester-Basya (Asya). "'She Who Seeks Shall Find': The Role of Song in a Hasid Woman's Life Cycle." *Journal of Synagogue Music* 35 (Fall 2010), 155–83.

Vallega, Alejandro A. *Heidegger and the Issue of Space: Thinking on Exilic Grounds*. University Park: Pennsylvania State University Press, 2003.

Van Den Broek, Roelof, and Wouter J. Hanegraaff. *Gnosis and Hermeticism: From Antiquity to Modern Times*. Albany: State University of New York Press, 1998.

Van der Leeuw, Gerardus. *Religion in Essence and Manifestation*, translated by J. E. Turner. Princeton, NJ: Princeton University Press, 1986.

Vandevelde, Pol. *Heidegger and the Romantics: The Literary Invention of Meaning*. New York: Routledge, 2012.

Vandevelde, Pol. "Translation as a Mode of Poetry: Heidegger's Reformulation of the Romantic Project." In *Phenomenology and Literature: Historical Perspectives and Systematic Accounts*, edited by Pol Vandevelde, 93–113. Würzburg: Königshausen & Neumann, 2010.

Vineis, Paolo. "Definition and Classification of Cancer: Monothetic or Polythetic?" *Theoretical Medicine* 14, no. 3 (1993): 249–56.

Vogt, Stefan. "The Postcolonial Buber: Orientalism, Subalternity, and Identity Politics in Martin Buber's Political Thought." *Jewish Social Studies: History, Culture, Society* 22, no. 1 (2016): 161–86.

Volkov, Shulamit. *Germans, Jews, and Antisemites: Trials in Emancipation*. Cambridge: Cambridge University Press, 2006.

Vries, Hent de. *Minimal Theologies: Critiques of Secular Reason in Adorno and Levinas*, translated by Geoffrey Hale. Baltimore, MD: Johns Hopkins University Press, 2005.

Vries, Jan de. *Die Märchen von klugen Rätsellösern, eine Vergleichende Untersuchung*. Helsinki: Suomalainen Tiedeakatemia, Academia Scientiarum Fennica, 1928.

Wach, Joachim. *The Comparative Study of Religions*. New York: Columbia University Press, 1958.
Wacks, David A. *Double Diaspora in Sephardic Literature: Jewish Cultural Production before and after 1492*. Bloomington: Indiana University Press, 2015.
Waldrop, Rosemarie. *Lavish Absence: Recalling and Rereading Edmond Jabès*. Middletown, CT: Wesleyan University Press, 2002.
Walton, Jeremy F. "Geographies of Revival and Erasure: Neo-Ottoman Sites of Memory in Istanbul, Thessaloniki, and Budapest." *Die Welt Des Islams* 56, no. 3 (2016): 511–33.
Walzer, Michael. "Introduction." In *The Jewish Political Tradition, Vol. 1: Authority*, edited by M. Walzer, M. Lorberbaum, N. Zohar, and Y. Lorberbaum. New Haven, CT: Yale University Press, 2003.
Ward, James F. *Heidegger's Political Thinking*. Amherst, MA: University of Massachusetts Press, 1995.
Ware, Rudolph. *The Walking Qur'an: Islamic Education, Embodied Knowledge and History in West Africa*. Chapel Hill: University of North Carolina Press, 2014.
Warnek, Peter. "Translating *Innigkeit*: The Belonging Together of the Strange." In *Heidegger and the Greeks: Interpretive Essays*, edited by Drew A. Hyland and John Panteleimon Manoussakis, 57–82. Bloomington: Indiana University Press, 2006.
Weber, Max. *The Protestant Ethic and the Spirit of Capitalism*, translated by Talcott Parsons. New York: Scribner, 1958.
Weidner, Daniel. "Reading Gershom Scholem." *Jewish Quarterly Review* 96 (2006): 203–31.
Weidner, Daniel. *Gershom Scholem: Politisches, esoterisches und historiographisches Schreiben*. Munich: Wilhelm Fink Verlag, 2003.
Weigel, Sigrid. "Scholems Gedichte und seine Dichtungstheorie: Klage Adressierung, Gabe und das Problem einer biblischen Sprache in unserer Zeit." In *Gershom Scholem: Literatur und Rhetorik*, edited by Stéphane Mosès and Sigrid Weigel, 16–47. Köln: Böhlau, 2000.
Weinstein, Roni. *Kabbalah and Jewish Modernity*. Portland, OR: Littman Library of Jewish Civilization, 2016.
Widengren, Geo. "La rencontre avec la *Daēnā*, qui représente les actions de l'homme." *Orientalia Romana* 5 (1983): 41–79.
Wiebe, Donald. *Beyond Legitimation: Essays on the Problem of Religious Knowledge*. London: Macmillan, 1994.
Wiebe, Donald. "'Why the Academic Study of Religion?' Motive and Method in the Study of Religion." *Religious Studies* 24, no. 4 (1988): 403–13.
Williams, Michael Allen. "Sethianism." In *Companion to Second-Century "Heretics,"* edited by A. Marjanen and P. Luomanen, 32–63. Leiden: Brill, 2005.
Williams, Michael Allen. *Rethinking 'Gnosticism': An Argument for Dismantling a Dubious Category*. Princeton, NJ: Princeton University Press, 1996.
Williams, Michael Allen. *The Immovable Race: A Gnostic Designation and the Theme of Stability in Late Antiquity*. Leiden: Brill, 1985.
Wilson, M. Brett."The Twilight of Ottoman Sufism: Antiquity, Immorality, and Nation in Yakup Kadri Karaosmanoğlu's Nur Baba." *International Journal of Middle East Studies* 49, no. 2 (2017): 233–53.
Windhager, Günther. *Leopold Weiss alias Muhammad Asad: von Galizien nach Arabien 1900–1927*. Wien: Böhlau, 2002.
Winkler, Rafael. "Dwelling and Hospitality: Heidegger and Hölderlin." *Research in Phenomenology* 47 (2017): 378–80.

Wisse, Frederik. "Stalking Those Elusive Sethians." In *The Rediscovery of Gnosticism: Proceedings of the International Conference on Gnosticism*, edited by Bentley Layton. 2 vols., 563–76. Leiden: Brill, 1981.

Withy, Katherine. *Heidegger on Being Uncanny*. Cambridge, MA: Harvard University Press, 2015.

Witte, Bernd. *Walter Benjamin: An Intellectual Biography*. New York: Verso, 1996.

Wittgenstein, Ludwig. *Tractatus Logico-Philosophicus*, translated by Charles K. Ogden, introduced by Bertrand Russell. London: Routledge, 1995.

Wittgenstein, Ludwig. *Philosophical Investigations*, translated by Elizabeth Anscombe. Oxford: Blackwell, 1958.

Wittmann, Rebecca E. "Telling the Story: Survivor Testimony and the Narration of the Frankfurt Auschwitz Trial." *German Historical Institute Bulletin* 32 (2003): 93–101.

Wolfson, Elliot R. *The Duplicity of Philosophy's Shadow: Heidegger, Nazism, and the Jewish Other*. New York: Columbia University Press, 2018.

Wolfson, Elliot R. "*Gottwesen* and the De-Divinization of the Last God: Heidegger's Meditation on the Strange and Incalculable." In *Heidegger's Black Notebooks and the Future of Theology*, edited by Mårten Björk and Jayne Svenungsson, 211–55. New York: Palgrave Macmillan, 2017.

Wolfson, Elliot R. "Heidegger's Apophaticism: Unsaying the Said and the Silence of the Last God." In *Contemporary Debates in Negative Theology and Philosophy*, edited by Nahum Brown and J. Aaron Simmons, 185–216. New York: Palgrave, 2017.

Wolfson, Elliot R. "Heidegger's Seyn/Nichts and the Kabbalistic Ein Sof: A Study in Comparative Metaontology." In *Heidegger and Jewish Thought: Difficult Others*, edited by Micha Brumlik and Elad Lapidot, 177–200. Lanham, MD: Rowman & Littlefield, 2017.

Wolfson, Elliot R. "Not Yet Now: Speaking of the End and the End of Speaking." In *Elliot R. Wolfson: Poetic Thinking*, edited by Hava Tirosh-Samuelson and Aaron W. Hughes. Leiden: Brill, 2015.

Wolfson, Elliot R. *Giving beyond the Gift: Apophasis and Overcoming Theomania*. New York: Fordham University Press, 2014.

Wolfson, Elliot R. "Skepticism and the Philosopher's Keeping Faith." In *Jewish Philosophy for the Twenty-First Century: Personal Reflections*, edited by Hava Tirosh-Samuelson and Aaron W. Hughes. Leiden: Brill, 2014.

Wolfson, Elliot R. "Nihilating Nonground and the Temporal Sway of Becoming: Kabbalistically Envisioning Nothing beyond Nothing." *Angelaki* 17 (2012): 31–45.

Wolfson, Elliot R. *Venturing Beyond: Law and Morality in Kabbalistic Mysticism*. Oxford: Oxford University Press, 2006.

Wolfson, Elliot R. *Language, Eros, Being: Kabbalistic Hermeneutics and Poetic Imagination*. New York: Fordham University Press, 2005.

Wolfson, Elliot R. *Abraham Abulafia—Kabbalist and Prophet: Hermeneutics, Theosophy and Theurgy*. Los Angeles, CA: Cherub Press, 2001.

Wolfson, Elliot R. "The Engenderment of Messianic Politics: Symbolic Significance of Sabbatai Ṣevi's Coronation." In *Toward the Millennium: Messianic Expectations from the Bible to Waco*, edited by. Peter Schäfer and Mark Cohen, 203–58. Leiden: E. J. Brill, 1998.

Wolfson, Elliot R. *Along the Path: Studies in Kabbalistic Myth, Symbolism, and Hermeneutics*. Albany: State University of New York Press, 1995.

Wolfson, Elliot R. "The Tree That Is All: Jewish-Christian Roots of a Kabbalistic Symbol in *Sefer ha-Bahir*." *Journal of Jewish Thought and Philosophy* 3 (1993): 31–76.

Yates, Frances A. *Giordano Bruno and the Hermetic Tradition*. Chicago, IL: University of Chicago Press, 1964.
Yerushalmi, Yosef H. Zakhor: *Jewish History and Jewish Memory*. Seattle: University of Washington Press, 1982.
Yovel, Yirmiyahu. *The Other Within: The Marranos: Split Identity and Emerging Modernity*. Princeton, NJ: Princeton University Press, 2009.
Yovel, Yirmiyahu. *Spinoza and Other Heretics, Vol. 1, The Marrano of Reason*. Princeton, NJ: Princeton University Press, 1989.
Zachos, Frank E. *Species Concepts in Biology: Historical Development, Theoretical Foundations and Practical Relevance*. Basel: Springer, 2016.
Zadoff, Noam. *Gershom Scholem: From Berlin to Jerusalem and Back*, translated by Jeffrey Green. Waltham, MA: Brandeis University Press, 2018.
Zadoff, Noam. "'Zion's Self-Engulfing Light': On Gershom Scholem's Disillusionment with Zionism." *Modern Judaism* 31, no. 3 (2011): 272–84.
Ziarek, Krzysztof. *Language after Heidegger*. Bloomington: Indiana University Press, 2013.
Zohar, Maor. "Scholem and Rosenzweig: Redemption and (Anti-)Zionism." *Modern Judaism* 37, no. 1 (2017): 1–23.

Index

Aaron 165–6
Abraham 114–16, 135, 240 n.2. *See also*
 Binding of Isaac
 continued presence at Mecca 123
 indirect inclusion in Sethian texts
  128–32
 interpretations of the God of 132–4
Abrahamic, the 118, 121–3
 and the desert 109–10
 as replacement for Judeo-Christian 116
 setting aside the category of 128, 134,
  247 n.7
 tropes of 103, 109
Abravanel, Isaac 159, 161–2, 168–9
 on the dangers of excessive wealth
  163–6
 personal wealth of 160
 on the value of the simple life 166–7
Adam 101, 106, 128–9, 131–4
Adorno, Theodor 29
aesthetics 63, 102, 203 n.66
Africa 140–1
agriculture 113, 161–2, 167
Akedah. See Binding of Isaac
al-Afghani, Jamal al-Din 111–12
Alami, Solomon 163
Almog, Oz 113
al-Wansharisi, Abu al-'Abbas Ahmad 168
Amichai, Yehuda 192
Amsterdam 152, 158
Andrea of Constantinople 168
androgyny 17–18, 217 n.51
angels 129–31, 133, 141
Anidjar, Gil 111, 243 n.53
anthropology 12, 46, 91, 253 n.16
anti-Christian 67–71
antifascism 3, 100, 120, 218 n.9. *See also*
 fascism
anti-Gnosticism 73. *See also* Gnosticism
anti-kabbalah polemic 67, 69, 71–2,
  221 n.45. *See also* kabbalah

anti-modernity 61, 63–4. *See also*
 modernity
antinomianism 32, 59, 63, 140, 149,
  206 n.100
anti-Semitism 106, 112. *See also* anti-
 kabbalah polemic
 of Blanchot 237 n.9
 of Heidegger 18
anti-Sufis 140. *See also* Sufism
anti-Zionism 172. *See also* Zionism
Apocalypse of Adam, The 128–32, 134. *See
 also* Sethian Gnosticism
apocalypticism 32, 127–9, 134, 149–50,
  155, 206 n.102
Apocryphon of John 91–2, 130
Aquinas, Thomas 68
Arabia 110, 114–15, 117–19, 123, 142, 145
Arabs 111, 113–15, 123
Argentina 66–9, 73
Asad, Muhammad (born Leopold Weiss)
  113–14, 116, 124, 243 n.45,
  245 n.18
 conversion to Islam 115, 119
 exegesis of the Binding 123
 on Islam as rational 120, 123
 a Jewish childhood 119
 need to address reality 120–1
 The Road to Mecca 114–15, 117–19,
  123
 on universality of Islam and
  particularity of Judaism 119
Asad, Talal 43, 115, 245 n.17
assimilation 103, 112, 168
atheism 29–31, 99, 105
Auerbach, Erich 124
 exegesis of the Binding 122–3
 exile in Turkey 119–20
 his Judaism and his secularism 117,
  120
 Mimesis 117, 120–2
 and the need to address reality 120–1

Index

Auschwitz 185–7
authoritarianism 40, 43, 59, 63, 67–8
Avesta, the. *See daēnā*; Zoroastrianism
Avestan language 227 n.30, 229 n.48, 230 n.54. *See also daēnā*
Axial age 40, 44

baptism 127–8, 130, 134
Barrett, Jack D. 93
Bartholomae, Christian 78–9, 85
Baudelaire, Charles 57
Bedouin 113–16
Benjamin, Walter 60, 215 n.1, 215 n.3
  The Arcades Project 57–8, 62–3
  concept of the urban symbol 57–64
  convergence with the Eranos Group 58–9, 63–4
  divergence with the Eranos Group 58, 61, 63–4
  influence on Scholem by 22, 26–8
  metrosophy 59, 61–4
  on the sacred and profane 60–2
Berlin 57, 59, 64, 114, 184, 188–9
Bernáldez, Andrés 161–2
Between Muslim and Jew 1, 7, 100. *See also* Wasserstrom, Steven
  on "enemy-brothers" 110
  on esoteric intimacies 138–9, 143–4
Bey, Essad (born Lev Nussimbaum) 113–14
Bible 160–5. *See also* Exodus; Galatians; Genesis; Hebrews; Romans
Binding of Isaac 109, 118, 121–3, 240 n.4
Blanchot, Maurice 99, 237 n.9, 238 n.26, 239 n.34, 240 n.43, 240 n.58.
  See also rupture
The Book of Questions 103–6. *See also* Jabès
Boym, Svetlana 58–9
Buber, Martin 109, 112–13, 115–16
Buckley, Jorunn Jacobsen 135
Buck-Morss, Susan 58, 62, 215 n.3
Buenos Aires 67, 69
Bush, Andrew J. 143–4

Cairo 91–4, 103
capitalism 41, 58, 61, 67, 113, 164
  Williamsburg Hasidim skepticism of 172–7

Castile 160–3, 167
categorization. *See* polythetism
Catholicism 94, 152, 160–2, 168
Catholic nationalism 67–9
Christian heretics. *See* heresiology; Valentinus
Christianity 2, 21, 30, 43, 48, 110–11. *See also* anti-Christian; Catholicism; Catholic nationalism; heresiology; Protestantism; Sethian Gnosticism; Valentinus
city. *See* urban
classification. *See* polythetism
Cogan, Nathan 181–2
coincidentia oppositorum 59–60, 63, 72, 216 n.29, 222 n.55, 238 n.26, 238 n.28
contact 4. *See also* interreligious contact
  and continuity 10, 49, 118–19, 157, 257 n.42
  as data for the study of religions 49, 56, 99–100
  as rupture 100–3, 106–7
  situations of 10, 13, 97, 99–100, 106–7, 116, 195 n.8
conversion. *See* converts
converts
  from Jewish to Christianity by force (*conversos*) 151, 157, 159–63, 167–8
  from Jewish to Islam 109, 112–19
  from Sufi to Salafi 137–44
  to Zoroastrianism 80
Copenhaver, Brian 50, 213–14 nn.19–20
Coptic codex 91–6
Coptic manuscripts 91, 133–4
Coptic Museum 91–3
Corbin, Henry 92, 94, 188, 238 n.26. *See also* Eranos Group
Crum, Walter 93

daēnā 2–3, 225 n.13. *See also* Zoroastrianism
  as a complimentary counterpart of milk 85–6
  difficulty defining 78–80, 225 n.11
  expressed through myth 80–4
  and sacrifice 84–5
Daumas, François 92, 233 n.30

David 115, 133, 153
Dead Sea Scrolls. *See* Qumran texts
death 4, 24–5, 32, 85–6, 101
    of god 30–1
    God is 189–90
    as God's prophet 192
    in two Zoroastrian myths 80–3
de Barrios, Daniel Levi 147, 151–3, 256 n.26
    exile and politics 155–6
    and the messianic restoration 154–5
    symbolic significance of politics 157–8
Deep Naturalism 13–14, 46, 56. *See also* naturalism
Deep Pluralism 12, 44, 46–7, 55. *See also* pluralism
De la Cábala al Progresismo (DCAP) 66, 70–2. *See also* Meinvielle
democracy 152–7. *See also* liberal-democratic states
de Planhol, Xavier 109–10
Derrida, Jacques 239 n.34
desert 137, 163–4
    and anti-Semitic tropes 111–13
    as metaphor 103–6
    as site for development of monotheism 109–10, 113–16
desert spirituality 110
dialectic 12, 43. *See also coincidentia oppositorum*
    historical/philosophical 47–9, 51, 55–6, 212 n.7
    individual/collective 81–2
    past/future 62–4
dialectical understanding 6, 12, 40–1
diaspora 155–7, 207 n.106. *See also* exile
disciplines 41–2, 45–7, 55
discourse and practice 79, 225 n.11. *See also* practice
Doresse, Jean 91–2, 93, 95–6
dualisms. *See* hermeneutic dualisms
Dumézil, George 182–3, 187–90

economics. *See* capitalism
Egypt 91–4, 96, 101, 163, 239 n.30
Egyptian Gospel, The 130–2, 134. *See also* Sethian Gnosticism
Ehrlich, Yom Tov 175–9
Eichmann, Adolf 68, 186

Eid, Joseph Albert 93–4
Eliade, Mircea 109, 183, 188–9. *See also* Eranos Group
empiricism 45–6. *See also* radical empiricism
epistemology 46–8, 51, 54–5. *See also* taxonomy
Eranos Group 94, 117–18, 232 n.5. *See also* Corbin; Eliade; Scholem
    and *coincidentia oppositorum* 60–1
    mystocentrism of the 58–9, 64–6, 77, 115
    and nationalism 63
    replacing ethics with ontology 121–2
Eriugena, John Scotus 69–71
esoteric 58–60, 139–44, 200 n.44
esoteric intimacies 139, 143–5
essentializing religions 111, 116, 123–4
ethics 5–7, 109, 131, 134. *See also* under Islam
Eve 132
exile 102, 179, 244 n.9. *See also* diaspora
    influence on Jewish messianism 148–51
    influence on Jewish perceptions of wealth 159–68
    influence on Jewish politics 152–7
Exodus 102, 149, 163–5, 178. *See also* diaspora
Exodus, Book of 132, 168
    2:22 206 n.98
    5:1 174
    24 154

farming. *See* agriculture
fascism 3, 17, 73. *See also* antifascism
    and aesthetics 63
    clerico-fascism in Argentina 67–73
    and the History of Religions 100
    and Scholem 65–6
Feldman, Deborah 171, 180
Ferdinand II, King 159–61
finance. *See* tax farming; usury
First World War. *See* World War I
footnotes as textual traces 87
Foucault, Michel 43, 189–90
Fowden, Garth 50–1
France 239 n.30. *See also* Paris
Frankel, Hertz 173–4

Freud, Sigmund 4, 181–2, 192
fundamentalist religious movements 42–3

Galatians, Book of
    4:21–5:1 131
gender. *See* androgyny
Genesis, Book of
    4:25 132
    6:2 131
    13:13 131
    17 131–2
    17–18 132
    18:16–33 131
    18:19 131–3
    18:20 131
    18:20–29 131
German Romanticism 57–8, 61–2, 73, 112–13, 218 n.7
Germans 112, 120, 172, 183–4
Germany 31, 34–5, 112, 121
Gnosticism 220 n.35. *See also* anti-Gnosticism; Sethian Gnosticism; Valentinus
    and the Germans 34–5
    and Heidegger 20–1, 31–2
    Jewish 69–72
    and Scholem 29, 31–2
    and the Study of Religion 73
Goethe, Johann Wolfgang von 4, 10, 181–2, 192
Golden Calf 165–6
Goldziher, Ignaz 111–12
Gomorrah. *See* Sodom and Gomorrah
Gospel of Thomas 95–6
Gospel of Truth 93, 95–6
greed 160, 163–6, 168–9, 172
Greek 34, 36, 188–9

Hamid, Adam Musa
    the conversion story of 140–2
    his shifting relationship with *jinn* 138–9
Hasidism 135, 150–1. *See also* Williamsburg Hasidim
Hebrew 20, 25–6, 31, 35
Hebrews, Book of
    11:13 132
Hegel, Georg Wilhelm Friedrich 72–3, 101–3, 238 n.29

Heidegger, Martin 72–3
    anti-Semitism of 18
    on anxiety 20–3
    on beyng and the failing of language 18–19, 22
    on beyng and the last god 30–1
    on Gnosticism 30–1
    and the kabbalists 20, 24
    on the poetic dwelling 32–7
    on poetic language 28–9, 33
    on translation 36–7, 210 n.129
Heideggerian phenomenology 59, 73
Hellenic. *See* Greek
heresiology 69–73, 89–90
hermeneutic dualisms 46
hermeneutics 41, 46, 57, 62
Hermes 49–50, 54
Hermeticism 45–6
    defining 47–50
    difficulties categorizing 50
    polythetic analysis of Hermetic texs 52–5
History of Religions. *See* study of religion
history. *See under* philosophy
Hitler, Adolf 3, 17, 107
Holocaust 105–6, 151, 171, 177, 264 n.18
Holocaust deniers 185–6
Homer 10, 121–2, 188
humor as form of critique 176–7
hyper-reality 14. *See also* real, the

idealism 73, 208 n.106, 209 n.116
identity 11, 171
innovations. *See* technology
inter-religion 2, 8, 10, 12, 14, 107
    and Abraham 116–18
    and the lives of Asad and Auerbach 118–21
interreligious contact 13, 44, 171. *See also* relationality
interwar period 109–11
intimacies. *See* esoteric intimacies
Irenaeus 89–90, 93, 95
Isabella I, Queen 159–61
Islam 110–15. *See also* Muslims
    as an ethical system 119–23
    converts to 109, 112–19
    and the ills of modernity 115–16
    and rationality 120, 123, 139

reformism within 138–9, 142–4
religious difference within 138–9, 144–5
Israel 5, 31, 133, 151
Israelites 153, 163–5, 178

Jabès, Edmond 99, 101, 103–7, 239 n.30, 239 n.34
James, William 14, 214 n.26
Jerusalem 88, 114, 186, 192
Jesus 130–4
Jewish Christianity 127–8
Jewish historiography 148, 155
Jewish Politics 254 n.1, 257 n.35. *See also* de Barrios
    analytical utility as a category 147–8
    and messianism 149–51
Jews
    metahistorical status of 32
    as Oriental 112–13
jinn 138, 253 n.10
    everyday relations with 140–5
    role in Sufi and Salafi healing 139
Job, Book of 168
Jonas, Hans 21, 91
Judaizing 68, 73
Jung, Carl 61, 91, 95–6
Jung Codex 95–6
Jünger, Ernst 183–6, 189

kabbalah 3–4, 17, 18–20, 24, 26–7, 58. *See also* anti-kabbalah polemic; Lurianic
    Ein Sof 20, 26–7
    pantheistic potential of 71–2
    and poets 28
    post-Scholemian developments in research of 72
    symbolism of 30
    theory of language 24–7
    typology of discourse about 71
Kellens, Jean 84–5
Kierkegaard, Søren 109, 122
King Lear 181–2, 186, 191–3
King Lear 4. *See also* Shakespeare
Kinus klali (General Assembly) 174–5
Kiryas Joel 172
kollel 173–4
Konuk, Kader 120, 122

Koran. *See* Qur'an
Kranzler, George 172, 176–7, 180
Ku Klux Klan 186

Lacis, Asja 59–60
Lamartine, Alphonse de 189–90
lament 22–8, 204 n.69
Landfahrer, Berl 190–1
language
    Blanchot on rupture and 99–103
    Heidegger on 18–19, 22–3, 28–9, 33–6
    and Judaism 99–107
    Scholem on lament as 22–8, 204 n.69
Lankarany, Firouz-Thomas 79
Levinas, Emmanuel 99, 101, 103, 109
liberal arts colleges 1, 39
liberal-democratic states 42–4
Lipstadt v. Irving 186
Logan Defenders 192
Long, Charles 195 n.8
luksus 171–80
Lurianic kabbalah 31, 71, 148–9

Mahamad, the 152–3, 156
Mandaeism 127, 133–5
Manichaeism 127–8, 132–4
manna 163–4
Marcion 132–4
Marxism 57, 68
masons 67
Masuzawa, Tomoku 88, 111, 232 n.5
Mašya 86
Mašyānī 86
materialism, critique of 165–6, 171, 173, 176
Mecca 118–19, 123
Mediterranean, ancient 49–50, 127, 133–4
Mehring, Walter 188–9
Meinvielle, Julio 3, 219 n.15
    anti-Judaism of 66
    anti-kabbalistic polemic of 69–72
    biography of 66–7
    and post-Scholemian kabbalah research 72–3
    reading of Scholem 71–2
Meisels, Dovid 174–5
Meisl, Mordechai 190–1

messianism 31–3, 148–9, 154–7
metaphor 23, 104–7, 133, 239 n.34
metaphysics 40, 42
methodology 6, 46–7, 52. *See also* theorizing
metrosophy 59, 61–4. *See also* Benjamin, Walter
Meyer, Conrad Ferdinand 190–1
Middle East, the 114, 117–19. *See also* West, the
military 67–9
Mina, Togo 91–3
miracles *(karamat)* 140–1
Miriam, Aunt 191–2
modernist urbanism 60–3
modernity. *See also* anti-modernity
  crisis of 28, 148
  Eranos Group and Benjamin split about 64
  gnostic 69–70
  Islam and the ills of 115–16
  and Jewish Politics 147–8, 150–2, 157
  and kabbalah 73
monarchy 152–6, 257 n.34
monotheism 109–11, 113–5
monothetism 48, 50, 52, 54. *See also* polythetism
Moses 133, 154, 163–5
Muhammad 114, 123
Müller, Max 9–10
Muslims 110–11, 114, 119–23, 137–8, 168. *See also* Islam
Mussolini, Benito 182
mysticism. *See* kabbalah; Scholem, Gershom
mystocentric approach to the study of religion 65–6
  Eranos Group's 65–6, 77
  Scholem's 71, 73, 147

Nag Hammadi 89, 92–6, 133–4
Naples 59–60
nationalism 63, 67–9
National Socialism 17, 31, 67, 70, 121, 172. *See also* Nazism
naturalism 41, 45–7, 214 n.26. *See also* Deep Naturalism
Nazism 17–18, 33–6, 184–6, 190. *See also* National Socialism

negotiation 3, 6, 12, 45–6, 211 n.1
Neher, André 99, 101, 103
Neoplatonism 48, 50, 212 n.6. *See also* Platonism
neo-romanticism 66, 112. *See also* German Romanticism
New Testament 134
Nietzsche, Friedrich 18, 30
"Nine Theses on the Study of Religion". *See also* Wasserstrom, Steven
  applied to Hermeticism 45–50
  applied to Williamsburg Hasidim 171
  on claims of truth and power 100
  on contact and continuity 99, 156–7, 257 n.42
  on relationality 121
  on religions existing in the plural 140
  on seeing from the outside 41
  on social relations 139
  on species-wide generalizations 159
Noah 128–9
nominalism 40–1
nomos 109
Nostradamus 187–9
Novalis 37, 112

occultism 9, 58–9, 63–4, 71, 190
Odyssey, The 121, 123
off-modern 59, 63. *See also* modernity
Old Testament 113, 186. *See also* New Testament
opposites. *See coincidentia oppositorum*
Orientalism 110–14, 143, 182

Pakistan 114–15
Palestine 31, 73, 113–14, 151
paradox 25–7, 29, 59, 103. *See also coincidentia oppositorum*
Paris 58–9, 61–4, 91–2, 103, 176, 183–4, 189
Pearson, Birger 129–30
persecutions of 1391, Castile 161
Perutz, Leo 190–1
phenomenology 56, 59, 80, 91, 214 n.26. *See also* Heidegger
Philip, The Gospel of 133
philology 6–7, 10, 89–91, 110–11, 169, 188–90

philosophy 30–1, 41–4, 189. *See also* truth-claims
and history 3, 6, 12, 39, 45–6, 56
Piemonte, Gustavo 69–71
Platonism 37, 42, 48. *See also* Neoplatonism
pluralism, religious 13, 40–6, 52, 254 n.21. *See also* Deep Pluralism
poetry 28, 32, 103
politics. *See* democracy; fascism; Jewish Politics; liberal-democratic states; monarchy; secularism; theocracy
polythetism 46–56, 225 n.11. *See also* monothetism
porosity 59–60
Porter, James 120–1
Portugal 159–60, 166–8, 189
power, claims to 13, 100
practice 79, 225 n.11
profane. *See* sacred and profane
progressivism 70
prophet 101–2, 154, 187
Protestantism 41, 43, 78, 84–5
psychology 29, 95, 120. *See also* Freud; Jung
Ptloemy 90, 132
Puccini 182–3
Puech, Henri-Charles 91–6

Quispel, Gilles 89–96
Qumran texts 40
Qur'an 113–17, 123, 138, 140–2

rabbinics 26, 71
race 110–12, 129–33
radical empiricism 14, 56, 214 n.26. *See also* empiricism
rationalists 39, 63, 120, 123, 139, 142, 150
real, the 121–4. *See also* hyper-reality
Reed College 5, 39–40
reformist. *See under* Islam
Reik, Theodore 4, 181–2, 192
Reitzenstein, Richard 21, 91
relationality 47–9, 63, 121. *See also* contact
Religion after Religion 1–2, 191. *See also* Wasserstrom, Steven
on contact 117–18, 156
on the Eranos group and symbols 61
on fascism and the Eranos Group 65–6, 100
on greatness 88
on mystocentrism 77, 109, 147
and potential rhetorical violence 73
on the skeptic and gnostic 29
religion. *See also* study of religion
definition of 5, 8, 49, 78–9, 82
religiosity 79–80
religious pluralism. *See* pluralism, religious
Religious Studies. *See* study of religion
Renaissance 50, 168–9
Renan, Ernest 110–14
revolution
conservative 59
literary writing's role in ruptures in history 101
of silence 22–3
ritual 77, 79–80, 84–5
Romania 63, 171, 173
Romans, Book of
9–11 131
romanticism. *See* German Romanticism
Rome 89, 91, 94
Rosenzweig, Franz 14, 32, 37, 207 n.106
Rottenberg, Yissachar Ber (Voideslaver Rav) 174–5
rupture. *See also* Blanchot
and contact 102–3, 106–7
as defined by opposing sides 100
Judaism at the center of 100, 103–6
between language and truth 99–100
language as 101–2
linked to violence 106

Saba, Abraham 162–3, 168–9
Sabbatianism 147–8, 150–2, 154–7
Sacheri, Carlos Antonio 68
sacred and profane 60–2. *See also* Benjamin, Walter
Said, Edward 110, 120
Said, Kurban. *See* Bey, Essad
Salafism 137–45
rationality of 139
Satmar Rebbe. *See* Teitelbaum, Joel
Schelling, Friedrich 72, 208 n.116
Schiller, Friedrich 183
Schmitt, Carl 40, 122, 173, 186

Scholem, Gershom 191. *See also* Eranos Group
  and fascism 65–6
  influence on Benjamin 58, 60–1
  influence on Meinvielle 70–2
  on Jewish Politics and messianism 147–51, 155–7
  on lament and language 22–3, 204 n.69
  mystocentrism of 71, 73, 147
  and secularization 29–30, 151–2, 157
  and zionism 25–6, 31–2, 66, 151, 217 n.50
scripturalism 141
Second World War. *See* World War II
sectarian boundaries 143–4
secularism 157
  and Auerbach 117, 120
  and Judaism 105–7
  role of theorists in the secularist-religious impasse 42–4
secularization 70, 151–2
  removal of God from history by 25, 29–30
Semites 111–13
Semitic languages 111
Senior, Abraham (Fernán Núñez Coronel) 161
Sephardi Jews, 15th C Spain 151, 159–63, 166–8
  greed of 160, 163, 168–9
  as manual laborers 161
  and shepherding 166–7
  and tax farming 162, 166
  wealth of 159–61
Sethian Gnosticism 92, 95, 243 n.54
  The Apocalypse of Adam 128–32, 134
  authoritativeness of Biblical texts for 133–4
  difficulty categorizing 127–8
  The Egyptian Gospel 130–2, 134
  and ethnic reasoning 131–2
  exegesis of Sodom and Gomorrah 128–33
  and interreligion 135
  Second Treatise of the Great Seth 133–4
  and the Seed of Seth 131–2
sexuality 17, 77, 80, 131
Shabbetai Tsvi 149–50, 152, 155
Shakespeare 10, 182. *See also King Lear*

shekhinah 149, 154
Shelley, P. B. 181
situations of contact. *See under* contact
Smith, Jonathan Z. 48
social class 160–2, 172, 176
sociology 138–9, 142, 145
Socrates 187–90
Sodom and Gomorrah 128–33
Solomon, King 133, 153, 166–7
Sombart, Werner 113, 172–3
Spain 149, 151, 159–68
Spanish expulsion 148–9, 159–67
Spinoza, Benedict 150, 152, 156
spirituality. *See* desert spirituality
Starobinski, Jean 103–4, 239 n.33
Strauss, Leo 190–1, 195
Stroumsa, Guy 128, 247 n.7
study of religion. *See also* "Nine Theses on the Study of Religion"
  data for the 49, 55–6
  mystocentric approach to the 65
  purpose of the 9, 169
  relationship between philosophy and the 41–2
  role of categorization in the 45–6
  the role of comparison in the 12, 40, 64, 99, 118, 159
  Wasserstrom's influence on the 1–8, 40, 116
subjectivity 82, 142
Sudan 137, 140, 142–3
Sufism 115, 137–40, 142
Sunna 138, 141
supernatural 109, 139, 253 n.16
supersessionism 102, 116, 118, 122
symbiosis 7, 143–4
symbolism
  Benjamin on urban 59–63
  Eranos Group on 61
  Scholem on 25–8, 30, 150–1, 200 n.45

Tacuara (Grupo Tacuara de la Juventud Nacional) 68
Talmud 67, 116, 176–7
tax farming 162, 166
taxonomy 46–7, 50–2, 55–6, 107
technology 13–14, 173, 177, 214 n.27
Teitelbaum, Joel 171–7
Tertullian 89, 94

Tetragrammaton 26, 28
theocracy 43–4, 66
Theodotus 90
theology 156
theophany 61, 109, 115–16, 156
theorizing 77–80, 83–6, 96, 100, 106–7.
    See also methodology
time 32, 59–60
Torah 119, 121, 123, 148, 166, 174
tradition
    as bridge across sociological
        differences 142, 144–5
    as reconstituted by literature 103
    structuring of social relations by
        138–9
translation 36–7, 207 n.106, 210 n.129
truth-claims 5, 13–14, 45, 47, 51, 100. *See
    also* philosophy
Turandot 182–3, 190
Turkey 117, 119–20, 122, 162

ultra-Orthodox. *See* Williamsburg
    Hasidim
United States 39, 40, 43, 179, 186–7
universalism 41, 119
urban 57–64, 167–8, 171–2. *See also*
    modernist urbanism
usury 67, 162
utopianism 11, 14, 31, 43, 70

Valentiner, Klaus 184
Valentinus 71, 89–91, 93–6, 132
Vatican II 68
violence 68, 73, 106–7, 216 n.11
Voegelin, Eric 69–70

Walzer, Michael 148
Wasserstrom, Dunia 183–7, 192
Wasserstrom, Steven M. *See also Between
    Muslim and Jew;* contact; inter-
    religion; negotiation; "Nine Theses
    on the Study of Religion"; real, the;
    Religion after Religion; symbiosis
    the concept of "religion after religion"
        61, 63–5, 78
    on esoteric intimacies 139, 143–5
    fascism and the History of Religions
        100

on the *ghulat* 128
his encounters as a teacher 1–8, 4–6,
    39–40, 87–8, 97, 193
on mystocentrism 77, 96, 118, 123,
    147, 156–7
as a teacher-scholar 1–8, 39–40, 87–8,
    97, 193
and understanding of religious
    difference 138
work on religion 4, 6, 73, 192–3
wealth 160–8, 172–7, 180, 191
Weber, Max 58, 88, 173
Weil, Simone 99
Weiss, Leopold. *See* Asad, Muhammad
West, the 43, 58, 112, 115, 119, 245 n.17.
    See also Middle East, the
Whitman, Walt 157
wilderness 163. *See also* desert
Williamsburg Hasidim 171–80
    anti-materialism of 171–8
    effects of gentrification on 180
    use of humor as a form of critique
        176–8
    views on women and materialism
        179–80
Wisdom of Jesus Christ 91, 93
Wittgenstein, Ludwig 24, 48
Woolf, Virginia 120
work on religion 4, 6, 73, 192–3
World War I 58, 123, 176
World War II 89, 117, 176, 187

Yaldabaoth 133
Yiddish 40, 171–3, 176–80
Yima, King 82–3
Yishuv 110, 113

Zionism. *See also* anti-Zionism
    and Buber 112–13, 115
    and Scholem 25–6, 31–2, 66, 151,
        217 n.50
Zohar, the 71–2
Zoroastrianism. *See also daēnā*
    Avestan myths 80–3, 86
    eras of cosmic history 83–4
    projection of Protestant assumptions
        onto 84
    from religiosity to religion 80–1

www.ingramcontent.com/pod-product-compliance
Lightning Source LLC
Chambersburg PA
CBHW050323020526
44117CB00031B/1592